THE

BENEFITS OF

MODERATE DRINKING

Alcohol, Health and Society

Gene Ford

Wine Appreciation Guild
San Francisco, California

Library of Congress Cataloging-in-Publication Data

Ford, Gene,

The benefits of moderate drinking: alcohol, health, and society / Gene Ford
   338 p.   cm.

Bibliography: p.
      Includes index.
        ISBN 0-932664-61-X : $24.95. ISBN 0-932664-1 (pbk.) : $1495
      1. Temperance. 2. Drinking of alcoholic beverages--United States.

      3. Alcoholism--United States. I. Title.
                                                HV5258.F67 1988
      613.8'1--dc 19   88-15496

The Benefits Of

Moderate Drinking

© 1988 by Gene Ford

Printed in the United States of America   10 9 8 7 6 5 4 3 2 1

ISBN 0-932664-60-1

Dedication

First, to the memory of Frank O'Hanlon, my doughty Irish grandfather who lost his Iowa tavern business to old temperance—the social delusion that alcohol prohibition would benefit society—here's a cold and frosty beer. Frank would have loved this book.

Next, to my friends and loved ones with whom I've bent many a convivial elbow, here's a spirituous toast to the warm companionship and mutual inspiration that we have found in an otherwise confusing world.

Finally, let's all raise a glass of wine in dedication to the reality that alcohol was given by God to man as a blessing and life enrichment, not as an abused or dirty drug.

Though we have a wide range of personal preferences in what we choose to drink, let us always drink responsibly and, in the practice, vivify the enduring wisdom of St. John Chrysostum, one of the great preachers of the fourth century, who wrote:

> Wine was given by God, not that we might be drunken, but that we might be sober. It is the best medicine when it has moderation to direct it. Wine was given to restore the body's weakness, not to overturn the soul's strength.

Other Titles by the Author

FORD'S ILLUSTRATED GUIDE TO WINES,
BREWS AND SPIRITS
  An illustrated textbook of all potable beverages

FORD'S ABCs OF WINES,
BREWS AND SPIRITS
  A cartoon encyclopedia of alcoholic beverages

SAFE SERVICE OF ALCOHOLIC
BEVERAGES
  A manual and videotape for on-premise operations

MODERATE DRINKING JOURNAL
  A bimonthly research journal on drinking

Contents

Foreword

It is not necessary to agree with every word in this book to recognize its value. The moderate use of alcoholic beverages has been with us for millennia; so has alcohol abuse. It is important to understand the difference.

But we have lost our way. In the fumbling approach to the prevention of alcoholism, phantoms have been created that obstruct, rather than further efforts to that end.

A massive effort has been mounted to discredit any use of alcoholic beverages, just as though prohibition had never cast its lasting shadow over this land. In many circles it is now high treason to say anything favorable about drinking. It is time that someone spoke out in order to make scientific inquiry about alcohol use respectable, regardless of where the truth may lead.

Gene Ford has made a commendable — and very readable — start in this direction and he merits attention.

It is usually overlooked that drinkable alcohol can be made in any household; indeed nature itself can do this unattended. So prohibition is both a biologic impossibility, and socially unrealistic in Western society.

It is imperative to draw common sense lines between moderate and excessive drinking; not to do so is self-defeating in terms of the prevention of alcoholism. Another erroneous notion links alcohol, which is legal, with "hard drugs," which are not. The former has a wide range of effects, depending on quantity; the impact of the latter is massively detrimental. Gene Ford is trying to bring light to these murky areas.

Thomas B. Turner, M.D.

[Dr. Turner is a former dean of the Johns Hopkins University School of Medicine.]

Preface

This book supplies an abundance of researched documentation upon which you can base personal decisions about drinking. It should not be viewed as another treatise on alcoholism or the latest twist in abuse therapy. I am neither advisor nor counsel to those with abuse problems. There are hundreds of informative books already in print on problem drinking.

As a moderate drinker, I am writing this book for the 115 million or so other moderate drinkers in this country who do not have the time or inclination to research the subject. As far as possible, I attempted to translate the arcane and often stilted language of the medical and social sciences into familiar terms. Any errors in the process are mine.

Born into the prohibition era of Czech and Irish stock, I have no distinct recollection about when alcohol first touched my lips. Until their passing, my parents were both light drinkers who attempted to inculcate in their offspring a sense of propriety about liquor. I have watched the heartache of alcoholism within my family circle though, and this ordeal brought home to me the tragedy which so many experience from excessive drinking and its consequences.

Fifty years of drinking, raising seven children to moderate habits, bartending in graduate school, and selling wine, beer and spirits for nearly two decades, added to my bank of experience. Twelve years in the college classroom teaching hotel and restaurant administration students how to manage alcoholic beverages and conducting seminars in bars on how to identify and avoid service to drunks has also provided valuable perspectives on the moderate use of alcohol.

Writing, speaking, publication of two major books and eight years in newspaper syndication as "The Wine And Liquor Uncomplicator" furnished my deepest insights. This past year of intensive alcohol-abuse research as publisher of the world's only pro-drinking research journal has given me a command of current thinking in the field.

I have expressed here my own, deeply-felt personal convictions that alcohol gives more than it takes from this society of ours, though that taking is often very dear indeed. Much that we value in life can be, and is all too often abused. Those who blindly oppose alcohol simply because it is abused are, in my observations, the true radicals.

We are a wet people. In 1933, through the endorsement of the Twenty-first Amendment, the majority of our states opted for legal drinking. Barring new adverse medical discoveries, we will continue to drink. The important questions we must face concern how we treat alcohol in our daily lives, in our literature, in our public media, in the education of our young, in health and social practices and in governmental affairs. There are no simple answers to these questions because a large minority does not drink and remains hostile to alcoholic beverages.

Often I recall my nearly two decades of travelling Washington and Montana as a salesman for the Christian Brothers' wines and brandy. I was always impressed with the relaxed approach to drinking in Montana compared to the strict formality of my home state of Washington. If a bar patron happened to see an old friend walking by in downtown Helena, he would think nothing of walking out onto the public street with a drink in hand.

In Montana motels, I have seen toddlers and teenagers playing and drinking soft drinks at the edge of the bar's dance floor late at night, allowing their parents a few extra moments of relaxation and sociability while on the road. In most Montana restaurants, you have to walk directly through the bar to reach the dining room. Won't these children learn more about proper adult drinking conduct in this congenial, home-like atmosphere? The forbidding, hidden-away, often gloomy rooms called bars in most states are far from the hospitality of our colonial inns.

A hope motivates me that I can contribute to a national reexamination of new temperance policies. Drinking is not a be-all or end-all objective in life but a comfortable expression of sociability, warmth and good will. Yet today, it seems that moderate drinkers are permitting another slip-slide into a new form of economic prohibition.

Those of us who support moderation should resent our federal and state officials characterizing alcohol as a dirty drug. We do not criticize those who abstain. We fully support their choice. But the majority of the people in this nation have already made the decision to drink, and they do so with full recognition of the terrible tolls of abuse.

We object to the association of alcoholic beverages with illicit street drugs. We challenge the Department of Health and Human Services' new policy that all references to substance abuse now must read "alcohol and other drugs." We resist legislation that would raise taxes to punitive levels, that would lessen reasonable availability and hours of service, that would eliminate normal advertising and price functioning in the marketplace.

These are radical political positions of civil servants in a nation where the majority of the citizens consume alcohol responsibly and in moderation. I have watched the step-by-step development of new temperance over the past decade. I have marvelled at the timidity of the industry, the inertia of the farmer and service businesses that thrive on the enormous economy of alcoholic beverages, and the befuddlement of the consumer. No one seems capable of rising to the challenge of organized anti-alcoholism. Like a tenacious brush fire, temperance has consumed the outbuildings and threatens the very homestead itself while the family of drinkers watches mutely from the porch.

This social-political imbroglio cannot be blamed entirely on the social activists. They see alcohol as a mortal enemy. Nor can we credit all blame to the media, legislators, religious and social agencies or the medical profession, though each is a part of the puzzle. To paraphrase Pogo, I have looked at all of the above and them is us.

We are all to blame because we shy from the truth.

I urge you to read this book with an open and inquisitive mind. Its purpose is a balanced and sympathetic consensus that will support equally those who abstain and those who exercise temperance while drinking. A moderate consensus will unite us once again in fighting the real devil of abuse. As Abraham Lincoln wrote:

> It is true that even then it was known and acknowledged that many were greatly injured by it. But none seemed to think the injury arose from the use of a bad thing, but from the abuse of a very good thing.

Acknowledgments

In writing this book, I depended on the expertise and experience of many in the academic, research and treatment disciplines. I am indebted especially to librarian Nancy Sutherland at the University of Washington Alcohol and Drug Abuse Institute Library, and to the diligence of Teresa Opsvig, my daughter and perceptive researcher.

As a sort of dynamic panel of experts, a number of scholars and professionals have reviewed portions of the manuscript, submitted materials or added special insights through interviews. I have used their incisive comments to introduce many of the findings.

For this privilege, I thank Karst Besteman, executive director, the Alcohol and Drug Problems Association; John B. Burcham, Jr., chairman, Licensed Beverage Information Council and executive director, National Liquor Store Association; John De Luca, president, the Wine Institute; Michael Q. Ford, executive director, the National Association of Alcoholism Treatment Programs; Paul F. Gavaghan, vice president, Distilled Spirits Council of the United States; Louis R. Gomberg, wine industry consultant; Augustus H. Hewlett, president, Alcohol Policy Council; Norman M. Kaplan, M.D., professor of medicine, the University of Texas Medical School; Philip C. Katz, Ph.D.,research director, The Beer Institute; Solomon H. Katz, professor of anthropology, the University of Pennsylvania; Mark Keller, editor emeritus, The Journal of Studies on Alcohol; Douglas W. Metz, executive vice president, Wine & Spirit Wholesalers of America; David J. Pittman, Ph.D., professor of sociology, Washington University; Ronald R. Rumbaugh, president, National Beer Wholesalers Association; Donald Shea, consultant, The Beer Institute; Thomas B. Turner, M.D., emeritus dean, Johns Hopkins Medical School; Robert S. Weinberg, professor of marketing management, Washington University; and Elizabeth M. Whelan, Ph.D., executive director, American Council on Science and Health.

Table of Research Findings

Part 1

THE BENEFITS OF MODERATE DRINKING

What's Right and What's Wrong with Our Drinking

1

Alcohol:

This Good Creature of God

*When members of a society have had sufficient
time to develop a widely shared set of beliefs
and values pertaining to drinking and drunkenness,
the consequences of alcohol consumption are not
usually disruptive for most persons
in that society.*
Mac Marshall
Beliefs, Behaviors & Alcoholic Beverages

*Bacchus turned a fruit into an enchantment
Which cheers the sad, revives the old, inspires
The young, makes weariness forget his toil,
And fear her danger, opens a new world,
When this, the present, palls.*
Lord Byron

*And malt does more than Milton can,
To justify God's ways to man.*
Anonymous

Alcohol serves many masters in our complex society. Drinking cannot be neatly categorized and classified.

The following explanation of drinking is a good place to begin our study. Morse makes good sense in his chapter from *Fermented Food Beverages in Nutrition*:

> Clearly, alcohol can serve many purposes through its pharmacological and symbolic characteristics. It gives pleasure, reduces pain, eliminates fears, raises self-esteem, solves conflict and so on. But basically the pleasurable experience from alcohol underlies all alcohol problems and perhaps all alcohol use. The alcoholic drinks to relieve tension, to celebrate, to become brave, to be sociable, to handle boredom, to

unwind, to get drunk, to feel good, to drown his sor-
rows, to get high — in other words, for the same reasons
everyone else drinks. In its nature and quality, however,
his drinking has changed from that of a nonalcoholic.

This book will not relieve the problems of alcoholism, but it will confront the problems created by the anti-alcohol lobby. It will do this by asserting the positive aspects of drinking which enrich the quality of life for the vast majority of the nonabusive drinkers. We have major alcohol problems today in the United States. Drinking problems plague Australia, South Africa and even West Germany and Italy where generally temperate drinking traditions dominate.

The greatest problem with alcohol today is not with the substance itself, or with our persistent core of problem drinkers. The difficulty lies in containing the reforming passions of well-meaning but misguided zealots. These do-gooders would plunge Western society once again into a pathological exercise of denial in trying to solve the riddle of human abuse. Alcoholism scholar and journalist Mark Keller created a name for these apostles of new temperance — the "alcoholismists" — individuals who are so consumed by the mechanics of fighting alcohol that they have lost sight of the clients they serve.

Alcohol abuse has been a constant in the history of man, as have physical, mental and carnal abuse. It probably always will be. But serious, debilitative drinking has been a minority problem through the long sweep of history. Morse in his thoughtful treatise suggests a new and refreshing approach which would involve the recognition and acceptance of the positive contributions of alcohol to mankind. "Perhaps a more rewarding strategy would be to ask why alcohol is not abused more or why everyone is not an alcoholic."

America's dilemma with alcohol today consists not so much in treating the drunks as in dealing with the political extremism of some highly committed public health administrators. These temperance partisans have control in many government and private agencies of public health. They seek stiff, punitive laws for alcohol control at a time when the nation is moderating its drinking habits. The statistics on drinking are trending down worldwide. We are gradually developing better clinical techniques for helping the alcoholic, although much research and treatment evaluation remains to be done.

Best of all, we are finally developing a moderate drinking consensus in America. It has taken a long time to shake the macho drinking image that developed in America at the end of colonial times. Thank the baby boomers and the yuppies that sensible, healthy, socially uplifting drinking is becoming the norm rather than the exception. Heavy drinking is out. Health and moderation are in.

But, we have failed to create a public policy which *supports* the propitious uses of alcohol. Over the last thirty years, we changed our drinking habits, but kept in place the negative attitudes about drinking left over from the repeal of prohibition. We repealed the laws, not the attitudes. Rather than tackle that serious and cumbersome debate, we resumed legal drinking in 1933, but left on the policy table all the myths and shibboleths about evil alcohol. Drinking is still only a tolerable diversion, not a blessing, as far as government is concerned. The only reason the Twenty-first Amendment worked was that the power to control alcohol was given the states. Each culturally distinctive region could reflect the will of its majority. This diverse control system has worked reasonably well. The only thing the federal government does is collect taxes and police generic matters such as advertising, labeling and purity of product. State alcohol control laws have adjusted and adapted to changing times and demands. That's what makes new temperance such a danger. Its advocates seek tight control at the federal level.

There is a resurgence of anti-alcohol fundamentalism.

In the 1950s and 1960s, thoughtful leaders in and out of American government began to grapple with the issue of how to define a proper role for alcohol. That is a real challenge in a nation where two-thirds of the population drinks and one-third abstains. As will be developed later in this text, several government commissions produced programs which would have accommodated all sides. A new federal responsibility was suggested in both research and the treatment of alcohol abuse but education and control would have remained on the state level.

Meanwhile, the old conservative temperance forces gained new momentum in the programs of the World Health Organization (WHO). A new control orthodoxy developed around the disease concept of alcoholism. In brief, that control theory holds that the numbers impacted by the disease of alcoholism would lessen in proportion to a society's reduction in drinking. The *availability* of alcohol became the primary issue. Since prohibition proved that alcohol cannot be eliminated completely, a reduction in its use is the second best target. That's what this book describes as new temperance. Twenty years ago, people of this persuasion set out to capture the mechanics of public health in the United States and elsewhere in the Western world, in and out of government. They've done a good job.

New temperance distorts and demeans the desirable, integrative function of alcohol for the majority who drink in a wholly responsible manner. Mark Keller has spent the past half century in the vortex of this ongoing debate. For four decades, he edited the prestigious *Journal of Studies on Alcohol.* In his essay "Alcohol Problems and Policies" in *Law, Alcohol and Order* (anyone seriously interested in the American alcohol problem should read this fine book), Keller writes with understandable indignation:

> That is where we stand today. Fifty years after the end of prohibition, we are being advised to enact inhibition. Along with the scientists, the alcoholismists — with still mainly alcoholics in their ranks and leadership — are in full cry against alcohol. I have heard the foremost leader among them say, "If it hadn't been for alcohol, I would never have become an alcoholic." What he meant was, alcohol is the cause of alcoholism. And that is what many alcoholics would like to believe: that, of course, there was nothing wrong with them; that they were not primarily weak or deficient; that alcohol just happened to get the best of them. Once they stopped the alcohol, they were all right. So alcohol was the cause.

And so we have the incredible irony (not to mention the economic lunacy) of the governor of California being asked to decide whether alcohol is a human toxin. Grapes are the largest cash crop in California. This is roughly akin to my state of Washington declaring that airplanes can be dangerous to health. Of course, alcohol is a human toxin. Of course, airplanes can fail and crash. But, broccoli, yams and carrots contain toxins. In some circumstances, drinking water can be dangerous. It's all a matter of degree and dosage. But the proposed toxicity warnings and the bottle label warnings never say anything about dosages. New temperance uses highly selective and bastardized science to single out alcohol. New temperance groups use the fear of fetal dysfunctions, drunk-driving and youth-on-drugs to garner public support for their draconian measures.

New temperance devotees are classical political progressives wearing the mantle of public health. Like stern mothers and fathers, they seek Orwellian control over the conduct of your most intimate personal lives. Progressives like to set standards for others. They suggest what you can eat, what you can drink, how you can exercise, the nature of your sexual practices, even what you and your children should read. Since the middle of the past century, when Christian progressivism evolved into a form of political fundamentalism, there has been a strong undercurrent of repression in American society. Historian David Kyvig in "Sober Thoughts," another essay from *Law, Alcohol and Order* writes:

> The prohibition amendment sought to redraw for all time the boundary between the public and private spheres of American life. From the founding of the republic, the right of the individual to be free from government intervention in purely private affairs received endorsement after endorsement. Only actions which had a negative impact on others were regarded as the proper concern of government. Prohibition redefined behavior once considered private and therefore beyond the proper reach of government as social and appropriate for government regulation. Adoption of the Eighteenth Amendment set a new standard for governmental intervention into personal lives, a step long discussed but not taken until 1919.

The inhibitionists and alcoholismists say that drinking is not a personal affair. They say it has negative public health consequences and, therefore, is in the realm of governmental concern. The progressives want more government intervention to make us behave according to their standards.

The Center for Science in the Public Interest (CSPI), a leading new temperance force, is a prime example. Their newsletters and publications tell how salt, saturated fats and alcohol — MacDonald hamburgers and Campbell's soup and drinking — are doing us in. On a nutritional advocacy level, their representations are appropriate. But, to purge these dangers, they call on Big Brother government to ordain what we eat, what we wear, and how we entertain ourselves. It's not that any or all of these health advocacies lack merit. It's the unrelenting dependency on governmental intervention and controls that makes CSPI and new temperance frightening and dangerous. Their vision is of a neatly ordered society in which we all weigh within ten pounds of the Metropolitan Life charts; we all jog three times a week; and we all wear Adidas runners and scruffy jeans. The real world is much more disordered and messy, but it is gloriously free and real.

Drinking is good for our society.

Science, history, sociology, anthropology, philosophy and most religions support the values in moderate drinking. Objective medical science supports the physical values in drinking, as the next chapter details.

History and anthropology show there are more practical benefits to a society from drinking than there are deficits in its abuse. This is not a Promethean discovery. It is fact based upon objective assessments of the assets and liabilities in alcohol usage. These values are especially apparent in America in the closing years of the twentieth century. All sorts of exotic cuisine and a new sophistication in the culture of eating have blended temperate drinking into our dining experiences. That is the best of all conditions for alcohol use—that it be consumed with food. This trend has led to many drinkers purchasing less in amount but better in quality. Though per capita drinking is down, the more expensive and food oriented beverages have increased in sales.

Alcohol's benefits are easily proven but few politicians would dare voice them on the political stump. Our lingering, temperance conditioned approach pretends that drinking is anti-social, immoral and self-indulgent. This book is written to challenge neoprohibition which is, in reality, a continuing, uninterrupted phenomenon. Alcohol bashing never went away. The repeal of the Eighteenth Amendment in 1933 merely legalized the mechanics of distribution and retailing. Society had to rid itself of the crime network and once again enrich the public treasury through legal alcohol taxes.

Alcohol ambivalence will never disappear completely in a society in which one-third of the adults do not drink. While these folks should never be made to feel uncomfortable in their abstinence, it no longer makes sense that their alcohol antipathies rule the roost. The majority that drinks correctly should assert itself. I say the time for that assertion has come.

The role of alcohol is very positive in history.

The shame of any radical alcohol temperance crusade is that it denies the integrative and humanizing functions of temperate alcohol usage. E. M. Jellinek, the father of the now widely accepted disease concept of alcoholism, was very supportive of drinking. As an historian, humanist and scientist, Jellinek recognized the positive contributions of moderate drinking. In "The Symbolism of Drinking: a Culture-Historical Approach" Jellinek writes:

> What led to the present inquiry is the fact that the act
> of drinking is an extremely old custom. To state this is
> almost a platitude. But it is important to stress that it is
> a custom which has persisted for thousands of years

despite the fact that at all times, and in all literate
cultures, it was realized that there were potential
dangers in the custom, and despite the fact that there
have always and universally been at least some opposition to it, and even at times highly systematic attempts
at eradication.

Jellinek saw drinking as inevitable. He suggested the disease
construct to help the abuser out of the morass of shame and moral
degradation. Still Jellinek continued to strongly support the traditional
role of alcohol in society. He found in both myth and religion that
drinking represented the very principle of life itself:

> Actually, it does not appear to matter whether the fluid
> is water, milk or an alcoholic beverage. The symbolism
> is the same: all are streams of life; all are fertility sym-
> bols...The equation of milk and wine still persists today.
> Thus we sometimes hear of wine as the "whole man's
> milk." Indeed, this symbolic equivalence is indicated by
> a multitude of examples in ethnography and
> folklore...Nor need the beverage be wine. It could be
> any alcoholic beverage; that is to say, it may be palm
> wine or beer or, later, distilled spirits.

Jellinek expressed a profound respect for the social function of
drinking. That is the message of this book. That there is a desirable,
health-giving aspect to sensible drinking. Yet, it is ironic that nearly
every authority interviewed over this past year warned against my
associating drinking with health benefits. I found this ambivalence in
all segments of our society. I found it even among men and women
who make and sell the products.

Yet, to avoid the conclusion that alcohol is health-giving is to
deny reality because of the passions and whims of the moment.
Alcohol has always been medicine in history, medicine in the
broadest, holistic sense as well as a specific medicine in clinical
practice. Hundreds of natural essences and oils affect our physical
and mental well-being, and we call these substances medicines.
Aspirin is one. Alcohol is one. Our problem lies in a ritualistic denial of
what we know to be true about drinking. In proper measure, it is
good for a person. Alcohol has always been considered a blessing to
the many, as well as a scourge to the few. Jellinek argues:

> I will not attempt to document the blood-alcohol, life-
> death equation further but I will add this: when the
> alcoholic beverage or water, but especially the

alcoholic beverage, was equated with blood, then the properties of blood were transferred to the substance with which it was equated. Since blood is food and medicine not only symbolically but actually, these properties are transferred to alcoholic beverages. Wines, spirituous liquors and beers have been considered "blood builders." If you donate blood, a friend may give you a bottle of port to compensate; one eats a good beefsteak because the blood one is taking in has great nutritional properties. Blood and alcoholic beverages mean two things to men: the restoration of health, i.e., medicine, and the maintenance of good health, i.e., food. Blood is par excellence the stream of life. Accordingly, the alcoholic beverage, too, becomes the stream of life, and the stream of life symbolism means power. All of these important properties of the alcoholic beverage—medicine, food, stream of life, power and death (the corollary of the blood-alcohol equation)—result in a tremendous prestige being attached to it. And this is the anchoring wedge for the general acceptance of alcohol in society: the prestige that lies in it, obtained through the act of drinking.

That is why new temperance relentlessly attacks the concept of responsible, moderate drinking Because, in appropriate use, alcohol has the power and majesty of human purpose. It belongs.

Alcohol helped to civilize wandering tribes.

These are not radical ideas. The anti-alcohol temperance advocacies are the radical ones. Alcohol helps to civilize today. It may well have been the most important single cause of civilization in ancient history. To civilize is to bring out from a savage, disorganized state. Katz in "The Evolution of Wine and Cuisine," and Katz and Voigt in "Bread and Beer" describe how nomadic man settled and domesticated both plants and animals. In this long process, humans sorted out and cultivated about one hundred from the thousands of edible plants used by nomadic hunter-gatherers. Grains and fruits for fermentation were common in every ancient society. In this civilizing process across the globe, alcohol became a dietary staple.

Man had to deal with the bothersome compounds called "anti-nutrients" in plant life—what modern day environmentalists call toxins and mutagens. Creating a "cuisine" by cooking raw plants provided an answer. The "anti-nutrient" in beer and wine was its intoxicating and often debilitating effect. The stone age civilizations solved the problem of excessive drinking by incorporating alcohol into religious and social practice. They worshiped together and drank together to make alcohol a unifying rather than a divisive element. Of course, they also set up rules of conduct—the first primitive alcohol controls.

Katz and Voigt found that the desire for a continuing source of alcohol may have been the most dominant civilizing decision. They speculate that the desire for a stable source of alcohol provoked the first domestication of wild grains. Alcohol brought us together as an organized society.

> First, the motivation for a change in behavior...was provided by the noticeable phenomenon—the "high" that people obtained from beer. Second, individuals and groups who consumed beer were better nourished than those who consumed wheat and barley as gruel or who ignored these wild resources. Beer would have had sustaining powers well beyond any other food in their diet except animal proteins. In biological terms, beer drinkers would have had a "selective advantage" in the form of improved health for themselves and, eventually, for their offspring. Third, cereals were a desirable resource because of the ease with which they could be harvested, transported and stored from year to year.

So the very beginnings of civilization evolved around the humanizing, the civilizing, the life-supportive, as well as the euphoric rewards of drinking.

> Our own explanation for the beginnings of cereal cultivation is consistent with the biocultural model for the evolution of cuisine. The key element in this explanation, the event that "primed the pump" and led people to choose to invest energy in the collection and propagation of wild wheat and barley, was the discovery of new food processing techniques—the sprouting and fermentation of grains.

The authors argue that the human effects of drinking were known long before the discovery of how fermentation worked. This was true because of the spontaneous, natural fermentation of ripe fruits and honey. Wine and mead were gifts of nature. "It is thus strongly suspected that this fermented food beverage was available before the start of agriculture. In other words, in a hunting-gathering society, wines were probably consumed at least on a seasonal basis when the grapes were ripe."

Each society must balance the good and bad in drinking.

The majority of us who consume with decorum, within deeply-held religious traditions and with profound cultural meanings have allowed those who despise alcohol to dominate the political stage. Consequently, our public alcohol policy is negative. That obeisance of the majority to the alcohol-hatred of a vocal minority has to stop before we slip into another period of social disunion. The moderates need to voice their resistance to this trend.

New temperance laws can adversely affect people's lives as prohibition did. They can really hurt people. They encourage the idea that drinking is synonymous with drunkenness. They raise the cost of drinking and encourage bootlegging. They embellish alcohol's racy, adult lure for teenagers. They establish a "forbidden fruit" attraction ready-made for the rebellious young. As this book goes to press, Wyoming became the last state to raise its drinking age to twenty-one under Congressional blackmail. They would lose highway funds if they didn't. This classic new temperance bill swept the Congress on a wave of emotion to protect our young people.

The May 1988 issues of _Status Report_, the Insurance Institute for Highway Safety newsletter, reports "The alcohol purchase age of 21 'reduced the involvement of 18–20 year-olds in fatal crashes by about 13 percent, saving about 1,000 lives in 1987,' the National Highway Traffic Safety Administration says." The report goes on to say that overall intoxicated fatalities had dropped 14 percent. These highway fatalities have been dropping for a decade, but new temperance will claim a victory. So the battle of the statistics is underway. Already, at least one state—Wisconsin—is reconsidering lowering the alcohol purchase age from 21 because after it was implemented, upper-teen alcohol offenses showed immediate increases.

Setting the minimum drinking age at 21 is one of a whole agenda of laws the new temperance people have in store. Product labeling is high on that agenda, as are heavy increases in excise taxation. The alcohol drinking moderate majority is left out of this political scenario because there is no advocacy group representing moderation.

Yet, the moderates have medical science on their side. They have history, art, culture and common sense on their side. Over the past several decades, cross-cultural studies in the discipline of anthropology have concurred that alcohol can be a unifying as well as a destructive force. Heath in "Alcohol Use, 1970-1980" from _Constructive Drinking_ sets forth the seven "...most significant generalizations that derive from these multidisciplinary evaluations of the role of alcohol in society:"

1. In most societies, drinking is essentially a social act, and, as such, it is embedded in a context of values, attitudes and other norms.

2. These values, attitudes, and other norms constitute important socio-cultural factors that influence the effects of drinking, regardless of how important biochemical, physiological, and pharmacokinetic factors may also be in that respect.

3. The drinking of alcoholic beverages tends to be hedged about with rules concerning who may and may not drink how much of what, in what contexts, in the company of whom, and so forth..

4. The value of alcohol for promoting relaxation and sociability is emphasized in many populations.

5. The association of drinking with any kind of specifically associated problems – physical, economic, psychological, social relational, or other – is rare among cultures throughout both history and the contemporary world.

6. When alcohol-related problems do occur, they are clearly linked with modalities of drinking, and usually also with values, attitudes and norms about drinking.

7. Attempts at prohibition have never been successful except when couched in terms of sacred or supernational rules.

Alcoholic beverages today are scapegoats. People drink more at times of stress and it is easier to blame alcohol or drugs than society's incapacity to provide for all its citizens. The biggest problem is our transition from an industrial worker society to a computer-based technocracy. The political and economic systems haven't figured out what to do with all those displaced workers. Shaefer in "Drunkenness and Culture Stress: A Holocultural Test" talks about how societies that have great unrest (i.e., the metropolitan areas in America) will experience increased substance abuse:

On the other hand, where political leaders have their
political organizations well attuned to the needs of the
people, and where the social structure provides a
variety of achievable statuses and roles, anxiety will
tend to be low, and feelings about personal power will
tend to be reinforced, and extreme, aggressive drunkenness will be highly unlikely.

Overdrinking is the issue, not wine, beer or spirits.

Since the discovery that malted grains would ferment, societies
have chosen to legalize the controlled use of alcoholic beverages.
That must say something about alcohol as compared to marijuana,
cocaine, barbiturates and other mind-altering substances that have
been generally discouraged or proscribed. Time and tradition
indicate that alcohol is not just another psychedelic as advocates of
new temperance strongly assert. Our oldest written record, a pottery
chard from ancient Egypt, depicts the brewing of beer. Katz and
Voigt report on this find:

> The most ancient documentary evidence for beer
> production comes from Mesopotamia, written in the
> Sumerian language on tablets that date to the 3rd mil-
> lennium B.C. The world's oldest recipe is for
> beer!...The purely personal pleasure that these people
> took in beer drinking is summed up in the following
> song, written to celebrate building of a tavern.

> Let the heart of the gakkul (fermenting) vat be our
> heart.
> What makes your heart feel wonderful,
> Makes also our heart feel wonderful.
> Our liver is happy, or heart is joyful.
> You poured a libation over the brick of destiny,
> You placed the foundations in peace and prosperity.
> May Ninkasi live together with you!

Ninkasi was the beer goddess. Bacchus, Isis, Priapos and the
many other male and female deities represented both alcohol and the
concept of fertility. Alcohol was the principle of life. In ancient times,
beer and wine were as much food and medicine as pleasant
beverage. Through all ancient and medieval history, the vintner,
brewmaster, distiller, and their merchants were prominent and highly
regarded members of the societies they served. Although various
societies attempted to moderate intake by rule-making, seldom was
the product itself reviled. Alcohol belonged.

True temperance seeks to moderate drinking.

It is not that these ancients didn't abuse. At times, the amount of drinking was prodigious. Reports of excessive drinking abound in the history of all western nations. French in the _History and Virtues of Cyder_ recounts the titanic alcohol abuse common in Alexander the Great's court. "Many of the competitors died during the contest or shortly after, but Torquatus Tricongius survived long enough to take the prize, having drunk his twenty-four pints." Some examples of our own American proclivities to heavy drinking are contained in Rorabaugh's _The Alcoholic Republic_ , but the historian qualifies the problem. Even in hard-drinking colonial times, a minority did most of the problem drinking. "Thus, half the adult males — one eighth of the total population — were drinking two-thirds of all the distilled spirits." Through the centuries, temperance movements invariably sought to moderate the misuse of the bibulous minority, not the moderate intake of the society as a whole.

Then came the late nineteenth century style of temperance. Early American temperance responded to another period of high stress in history. After the revolution, we entered a period of disgraceful, endemic overindulgence. But, all of Western civilization was impacted: first, by the agricultural revolution which encouraged vast expansion in population; and then by the industrial revolution which introduced machinery. It was an epoch of uncertainty, transition, of joblessness and widespread disillusion, particularly in the young American Republic. The new machines could more quickly accomplish the tasks that hands and beasts of burden had shared since the beginning of time. Alcohol was inexpensive and drinking was a way of escaping from seemingly insoluble problems.

Through a fitful and traumatic first fifty years of the nineteenth century, the industrial revolution gradually bore its magnificent fruits of full employment, stability and economic progress. Hill in "Ethnohistory and Alcohol Studies" from _Recent Developments in Alcoholism_ paints that terrifying period which preceded this economic turnaround:

> But the series of events since the American Revolution had a significant psychological impact on them [American workers]: they had lost their self-esteem and self-confidence and were uncertain as to the value of their culture and their abilities to survive as a people. Wallace sees their psychological difficulties reflected in increased drinking, drunken violence, frequent witchcraft accusations, depression, and suicides.

By 1850, employment was up and drinking was down. Americans had again moderated their alcohol intake to responsible levels. The majority went about building a nation as a sobersided people. Many are surprised to learn that the level of drinking in the 1860s, after the trauma of the civil war, became very close to what prevails today. The temperance movement, prohibition and repeal were a virtual waste of time in terms of per capita consumption.

But the temperance movement did not die with the elimination of its root cause—overdrinking. It radicalized and politicized its operations. It created a vindictive devil of drink, of this natural substance that Puritan leader Increase Mather had called "this good creature of God." The rest is history, sad and bad history. Mobsters became the kingpins of the alcoholic beverage commerce. Prohibition made lawbreakers and scofflaws of the majority of citizens who routinely made gin in the bathtub and beer in the basement. Harrison in *Drink and the Victorians* describes the populist, conservative-Christian base for political temperance that still dominates the movement today. This is populist progressivism. It seeks to incorporate Christian paternalism by an intervening government:

> A German miner who visited Newcastle in the 1890s found two aspects of British Society unfamiliar. He noted that the middle and the working class are on very friendly terms...because they are brought together in clubs and religious organizations and that the sects try to outdo one another in the exercise of practical Christianity. Both of these aspects of British Society have been actively promoted by the temperance movement...The temperance movement was, in fact, one of several transitional organizations channelling religious energies into party politics.

Today, the American society is faced once again with a highly motivated and articulate new temperance crusade, one which is far more political and power-oriented than health and care-oriented. It has insinuated its disruptive philosophy into a wide spectrum of both governmental and private public health, alcoholism, and drug treatment and rehabilitation agencies.

Temperance today is a minority of public health radicals.

Yet it is, for all I can discover, a minority within a minority. This temperance vanguard today lacks the millions of teetotaling foot soldiers of yesteryear. So new temperance relies on slick publicity and public information programs that sell fear. Fear of youth drinking and drugging. Fear of death on the highways. Fear of the addictive properties of alcohol. Fear of cancer. Fear of drinking even small amounts when pregnant. Its leaders deny that they are prohibitionists, though their highly structured propaganda stimulates the anti-alcohol atmosphere of the 1930s. That's why so few people recognize the real dangers. Temperance leaders loudly protest that they do not want prohibition, just a few laws and rules here and there. The sum of these laws would be a wet-prohibition.

This book looks at the other side. The good side of drinking. It does not support abusive or heavy drinking. Indeed, it argues that a better public attitude toward alcohol will reduce abuse. It does not suggest that everyone should want or need to drink. It suggests that society, as a whole, should determine what's of value and what's worth retaining in our drinking practices. As it is, those who are describing the parameters of correct drinking are mainly Keller's "alcoholismists", many of whom have had personal problems with alcohol. These radicals definitely do not share open and objective viewpoints on the subject.

This text suggests that temperate drinkers must define for themselves what constitutes moderate, responsible drinking. It argues that the federal government has become a leading proponent of new temperance. The concluding chapter suggests that the price will be high. If moderate drinkers persist in ignoring this accelerating social phenomenon, they risk easy access to their single malt scotches, their favorite brews, and their mellow cabernets. Their sons and daughters will also be tempted to misuse. It is a lesson we apparently have forgotten.

The book focuses specifically and intentionally on the role of the federal government, and with good reason. In the alcohol and public health field, there is no more important or valuable tool than to control the statistics and to dominate communication. That's what the Department of Health and Human Services provides for new temperance. A shield and a voice.

The time has come to do battle with the pseudo-scientists of new temperance, and to create a firm and lasting political consensus which incorporates "this good creature of God."

2

The Good News
About Alcohol and Health

*It keepeth the stomach from wambling
and the heart from swelling:
the bellie from wirtching,
the guts from numbing, the hands from shivering
and the sinews from shrinking, the veines from
crumpling, the bones from aking and the marrow
from soaking. And truly it is a
sovereign liquor if it be orderlie taken.*
Raphael Holinshead, 1577

*The popular mythology of alcohol is
a vast and vehement book. It is also a
book of massive durability. Almost every
vision of alcohol that the human imagination
has summoned up during some six thousand
years of fascinated scrutiny may still
be found among its pages. As a compendium of
ageless errors, of phantom fears and ghostlier
reassurances, it probably has no equal. It is,
perhaps, the classic text in the
illiterature of medicine.*
Berton Roueche'
Alcohol: The Neutral Spirit

*Scientifically, only risks can be measured;
the absence of risk (absolute safety) can
never be conclusively established.*
Henry Rosett, M.D. and Lyn Weiner
Alcohol And The Fetus

Is moderate drinking good for you? Does the moderate daily
intake of alcohol cause any physical harm? How does the rate of
drinking affect health?

Don't look to the medical profession for a clear, unequivocal answers to this questions. For the better part of two centuries, alcoholic beverages have endured calumny and defamation in this country without respite. Doctors are no different in the ambivalence department than the rest of us. Most physicians are as confused about moderate drinking as the rest of us, and the medical profession has been cowed by the constant threat of liability lawsuits. Individual doctors routinely and quietly recommend light or moderate drinking within their medical practices. They aren't apt to do so publicly until the whole, complex issue of alcohol and health has been aired. New public policy must be formulated which encompasses a healthful, socially acceptable level of drinking for those who choose to drink.

The California Wine Institute has sponsored several wine and health symposia and has published several books and pamphlets on the voluminous research concerning wine and health. Institute president, John De Luca comments, "The doctors are intimidated by malpractice suits. There is a lot of timidity around now."

Yet, amid all this confusion, there is a fascinating story in the medical literature that is not at all tentative. Here are the findings from my search of the literature on alcohol and health.

Research Finding 2.1

Alcohol has been the mistress of medicine
through all recorded history.

> *Sweet drink put far away their cares. As*
> *they drank liquor their bodies became satiated.*
> *Much they bubbled and their mood was exalted.*
> **Epic of Creation, 2225 B.C.**

> *After Mass there was often a distribution of unconsecrated wine*
> *as well as pain benit; Wine was also used for salving cuts and*
> *wounds...being the only known disinfectant. In fact,*
> *it was universal medicine.*
> **Desmond Seward**
> *Monks and Wine*

Alcohol has always been a medicine and drinking an effective therapy. The pertinent question is why historians so often ignore the role of alcohol in the telling of the past. Fleming in *Alcohol: The Delightful Poison* says, "Alcohol is seldom mentioned in history

books, but it has affected, and been affected by, many of the events
that are."

Most historical references on the therapeutic values of alcohol
involve wine. As the Jewish Talmud advises, "Wine is the foremost of
all medicines. Wherever wine is lacking, medicines become
necessary." St. Paul writes, "Drink no longer water but use a little
wine for thine stomach's sake and thine often infirmities." Euripides
exulted, "Wine removes the cares pressing upon the minds of
sorrowing mortals, who, when filled with this juice of the grape, no
longer need sleep, and no longer remember their daily miseries."
Classical literature and poetry abounds in the praise of alcoholic
beverages.

Straus writes in "An Historical Perspective on the Clinical Uses
of Wine" that wine was a common medicine in ancient times:

> Wine began to be used as medicine by ancient man,
> and there are 191 references to wine's medicinal
> properties in both the Old and New Testament. The
> numerous references in the Bible indicate that not only
> wine but stronger beverages were made, as indicated by
> the following words: Yayin — the Hebrew word most
> frequently used to describe wine; Homer — young,
> unmixed wine; Tiros — strong wine; Sekhor — strong
> drink; and Meseg — mixed wines.

> For example, in the Book of Psalms, it is written that,
> "wine maketh glad the heart of man." Furthermore,
> two Biblical precepts indicate that the ancients knew
> well of wine's tranquilizing effects. One precept is:
> "Give strong drink unto him that is ready to perish, and
> wine to those of heavy hearts." The other is: "Let him
> drink and forget his poverty, and remember his misery
> no more."

Koch in _Alcohol: Gift of God_ writes:

> While it was common to mix wine and water, undiluted
> wine was a prized possession. Notice in Isaiah 1:22 that
> choice wine diluted with water is considered as
> devalued as silver becoming dross...In each of these
> verses, wine is referred to in speaking of God's bless-
> ings to His people. The Old Testament verses include
> wine as one of the specific benefits from God.

Distilling probably wasn't discovered until many centuries after Christ. It is conjectured that the Biblical references to strong drink referred to wine diluted with herbs—what we call tonics today. Often, these mixtures included psychedelic herbs. Wasson, Ruck and Hofmann in *The Road To Eleusis* describe the common practice in ancient Greece:

> The solution to this apparent contradiction is simply that ancient wine, like the wine of most early peoples, did not contain alcohol as its sole inebriant but was ordinarily a variable infusion of herbal toxins in a vinous liquid. Unguents, spices, and herbs all with recognized psychotropic properties, could be added to the wine at the ceremony of its dilution with water...The fact is that the Greeks had devised a spectrum of ingredients for their drinks each with its own properties.

The hippies of the 1960s thought they discovered a new euphoria by combining marijuana and "pop" wines. They were merely repeating an ancient Greek practice. Wine not only enlivened the terrible drudgery of foot-soldiering in early times, but it also helped its users win great battles. Straus writes, "Twenty-five centuries ago, in 539 B.C., Cyrus the Great had his troops carry wine on their march to Babylonia as a prophylactic measure against waterborne diseases." And the great legions of Rome conquered most of Europe carrying their health-protecting wines with them. Many of today's European wine growing regions were developed by the conquering Romans.

The Greek, the Roman and other Mediterranean people used wine as a dietary staple. And they drank beer regularly even in pre-Christian times. Nations to the north, lying beyond the grape cultivation regions, substituted mead (fermented honey) for wine and made beer a staple. Grain was common in their husbandry. Hunter in *Fermented Foods and Beverages* tells of the use of honey as both a medicine and an intoxicant, "Hydromel, the mead of the Greeks, was for centuries not only a popular drink but was considered a salutary medicine...Pliny said...'it invigorates the body, is soothing to the mouth and stomach...is well suited for persons of chilly temperament, or of a weak and pusillanimous constitution.'"

Distillation was a more recent phenomenon.

The distillation of wine and beer first began around 800 A.D. The medical fraternity was captivated by its magic. Marrison in *Wines and Spirits* traces the perfection of distilling skills to the production of prized perfumes and cooking oils by the Arabs. The north Africans,

"...had built a flourishing trade in these commodities, which were almost necessities for those who could afford them...By the twelfth century, Salernus was writing about distillation, and a hundred years later Albertus Magnus gave a description of the process." Forbes' *Short History of the Art of Distillation,* one of the rare texts on distilling, attributes a major scientific benchmark in the development in Europe of liquor distillation. "The discovery of mineral acids and somewhat earlier (eleventh or twelfth century) that of alcohol may be said to mark the beginning of a new stage in history, the transition of the old and the new chemistry."

In every language, the root words for distilled spirits mean the "water of life." Arnald of Vilanova first tabbed spirits thusly, "The true water of life will come over in precious drops which, being rectified by three or four distillations, will afford the wonderful quintessence of wine. We call it *aqua vitae*." The French called it *eau de vie*, and the Celts tabbed their fiery spirits *uisge beatha*, meaning the water of life. That Celtic phrase is the root for our word whiskey.

By 1519, the most prominent surgeon of his day, Hieronymus Braunschweig testified to the prestige accorded spirits in medieval medicine:

> Aqua vitae is commonly called the mistress of all medicines. It eases the diseases coming of cold. It comforts the heart. It heals all old and new sores on the head. It causes a good color in a person. It heals alopolecia [baldness] and causes the hair well to grow and kills lice and fleas. It cures lethargy. Cotton wet in the same and a little wrung out again and put in the ears at night going to bed, and a little drunk thereof, is good against all deafness...It causes good digestion and appetite for to eat, and takes away all belching. It draws the winds out of the body. It eases that yellow jaundice, the dropsy, the gout, the pain of the breasts when they be swollen and heals all diseases of the bladder, and breaks the stone...It gives also young courage in a person, and causes him to have good memory and remembrance.

Darby in *Wine and Medical Wisdom through the Ages* extols the virtues of drink but warns of the tempting promises of medical quackery:

> The strong conceptual bonds between religion and healing and the magic-medical property of wine explain the

associations of wine, the healing arts, religion, the elitists, the learned priests. Throughout history, wine has been regarded as...aliment, medicine and poison. The palliative relief, albeit temporary, from anxiety or discomfort that it affords and the absence of specific medical therapies gave rise to an extraordinary diversity of medical "uses" of wine in folk medicine, by legitimate physicians, and by promoters of nostrums and quackery.

Health literature generally favors alcohol.

It's not that you can't find praise for alcohol in the popular media. Many contemporary books and magazine articles attest to the health and therapeutic values in moderate alcohol consumption. There is a strong association of wine and beer in medicine and therapy, as detailed by many of the scholarly references in the bibliography. A host of pop-culture advisories are in print today, such as Michaels' book *Stay Healthy with Wine* and Maury's *Wine Is The Best Medicine*. The latter book has dosages and wine types for everything from bronchitis and diarrhea to weakness of the liver!

The vintners have more thoroughly defined the rich vein of alcohol-based remedies and therapies though the centuries, but all alcoholic beverages have been generously involved in both folk and authoritative medicine. In recent decades, the Wine Institute has added greatly to an understanding of wine in modern medical practice in a seminar series called Wine, Health & Society. Many practicing physicians also use the Wine Institute's very practical and informative *Wine And Medical Practice* pamphlet.

Beer and spirit interests have also been active in the medical information field, particularly in the financial support of basic research on drinking and health. The Distilled Spirits Council of the United States (DISCUS) has generously supported basic research on alcoholism at Harvard University and at other famous research centers. The American and Canadian brewing industries have funded the independent Alcoholic Beverage Medical Research Foundation. Many scholarly and insightful studies have been produced at the these research centers. Among them is the important 1981 report by Turner, Bennett and Hernandez titled "The Beneficial Side Of Moderate Alcohol Use" upon which this book's upper limits of consumption are based.

Very little of the research in the literature mentions specific types of drinks. In most projects, participants report on their drinking patterns, and that information is translated into ounces of ethanol for purposes of analysis. A few of the projects, such as the drinking questionnaire in the Canada Health Survey, kept separate statistical analyses for wine, beer and spirits. Most of the scientific studies cited below demonstrate the effects of alcohol on health without reference to types or sources.

While many of us partake of a variety of beverages, the alcohol of choice in our nation today is beer. Americans consume more than twenty-three gallons of beer per person annually compared to around three gallons of wine and slightly under two of spirits. This book is not interested in proving (or disproving) any specific advantage in the consuming of any particular alcohol beverage. That's for partisans to do. Its objective is to establish an image for alcohol in America that is common in the Latin nations in Europe.

Alcoholic beverages have always been respected as a medicine. Even though their abuse was also manifest.

Research Finding 2.2

National health surveys find better
health among moderate drinkers.

> *It is very dangerous to make health claims for*
> *alcohol. It's mainly used for relaxing, for sociability.*
> *It creates warmth, a glow; it's for individuals to enjoy*
> *with their meals.*
> **Interview with David J. Pittman, Ph.D.**
> Washington University

Some researchers are outspokenly favorable to moderate drinking, though nearly all express caution and prudence. In 1982, John Pickering, a Philadelphia cardiologist, reported on a seven-year study titled "The Multiple Risk Factors Intervention Trial," and he suggested a regimen likely to "rustproof" your heart. "Lose weight if you are heavy. Stop smoking. Exercise regularly. And drink one and one-half ounces, not more, of alcohol every day."

When is the last time you heard a physician advising daily drinking? One wonders why such positive data aren't given wider currency in public media. One reason is that few of these positive studies find their way into the alcohol public information reporting system of the National Institute on Alcohol Abuse and Alcoholism (NIAAA).

You do not read in NIAAA literature of Dr. Pickering's recommendation of daily drinking or of Turner et al. and their scientific analysis of permissible upper limits. These positive statements would help us better understand the values as well as the dangers in drinking. The absence of any support for moderate drinking in NIAAA publications is significant. There are cardinal sins of omission as well as commission.

Studies consistently demonstrate better health standing among individuals who drink between one and four standard drinks daily. Here are three excerpts from major American surveys which are typical in their conclusion that moderate, daily drinkers form a healthier population segment than do abstainers or heavy drinkers.

The Alameda County Study

Wiley and Camacho, in "Life-Style and Future Health: Evidence from the Alameda County Study," report the results of a nine-year, longitudinal study of 3,892 adults under the age of 70 in Alameda, California:

> Moderate alcohol consumption (17–45 drinks per month) in 1965 is associated with the most favorable adjusted health scores. The extreme categories — abstention or consumption of 46 or more drinks per month — are associated with the least favorable scores....it is not likely that our results are due to the effects of ill health on abstention, because the health outcome measure we used is adjusted for initial level of health.

Even when the statistics were adjusted to eliminate participants with pre-existing adverse health conditions, such as might occur with former alcoholics, the moderate drinkers in the Alameda study were healthier. This is important because critics of these studies often say that the abstaining segment necessarily contains former alcoholics and others with illnesses or conditions that skew the findings.

The Canadian Health Survey

Another national health survey, this one in Canada in 1984, involved 17,249 respondents. Richman and Warren in "Alcohol Consumption and Morbidity In the Canada Health Survey" not only reported substantially improved mortality among moderate beer drinkers. The authors also raise the vital question as to why so little time and research money is spent on determining why moderate drinkers manage to stay moderate:

Excessive drinkers constitute an extreme subset of all drinkers, and it cannot be assumed that relationships observed in excessive drinkers can be extrapolated to moderate drinkers...Overall morbidity rates and both frequency and quantity dimensions of the dose-response relationship varied markedly as a function of type of beverage consumed. Beer drinkers, in particular, varied from other consumers. They had significantly lower rates of morbidity than expected. Increases in frequency of beer drinking were associated with reductions in morbidity, but mildly deleterious effects were associated with excessive consumption.

The American Health Survey

Yet another health survey was taken across the United States. One statistical segment involved 17,600 men and women who met certain exclusive criteria designed to *eliminate* adverse conditions due to age, sex, or smoking. Titled "Associations between Alcoholic Beverage Consumption and Hospitalization, 1983 National Health Interview Survey", the report by Longnecker and MacMahon found:

Figure 1 shows the OR (ratio of odds) of hospitalization in females by level of alcohol intake. A U-shaped relationship is seen, with the lowest risk for those consuming 29–42 alcoholic drinks in the two-week period — more than two and up to three drinks per day on average. Comparable data for males given in Figure 2 show the same trough at 29–42 drinks, although the U-shaped pattern is not so clear.

The authors go on to say that, "A U-shaped association between ethanol consumption and ischemic heart disease and mortality is evident in the data reported by investigators. It is likely that the U-shaped association between alcohol consumption and hospitalization noted here reflects this known association."

These U-shaped curves have great significance in epidemiology since they identify a segment within the study that stands apart. These three broad-based surveys show nearly identical U-shaped curves which depict moderate drinkers as better off than abusers or nondrinkers. They illustrate favorable patterns for moderate drinkers similar to many of the heart studies reported below with U-shaped response curves.

Daily drinkers found to have 15 percent less disability.

Observation of these better health patterns among moderate daily drinkers raises a simple question. If alcohol researchers know of these studies, why shouldn't the moderate drinking public know more of them too? If federal and state health authorities know about these studies, why should they fail to inform the drinking population of a critical relationship between drinking and well-being?

Richman suggested promising avenues for new research on these health values which may pertain in daily or frequent drinking. Here are his comments as reported in *Research Insights* from the United States Brewers' Association:

> As expected, persons who drank more reported progressively more accidents. Was there a similar dose response with disability? One would expect that higher or more frequent alcohol intake would be associated with more disability. However, there was no dose-response with disability in this sample of the general population. Persons who drank more or on more occasions did not have corresponding increase in disability.
>
> In fact, persons who drank once a day had 15 percent less disability than the general population. The data support the need to assess not only the risks of high alcohol intake, but the potential benefit of moderate alcohol intake in the general population.

Obviously, the moderate beer drinkers who responded in Canada, the moderate drinkers surveyed in Alameda, California and the men and women who answered the hospitalization survey are living longer, healthier lives than the nondrinkers or abusers who responded to those same surveys. Are these atypical studies chosen simply because they demonstrate favorable results? Hardly. Consider the many citations which follow.

Research Finding 2.3

Heart and cardiovascular research
shows better health among moderates.

*The evidence is very strong that low
levels of drinking may reduce the risk of
cardiovascular disease. At these low levels,
there is little risk of organ damage from
alcohol for most people.*
Richard D. Moore, M.D.
Alcohol Research

The NIAAA uses the words "caused by" to show negative statistics and avoids reference to positive values of alcohol. NIAAA publications say it *causes* crime, suicide, and wife-beating while the agency is indifferent to the positive relationships of moderate drinking. One wonders at NIAAA's timidity in finding similar "causal relationships" between moderate alcohol intake and heart health, so clearly defined are these studies.

Here are excerpts from recent studies which describe how regular daily drinkers are enjoying better health than nondrinkers or abusers. Sources of these studies are cited in the bibliography.

Yano studied 7,705 Japanese men living in Hawaii and found a stepwise decline in coronary heart disease (CHD) from a mean daily intake of from zero to 31.5 grams of alcohol daily.

Ramsey in Glasgow studied 1,505 men with hypertension finding a significant trend away from heart attacks in each age level of moderate drinkers.

Vaillant studied core city men and alcoholism over a 45 year span and found that control problems are rare in men who did not exceed four drinks daily.

Hennekens et al. studied 568 married white men in Florida aged 30 to 70 and found the risk of heart disease significantly lower for those drinking 2 ounces of ethanol daily (four standard drinks).

Marmot et al. in a longitudinal study of civil servants including 1,422 men over 10 years found the mortality rate was lower for drinkers of 34 grams per day and cardiovascular mortality was greater in nondrinkers.

Ashley in Canada found that IHD (ischemic heart disease) and cerebrovascular disease accounted for 30 percent of all deaths and that up to 4 standard drinks per day is protective against these two diseases.

Jackson in New Zealand studied blood pressure in 1,429 men and women from 35 to 64 and found that those with light to moderate drinking at 34 grams per day had lower blood pressure than nondrinkers and heavy drinkers.

Gordon reporting on the Framingham, Massachusetts 22-year follow-up study of residents found that frequent drinkers were less likely to die of CHD, and the lowest risk was among men who consumed 30–59 drinks per month equivalent to 1.7 to 3.4 drinks per day.

Gordon and Doyle in Albany in a study of men over 20 years of age concluded that nondrinkers had higher death rates than drinkers of less than 30 ounces of alcohol per month.

Wiley and Camacho in a longitudinal study of 2,892 white adults under 70 found that the extreme categories of abstention or consumption of more than 46 drinks per month had the least favorable health.

Kozarevic et al. in Yugoslavia studied 11,121 men aged 35 to 62 in which daily drinkers had fewer heart attacks than occasional drinkers.

Dyer et al. in Chicago studied 1,832 white male employees at General Electric and found that over 6 drinks per day increased death rates for all causes while CHD (coronary heart disease) and CVD (cardiovascular disease) rates dropped for those who drank 1 to 4 drinks per day.

Klatsky et al. in California found nondrinkers have significantly higher cardiovascular mortality.

Colditz et al. in Massachusetts in a cohort study of men over 66 found the famous U-shaped curve providing maximum protection in those drinking up to 34 grams per day.

Barboriak et al. in Milwaukee studied 909 nondiabetic males and found that coronary occlusions were higher in nondrinkers than in those drinking less than 180 milliliters of alcohol per week.

Camargo et al. in Washington state studied HDL (high density lipoprotein) and found that a rate of 2 to 3 drinks a day kept a high protective level of HDL while cessation of drinking dropped that level.

Diehl et al. in London observed the protective effects of alcohol intake on CHD risk through the HDL3 subfraction.

There is danger in extracting these few lines from the reports of complex research projects. But, obviously, there is a pattern found. They are cited because they demonstrate that drinkers are found to enjoy better health. A level of consumption between two and four drinks repeatedly shows health benefits. One cannot read these reports and not wonder whether the *real* health risks lie in the current campaign of the Department of Health and Human Services (DHHS) to lower per capita consumption.

People who now enjoy the benefits of their moderate consumption could be placed at *greater risk of heart disease* through reduced consumption. That is at least a valid research assumption.

Research Finding 2.4

Specialists show cautious support
of the benefits of moderate drinking.

> *Modest alcohol consumption*
> *has been associated with beneficial effects.*
> **American Heart Association**

Recognizing the growing evidence of well-being of individuals in these surveys and studies, the American Heart Association (AHA) recommends a cautious approach to drinking. Their 1984 publication titled "Report of Inter-Society Commission for Heart Disease Resources" states:

> Therefore, alcohol should be prescribed by the physician with caution, although there is no contra-

indication to its regular use. An increased HDL-cholesterol level appears to be a dividend of moderate consumption of alcohol...AHA guidelines for daily consumption are not to exceed 50cc or 2 shots of whiskey, 2 beers or 2 four ounce glasses of wine and no more than 15% of daily calories.

The AHA publication indicates there is nothing which would recommend against alcohol's "regular use." This contrasts with the NIAAA's current attitude that drinking is "risk taking." The NIAAA Scientific Advisory Board's recommendations for future research state, "Several epidemiologic studies have reported that moderate drinking (one or two drinks a day or less) may reduce the risk of coronary heart disease (CHD)...Thus the question of whether moderate drinking protects against coronary heart disease continues to generate considerable controversy."

Contrast NIAAA's skepticism with the following series of excerpts from the medical literature.

Moore and Pearson in "Moderate Alcohol Consumption and Coronary Artery Disease." "The incidence of both CAD (coronary artery disease) and death from cardiovascular causes decreased with increasing consumption up to a level of 4 to 5 drinks per day."

Klatsky in _The Proceedings of the Wine Health and Society Symposium._ "Non-drinkers had a higher mortality rate due to coronary disease than did users of (plus or minus) 2 drinks. The (plus) 6 drinkers and the (plus or minus) 2 drinkers had the lowest incidence of acute myocardial infarction, but mortality from ischemic heart disease was highest in the (plus) 6 group."

NIAAA's _Second Special Report to Congress on Alcohol and Health, 1974._ "The use of alcoholic beverages thus appears not to have any detrimental effects leading to coronary heart disease, but present knowledge is insufficient to establish that alcohol has a protective effect."

Gordon and Kannel in "Drinking Habits and Cardiovascular Disease: The Framingham Study" in _American Heart Journal, 1983._ "Based on this information (with 5,206 residents), it was found that the incidence of cardiovascular disease in general, and of CHD and IC (intermittent claudication) in particular, was inversely related to the amount of alcohol regularly consumed."

La Porte, Cresanta and Kuller in "The Relationship of Alcohol Consumption to Atherosclerotic Heart Disease." The authors reported that the countries with the highest alcohol intake such as France, Italy, Spain and Portugal had the lowest death rate from heart disease.

Alcohol Consumption and Blood Pressure in the *New England Journal of Medicine*, 1986. "These findings suggest that in men and in women aged 50 years and older, there is a nonlinear relationship between blood pressure and alcohol consumption, and that there is a level of alcohol consumption, of approximately four drinks per day, below which drinkers have either similar or lower blood pressure levels compared to nondrinkers."

Gill et al. in "Stroke and Alcohol Consumption" say "Among men, the relative risk of stroke (adjusted for hypertension, cigarette smoking, and medication) was lower in light drinkers (those drinking 10–90 g of alcohol weekly) than in nondrinkers."

Pikaar et al. in *"Effects of Moderate Alcohol Consumption on Platelet Aggregation, Fibrinolysis and Blood Lipids"*. "*Epidemiological studies have shown a* U-shaped relationship between alcohol consumption and cardiovascular disease...A decrease in the aggregability (of platelets) of alcohol in the blood is known, but little is known about the long-term effects ...it appears from our study that regular moderate drinking of red wine in a 5-week period has scarcely or no effects at all on liver function, hematologic values, and blood pressure."

Kane in "Atherosclerosis, High Density Lipoproteins and Ethanol". "Studies in the centripetal transport of cholesterol suggest that a subspecies of HDL may play a part in the removal of cholesterol from the peripheral

tissue cells and possibly in the reversal of
atherosclerosis."

The McConnells in *The Mediterranean Diet,* 1987. In
promoting an ideal heart diet and stress factors, particularly of a wine and olive oil-based diet and its relation to coronary artery disease, the McConnells write,
"In recent years, we've been losing around a half a million people a year to coronary heart disease; paying the
medical bills for CHD has cost us $2 billion a year; and
in 1985, American surgeons performed 160,000
coronary bypass operations."

The NIAAA dismissed the whole cumulative panoply of research
and fact with a single line in the *Sixth Special Report to Congress on
Alcohol and Health*::

> Several studies indicate that alcohol consumption is
> associated with hypertension and blood coagulation
> disorders, but evidence that moderate drinking has a
> protective effect against coronary heart disease con-
> tinues to be controversial.

Controversial to whom? Only to those whose agenda is the
reduction of all alcohol consumption. What this country must
comprehend is that the NIAAA is favoring a political agenda that
could, in some respects, be inimical to the general health of the entire
population of drinkers.

The public should be apprised of both good and bad data.

The reluctance of our public health establishment to trust the
citizenry with medical findings is insulting and naive. In a recent
Seattle heart study, researchers found that the men in the study
actually *lost* their heart-protective HDL (high density lipoprotein)
levels when they ceased their normal moderate drinking. Yet,
Camargo et al. concluded their report, "The Effect of Moderate
Alcohol Intake on Serum Apolipoproteins A-I and A-II," with the
following warning:

> Although the adverse effects on health are "rarely"
> seen at this level of intake, there are uncertainties con-
> cerning the effect on the fetus, the relationship to
> motor vehicle accidents and to the addictive potential
> of moderate drinking...Furthermore, recommendations
> that everyone drink at even moderate levels must be
> seriously questioned in light of the potential dangers

associated with this level of intake and the likelihood of increased consumption by some individuals.

First, none of the studies reviewed here has recommended that everyone drink. Nor does this book. Second, a question must be raised about the addictive potential that the authors found for moderate drinkers. There is none in the research literature that I have surveyed. Third, what are the potential dangers to those who stop drinking moderately? The authors find, on the same page, that:

> Our results suggest a causal relationship between moderate alcohol intake and increased serum apo A-I and A-II concentrations...The decrease in both apo A-I and apo A-II serum concentrations during abstention from alcohol in these men is consistent...There were also concomitant increases in serum apo A-I and apo A-II when drinking was resumed.

Cessation of moderate drinking specifically placed the Seattle men in greater long-term risk of heart trouble. When these healthy men stopped "consuming approximately two to three drinks per day, a six week cessation of alcohol intake significantly reduced apo A-I and apo A-II concentrations relative to control group levels."

The answers on alcohol and heart health are not yet decisive, but some observations are certain. The primary tenet of new temperance to lower the per capita level of consumption has to be evaluated in terms of increased danger of heart disease.

Research Finding 2.5

Moderate drinking is found beneficial to general health.

It is concluded that while some causes of hospitalization are clearly increased among drinkers, the overall acute care hospitalization experience of moderate drinkers appears favorable.
**Matthew Longnecker, M.D.
and Brian McMahon, M.D.**
American Journal of Public Health

This book distinguishes between drinking for health and healthy drinking. Physicians often recommend health drinking, particularly with the very young and elderly who lack appetite. But, for the majority, drinking is not done specifically to achieve a health goal, though better mental disposition and physical health may be tangible consequences. What this book maintains is that moderate drinking is a healthy practice, one which benefits both the individual and the society as a whole.

With this distinction in mind, here is a potpourri of excerpts from the medical literature demonstrating a variety of positive therapeutic and health aspects in drinking.

> **General mortality:** *The Second Special Report to Congress on Alcohol and Health* finds "All-in-all, the data on general mortality suggest that for the amount of drinking, apparently unlike amount of smoking, there may be some kind of threshold below which mortality is little affected. In the absence of further evidence, in fact, the classical "Anstie's limit" seems still to reflect the safe amount of drinking which does not substantially increase the risk of early death."

> **Alcohol and the brain:** Bowden in "Brain Impairment in Social Drinkers? No Cause for Concern" studies alcohol and the brain and attacks the popular myth that alcohol destroys inordinate numbers of brain cells. The author states, "In contrast, this paper shows that on the basis of available evidence there may be a level of alcohol consumption which is quite benign. It will be argued that there exists no convincing data warranting concern that moderate alcohol consumption elevates the risk of long term impairment in mental capacities." Bowden also reports in "Cerebral Deficits in Social Drinkers" that, "...the research is not capable of elucidating a cerebral effect."

> **Temporary effects of alcohol:** *Biology, Third Edition* has the following passage: "With the passing of time, cells progressively lose power to replace themselves...The brain loses 10 to 12 percent of its normal weight in the course of a normal lifetime. At age 35, a person begins to lose an estimated 100,000 brain cells each day." Another passage in Roueche's *Alcohol The*

Neutral Spirit states, "Alcohol does not, in the concentrations present in the blood, cause organic damage in the brain....It does not destroy the cells. Alcohol does not corrode them or dissolve them....Its effects are functional and temporary. When the tide of alcohol recedes, the brain awakes and resumes its normal round."

Beer drinking and general health: Richman and Warren in "Alcohol Consumption and Morbidity in the Canada Health Survey" wrote "In sum, the results with respect to quantity of alcohol use suggest a generally inverse [beneficial] relationship to health status for moderate consumption of beer, with some suggestions of deleterious effects at the upper quantity extreme. There is no evidence, however, that the somewhat poorer health of excessive drinkers occurs with the frequency sufficient to offset the apparently better health of the majority of moderate beer drinkers. Consequently, the net health status of beer drinkers, considered as a group, remains significantly better than expected."

Alcohol as a beverage: Lucia in *Wine and Your Well Being* says, "Water, milk, fruit juices and fermented beverages — especially those derived from the grape — are among the most natural and essential dietary accompaniments to solid food in human nutrition. Wine was appraised by Louis Pasteur — one of the greatest scientific minds of the nineteenth century — as the most healthful, the most hygienic dietary beverage of all."

In geriatric care: The column "Happy Hour Therapy" in *Human Behavior,* 1974, says, "After about 12 ounces of beer each, the tippling group proved much more sociable than did the fruit-juice crowd, who remained unchanged. The test lasted 11 weeks, the happy-hour bunch responding with a much higher rate of positive outlook, cheerful mood and sociability." Mishara and Kastenbaum in *Alcohol and Old Age* find, "Research over the past 15 years suggests that the moderate use of alcoholic beverages for institutionalized elders has beneficial psychosocial effects and rarely produces physical difficulties."

In nursing homes: Sarley and Stepto in "Wine is Fine
for Patients' Morale and Helps Stimulate Their
Appetite" found, "There were no undesirable side
effects...The use of wine in this group made the
patients' stay and recovery more rapid...The nurses felt
that those who were taking wine with their meals
needed less sedation and less sleeping medication...Overall, the wine patients were satisfied with their
environment, with treatments and with general conditions of their stay."

For the diabetic: McDonald in a Wine Institute symposium on Wine, Health and Society stated, "Alcoholic
beverages are quite suitable for well-controlled diabetic
patients. They can drink safely provided there is medical approval and no contraindications. Wine is particularly suitable for use in diabetic diets, particularly
dry wines because they are very low in sugars."

Antibiotic against bacterial infections: The antibiotic
effect of wine resembles most closely that of penicillin.
At the Bonn Institute, the anti-bacterial action of wine
and penicillin were compared, and water and wine was
substantially more potent against colonies of specific
bacteria than strong combinations of penicillin.

These reports may seem to favor wine over beer or spirits
because wine therapy has been more widely applied through history.
(However, many studies indicate that any ethanol produces similar
therapeutic results). The Wine Institute's fine pamphlet titled *Wine
and Medical Practice* contains many specific recommendations for
physicians. Here is a random collection of the pamphlet's findings:

In the gastrointestinal system. "The crucial problem
centers about the occasional use of moderate amounts
of alcoholic beverages. It seems that temperate
amounts cannot be considered deleterious, and...may
even effect digestion favorably if taken with meals." For
hypertension. "It has been stated by many observers
that alcohol, especially in the form of wine, may
provide effective and long lasting relief of the apprehension and general discomfort at times associated with
high blood pressure." For the diabetic. "In the normal
diet of a diabetic, dry wines (i.e., not containing fer-

mentable sugar) can serve as an excellent and regular source of energy." **For emotional tension.** "The traditional use of wine as a tranquilizer has been confirmed in laboratory studies." **In gastroenterology.** "In moderate amounts, it stimulates gastric secretion and motility, increases the bile flow, and assists the natural processes of evacuation of the colon." **In terms of a regular diet.** "In studies on experimental animals, Richter has shown that weight and general health can be maintained so long as consumption of alcohol is kept below 40 percent of total caloric intake."

Some writers seem carried away by their enthusiasm for wine or other alcohols as medications and therapeutics. Dr. Maury in *Wine Is The Best Medicine* actually prescribes specific wines and dosages for everything from allergies to menopause. But the historical verity of alcohol and medicine is best expressed in the introduction to the manual *Wine and Medical Practice*:

The oldest of all human ailments is anxiety, the offspring of fear. It is still the most universal of all complaints. The widespread desire for relief from it is attested to by the use of one million Miltown tables in its second year. The caveman threatened by the saber-toothed tiger had the same anxiety as the Wall Street broker in a bear market. The caveman and the broker have found in naturally fermented products a certain measure of relief. Every race and tribe that could get it has used and appreciated this surcease from worry, depression and stress. All this goes into the experience which has contributed to our knowledge of the benefits of wine.

Alcoholic beverages do contribute to the health and well-being of many users. Here is a final thought by Richman who directed the Canada survey:

Finally, although a recent report by the National Academy of Science noted that the benefit resulting from drinking is usually conceded even by those who are most appalled by the damages, few studies have tried to document those beneficial consequences and even fewer have tried to evaluate how different beverage types contribute to them.

Many of these authors prudently stress that it is uncertain whether health advantages in these groups have any direct relationship to their daily drinking habits. This remains a valid question for additional research. It may well be that other living habits among the healthy middle span contribute more to their well-being than does their drinking. But the salient observation is that coronary and heart health of moderate drinkers—without question the majority of American adults—are not being harmed by daily drinking. Indeed, that drinking may well be contributing to some kinds of specific heart health benefits particularly in lowering the effects of low density lipoprotein collected in the blood vessels.

Very few people drink for health reasons alone. Most people would be satisfied with assurance that moderate intake of alcohol was doing them no bodily harm. These studies prove to my own satisfaction that moderate drinking does not bring harm to otherwise healthy individuals, and that may be the most important finding in this book.

Research Finding 2.6

Danger of breast cancer was modified in recent studies.

> _The danger of breast cancer in women from moderate drinking is qualified in recent research projects. For a person who is consuming 2 glasses of alcohol per day, and is not a cigarette smoker, there is probably very little risk of cancer._
> **Professor McMichael as reported in**
> _Alcohol Insights_

The controversy over the danger of breast cancer heated up in the spring of 1987 upon the release of two studies in the _New England Journal of Medicine_. Schatzkin et al., in "Alcohol Consumption and Breast Cancer in the Epidemiologic Follow-up Study of the First National Health and Nutrition Examination Survey," studied 7,188 women (21 to 74 years of age) over a ten year period. In the second and larger of the two studies Willett et. al. reported in "Moderate Alcohol Consumption and the Risk of Breast Cancer" on a follow-up survey involving 90,000 nurses. Both studies concluded that women who drink, even at moderate levels, are more likely to get breast cancer in later life than those who abstain. Willett reported:

> Nevertheless, the consistency between the different studies is rather remarkable. So one has to give this pos-

sibility of a cause-and-effect relationship very serious consideration.

Time magazine reported Willett as saying:

> We're also missing one piece of information — specifically whether decreasing or stopping in middle life will influence the risk of breast cancer. It's possible that whatever damage may have been done early on cannot be reversed.

Every media outlet in this nation carried these stories along with the headlines that one in ten women is in danger of breast cancer. I did the arithmetic on the two samples reported by Schatzkin and Willett. There was a .02 percent cancer rate in the first group and an even lower rate of .01 percent among the large nurse population. Relating these figures to the one in ten confused me so I checked with Dr. David Thomas at the Fred Hutchinson Cancer Center in Seattle. Here is an excerpt of his interview that appeared in the *Moderate Drinking Journal:*

> It doesn't mean that one woman in ten alive is going to get breast cancer. What it essentially means is that if every woman lived to reach 85, about one in ten would get breast cancer...The cumulative probability of breast cancer at age 85 is about one in eleven.

Since this highly publicized scare, other letters have appeared in the learned journals on the subject. Skegg in a letter to the *British Medical Journal* states:

> The hypothesis that dietary fat may cause breast cancer has been a central theme of research for sound reasons. Firstly, abundant evidence from animal studies shows that mammary carcinogenesis is enhanced by high fact diets and inhibited by calorie restriction. Secondly, mortality rates for breast cancer in different countries are highly correlated with fat consumption...In Japan where breast cancer is uncommon, a rapid increase in the fat intake has been accompanied by a rise in the death rate from breast cancer.

More correspondence in the *New England Journal of Medicine* also casts doubt on the alcohol and breast cancer relationship. Lindegard in a letter to the editor regarding "Alcohol and Breast Cancer" writes, "The editorial on alcohol and breast cancer (May 7 issue) underscores the need for more research because of several shortcomings of the epidemiologic information...in the general population of Gothenburg, no association at all was evident between breast cancer and alcohol-related conditions." Similarly, Andrianopoulos hypothesized in another letter, "However, the results from epidemiologic and animal studies indicate that emotionality (depression) and stress modify the risk of cancer."

As reported in the June 1988 University of California *Wellness Letter*, Dr. Susan Chu of the Atlanta Centers for Disease Control recently announced the results of a study of 7,000 women from ages 20 to 54 in which, "We found no increased risk of breast cancer with alcohol use." Commenting on this study, Lawrence Garfinkel, a vice-president of the American Cancer Society was quoted by the Associated Press: "The jury's still out. If there is a risk, it has to be very, very minimal."

These are comforting commentaries by competent medical authorities. The positives, however, never attain the same kind of national attention as the reports which identify even moderate alcohol consumption with physical harm. A recent issue of the *University of California Wellness Letter* sums up the conflicting data:

> Clearly a lot more medical research needs to be done. If you're a woman wondering whether an occasional drink will do you good or harm, the answer is still up in the air. No cause and effect relationship between alcohol and breast cancer has been developed.

The Licensed Beverage Information Council (LBIC) has submitted these studies to an expert panel and we look for further clarification of these often confusing data. In the meantime, moderation again seems the right course for those who choose to drink.

Research Finding 2.7

Reports of danger of fetal alcohol dysfunctions have been inflated.

The danger of fetal dysfunctions are deliberately enlarged and distorted by anti-alcohol lobbies. Louis Harris and Associates found that "...92 percent of women aged 18 to 44...were aware of the effects of overconsumption."
DISCUS News Release

*This is an astounding rate of FAS awareness. It
surpasses the American literacy rate. I doubt
if 92 percent of the population of Baltimore
over the age of 18 would be able to identify
the newly elected Governor of Maryland.*
Interview with Augustus Hewlett
Alcohol Policy Council

*The fact is that there is no evidence
suggesting the daily consumption of one
or two glasses of wine is harmful to the fetus.*
David Whitten, M.D. in
Wines & Vines

Imminent danger to the youth of America can move the political
machine like few other issues. The danger of fetal alcohol syndrome
(FAS) is used mercilessly as a tool to push the anti-alcohol political
agenda of new temperance. There is clearly more heat than light
surrounding the medical data on drinking and pregnancy.

The Department of Health and Human Services (DHHS), the
Center for Science in the Public Interest (CSPI), the American Public
Health Association (APHA), the National Council on Alcoholism
(NCA) and many other public health organizations are promoting
warning labels on the supposition that pregnant mothers will drink
less as a consequence. The danger of FAS has been the primary
argument in support of alcoholic beverage labeling over the past two
decades.

In California, over sixty advocacy groups are pushing for a fetal
warning on every bottle of wine, beer and spirits. At least four other
states have similar bills under consideration. In California, the labeling
coalition is not satisfied with the compromise reached by state
authorities which would place warning posters where alcohol is sold.
Much research indicates that labels have little effect and that the age
group affected is already aware of the dangers in overconsumption.
Here are some of the pertinent findings in the medical literature
concerning FAS.

Sokol, writing in the *Journal of the American Medical
Association* in 1987, reported on a study of 8,300
mothers and found that only 2 percent had placed their
babies at risk from drinking up to four drinks per day.
"A broad edict against alcohol ingestion is likely to be

less effective than one which targets those shown in the study to be at increased risk."

Rosett and Weiner, writing in their book _Alcohol and the Fetus: A Clinical Perspective,_ report on a review of the 400 cases of FAS worldwide. "Every one was a chronic alcoholic who drank heavily in pregnancy... Women place their babies at risk when they have five or more drinks on one occasion...However, there is no evidence of damage to the fetus if a woman chooses to drink less than one ounce (two standard drinks) of absolute alcohol on any given day." Dr. Ernest Noble, the original advocate of warning labels, wrote the foreword to the Rosett and Weiner book. At the time Noble held this opinion. "The authors thoughtfully weave through the fabric of the book basic science, clinical and epidemiological information...where dissent, ambiguity, lack of definition and even emotionalism are prevalent."

Rosett and Weiner warn that many in public health are _misrepresenting_ the FAS dangers by commenting on the often repeated phrase that ingestion of alcohol by pregnant women is the third leading cause of mental retardation.

Many FAS programs have incorporated this statement [concerning alcohol being the cause of mental retardation] in prevention campaigns. These statements are misleading. In fact, only 10 percent of the cases of mental retardation are of known origin; in 90 percent the causes are unknown.

A review of the clinical and experimental evidence suggests that there is no measurable risk from consuming less that 1 ounce [of absolute alcohol] per day. Others agree that no risks have been observed, but protest that safety has not been proven. Scientifically, only risks can be measured; the absence of risk (absolute safety) can never be conclusively established.

Mills and Grauberd report in "Is Moderate Drinking During Pregnancy Associated With An Increased Risk For Malformations?" that their data on 32,870 mothers demonstrated the following. "Total malformation rates were not significantly higher among offspring of women

who had an average of less than one drink per day
(77.3/1000) or one to two drinks per day (83.2/1000)
than among nondrinkers (78.1/1000)...Likewise, major
malformations were not increased in these drinking
groups...Nonetheless, the possibility that there are
some malformations for which no safe drinking level
exists requires additional investigation."

Despite the emphasis of nearly all researchers on the dangers of
heavy drinking during pregnancy, an *ADAMHA News* article reports,
"...the Surgeon General and the National Institute on Alcohol Abuse
and Alcoholism recommend that women abstain from using any
alcohol at all during pregnancy. This position has been adopted by
the American Medical Association, the National Council on
Alcoholism and other authoritative groups."

Perhaps that should read *authoritarian* groups. Any woman who
has the slightest fear should follow her conscience and not drink.
However, the DHHS pamphlet titled "My Baby...Strong and Healthy"
establishes a larger prohibitionary intent. It opens with this forthright
and noncontroversial statement, "The safest choice is not to drink at
all during pregnancy..." Then it continues with a much broader and
questionable suggestion "... or *if you are planning
pregnanc*y [emphasis added]." The pamphlet also recommends
abstinence during nursing periods. "In addition, women who breast
feed should continue abstaining from alcohol until their babies are
weaned." It is fair to wonder whether the DHHS objective is *safety* or
simply a *reduction in the amount of per capita* alcohol consumed in
the United States.

Research Finding 2.8

Health hazards from drinking
apply mainly to heavy drinkers.

*The health hazards in alcohol use are numerous
but they impact primarily the heavy drinker.The National
Institution Alcohol Abuse and Alcoholism and the Alcoholic
Beverage Medical Research Foundation should work together
Medical Research Foundation should work together to provide at
least as much scientific research to support the 90 percent who
are not at risk as the as the 10 percent who are.*
Peter Stroh
National Beer Wholesalers Association

This finding sets forth the primary and tragic medical problems which result from heavy drinking as described by Eckhardt et al. in "Health Hazards Associated With Alcohol Consumption." Table 4 in the *Sixth Special Report to Congress on Alcohol and Health* lists the following alcohol-caused deaths for the year 1980. While I dispute the attribution of *causality* in some of these categories, there is no question that heavy alcohol use is *involved* in this many deaths each year (and probably many more).

Alcohol, main cause	19,587
Alcohol, contributing	7,269
Other diseases	11,679
Accidents	37,849
Violence	21,144
Total	**97,528**

It matters little whether all of these needless deaths were *caused by* or simply *involved with* alcohol. What matters is the terrible persistence of alcohol as a factor in misbehavior and human self-destruction. Here are the main hazard areas outlined in detail in the article by Eckhardt:

Pharmacology. With low doses, ethanol possesses transient stimulatory properties...as the dose is increased, ethanol produces a full spectrum of CNS (central nervous system) depression, ranging from sedation to general anesthesia to death.

Drug Interactions. It has been well documented that ethanol can affect the pharmacological and therapeutic actions of a number of other drugs...

Liver Disease. Although cirrhosis was once thought to result from poor nutrition...heavy alcohol consumption can lead to cirrhosis...

Nutritional Deficiency. Heavy alcohol intake contributes to nutritional deficiency...

Nervous System. Long-term alcoholism, especially when combined with malnutrition, often results in severe neurological and cognitive deficits...

Alcoholism. Alcoholism is a chronic, progressive and potentially fatal disease...

Affective Disorders. An association has been made between alcoholism and unipolar affective disorders such as depression..

Suicide. Long term problem drinking effects have been considered precipitants of suicide.

Cardiovascular disease. Patients in whom heavy use of alcoholic beverages leads to cardiac disease...

Cancer. The observation that many patients with cancer of the mouth, pharynx, esophagus, and liver are found to be alcohol-dependent...

Accidents. Those who are alcohol dependent have a considerably higher rate of accidental death...

Crime and Abuse. It is unclear whether alcohol is causatively related to crime or merely associated with its occurrence...

The authors note the uncertainty of the association between alcohol with crime and abuse.

Research Finding 2.9

A worldwide crusade seeks
to label alcohol as a toxin.

There are large numbers of mutagens and carcinogens in every meal, all perfectly natural and traditional. Nature is not benign.
Bruce Ames in
Science

Because the issue is seen as so good, where you would normally hold people to certain standards on statistics and research, there is a weakening because the cause is considered to be so important that the criteria is compromised.
Interview with John De Luca
The Wine Institute

New temperance believes it can solve the dilemma of alcohol dosage by branding all alcohol as toxic to the human body.

On the surface, warning labels seem perfectly logical. Just put that little line on the label (like cigarettes or poisons) and warn us that cancer or cardiovascular disease might result from usage. It's true, isn't it? Yes and no. In a broad sense, it is true that too much alcohol over too long a time can be physically harmful. But the problem with this logic is that it singles out alcohol among hundreds of toxins we ingest or use regularly in cooking. Tierney in "Not to Worry" talks of the work on toxins done by Bruce Ames at the University of California.

> But now he has a bemused look as he picks up an organic mushroom. "Filled with carcinogens," he says and moves on to the cabbage and broccoli, which contain a compound similar to dioxin, the dread contaminant in the herbicide Agent Orange..."Alfalfa sprouts are full of some really nasty chemicals that cause lupus if the dose is high enough...How silly can you get? The charcoal [marked No Artificial Additives] itself is just pure carcinogens.

Ames in "Cancer Scares Over Trivia" testified to a California Senate Committee:

> My estimate is that more than 99.99 percent of the carcinogens we ingest are from natural or traditional sources...What we do need are some sensible regulations about pollution. We should also remember that life expectancy increases every year.

Every shred of credible evidence indicates that these warnings don't work. Why propose something that does not work except to demean the substance? The evidence of toxicity is flawed says pathologist Rubin in "An Overview of the Evidence Concerning the Hypothesis that Alcohol Causes Cancer," which was given to the California Proposition 65 scientific panel:

> As discussed in this overview and the more detailed accompanying papers, the available evidence does not support a finding that alcohol consumption causes cancer. The epidemiological data are equivocal and flawed; the animal studies are consistently negative; and there is no evidence that has established a mechanism by which alcohol causes cancer. It is impermissible to accept an association that neither

demonstrates dose response nor adequately controls
for confounders. It is, moreover, inappropriate to
accept a weak, inconsistent association only at the
highest level of alcohol use as evidence for the proposition that alcohol, rather than other factors, causes these
cancers.

Despite these scientific doubts, there is little doubt about this
toxicity question at the World Health Organization(WHO) and its
International Agency for Research on Cancer (IARC). The Center For
Science In the Public Interest and Senator Strom Thurmond in
Washington, D.C. seek to label alcoholic beverages as carcinogens,
toxins and proximate causes of hypertension, cardiovascular and
liver disease as well as cancer. In reality, dozens of things we eat and
drink daily contain carcinogens, mutagens and toxins. But we ingest
them at such low levels as to be meaningless. The only reason to
single out alcohol is to place drinking in disfavor. That's the objective
of new temperance.

Warning labels will deter the wrong people from drinking.

Senator Thurmond introduces container labeling legislation in
every session of Congress (though he apparently has less concern
for the toxicity of tobacco produced in his home state). In California,
the legislative coalition promises to be back with a state labeling bill
in 1988 and similar bills have been introduced in legislatures around
the nation.

Not surprisingly, the product label method of communicating
health risks was first suggested by Dr. Ernest Noble twenty years ago
when he ran the NIAAA. The issue needs wider airing today so it can
be permanently put to rest. Labels will most certainly discourage
more of the light to moderate drinkers with their scare tactics than the
heavy abuser types. The heart protection and other therapeutic
values in moderation would certainly be diminished by warning labels.

As in the first two decades of this century, the anti-alcohol forces
are employing questionable and narrowly interpreted scientific data.
Warning labels are another device to discourage everyone from *any*
drinking. The proposed warning labels are never dose specific. The
stated objective of new temperance is the reduction of per capita
consumption across the board.

The alternative would be honest labels.

I have written to the sponsors of the labeling bill and to the entire
senate committee suggesting that their warning labels also contain
the following line if labels become mandatory:

> Recognizing, however, that moderate use of this
> product may help to prevent cardiovascular and other
> life threatening diseases and add to the general well-
> being of the user.

Anyone who has read this far will concur that my statement is a reasonable expression of scientific research. As expected, I have not heard from the sponsors. Any expression of value in drinking is anathema to their objectives. Proponents of labeling have read and heard all the expert testimony which demonstrates that warning labels on commonly used objects (e.g. alcohol containers) have little or no effect. Proceedings of the Human Factors Society, 1984, are a typical example:

> In spite of the widespread use of warning labels,
> searches for scientific evidence have yielded virtually
> no reason to anticipate that warning labels on con-
> sumer products serve as effective warning mechanisms
> to increase safety.

I have not said that everyone who advocates product labeling is an enemy of drinking. Many supporters may be confused and willing to err on the side of safety. But, the primary proponents of labeling—Senator Thurmond, Senator Kennedy, the NIAAA, the Center for Science in the Public Interest, the National Council on Alcoholism—know of this adverse research.

Urethane in alcohol is another specious danger.

Another current toxicity controversy pushed by the Center for Science in the Public Interest involves a naturally occurring chemical in many fermented products, urethane. Very little research has been done on this common substance since it exists at levels which require very sophisticated equipment for measurement. Some urethane develops after bottling depending upon exposure to heat and other factors.

It is a telling comment that in the Center For Science campaign against urethane, this "nutrition-based" advocacy group has petitioned the Food and Drug Administration to create standards for urethane content only for alcoholic beverages. How could a scientific organization neglect urethane's presence in other fermented foods such as pickles, cheese and sauerkraut? This singular focus on alcohol betrays an unscientific animus.

Readers are advised to look for the reasons behind the singling out of alcohol. Commenting on the WHO conclusion that alcohols are carcinogenic, Rubin notes:

At least two types of bias may occur in epidemiological studies — selection bias and reporting bias. Both seriously complicate the reliability of the studies reviewed by IARC...The introduction of this kind of selection bias throughout the key studies relied upon by IARC compromises their reliability.

Research Finding 2.10

Alcoholism and moderate drinking
both justify more research funding.

It is important to acknowledge that drinking by most members of society is not accompanied by problems and may ease the loneliness of old age, the burden of intolerable pain, foster healthy psycho-sexual attitudes or encourage social intercourse.
Editorial
British Journal On Alcohol and Alcoholism

My contention is that in the privacy of their offices, that even those who deal with alcoholics agree its one of the best sedatives ever discovered.
Interview with Karst J. Besteman
Alcohol and Drug Problems Association

The important question is whether we are spending enough, not too much, on research into the causes of alcoholism and on its treatment.

There follows two comparisons created by Fein in *Alcohol In America: The Price We Pay* . They show a gross imbalance of research funding, at least according to the raw numbers of affected people. A new consensus on alcohol use would undoubtedly encourage the investment of significantly higher expenditures for basic research. Among the questions would be a determination of why the majority of drinkers remains moderate.

Here are Fein's computations for 1980 taken from the National Center for Health Statistics:

	Deaths	Persons **Affected**
Heart Disease	761,085	17,186,000
Cancer	416,509	5,000,000
Cerebrovascular	170,225	1,869,000
Alcohol	127,385	14,700,000
Diabetes	34,851	5,500,000

According to these figures, three times more people are affected by alcohol disease than cancer but there are about one-third fewer deaths. Obviously, cancer kills over a shorter time period. Fein's point, however, is that skewed national disease priorities are demonstrated in the following 1981 allocations for basic research funds.

Disease	**Research Funds**
Cancer	$772,000,000
Heart and vascular disease	$327,000,000
Respiratory disease	$ 80,000,000
Alcoholism and abuse	$ 22,000,000

Of course, millions are expended in care and treatment of alcoholism but this minimal investment of research dollars indicates a lack of serious national purpose to discover the root causes of alcoholism.

Research Finding 2.11

The anti-alcohol strategy is
called the control of availability.

*I see us within the next two to four
years forging a new consensus in America
about our product. There will be a
confluence between a new emergence of
thinking about alcoholic beverages, and
this all comes out of sorting and shifting
of the issues such as Proposition 65.*
Interview with John De Luca
The Wine Institute

The phrase "control of availability" is used today to describe a research theorem suggests that abusive drinking control is tied mathematically to the total amount of alcohol consumed.

It theorizes that a nation which lowers consumption overall will experience a compensatory reduction in heavy drinking. To enforce the reduction, there must be pervasive governmental intervention into the marketplace. NIAAA's *Fifth Special Report to Congress on Alcohol and Health* established lowered consumption as a specific policy goal of the government of the United States. The report also set forth specific legislative goals:

> Lowering of alcohol consumption levels is associated with reduction in a number of adverse effects of drinking such as alcohol-related traffic accidents (especially by youth) and diseases such as cirrhosis of the liver. Some effective efforts, documented through research, are:
> Increasing taxes on alcoholic beverages.
> Increasing the legal age for purchase of alcoholic beverages.
> Altering the number and location of outlets
> for purchase of alcoholic beverages.

The justification for these radical control measures is *public health*. Therefore, to promote this set of government interventions, new temperance has sought to create a *crisis mentality* about alcohol abuse. The highly visible and emotional issues of alcohol-related automobile deaths and drug corruption of youth are employed as evidence of the crisis.

NIAAA's *Sixth Special Report to Congress on Alcohol and Health*, released in January 1987, completed the anti-alcohol turnabout. It eliminated any reference whatsoever to the traditionally accepted health values in moderate drinking, with the single exception of one mention of some possible, as yet unproved, cardiovascular benefits.

Alex Richman, director of the Canadian beer study "Alcohol Consumption And Morbidity In The Canada Health Survey," cautions that the positive results of their study do not necessarily prove that beer promotes good health. Rather, the results may demonstrate that beer drinkers may have more healthy lifestyles than other people, or they may imply that moderate drinking people do not as readily admit to being ill.

Many things can contribute to better health.

Richman raises an intriguing question that goes to the worth and efficacy of massive beer advertising as potentially a *promoter* of healthy lifestyles rather than a corrupter of youth. This could open an intriguing line of research.

> Healthy lifestyles, in particular, fitness and friends are increasingly present in television portrayal of beer-drinking lifestyles. Rarely do these commercials associate negative lifestyle habits, (e.g., smoking, drug use, stress, obesity) with consumption of beer...Thus, the positive health levels of beer drinkers observed in this study may be simply mute testament to the success of mass advertising—with healthier individuals increasingly indicating beer as their beverage of choice.

This line of reasoning runs counter to the Center For Science in the Public Interest SMART Campaign (Stop Marketing Alcohol On Radio and TV). SMART promotes the concept that breweries should sponsor ads warning of health problems with drinking. Our alcohol prevention leadership does not tell us that both British Columbia and Saskatchewan provinces have experimented with bans on advertising. When no positive impact on drinking habits could be measured from the bans, they returned to advertising. Why do our governmental authorities ignore this reality, and the fact that Chairman Gorbechev's control of availability is a flop in Russia?

DHHS and NIAAA ignore this vast body of positive health data and dismiss the whole cumulative argument of alcohol and health with a single line in their report to Congress.

> Several studies indicate that alcohol consumption is associated with hypertension and blood coagulation disorders, but evidence that moderate drinking has a protective effect against coronary heart disease continues to be controversial.

Controversial to whom? Only to those whose agenda is the reduction of all alcohol consumption. What the taxpayers of this country must understand is that the NIAAA is pushing a political agenda, not completely a health agenda. The result in alcohol use could be *inimical* to the general health of the population.

Americans are going to continue to drink. That is not at question. How they view their drinking is an important medical and public health question.

Research Finding 2.12

Confusion discourages public debate
of health values of moderate drinking.

> *Now our progress is being threatened by a plethora
> of unnecessary controls on alcoholic beverages and
> negative messages to the consumers of these products.*
> **Interview with Augustus Hewlett**
> Alcohol Policy Council

> *While I was on the National Council on Alcoholism
> board, there was never any discussion of warning
> labels or raising excise taxes or advertising bans.
> Marty Mann and others were looking for ways to
> treat and help individuals.*
> **Interview with John De Luca**
> The Wine Institute

The national Congress forms policy and passes alcohol
legislation—such as the proposed warning labels—based, in part,
upon the series of special reports on alcohol and health produced at
NIAAA.

These reports have gradually become the propaganda position
papers for new temperance. The *Second Report to Congress on
Alcohol And Health,* published in 1974 by Dr. Morris Chafetz and
edited by alcoholism historian Mark Keller, contained an appendix
article which outlined several philosophical approaches to the
prevention of alcohol problems. This thoughtful treatise is still sound
advice for legislators today:

> The time has come for a redirection and reemphasis
> toward prevention of alcohol misuse and alcoholism
> and the development of healthy drinking patterns that
> are based on certain assumptions.
>
> Alcohol as a social instrument is available and is used
> by many large populations, and efforts to remove it
> have failed. In many ccultures that experience minimal
> alcohol problems, alcohol is used early and often.
> Studies of drinking cultures without significant alcohol
> problems, combined with an understanding of the phar-
> macological action of alcohol, indicate that there are
> ways of drinking that do not result in alcohol problems.

These two quotes show how the original mandate at NIAAA was considered to encompass the interests of the entire population, user and abstainer alike. The Chafetz "responsible drinking" philosophy was emphasized in a study done for NIAAA by the Booz, Allen research firm titled "Parameters of Responsible Alcohol Taking." This document charged NIAAA to maintain the distinction between those who abuse alcohol and those who drink responsibly. The report suggested that NIAAA should:

> Provide support for those people who choose to take alcohol in moderation or to abstain.
> Reduce the guilt feelings surrounding alcohol taking when it is taken in moderation.

These are still the only acceptable parameters for federal alcohol administration in a nation where the majority of adults drink — without abusing. However, in Dr. Ernest Noble's *Second Special Report to Congress on Alcohol and Health*, June 1978, the focus had shifted dramatically from "support for those who choose to take alcohol in moderation" to the implication that any drinking carried certifiable risks. Noble wrote, "People who choose to drink alcoholic beverages must be made aware of the consequences to the extent we know them...the corresponding degree of risk they are assuming."

Risk and heavy use concepts were broadened by NIAAA.

Fair enough. No one denies the serious risks of overuse. But Dr. Noble's new emphasis eliminated the *benefits* side of the ledger and stressed only those risks. The benefits side has never been restored at NIAAA. No longer do our federal alcohol abuse administrators feel responsible for lifting the guilt associated with innocent drinking. Precisely the opposite pertains. By the fifth special report in December 1983, written under direction of Dr. Robert Niven, a new "heavy use" category was introduced. Anyone consuming at the rate of 14 drinks per week could be considered a heavier consumer!

A certain conservatism is understandable, particularly from individuals who have been personally impacted by alcoholism. Dr. William Bennett, editor of the Harvard Medical School Health Letter puts his position bluntly in a recent article "The Drink-a-Day Lore." "People who drink any amount of alcohol for their coronary health would be well-advised, I think, to go instead for a brisk walk at the cocktail hour." But Bennett telegraphs his punch by informing us in the article that his father, a "classic meat-and-potatoes alcoholic" died shortly after his 48th birthday. I can understand Dr. Bennett's honest conservatism. But, my own father passed away in my home at 82 not long after sharing dinner and a friendly drink. His modest daily alcohol consumption was always an admirable standard for me. I am certain that Dr. Bennett can understand my liberal attitudes about alcohol just as I sympathize with his conservative stance.

But it is difficult to understand the indifference of Ferrence, Truscott and Whitehead in "Drinking and the Prevention of Coronary Heart Disease:"

> Promoting moderate drinking or revising recommendations for preventing alcohol-related damage poses many problems...Many light and moderate drinkers would already derive any protective effect of alcohol at their current levels of consumption.

As a practical matter, how are light and moderate drinkers to _retain_ "any protective effect of alcohol" if organized medicine, the federal government and powerful public advocacy groups frighten them away from any drinking. And, what of young people entering the drinking age? Is it necessary that they stumble accidentally over these positive data when the long-term health of their hearts could be involved?

Aspirin Over Alcohol: a Tale of Two Drugs

A dramatic example of selective medical enthusiasm occurred in early February, 1988. The American Heart Association (AHA) reported widely on the findings of an aspirin and heart risk study. Every medium of communication in the nation trumpeted the impressive data of Dr. Charles Hennekens, Harvard University researcher. The four- year health study involved 22,071 physicians. The AHA news release stated:

> Originally scheduled to end in 1990, the investigation was terminated early because of its "statistically extreme" beneficial effects in reducing nonfatal heart attacks...The four year study showed a 47 percent reduced risk of heart attack among physicians taking one aspirin (325 mg) every other day, compared to doctors taking a placebo.

A January news release from the AHA identified heart disease as the nation's number one medical problem. "In a single year, heart and blood vessel diseases in the United States killed 991,332 — about 50 percent more than the combined tolls of World Wars I and II plus the Korean and Vietnamese wars." Before the month was out, I received from AHA a printed leaflet accompanied by a question-and-answer sheet on the efficacy of aspirin in heart health.

Obviously, the AHA wanted me, as a journalist, to be aware of the positive aspirin report.

Two months earlier, the same American Heart Association mailed me a packet of reports on their annual research meeting containing an unheralded report on alcohol and heart risk taken from another study by the same Dr. Hennekens:

> Analyses showed that compared with nondrinkers, people who drank "moderate" amounts of alcohol every day—defined as two beers or wines or one mixed drink—had a 49 percent lower risk of having a heart attack.

Though the control group in this second Hennekens project was much smaller than in the aspirin survey—22,071 to 423— Hennekens' conclusion on alcohol and heart disease is remarkably similar to dozens of other studies accomplished over the past half century. There is no real statistical difference between the 47 percent lower risk with aspirin and 49 percent with daily alcohol intake. Why did AHA back the aspirin survey so eagerly and lightly pass over the alcohol results? Could it be, as Roueche' mused, AHA officials are concerned that, "If human experience demonstrates that a drink can provoke the same response as a pill with a good deal more sociability, humans are going to choose the pleasure of the drink."

An inquiry to the public information office at AHA revealed that the scientific committee had made the choice to *back* the aspirin results and simply report the alcohol findings—and there was always "the addiction problem." It won't wash. The AHA knows full well that addiction to alcohol is a minority problem in this nation and that heart disease is a majority problem. Dr. Elizabeth Whelan, executive director of the American Council on Science and Health, provided the rationale for promoting both alcohol and aspirin for health in an article in "Across the Board:"

> Probably the best-established health effect of alcohol is its role in decreasing the risk of coronary heart disease. This phenomenon was first observed in 1904 and has since been confirmed in at least 30 studies on more than 100,000 people around the world, using several methods of analysis...According to data going back to 1926, and confirmed in tens of thousands of people since, light or moderate drinkers tend to live longer than abstainers and heavy drinkers.

The politics of medicine, as represented by the medical societies, probably will continue to reflect alcohol hostility. Many anti-alcohol professionals are actively pursuing new temperance goals. But society should expect more from the scientists and epidemiologists on the national payroll. NIAAA civil servants are paid for their objectivity, not their political predilections. As long as the constituency of NIAAA remains essentially recovering alcoholics and right-wing public health advocates, it will lack that critical scientific objectivity. Perhaps, as one critic suggested to me, the NIAAA should be placed among the National Institutes of Health to get it out of the politics of alcohol.

This book does not suggest that the medical profession or the NIAAA (or anyone else, for that matter) promote drinking. The medical profession has no business promoting any products. But, I urge that both sources speak more objectively to this subject which impacts the lives of all 127,800 million drinkers, not just those who abuse. This obsession with abusers and abuse disserves the total public health. Chafetz makes an important distinction in his book *Why Drinking Can Be Good For You:*

> I don't think you have to drink to be an alcoholic. I think Carry Nation was an alcoholic — a nondrinking alcoholic. She couldn't take care of her daughter. She couldn't live with her husband because she was so obsessed with demon rum. Didn't she have an alcohol problem?

It is quite obvious that many in the public health profession today are Carry Nation nondrinking alcoholics.

Research Finding 2.13

Alcohol should be restored to the medical pharmacopoeia.

Although I have couched my remarks in terms of what New Drys need to know about wine, it is primarily the physicians of this country who need to know the things I have talked of tonight. It is up to us, the enlightened and knowledgeable, to educate our patients, but more importantly, our colleagues and political representatives, of the important health and social benefits of wine.

David N. Whitten, M.D.
The Medical Friends of Wine

It is easy for me to criticize organized medicine for its lack of enthusiasusiasm about alcohol and health. I've read the literature.

There's an inexplicable gulf between these favorable data and the occasional positive article on drinking in the public media. Yet, I appreciate how difficult it would be, from an organizational point of view, for alcohol-friendly members of the American Medical Association (AMA) or the American Heart Association (AHA) to process a clearly pro-alcohol statement through their ruling bodies. The AHA, to their credit, established dietary guidelines which include drinking. But, in general, the professional medical societies are houses divided when it comes to drinking. The general public is poorly served by this institutionalized equivocation and ambiguity.

The truth of the alcohol and health muddle lies somewhere between the effusive panegyric for distilled spirits written by Holinshead in 1577 and the biting, satirical observations of Roueche' in 1960 (from the two quotes which opened this chapter). Roueche's point is that, from a strictly scientific viewpoint, the molecule ethyl hydroxide (ethanol) is neither good nor bad. It is simply another of hundreds of potentially toxic chemicals taken from plant life which mankind has chosen, over thousands of years, to incorporate into a diet.

It would amaze the casual reader today to discover the princely role that alcohol once had in medicine and in folklore. Aside from its commercial contributions, alcohol was venerated beyond belief. McNulty in *Drinking In Vogue* describes this exalted status. "Actually, the making of alcohol, though a perfectly natural process, has had quasi-religious associations since the very beginning. It has also been associated with health and well-being. The medieval alchemists, for instance, believed that wine synthesized the four essential elements of life: earth, air, fire and water."

While alcoholic beverages are no longer mythologized as the four elements, they are elemental components in our lives and quite natural components in our bodies. Chafetz in *Liquor: The Servant of Man* provides another perspective on how the body produces alcohol *naturally* along with other virulent body fluids:

> That alcohol is a poison and will kill you quickly and surely, but no more quickly and no more surely than distilled water, if you drink too much of it at one time.
> That alcohol is manufactured in the human body but is

less poisonous than most of the other natural secretions
such as thyroid, pituitary, adrenal, pancreas and bile.
That alcohol, if taken in anything remotely approaching
customary amounts, is harmless to the body and in
many cases beneficial.

Die-hard opponents of drinking in public health, particularly
those supporting product labeling, conveniently ignore the fact that
the body produces alcohol normally. It is not a foreign substance to
man or woman. Mammalian livers produce an abundance of
dehydrogenase, the enzymes which break down the alcohol
molecule releasing its energy for human use. Pearson in *Life
Extension* reports, "All healthy mammals, including people, make a
small amount of alcohol in their bodies as a part of normal
metabolism. The average person makes about one ounce of alcohol
every day...In order to metabolize this internally created alcohol, man
and the other mammals have special enzymes, particularly in their
livers."

In proper dosage then, the chemical ethanol is a potable,
naturally occurring substance in human physiology, hardly the "dirty
drug" described in much of the National Institute on Alcohol Abuse
and Alcoholism (NIAAA) literature. A glass or two of an alcoholic
beverage, taken with food, may release only a scant trace of ethanol
into the bloodstream, or none at all if taken slowly enough. Alcohol
only becomes a human problem when consumed in excess, which it
quite often is.

In 1987, an Everett, Washington teenager arrived DOA at a local
hospital from alcohol poisoning. The lad had forfeited his life to win a
$15 bet that he could down a bottle of brandy within a certain period.
He drank it so fast that a mortally toxic level was attained before his
body had time to regurgitate or pass into a coma. Many things we eat
and drink can and do contribute ultimately to our demise, slowly in
the case of sugars and saturated fats, and more rapidly in the case of
excess ethanol. But the excess is a human failing, not a product
deficiency.

Mead in "Health Warning" tells of another rare display of
excess. A 57 year old San Antonio man died from a water- drinking
binge. It seems that the heavy water intake lowered the sodium in his
blood causing his brain to swell and his life to end.

Yet, despite the accumulating evidence found in research
studies defining moderate alcohol intake as harmless, the medical

world remains indecisive and incapable of presenting this reality directly to its constituency.

Alcohol should again be recognized as a therapeutic drug.

A long-range objective of my informal organization, Citizens for Moderate Drinking, is the restoration of alcohol to America's pharmacopoeia of approved drugs. I have no illusions about the difficulty of accomplishing this task. The suggestion will be met with entrenched resistance in many, if not most, medical circles. But the idea needs serious debate. Much of the confusion surrounding alcohol's proper use would be allayed by this restoration. If alcohol is again recognized as a therapeutic drug, as is aspirin, its producers would be subjected to fewer capricious lawsuits. New temperance advocates could hardly continue to describe it a "dirty drug."

Here is the history. Alcohols were summarily removed from the U.S. pharmacopoeia as a sop to old temperance just after the turn of the century. By mid-century, advances in the science of microbiology added dozens of wonder drugs to our culture. Traditional alcohol remedies have become anachronisms along with thousands of herbal remedies.

So, it is difficult today for a conscientious person to look to the medical profession for scientific objectivity when it comes to alcohol. Indeed, where one would expect objectivity there often occurs hostility and obfuscation. Sinclair in *Era of Excess* points to the early use by temperance forces within medicine of highly selected scientific data in the prohibition battle. "Widespread use was made of medical statistics to win over the intelligent. The dry propagandists were among the first to discover the modern device of bemusing the opposition with facts and figures, while forgetting to mention any contrary evidence."

Physicians have continued to use alcohol in therapy.

It was on June 6, 1916 that alcohol was officially removed from the U.S. pharmacopoeia. On June 6, 1917 the American Medical Association House of Delegates passed the following resolution:

> Whereas, We believe that the use of alcohol as a beverage is detrimental to the human economy, and Whereas, its use in therapeutics, as a tonic or a stimulant or as a food has no scientific basis, be it Resolved That the American Medical Association opposes the use of alcohol as a beverage...

Sinclair continues that this action was a sham and pretense:

If the American Medical Association membership had really believed that alcohol was detrimental to the human economy, the association's condemnation would have been justifiable. But alcohol was still being widely prescribed as a medicine in 1917... It was recommended by many doctors in cases of fainting, shock, heart failure, exposure, and exhaustion. It was believed to be an antidote to snake bite, pneumonia, influenza, diphtheria, and anemia. It was used as a method of feeding carbohydrates to sufferers from diabetes. It was given to cheer and build up the aged. Insufficient research had been done to state definitely that alcoholic drinks possessed no food value. Nothing was said in the resolution about the fact that small quantities of alcohol taken with meals might aid the digestion and relax the mind. The wording of the resolution did not mention the use of alcohol as a narcotic and depressant.

The exclusion of alcohol from the list of recognized drugs remains a sham and pretense to this day. American doctors recommend it as therapy every day, even to pregnant females when taken in proper dosage. The real world is full of examples of this therapy. The oddest I have found was told to me by a practicing Mormon. The lady's doctor advised the use of vodka for bleeding during an early stage of pregnancy. While I would certainly advise a second opinion on that one, the fact is that it is the politics of medicine, not its practice, that keeps alcohol in a state of limbo.

Ironically, during the early years of prohibition, doctors were the only legal alcohol game in town. Physicians wrote millions of prescriptions for "medicinal" alcohols, but eventually Al Capone and his associates in the beer and liquor business created a distribution network that covered the nation, just as marijuana and cocaine are universally available today. This ready availability rendered the cumbersome physician/prescription/drug store route obsolete. But the medical profession was a part of the subterfuge of drinking for a time during prohibition. Unjust laws corrupt universally.

Alcohol's uniqueness should be supported medically.

The generalized health benefits shown in this chapter are enough to merit open and cautious support of moderate drinking by the medical profession. The journey through life demands constant balancing of choices. We continue as a people to overeat fast food hamburgers and heavily salted potato chips, fully aware of the short and long range trade-offs. Saturated fats and sugar are killers. Yet, no one at DHHS or the American Medical Association suggests placing warning labels on Big Macs or Baby Ruths, though both are demonstrably dangerous in excessive use.

Even while extolling the substantial contributions to nutrition of wine, Dr. Janet McDonald in an article titled "Wine and Human Nutrition" in *A Symposium on Wine, Health and Society* states: "From a biomedical standpoint, it is not yet known what constitutes a safe limit of alcohol use...It should be the physician's responsibility, with adequate knowledge about his patients, to weigh potential risks and benefits for each individual."

Many alcoholism and research professionals disagree with the advocacy of control of availability programs by their professional organizations. Whatever the risks, Americans have determined to drink and they should not be hectored by the federal government or conservative medical authorities into feeling guilty about their temperate drinking practices.

Roueche' writes:

> Although alcohol is generally conceded a place in mid-twentieth century medicine, the position it occupies there falls somewhat short of imposing. That it has one at all, however, is something short of a triumph. It can smother pain. It can summon sleep. And it can, above all, placate the troubled spirit and rest the racing mind...There are other analgesics, other soporifics, and many ataractics which are not merely as good but, in almost every respect, almost immeasurably better. Their only flaw, is excellence. Unlike alcohol, they are all so efficiently potent — and hence, at least potentially, so dangerous — that their use is confined to conditions of comparable stature. They are also, unlike alcohol, incapable of giving pleasure. They can only offer the chilly charity of relief.

Roueche' makes an important point. If human experience shows that a drink can provide the same relief as a pill — with a good deal more pleasure in the taking — some humans are going to choose the pleasure of the drink. Until humans are absolutely certain that alcohol is specifically and ineluctably harmful — as has been established with tobacco — they will continue to opt for its use. Even if found to be harmful in *any* dosage, alcohol would undoubtedly survive, so deep are its historical roots and firmly entrenched are its pleasurable usages.

Summary of Chapter 2

> *It is very difficult to create an incentive*
> *for a sick person to manage a stigmatized disease.*
> *If, in so doing, he or she is admitting*
> *to some sort of wrongdoing tacitly.*
> **Interview with Michael Q. Ford**
> National Association of Alcohol Treatment Programs

Drinking *can* be good for you.

Evidence of this benevolence occurred recently in my own family. One of my daughters returned home with her firstborn child. When her nursing milk refused to come down, she called another daughter who had nursed three children. "Just sit down, put up your feet, and have a beer." advised Susan. While the new mother is not much of a drinker, she followed this "old wives tale." In a matter of minutes, after a few sips of the beer, she relaxed and the milk of life flowed. I recognize that the mother could have practiced yoga, taken a tranquilizer, or exercised vigorously to release her obvious tensions. But, the beer worked and mother and baby were again one.

It is prudent that the medical and public health professions should register concern that positive alcohol and health data could be used as an excuse for overdrinking. It probably will be no matter what any of us do. Overdrinkers use dozens of excuses. But certainly that fear would pertain only for the abusing minority or for those in high risk categories.

The majority does not abuse. I have found no evidence that the majority would overdrink for health or any other reason. We are a mature, sophisticated society, capable of making critical and informed choices. If the medical profession intends to maintain such caution concerning alcohol (and it gives every evidence of maintaining that position), the citizens of this nation should look elsewhere for valid data on alcohol and health.

At the DHHS November 1987 conference on alcoholism in Washington, D. C., Secretary Otis Bowen stated unequivocally, "I'm not here to announce a new prohibition movement. Instead, we do want to stress that alcohol consumption is a risk-taking behavior." Perhaps Bowen's conciliatory words on prohibition would have meant more had he not announced also a cooperative effort with the National Council On Alcoholism to organize the new citizen's movement. The NCA is the largest, private neoprohibition lobbying agency in the nation. As of this writing, the citizen's group is in the final stages of formation. It is bad policy and bad politics for our major alcohol health agency to be formulating a lobbying group under the direct auspices of the NCA.

Restigmatizing alcohol could put the drunk back in the closet.

The loudest burst of applause during the secretary's speech at the conference came when he affirmed his intent to have all departmental communications in the future read "alcohol and other drugs" rather than "substance abuse." The danger in this new approach (now in full swing) lies in a restigmatizing of alcohol. Getting alcoholics out of their shame closets has been the greatest accomplishment of this century in alcoholism treatment.

In their misguided drive to lower per capita drinking, the DHHS, NIAAA and Alcohol, Drug and Mental Health Administration (ADAMHA) are relentlessly associating alcohol with "dirty" street drugs. This chapter has shown that, for the majority, alcohol is not a danger and may even be a blessing. Dr. Norman Kaplan of the University of Texas Medical School says, "Two drinks a day, on the average, have no deleterious effects on health and are actually beneficial." His phrase is "Up to two are good for you." Presuming no other medical contraindications, that advisory for drinkers remains well within the safe levels of human physiology.

Dr. Elizabeth Whelan says that society is plagued with frightened people who are extraordinarily preoccupied with bad things that might happen to them. In "Consumerism and the Misdirected War Against Alcohol Advertising" Whelan comments:

> We are in a nation, in a society, which is in the grip of an unprecedented level of nosophobia. Nosophobics are everywhere. They dominate the airwaves, the electronic media. They work for self-appointed consumer advocacy groups. They have infiltrated high level offices of our regulatory agencies. If you are having a temporary lapse on what exactly nosophobia is, let me remind you that it is like hypochondria, but it is different. Hypochondriacs think they are sick. Nosophobics think they will in the future be sick, because of the lurking factors in the environment in which they live.

Historian and editor Mark Keller warned in the *Second Report to Congress on Alcohol and Health* in June 1974 of the danger of focusing alcohol research exclusively on the sick. This wisdom should again be evoked in choosing new leadership at NIAAA and DHHS. The health of the moderate drinker is as important as the health of the abuser.

> The question of a general relationship between drinking and increased risk of mortality has a long history. In the 19th century it took the form of whether there was a "safe level" of drinking which would not cause disease. The common answer was Anstie's limit: the equivalent of 1.5 ounces of absolute alcohol per day...This concern has more or less disappeared from view in the twentieth century. In the heyday of the teetotal temperance movement, the issue became one of drinking or non-drinking, and the question of a safe amount became irrelevant. Later the medical concept of alcoholism, as a specific disease defined by the loss of control over drinking, diverted attention from studying the risks of drinking by "normal" people to studying clinical samples.

As Selden Bacon prophesied twenty years ago, a leadership cadre has emerged at the helm of the alcoholism research and treatment professions "...for whom what should be taught [moderation and responsible drinking] remains uncertain and frightening."

3

How To Measure
Moderate Drinking

Our diverse ethnic and cultural back-
grounds make it hard for us to accept
each other's ways of drinking or nondrinking.
Therefore, it is more difficult for us to arrive at a
workable consensus on standards for appropriate
conduct than is true in countries with much
longer continuity of cultures, such as
Sweden or Japan.
Don Cahalan
Understanding America's Drinking Problem

Only Irish coffee provides in a single glass
all four essential food groups: alcohol, caffeine,
sugar and fat.
Alex Levine

This chapter has two objectives — to show how alcohol affects
the human body and to suggest what constitutes reasonable
drinking.

The first task, outlining the physiological aspect, is relatively
straightforward and noncontroversial. The second, ascertaining
reasonable levels of drinking, is loaded with controversy. Each of us
must determine what's reasonable by objective standards. What is
reasonable for one person can be extreme for another.

Any workable concept of responsible drinking must encompass
a broad perspective. One which ranges from one or two drinks a
month for the very light drinker to, possibly, a full bottle of wine daily
for an Italian-born immigrant. A tolerance for these broad parameters
is essential to any real national consensus on drinking. The objective
should be to construct a drinking consensus which will be sufficiently
narrow to ward off physical harm, but broad enough to encompass
very different ethnic and cultural drinking patterns.

Baus in *How To Wine Your Way To Good Health* suggests that moderation in drinking, like moderation in everything else, lies in personal control of human behavior, not in precisely measured fluid amounts:

> But what is moderation? What it is not is abstinence. Abstinence and alcoholism are the two extremes: moderation is the middle way, the good way in drinking and politics. Moderation is an individual thing, much as the woman you love or the size of your shoes or the tone of your voice or your mannerisms. Moderation to one man is a glass; to another a bottle. A bottle to one man is a pint; to another a magnum. Your size, your tolerance, your capacity, your hangover range, your age, your very mood at the time of drinking all help to measure it — and you can measure it.

One thing positively wrong is drinking to insensibility. The image of the two-fisted drinker is a sorry one. In the strongest terms possible, this book criticizes the macho drinking image found in so much of the literature and folkways of pioneer America. Don Cahalan, discusses this excess in *Understanding America's Drinking Problem* :

> Our individualism and our made-in-Hollywood folk legends about rough pioneers and cowboys make us sympathetic to macho heroes who can drink anyone under the table and still outshoot all foreign hordes that try to overpower them...Our diverse ethnic cultural backgrounds make it hard for us to accept each other's ways of drinking or nondrinking. Therefore, it is more difficult for us to arrive at a workable consensus on standards for appropriate conduct than is true in countries with much longer continuity of cultures, such as Sweden or Japan.

The macho image is good for the box office but bad for the barroom. The first step toward moderation in drinking is to downplay the abuse-prone drinking fads (shooters, slammers, beers with a shot back, etc.). In their place, use what follows to develop a precise, moderate drinking methodology.

A drinking segment should be required in driver education.

In the best of all scenarios, state legislatures would mandate their liquor control agencies to produce completely objective alcohol training manuals and tests similar to those used for driving licenses. Since those legislatures have virtually preempted real learning experiences for the upper teens by insisting on age 21 as the lower limit for drinking, they should provide alternative methods of instruction. Examinations could parallel or even be extensions of existing driving examinations. We might wish otherwise, but we know that many young people will drink and drive long before reaching their twenty-first birthdays.

There are dozens of comprehensive training pamphlets already available on drinking. There are excellent brochures produced by the federal Department of Transportation, the American Automobile Association, and the Insurance Institute for Highway Traffic Safety, to name a few. These instructional materials are generally conservative in approach, but there is nothing wrong with being conservative when dealing with the lives of the young and the safety of the rest of us. Instructions should avoid anti-alcohol preaching which would likely be ignored by the student anyway.

The positive impact on young drivers could be substantial. Alcohol training examinations could require each new driver to answer basic questions about blood alcohol concentrations, loss of motor skills due to alcohol or medications for common illnesses like the flu, the synergistic effects of alcohol and drugs, and the legal responsibilities of drinking drivers. Premature death and the maiming of millions is the consequence of ignorance among beginning drinkers who do not fully understand the demands of performing life-threatening tasks like driving, skiing and boating while under the influence of alcohol or any other mind-altering substance.

This chapter presents findings about the physiology of drinking and presents easy-to-use guides to compute, by body weight, the upper limits of alcohol ingestion. It shows how to compute safe rates of consumption over drinking periods, to compute blood alcohol concentration (BAC) and to understand what alcohol does inside the body. What a safer world this would be if every driver knew these basics.

Unfortunately, along with these data, it is necessary for me to disclaim any personal responsibility for what any individual does after reading this book, particularly while driving or operating dangerous machinery. Drinking involves serious personal responsibilities, particularly in this litigation-prone era. Every person must be responsible for his or her own actions, sober or intoxicated. But, there is much that can be learned about personal drinking by studying these findings.

Research Finding 3.1

There is a formula for calculating
the upper limits of consumption.

> *Keep in mind one serious error is made by*
> *virtually all drinkers when subjectively trying*
> *to estimate how much and how often they drink.*
> *They consistently underestimate both*
> *frequency and quantity.*
> **Elliott J. Howard, MD**
> *Drink To Your Health*

How much drinking is safe from a physiological viewpoint? That question does not ask how much should a person drink. This first finding relates only to the upper limits for organic health, not for advisable or even safe limits in terms of individual daily performance standards.

Intelligent limits for drinking must be based on many unique, personal factors, such as general health conditions, blood pressure, age, the individual drinker's degree of alcohol tolerance and so on. These judgments must be guided by experience in drinking, family or ethnic proclivities. A person should be forewarned of the dangers of a history of alcohol or drug abuse in the family. A different decision is required when alcohol is taken with food or on an empty stomach, when the drinker intends to surfboard, drive an automobile or operate a power lawn mower near the time of ingestion.

The American Automobile Association's (AAA) manual, *One Drink Can Be Too Many*, focuses on the driving issue but its warnings pertain to any drinking occasion:

> Of course, the amount of alcohol consumed by the driver, and the alcohol content of his blood are both major factors determining his capability to operate a car.
>
> But there are many variable factors which enter the picture. These include how tired the potential driver is; how much, what and when he has been eating; whether he is on medication of any kind; what type of a day he has had at work or at home. These and other factors may help determine how alcohol — in any amount — is going to affect the driver's ability.

There is a very serious debate going on within the medical profession as seen in the recent series of papers in the British Journal of Addiction under the umbrella title of "Drinking Sensibly." Responding to Kendall, Pittman, Tuyns, Caetano and others have broadened. Caetano agrees with Kendell in supporting "...decreasing per capita consumption by manipulating taxation and other alcohol control measures..." Tuyns offers a more sensible approach comparing drinking to driving an automobile, risky but, "Let us teach people how to drink sensibly." Pittman points to a more balanced approach since, "...the overwhelming majority (96.6%) of those drinking below the 50/35 limit had not adverse effects."

Yet these serious commentaries show how deeply the control arguments have invaded the public health construct. The question remains how much can a person consume daily without harming organs or general health? The answer is no one can say with absolute certainty, but Dr. Pittman's 99.6 percent statistics is good enough for now. Here is a simple formula for computing limits from "To Your Health" by Dr. Elizabeth Whelan, executive director of the American Council on Science and Health. Whelan developed her handy divisors from an article by Turner, Bennet and Hernandez titled "The Beneficial Side of Moderate Alcohol Use." Whelan writes:

> Dr. Turner and his colleagues...have devised a formula that enables each individual to calculate the precise amount that can be safely consumed on a daily basis by most people in most circumstances. The simplified guidelines for determining the amounts allowable during any 24 hour period are as follows.

> For the number of ounces of 80 proof spirits, divide your weight in pounds by 30.
> For the number of ounces of table wine, divide your weight in pounds by 9.
> For the number of ounces of beer, divide your weight in pounds by 3.

Whelan's article provides the breakdown shown in the box which follows. The spirits, beer and wine are shown in ounces and the weight in pounds. But remember that the formulation does not recommend that a 150 pound person drink 5 shots of 80 proof, 16.7 ounces of wine or 50 ounces of beer, on any one day. The data merely provides the upper limits without harm as found in the scientific literature. Whelan warns against misuse of the limits.

Weight lbs.	Alcohol oz.	Spirits oz.	Wine oz.	Beer oz.	Drinks no.
120	1.7	4	13.3	40	3
150	2.0	5	16.7	50	4
180	2.5	6	20.0	60	5
210	3.0	7	23.3	70	6

This is not to suggest, however, that teetotalers should be encouraged to drink if that is not their preference. There are many reasons that people do not drink. Some simply don't care for either the taste or the effect of alcohol; others abstain for religious reasons. Still others must avoid the substance for medical or psychological reasons...Such people clearly should not be urged to imbibe, even on "doctor's orders."

Limitations are essential with all drugs.

The Turner upper limits formulation provides a vital link that has been missing in public discussion of drinking. It provides an unequivocal, understandable, easily measured, upper health measurement for daily drinking in terms of body weight. Nothing more. But, an established upper limit is also a tool to limit harmful drinking among the abusing population. No person can argue successfully that it is safe to drink above these limits.

Let's be specific. The formula indicates that it would be dangerous for a 150 pound person to drink more than five shots of spirits daily. That upper limit certainly conflicts with the current statement of Secretary Otis Bowen of the Department of Health and Human Services (DHHS). Bowen says that drinking as many as five drinks on any one occasion constitutes heavy binge drinking. Those four or five glasses of wine, beer or spirits may well constitute heavy drinking from a moral, ethical or caloric viewpoint. They do not constitute dangerous drinking from a medical point of view. Dr. Bowen asserts his own personal feelings, but certainly not any known medical standard.

It will be argued by the "drys" that the mere enunciation of such a safe upper limit will provide the heavy drinker with another excuse to overdrink. Serious drinkers do not need new arguments. Abusers use many creative excuses to justify their excesses. Even granting this danger, moderate drinkers outnumber abusers ten to one and it is the nonabusers who need some basic, unequivocal standard. The Turner data provide that credible, scientific guideline.

We are accustomed to dosage constraints for the intake of salt, saturated fats and aspirin, as well as for prescription drugs. There are uncertainties and risks in the consumption of aspirin, dyazide, turnip greens and dozens of other common foods and medicines. Nearly every medicine we take has a side effect of some sort.

Life itself is uncertain and unpredictable. No one is urging the medical profession to advise everyone to drink. But establishing safe limitations is an important issue that has been ignored by the National Institute on Alcohol Abuse and Alcoholism (NIAAA) and Department of Health and Human Services (DHHS). We need widespread discussion in the popular media of this new formula for upper limits of consumption.

A rational drinking limit was first suggested in 1874.

The Turner upper limit for drinking is not a novel computation. Babor, Kranzler and Louerman in "Social Drinking as a Health and Psychosocial Risk Factor Anstie's Limit Revisited" provide the most famous historical reference. "Initially, the historical debate over moderate drinking was formulated in terms of the relative risks associated with consuming beverages containing low concentrations of alcohol...versus high concentrations...At nearly the same time (1874), the English physician Francis Anstie proposed a limit of not more than 1.5 ounces of absolute alcohol daily as the amount that an adult man could drink without adverse effect to his health." Absolute alcohol is the precise amount of alcohol (ethanol) in any drink. As example, 40 percent of an 80 proof drink is alcohol while 12 percent of a glass of dry wine is alcohol.

The Whelan body weight divisors (based on the Turner article) are 3 for beer, 30 for spirits and 9 for wine. These calculations will produce amounts very close to the Anstie 1.5 ounces of absolute alcohol daily. The abstract for the Turner article states, "Accumulating data indicate that the moderate use of alcoholic beverages by adults may reduce the risk of myocardial infarction (heart attacks), improve the quality of life of the elderly, relieve stress, and contribute to nutrition."

The article reviews the literature on cardiovascular disease, alcohol and aging, relief of stress in drinking, and the nutritional contributions of alcohol. These various and diverse findings are used to establish their suggested limitations for healthy use:

Data accumulated more recently show that chronic ill effects in man are rare below a daily intake of 80 g (grams) and thus permit upper limits of moderate drinking to be established on a more rational basis. It is proposed that to qualify as "moderate", intake of ethanol should exceed neither 0.8 g (grams) per kg (kilogram) on any one day (and an absolute limit of 80 g (grams)) nor an average of 0.7 g/kg/day (grams per kilogram per day) in any 3 day period.

The Turner study distinguishes between the absolute upper limit of 8 grams per kilogram on any one day and a maximum of 7 grams per kilogram on any three days. This accommodates a larger intake on a day which includes an extended social event such as a football game and dinner following. That would work out to four beers for a 132 pound person or six beers for a 200 pound person.

There is always a danger of overstating research data taken out of context, a common practice on the media talk shows of America. Yet, the growing body of research about the positive aspects of moderate drinking is compelling. Chapter 2 contains many citations, positive and negative, about health and drinking. These data demonstrate that many moderate drinkers are living healthier and longer lives, particularly where heart disease is concerned.

The point in this finding is that individuals who are normally light drinkers may safely consume more on special occasions. They can probably stay within these upper limits at a party or while on vacation without concern, except for the physical dangers that might result from the loss in motor dexterity. Finally, Dr. Turner points to the inevitability of alcohol consumption in the society as the most compelling reason why we should devise understandable limits on its use:

What most people forget is that prohibition is a biological impossibility. You can make alcohol in any kitchen. There is no way you can prevent alcohol from being used.

Research Finding 3.2

Calories are another important consideration in drinking.

Everywhere the evidence is overwhelming.
Americans are finding it increasingly
acceptable — and sometimes desirable —
to try to alter other people's behavior.
Daniel Moskowitz
Business Week

There is only a small group of clinicians who are
interested in alcoholism. Generally clinicians who
write on it are those who are seeing people who
have had problems. The same problem exists for
psychiatrists. They generally talk
about pathological behavior.
Interview with David J. Pittman, Ph.D.
Washington University

Common sense suggests that a second important factor in
drinking is the contribution to body weight of ethyl alcohol. Ethanol,
or ethyl alcohol, is a rudimentary form of food since it releases
calories which are burned as energy inside the body. Of even greater
concern is the fact the body burns those free alcohol calories first,
allowing other foods to be stored in the body as excess fat. So,
moderate drinkers need to define the maximum number of calories
that their health regime may tolerate from this source.

Most diet plans contain comprehensive inventories of calories
from drinks. The upper limit formula for my personal body
size — around 200 pounds — would permit me occasionally to drink
six cans of beer per day (200 divided by 3 equals 66 ounces). Now a
daily six pack at 15 calories per ounce would contribute a prohibitive
990 calories or an untenable 41 percent of my daily goal of 2,400
calories. I personally restrict alcohol to within a 15 to 20 percent
daily caloric window. Recall that the American Heart Association
suggests a 15 percent limit on calories from alcohol.

Light beers contain about 100 calories compared to 140 for a
regular lager. Table wines average 24 calories per ounce and 80
proof spirits weigh in at 120 calories per ounce. Williamson in
"Alcohol and Body Weight in the United States" says that American
drinkers average 10 percent of their calories from alcohol but that
generally it has an "... independent association with lower body
weight in men..." Drinking the upper permissible limits daily, however,
would develop a serious new health problem called obesity. By
contrast, If a moderate drinker occasionally reaches the upper limit,
there is no physical harm. But there are those extra calories.

So, the regular drinker who wishes to avoid obesity must count calories anticipated from this source. Turner cites several approaches. Many Europeans regularly consume up to 20 percent of their calories from ethanol. Wine alone constitutes 10 percent of a French housewife's food budget. New York state drinkers surveyed in 1950 ingested 105 alcohol calories per person per day. Another study estimated that alcohol constitutes 8 percent of the total calories in the diet of American drinkers.

Following this plan, a 150 pound man or woman could ingest three beers or glasses of wine in a day without guilt or danger to health but with as many as 350 additional calories affecting the waistline.

Research Finding 3.3

Blood alcohol content should
always be computed.

*The NIAAA approach is to
inadvertently or purposely downgrade
the question of quantity in drinking... This is
the key to the alcohol problem. There is just no
relation to what happened at one level of drinking
with what happens at
different levels.*
Interview with Thomas B. Turner, M.D.
Alcoholic Beverage Medical Research Foundation

There is no substitute for a BAC card.

Every party-goer should carry a wallet-sized Blood Alcohol Content (BAC) reference card. These graphs can solve many an argument and save many lives. Every public bar should be required to post BAC cards for the benefit of their patrons. These standard guides measure the levels of intoxication by the amount of alcohol related to body size. Public comprehension of these drinking guides would provide far more safety than the proposed product labels or fetal alcohol syndrome posters.

Handy wallet or purse-sized cards are published by the Distilled Spirits Council of the United States, the American Council on Alcoholism, and by many beer, spirit and wine companies and agencies. The BAC card shown here is published and widely distributed by the Washington State Liquor Control Board.

Moderate drinkers should learn to compute their own and the appropriate drinking limits for social guests by making general estimates of body weights. The Washington card states that an ethanol concentration in the blood system of .10 percent (Washington law) is legal proof of intoxication. It is at this level that an operator of a motor vehicle breaks the law and may be convicted of drunk driving.

One of the new temperance proposals being considered within the American Medical Association and in several state legislatures

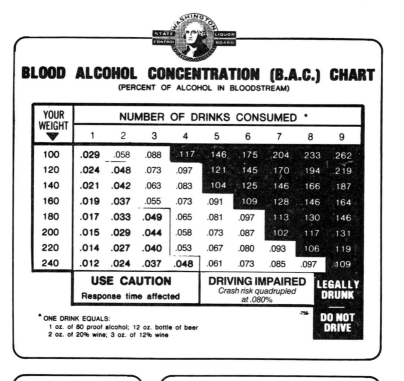

BLOOD ALCOHOL CONCENTRATION (B.A.C.) CHART
(PERCENT OF ALCOHOL IN BLOODSTREAM)

YOUR WEIGHT ▼	NUMBER OF DRINKS CONSUMED *								
	1	2	3	4	5	6	7	8	9
100	.029	.058	.088	.117	.146	.175	.204	.233	.262
120	.024	.048	.073	.097	.121	.145	.170	.194	.219
140	.021	.042	.063	.083	.104	.125	.146	.166	.187
160	.019	.037	.055	.073	.091	.109	.128	.146	.164
180	.017	.033	.049	.065	.081	.097	.113	.130	.146
200	.015	.029	.044	.058	.073	.087	.102	.117	.131
220	.014	.027	.040	.053	.067	.080	.093	.106	.119
240	.012	.024	.037	.048	.061	.073	.085	.097	.109

USE CAUTION	DRIVING IMPAIRED	LEGALLY
Response time affected	Crash risk quadrupled at .080%	DRUNK
		DO NOT DRIVE

* ONE DRINK EQUALS:
  1 oz. of 80 proof alcohol; 12 oz. bottle of beer
  2 oz. of 20% wine; 3 oz. of 12% wine

-756-

YOUR DRIVING ABILITY IS RELATED TO YOUR BLOOD ALCOHOL CONCENTRATION.

ALCOHOL IS A DRUG THAT AFFECTS YOUR JUDGEMENT AND SLOWS YOUR REACTIONS.

WHEN YOU HAVE BEEN DRINKING—DON'T GAMBLE. CALL A CAB. CALL A SOBER FRIEND.

DO NOT DRIVE UNDER THE INFLUENCE!

TIME IS THE **ONLY** WAY TO REDUCE YOUR B.A.C.

ALCOHOL IS BURNED-UP BY YOUR BODY AT .015% PER HOUR.

THIS CHART SHOWS HOW MANY HOURS IT TAKES TO REDUCE YOUR B.A.C. FROM VARIOUS LEVELS.

IF YOUR B.A.C. IS ▼	HOURS TO REACH B.A.C. % BELOW		
	.000	.050	.100
.025%	1.7		
.050	3.3		
.075	5.0	1.7	
.100	6.7	3.3	
.125	8.3	5.0	1.7

WALLET SIZE BLOOD ALCOHOL CONCENTRATION CARDS ARE AVAILABLE AT ANY STATE LIQUOR OUTLET.

would reduce the percentage for legal intoxication to 0.05 percent. This is an unrealistic BAC that would virtually prohibit any public drinking among drivers of smaller physical stature. Obviously, the large minority of repeat drunk drivers now on the road would ignore that new limit as they ignore the present one. The 0.05 percent BAC proposal is simply another tool in the campaign to lower overall per capita drinking.

How to compute your blood alcohol content.

Let's see how the BAC works. The card defines one drink as the equivalent of 1 ounce of 80 proof alcohol (a 12 ounce bottle of beer, 2 ounces of dessert wine at 20 percent alcohol or 3 ounces of 12 percent wine). Other cards use different base amounts for their computations. The "Know Your Limits" card published by the Distilled Spirits Council of the United States (DISCUS) uses 1 1/4 ounces of spirits in place of the single ounce in the Washington card. This is an important distinction. A 200 pound man could theoretically consume seven drinks in a single hour before reaching legal intoxication using the Washington card. Intoxication would be achieved with only five drinks with the DISCUS card. So, scrutinize the definitions carefully on whichever card you obtain.

Almost all the cards show three performance zones. The first is a generally safe drinking zone in which the BAC remains at or under 0.05 percent of alcohol in the bloodstream. The danger of physical accidents at this level is relatively low, though any drinking lessens, to some degree, physical dexterity. The next performance level of BAC readings from 0.05 through 0.09 percent are generally termed caution or danger zones. The likelihood of accidents or poor judgment is quite high with this amount of alcohol in the system. The AAA's _One Drink Can Be Too Many_ pamphlet says the following about these relative risks:

> A National Transportation Safety Board study showed that a driver's likelihood of causing a highway accident increased measurably at .04 per cent; at .06 it's about four times as great; six times as great at .08; and about eight times as great at .10 per cent — the level at which most states charge a person with driving while intoxicated. Note in particular that a 100 pound individual reaches that intoxication level from as little as 4 drinks.

Of course, the danger is not restricted to driving an automobile. Chopping vegetables with a sharp knife, climbing ladders, skiing and even tennis can be hazardous activities when the BAC rises above the 0.05 percent BAC. For this reason, Vogler and Bartz in _The Better_

Way to Drink have developed a system by which drinkers choose to maintain a target level of BA (Blood Alcohol) of 55 (another way of saying .055 BAC). They provide convenient weight charts calibrated by the hours of drinking to facilitate that objective. The authors recommend:

> How much, how often and how long someone drinks are important basic measures of the habit. The more people drink, the more frequently they do it, and the longer they stay at it when they drink, the greater the drinking habit...There are still big advantages to setting some limits. Even though you might drink an excessive amount, you can remain below a BA of 55, which is very important because you will avoid the negative consequences.

How equivalency relates to blood alcohol content

The next finding explains the controversy over comparative rates of absorption between wine, beer and spirits. As a practical matter, few drinkers will pay any attention to these rates of absorption when choosing what to drink. For the conscientious host, the only equivalency that makes sense is to know the total amount of alcohol consumed by guests. And that requires some kind of rudimentary equivalence or a drink counting system. Counting drinks is far more important than knowing the relative absorptive levels of each type of beverage.

In my professional training seminar for bars titled Safe Service of Alcoholic Beverages, I suggest a system based upon the numerical value of 1 for each standard drink — the equivalency of one-half ounce of absolute alcohol. Each numerical 1 represents either a shot of liquor, a bottle of beer or a glass of dry wine. This system enables bar servers to keep an approximate numerical count of the BAC of every guest they serve. This is accomplished by making an arbitrary upper limit of service for each guest decided by body weight. For convenience, I advise three categories — small, medium and large — with top limits for each grouping. This would limit the small guest to no more than 3 drinks at any one setting. No more than 5 drinks would be served a heavy-set person.

Consider the quandary facing a conscientious social host or professional bar server. Guests may range from twelve to a hundred on any evening. Trying to keep track of varying rates of absorption by guests enjoying several different types of beverages, or even mixing them, is nearly impossible. Classify each person by upper limits and

How Alcohol Impacts at Increasing Levels

From National Institute on Alcohol Abuse and Alcoholism Approximations for Statistical Populations)

CONCENTRATION   EFFECT

0.05 percent BAC   *Loosening of judgment, thought and restraint*

0.08 percent BAC   *Tensions and inhibitions of everyday life lessened*

0.10 percent BAC   *Voluntary motor action affected, hand and arm motion, walk and speech clumsy*

0.20 percent BAC   *Severe impairment: loud speech and staggering, emotionally unstable*

0.30 percent BAC   *Deeper areas of brain affected, response poor, stuporous and confused*

0.40 percent BAC   *Generally comatose, incapable of voluntary action, anesthesia*

0.50 percent BAC   *Certain anesthesia, difficulty breathing, toxic death likely*

count the numbers of drinks served. This is the only rational and safe method.

If you serve cocktails and high proof beverages — always the case in a bar — you must also determine how many numerical units (how many ounces of absolute alcohol) each specialty drink contains. It's not very hard. Although bars vary the drink ingredients, I recommend either *Mr. Boston Official Bartenders Guide* or *Jones Complete Barguide* as ready sources for recipes on mixed drinks.

Drinks are easy to count.

A Long Island Iced Tea, for example, constitutes a minimum of 1 1/2 drinks by my counting system (and often more depending on house policy) because it includes equal portions of rum, vodka and gin. A Manhattan has an ounce and a half of whiskey plus a small amount of vermouth so it becomes 1 1/2 numerical drinks.

There are so many hundreds of variations of alcoholic drinks that there is no space in this book to identify them all. As example, a high potency beer can contain triple the amount of alcohol as a light beer and double that of a standard lager. Creamy dessert sherries often have double the alcohol of a fruity Liebfraumilch. This is where knowing drink potency, pre-planning and drink counting become effective. If you are going to drink, you simply *must* determine the potency of each type of drink. Hopefully, the federal government will soon mandate potency as a percent of the fluid as the British now do and the French always have. The amount of ethanol is important.

In these litigious times, we are truly becoming our brother's keeper, at least when we are called to stand before the legal bar. The knowledge that you could be sued suggests caution also before the *wet* bar.

In *The Better Way To Drink,* Vogler and Bartz remind us, "... the vast majority of people can use our guidelines to become and remain successful drinkers. The first step in being a successful drinker is setting appropriate limits." Of course, each of us must personally count our drinks and compute their potencies. It is best to plan ahead so you know before the party begins, approximately how much you will consume.

Research Finding 3.4

The rate of absorption helps
determine the impact of drinking.

*We call it the pleasure paradox. You
think the more you drink the more pleasure
you get, but research shows that the less
you drink the more pleasure
you get from each drink, so to speak.*
Interview with G. Alan Marlatt, Ph.D.
University of Washington

*I don't think we would take back or change anything
we said in our moderate drinking article. The only thing
that comes to mind is that there is now pretty good
evidence that women should drink somewhat less than
men because of more fat that they have and alcohol is
not soluble in fat.*
Interview with Thomas B. Turner, M.D.
Alcoholic Beverage Medical Research Foundation

Nothing is as controversial today within the alcoholic beverage industry than the concept of "equivalency." It is a catchword designed to relate the intoxicating potential of wines, beers or spirits solely by the amount of absolute alcohol each contains.

Recently, a public education campaign stating the equivalency of standard servings for all three beverages was mounted by the Distilled Spirits Council of the United States (DISCUS) and its member companies. Their argument was that consumers should recognize the relative potencies of their chosen beverages. Beer and wine people answered with a counter effort involving sophisticated research studies to prove different ranges of alcohol absorption between wines, beers and hard spirits.

Merit is found on both sides of the issue. My own system of drink counting explained above is a practical compromise with equivalency. I recognize that there is a significant range in absorption, depending on the beverage and the manner in which it is consumed. I also know that the social host and the bar server need a simple working tool to maintain sobriety among guests. I have taught thousands of alcohol servers to simply count the drinks. The general public needs this facile tool. Counting drinks will help them stay within the target level of a 0.05 blood alcohol content (BAC).

So, without taking sides on the specific issue of equivalency—an issue which involves comparative excise taxes as much as comparative absorption—here is an explanation of what happens when you consume alcohol. To be a safe, intelligent drinker, it is important to understand the rate of entry and the rate of metabolism or dissipation of alcohol. This is the kind of information many Italian or Spanish youngsters learn naturally and artlessly by drinking appropriate amounts while growing-up.

Different people absorb alcohol at differing rates.

The equivalency issue does serve to highlight the many variables for both individuals and beverages. For this reason, a BAC card and other research data must be humanized, personalized and internalized by individuals. We are not laboratory mice and our physical dispositions at the moment of drinking can tangibly impact both absorption and elimination. Drinking is not an exact science. Gardner and Stewart in "Blood Alcohol and Glucose Changes After Ingestion of Ales, Wine and Spirits" demonstrate the wide absorption range between types of drinks and drinkers in controlled tests:

> Since blood samples were taken at 10, 40 and 130 minutes after the last dose was dispensed [blood was taken before drinking and at 60, 90, 180 and 240 minutes] it is possible to estimate only the time at which maximum blood alcohol level was reached. After the ales, the majority of the subjects showed their highest blood alcohol at 90 minutes while the remainder reached the maximum in 60 minutes. After wine in the fasted state, 13 of 19 subjects reached the maximum recorded level at 90 minutes and the remainder showed peak level at 60 minutes.

Participants who consumed wines and ales had the slowest rates of absorption, some reaching peak only after 90 minutes. But, the authors also found a quite diverse pattern. As example, among the wine drinkers, 13 required 90 minutes to peak while the remaining 6 wine drinkers, a full one-third of the group, experienced peak absorption within an hour. Those 6 wine drinkers had different physical constitutions and alcohol tolerances. What these tests provide are average absorption rates. In the bar, we are dealing with human beings who are seldom average.

Another neglected factor in absorption is the congeneric constituency. Congeners are a family of organic chemicals which are formed in fermentation and distillation. They provide the distinctive flavors, smells and tastes in most spirits and in many wines and beers. Included are such chemicals as furfural, esters, tannins, aldehydes and acids. A blended American whiskey, as example, will average 0.116 percent of these congeners compared to a cognac which will exceed 0.240. Mendelson and Mello in *Alcohol: Use and Abuse in America* comment on this congeneric factor in absorption:

> The rate of absorption from the small intestine is also influenced by the congener content of the beverage... Low congener beverages, such as vodka, are absorbed more rapidly than high congener beverages, such as brandy. Distilled spirits, which have a higher congener content, will be absorbed more slowly than wine or beer.

Ingesting food while drinking slows the absorption rate.

Much more to the point of this book (and a much better argument for wine, beer and spirit producers) is that all alcoholic beverages should be taken with food. Pelletier in "Wine and Health" from A Symposium of Wine, Health and Society reports:

> How and when an alcoholic beverage is consumed — with or without food, etc. — is an important point. If you reexamine the literature, wine tends to be consumed with food, which is the most beneficial way to moderately consume any alcoholic beverage. Secondly, there is an enormous variation (I think this has a genetic base and it certainly points to wide individual variants) where peak blood alcohol levels vary between 30 and 133 percent impact when an individual consumes distilled alcohol on an empty stomach.

How to figure absorption over time.

Using the Washington state BAC figures shown above, five drinks in a single hour would be required for a 180 pound person to reach a BAC of .081, just under legal intoxication. The card also says that an average of .015 percent of alcohol is eliminated in a single hour. That elimination rate applies to everyone, large or small, since it is the rate at which a healthy liver oxidizes alcohol.

If a 180 pound man drank five beers in the first hour of a three hour party and nothing more, his maximal BAC would be .081. This level would be reached in the first third of the evening. Let us assume, however, that our 180 pound man actually consumed those five beers over the first two hours. Then he sipped a soft drink and munched hors d'oeuvres in the final hour. What would be the BAC of our hypothetical drinker when he prepared to depart and fished his car keys from his pocket?

Let's compute it.

Five drinks on the BAC card would place our typical drinker at a concentration of .080 BAC (blood alcohol content). The elimination rate given on the Washington BAC card is .015 percent of the BAC per hour. Multiply that by three and you have .045 percent elimination over the time at the party. Subtract that from the maximum .080 BAC and at departure time, our guest would theoretically have a .033 BAC.

Under these contrived circumstances, our subject could drive safely, but with a somewhat diminished reaction time. His presumed .033 BAC level suggests caution in the operation of a motor vehicle, but not absolute danger. This computation presumes that our man drank steadily over two of the three hours, and that the five beers were of single potency each. If our drinker consumed food from the very beginning of the evening along with his beer drinking, the absorption would have been further slowed and the peak BAC would have been reduced.

Unfortunately, that is often not the scenario. More often, food is presented late in the evening after absorption has already been accomplished. Safety suggests that the host keep the food moving at the same pace as the alcohol. Both the absorption and the elimination rates are affected by the amount of time involved, the potency of the drinks and the presence or absence of food in the gut.

Every drink and every drinker Is different.
Drinking is a serious and personal matter so it must be computed differently by each drinker. If our typical man was drinking Manhattans and his date was drinking scotch and water, he would absorb nearly one-third more alcohol from the same number of drinks because a Manhattan is the equivalent of one and one-half standard scotch and water cocktails. This does not say that mixed drinks or strong beers should be eliminated from the party. It does say that potency must be calculated, preferably in advance of drinking, with a clear head and a stern resolve. With these two factors of drink potency and time, you can compute your way in advance through any difficult drinking situation and maintain the glow of a 0.05 BAC.

It is essential also to understand that every single drink lessens physical abilities to some degree. The tranquilizing impact of ethanol on the brain progressively lowers physical coordination and manual dexterity. The following page shows one of a series of splendid moderation ads from the House of Seagram that graphically depicts this progressive impact.

The party begins.

I can drive when I drink.

2 drinks later.

I can drive when I drink   .

After 4 drinks.

I can drive when I drunk.

After 5 drinks.

I can drin when I drin   .

7 drinks in all.

I can drven drn

The more you drink, the more coordination you lose. That's a fact, plain and simple.

Still, people drink too much and then go out and expect to handle a car.

When you drink too much you can't handle a car. You can't even handle a pen.

The House of Seagram

A partially full stomach is the best insurance policy.

Fitzgerald and Hume, in "The Single Chemical Test for Intoxication: A Challenge to Admissibility," discuss the impact of food in the gut:

> It is only when it is absorbed into the blood that it reaches the nervous system and produces its characteristic effects...Direct absorption from the stomach is slow and inefficient...usually between 5 and 10% on the low side to about 20%...Although alcohol requires no digestion and can be absorbed rapidly and efficiently in the small intestine...A beverage which is essentially water and alcohol without significant amounts of carbohydrate, fat or protein—such as vodka—when taken on an empty stomach passes almost immediately into the small intestine and is absorbed...If the stomach is not empty, or if it is empty but the beverage contains digestible materials such as sugars or other carbohydrates, the situation can be very different. The function of the stomach is to retain and process (digest) foodstuffs—whether liquid or solid—until large molecules are broken down into smaller molecules or otherwise converted into the bloodstream by passing through the walls of the small intestine.

So when you think of alcohol, think of food.

Body fat and psychological factors affect alcohol's impact.

It's unfair, but women and older folks are able to drink less alcohol. Canada has a separate BAC chart for women. This is because female and elderly bodies have more fat in proportion to body size and less body water on average. Whelan explains:

> Alcohol is more soluble in water than fat. A person with higher body fat will have proportionately less body water; this in turn slows the rate of distribution and metabolism of the alcohol and results in a higher blood alcohol level. If two men of the same size and weight, but with different quantities of body fat, drink the same amount of alcohol, the fatter man will have a higher blood alcohol level. Because women and the elderly tend to have proportionately more body fat, they generally are able to drink relatively less than men or younger people before risking effects on their health.

Another important factor for women is the added danger of liver damage from excessive drinking. Norton in "Alcohol Consumption and the Risk of Alcohol-Related Cirrhosis in Women" stresses the advisability for females who drink daily to remain at 3 or under normal drinks. More research is being done in this area.,

Groups of the same sex tend to drink more and faster. Emotional stress tends to slow emptying of the gut which can delay the alcohol impact. Larger individuals have a greater mass of blood vessels and body water to dilute more alcohol. factor. New drinkers simply can't handle as much alcohol because they are unused to the novelty of mental euphoria and the subtle losses of physical dexterity. The beginning drinker and those who drink infrequently are more quickly impacted, and at lower BAC levels, than experienced drinkers.So, a combination of discretion, common sense and a well-worn BAC chart should be coupled with a large dose of caution in determining how much and when.

Research Finding 3.5

Alcohol is metabolized naturally in the body.

I have to tell you that even though I have been in public health 15 years, I was basically shocked at the amount one can consume before one begins to get into adverse effects.
Interview with Elizabeth M.Whelan, Ph.D.
American Council on Science & Health

My feeling is that it is primarily genetic. Now genetics are very complicated. People handle alcohol differently. We're trying to get a handle on this but it is very complicated.
Interview with Thomas B. Turner, M.D.
Alcoholic Beverage Medical Research Foundation

A person does not need a degree in biology or body chemistry to understand the physiology of alcohol. Ethyl alcohol is not a *foreign* substance, but a natural chemical produced within the body every day. We are all born to produce alcohol and wenaturally manufacture the enzymes which are required to break down alcohol into energy and waste components.

THE PHYSIOLOGY OF ALCOHOL

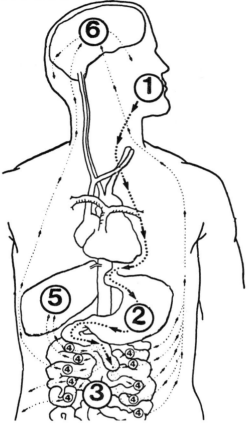

Alcohol passes from the mouth to the stomach (2) where small amounts are absorbed, depending upon the amount of food in the gut. More than 90 percent of the alcohol is passed by the small intestines (3) directly into the bloodstream (4). This occurs without digestion or any other chemical change of the alcohol. Oxidation or reduction of the alcohol into its constituents of water, carbon dioxide and energy occurs in the liver (5). Since this organ can oxidize slightly over one half ounce of absolute alcohol hourly, the remaining portions of alcohol continue to circulate in the bloodstream. The primary impact of the alcohol in the bloodstream occurs in the brain (6) and on the central nervous system.

In rare cases, this internal alcohol production can be a serious physical problem. In 1983, a San Francisco lad's immune system faltered allowing the production of abnormal amounts of yeast in his stomach and bloodstream. The youngster was continuously intoxicated from this internal fermentation. The problem eventually was controlled by a combination of drugs and diet.

But no one should be confused about why human beings consume alcohol. We drink for effect. Here are some comparative levels of impact in the brain at high BAC levels as reported by Dr. Joseph Pursch in a column titled "Alcohol's Effect on [the] Brain is Easy to See:"

> At a concentration of .10 the frontal lobes of the brain, the parts right behind the forehead, are affected...At .10 to .20, the parietal lobes (the area directly above his ears) become affected with slurred speech, mild tremors and loss of motor skills...A concentration of .20 to .30 hits the occipital lobes located in the back of the head. Now there is double vision...

Obviously, the objective is to keep alcohol at or below the .05 BAC level so that these untoward effects never occur in your brain. Once alcohol enters the bloodstream, it travels relentlessly around and around the body until the liver oxidizes it completely. An important distinction between ethanol and other drugs is that it does not remain in the cells and tissues as a foreign deposit as does marijuana and other drugs. Goldstein in "How Ethanol Really Works" explains the often misunderstood impact of ethanol on cell membranes during this residual period. "The cell membranes are disorderly when treated with ethanol. 'Disorderly' is not quite the approved terminology, but we do call them disordered."

This "disordering" produces some of the anesthesia, and there is hope among scientists that study of these effects will reveal a genetic marker which would unlock the mystery as to why some individuals become alcoholic and others do not. Mendelson and Mello in *Alcohol: Use and Abuse in America* explain that this disordering is what makes alcohol at once both a powerful and an acceptable drug:

> Lipids are one of the major constituents of all cell walls or cell membranes. To travel from the bloodstream into the brain, and into the nerve cells, alcohol has to pass through cell walls...The alcohol molecule is unique in the ease with which it can enter nerve cells and return

to the blood. The passage of most other substances into the brain is prevented by barriers formed by the cell walls....Many substances are trapped in lipids for hours, days or even permanently. When the substances are drugs, their effects may be adverse because they persist for such a long period of time.

The oxidation of ethanol occurs in the liver.

These phenomenal attributes of alcohol should be kept in mind when considering the assertion by Dr. Ernest Noble, second director of NIAAA, that alcohol is a dirty drug. Alcohol is really a remarkable drug in its biochemistry. The metabolizing of the alcohol molecule is accomplished in the liver by the action of enzymes and coenzymes, principally by alcohol dehydrogenase. Most mammals possess these enzymes for the processing of naturally occurring alcohol created daily through bacterial fermentations.

A person may choose to abstain from ingestion of alcohol, but none of us can be total teetotalers. It is in this catalyzing of the ethanol molecules that energy becomes available to the body in much the same process as sugar is metabolized. Since the liver is the primary organ involved in transforming the alcohol molecules into carbon dioxide and water, its functioning is diverted from the routine handling and detoxification of other substances. This is where the danger occurs in taking multiple drugs. A synergism of effects occurs since the liver, active in processing the ethanol, works more slowly on the other substances, heightening their toxic effects on the system.

The rate of degradation of alcohol can also be affected by the amount of sugar in the liver. A person who has fasted for a long period will break down the alcohol more slowly than one who has recently eaten. A person more tolerant to alcohol is a person whose body has experienced alcohol often enough to accommodate the intoxicating effects. The intoxicating effects do not disturb the more tolerant person to the same degree as the beginning drinker.

Mendelson and Mello explain:

> The experience of many social drinkers suggests an exception to the general rule that the rate of alcohol metabolism is unalterable. Many have noticed that the more they drink, the more they are able to drink without incapacitating intoxication.

This observation is valid and reflects the pharmacological phenomenon known as "tolerance." Alcoholics may develop enormous tolerance for alcohol. Since a practicing alcoholic may consume a full bottle of spirits daily, a great deal of tolerance is required for that person to perform routine daily tasks in a seemingly sober manner. Remember, however, that, despite this practiced conditioning, the physical dexterity of the drunken person is reduced according to the amount of alcohol in the bloodstream. That is why there is such a high rate of all types of physical accidents and injuries among heavy drinkers. While they may seem stable, they lack physical control.

Beware of operating a vehicle or riding with someone whom you are certain has exceeded a tolerable intake. No matter how seemingly calm and deliberate, a person above .05 BAC is a menace behind the wheel. The only sensible approach is found in a small box on the back of the Washington State BAC card which reads:

TIME IS THE ONLY WAY TO REDUCE YOUR BAC.

The card states that the body excretes alcohol at the rate of .015 percent of its concentration in your blood stream per hour — any body, large or small. That's the rate at which a healthy liver oxidizes or breaks down the components of ethanol.

What alcohol does as it circulates in the body.

The most observable influence of alcohol is upon the central nervous system. This is demonstrated both on the emotional and autonomic levels. Depression of the central nervous system produces what is known as the release phenomenon. This state often initiates heightened physical activity and excess vitality in the short run. This is because the alcohol has a panoply of therapeutic effects including tranquilization, sedation, anesthesia to pain, a lowering of cholesterol and the dilation or expansion of capillaries as blood surges to the extremities. We drink alcohol because of these desirable side effects.

Appetite is generally stimulated because the mouth and stomach acids flow more freely. This is why doctors often recommend a drink for the young or the aged who lack appetite. Olsen in "Wine and Health" describes this internal organic response:

> The healthful effect of the alcohol in such beverages is achieved by relaxation of walls and resultant dilation of blood vessels serving the autonomic organs, specifically those concerned with nutritive, glandular, vascular, sensuous and reproductive activities. This means blood pressure is lowered and there is an increased ease of flow of blood to these organs; senses are heightened

and function is improved...The initial effect is the same for a Graves (Bordeaux wine) as for a Gallo as for a Grasshopper (cocktail). Once the ethanol has reached the circulatory system, its origin is unimportant. Some slight amount of ethanol is absorbed into the bloodstream through the mouth and the lining of the stomach walls, but up to 85 percent is transmitted through the small intestines. This absorption process is rapid when the gut is empty and slowed considerably when the stomach is full and is contending with foods such as protein or milk products, which line the stomach walls interfering with the alcohol absorption.

As explained above, a review of the literature does show an absorption variance between types of alcoholic beverages. However, other more significant variables relate to physical makeup, the amount of food in the gut and alcohol tolerance. It is quite evident that alcohol absorption reflects the individuality of the drinker as much as the nature of the beverage. That's the really important point. As in most other human activities, we are unique in drinking. Mood, alcohol tolerance, age, physical health and drinking experience must be taken into consideration.

We drink primarily to alter our moods.

Any honest analysis of moderate drinking should face the reality that we drink essentially because alcohol alters our moods. Every now and then, as a public speaker on alcohol matters, I am urged to engage in a futile debate with the aficionado of one beverage or the other who insists that his or her consumption is cultural and not physiological.

It is both. We drink beverages, aside from water, both for their taste and their psychosomatic effects — coffee and tea because they stimulate, alcohols and warm milk because they relax us and make us feel better. It does no disservice to our favorite alcoholic beverages to say so. After all, it's difficult to get through this stressful life without palliatives of one sort or another. A most compelling example of affluence in America is the fact that purchased drinks have surpassed water in total fluid intake. We purchase everything from wine to exotic bottled waters to avoid ingesting the 180 gallons of straight water necessary annually to maintain life.

However, we have to recognize that altering our moods with alcohol can be a mixed blessing. Pace and Cross make the point in *Guidelines To Safe Drinking* that alcohol can also bring out the beast in us. "Depending upon the amount of alcohol ingested, the *individual loses many of the more civilized assets that have been acquired, such as consideration for other people, politeness, modesty, reserve, prudence, and anxiety or concern."*

Shakespeare wondered why we put an enemy in our mouths to steal away our brains. Is that why we drink, to deliberately lose our civilized reserve? Of course not. But, the partial loss of decorum—the ability to sit back and shrug off the burdens of the day—is an important, congenial reward of responsible drinking. The authors describe this function through an explanation of the excitatory and inhibitory cells of the brain. Alcohol impacts the inhibitory cells first, lowering inhibitions in an otherwise reserved person. This process gives the appearance of stimulation in the form of a short-lived euphoria which fades as depression inevitably occurs on the excitatory cells.

The most important lesson in the learning-to-drink odyssey lies in taking advantage of the release·phenomenon. The relaxation and euphoria we obtain must be matched by a recognition of a relative loss of skills and good judgment. Weil and Rosen in *Chocolate to Morphine* distinguish between feeling skilled and losing skills through the depressive effect of alcohol:

> It is important to note, however, that some of the sensation—especially the sense of confidence—produced by low doses of alcohol may be false. Unlike stimulants, alcohol and other depressants slow the functioning of the nervous system, including reflexes, reaction time, and efficiency of muscular response. Though people often feel they are performing better after a few drinks, scientific tests show otherwise.

Research Finding 3.6

The alcohol elimination process
is natural and regular in operation.

*Once alcohol is in the bloodstream, it must
be broken down by the liver and oxidized—
that is, turned into water and carbon dioxide.
The liver is able to convert less than one-half
ounce of alcohol per hour into
these harmless chemicals.
From One Drink Can Be Too Many*

*Safe drinking seems to be drinking that is used
to enhance the quality of life for the individual;
unsafe drinking is drinking that is a goal in itself.*
John A. Ewing, M.D.and Beatrice Rouse, M.Ed.
Drinking

As soon as alcohol enters the bloodstream, the body begins to dispose of it through enzymatic oxidation. The lungs and the kidneys expel directly, at most, about ten percent of the alcohol. That is why the telltale drinker's breath provides such an accurate gauge of blood concentrations. That is why the police breathalyzer is accepted as legal proof of intoxication. There is the same amount of alcohol in 2.1 liters of alveolar air as in one milliliter of blood. It's a foolproof measuring system.

Ninety percent of ingested alcohol is changed to carbon dioxide and water by oxidation in the liver. There are several chemical steps involved beginning with the creation of acetaldehyde, the primary culprit of the hangover. This acetaldehyde transforms to acetate, the familiar acid in vinegar, and eventually changes into water and carbon dioxide. Through this complicated chemical pathway, heat or usable calories are released which the body employs immediately for its functioning. The signal difference between alcohol and other sources of energy such as sugar is that it may not be stored for future use. Alcohol energy is utilized immediately upon release.

The *Manual on Alcoholism* published by the American Medical Association describes the rate of metabolism as slightly under one standard drink per hour. "The rate of metabolism in man is fairly constant at about one gram per 10 kilograms body weight per hour. In other words, an average 150 pound (70 kg) adult male under ordinary circumstances metabolizes approximately seven grams of ethanol (the equivalent of about two-thirds ounce of straight whiskey or eight ounces of beer) in an hour."

There is, of course, some individual variation, which is reported to be as great as 50 percent more or 50 percent less than the average figure. The Washington State BAC card, based on Rutgers University computations, settles for the easy-to-remember average of a single drink per hour. It's pretty close for most of us.

Drinking can impact human nutrition.

This abundant release of energy in the form of non-nutritive calories is also why the habitual inebriate will eventually starve his organs of their needed daily requirements of vitamins and minerals.

Individuals who drink 6 or 8 drinks a day derive as many as half their functional calories from alcohol but those ethanol calories lack the nutrients of a balanced diet. This is why the counting of the calories to be consumed in alcohol is important for the moderate drinker.

While other foods, such as fats and sugars, are stored in cells and used as the body needs them for energy, the liver acts relentlessly to eliminate the alcohol as fast as it comes in. This may be the reason why civilizations so universally legalize alcohol. Its effects are transitory. In moderation, alcohol enters, gives euphoria and usable calories, and often nutrients, before exiting at a quite rapid rate and without physical harm. Only, though, in moderation.

As Pelletier points out in "Wine and Health," there are functions aside from the release of calories involved in wine metabolizing. "The first issue is increased nutrient absorption. There are some nutrients which are known to be absorbed more efficiently in the intestinal tract in the course of wine consumption in addition to the nutrients _per se_ in wine." Since they are essentially cereals and fruit juices, beers and wines bring with them trace elements of all the vitamins and minerals necessary for human survival. These beverages have been determined in metabolic research projects to enhance the absorption of calcium, phosphorus, magnesium and zinc when compared to solutions of plain ethanol in water.

Distilled spirits are often consumed in other health-giving beverages such as orange juice, tomato juice and in cocktails and liqueurs which often contain foods or herbal additives and a wide array of therapeutic oils and essences. While drinking is not essential to human existence, there is accumulating medical evidence that moderate intake can add to physical well-being just as excess can cause great bodily harm.

Alcoholic beverages are unfairly compared to street drugs.

Keep these distinctions about alcoholic beverages firmly in mind when you read propaganda comparing them to street drugs. This is the line of the National Council on Alcohol Abuse and Alcoholism, the National Council on Alcoholism, the Center for Science in the Public Interest or other public and private health agencies which associate alcohol with tobacco, marijuana, cocaine and other street drugs. Tobacco is harmful in any use, and street drugs are illegal, generally harmful, and often addictive.

For over ninety percent of its users, alcohol is not addictive or harmful. Furthermore, many street drugs contain chemicals that remain in the body sustaining detrimental effects for long periods of time. Outside of the obvious observation that wine, beer or spirits can be abused, there is no rational basis for comparing alcohol and street drugs—the current campaign at DHHS and NIAAA. An unfortunate side effect of that campaign is the denigration of the word drug itself. Weil and Rosen in *Chocolate to Morphine* define the word:

> A common definition of the word *drug* is any substance that in small amounts produces significant changes in the body, mind or both. This definition does not clearly distinguish drugs from some foods...Most people would agree that heroin is a drug. It is a white powder that produces striking changes in the body and mind in tiny doses. But is sugar a drug? Sugar is also a white powder that strongly affects the body, and some experts say it affects mental function and mood as well. Like heroin, it can be addicting. How about chocolate? Most people think of it as a food or flavor, but it contains a chemical related to caffeine, is a stimulant, and can also be addicting. Is salt a drug? Many people think they cannot live without it, and it has dramatic effects on the body.

As a commonly ingested drug, ethyl alcohol is unique. It is certainly not harmful to the system in the same sense as are most of the other illegal psychotropic substances. And, of course, it is legal. Alcohol enters and exits the bloodstream and cells of the body without harm. The body actually shuts down completely by becoming comatose should a person ingest sufficient quantities so quickly as to threaten total toxicity—the only common drug to act in this manner.

Research Finding 3.7

Fats and proteins foods are
good absorption blockers.

> *Eat before or while drinking. The absorption*
> *rate for alcohol can be slowed by as much as*
> *one-third. Foods that are high in protein*
> *and starch are best for this purpose.*
> **" If You Drive What About Drinking?"**
> American Automobile Association

There is no digestion necessary in alcohol absorption. Alcohol is accepted into the bloodstream in its original form. As it circulates through the blood system, the alcohol is distributed evenly in the water of the body residing in the tissues. While the body is over 70 percent water, parts of the body such as the blood have higher water content. The fact that blood is ninety percent water is the reason alcohol content can be so precisely measured from a blood sample. Our objective should be to slow the absorption process so we gain the benefits and lessen the dangers. Food is the best way to accomplish this tempering effect.

Fitzgerald and Hume reported:

> Carbohydrate meals empty fairly rapidly. Protein meals empty more slowly, but if lumps of meat, for example, are present, they may remain in the stomach for as long as nine hours...a meal containing a considerable amount of fat is passed slowly into the small intestine over a period of four to six hours.

Amerine in "Absorption of Ethanol From Alcoholic Beverages" confirms this slowing of metabolism particularly by fatty foods. "The lowest BAL [Blood Alcohol Level] is obtained when the alcoholic beverage is consumed with a meal or within two hours after a meal. If the stomach is full, the peak BAL may be only 30 to 70 percent of that when alcohol is taken on an empty stomach...the composition of the meal is important. Meals containing fat or high carbohydrates inhibit gastric emptying and also speed up ethanol absorption."

Think of that. After a full, fatty meal, alcohol peaks may be from 30 to 70 percent lower. It is no accident that the Italian often ingests a morsel of food with the glass of wine. This practice embodies hundreds of years of experience and practical wisdom.

Goldstein in *Pharmacology of Alcohol* explains the two reasons for always eating when drinking. As her book outlines, blood alcohol content samples taken from the fingertip vary dramatically between persons drinking with empty and full stomachs. But, more importantly, the presence of food in the gut lowers the total amount of alcohol that ever reaches the brain:

> Furthermore, taking food with drink sharply reduces the total amount of ethanol that reaches the brain. You will notice that the ethanol is totally eliminated in about the same time in both cases and that the area under these curves, the total exposure of the brain to ethanol under the two conditions, is not the same at all.

Goldstein's explanation for this phenomenon is that the ethanol passes through the liver first along with the food and in rather low amounts. The liver can dispose of these small amounts of alcohol immediately as compared to the large doses that enter the bloodstream from the intestines after consumption on an empty stomach. She conjectures that the same dosage, taken slowly in sips over a full day, would never allow any ethanol to enter the bloodstream. Obviously, the correct time to serve and consume food is before and during the drinking period, not, as is most often the custom, at the end of the social event. This is why temperate nations historically associate drinking with meals and large feasts in which alcohol appears only in association with food.

Finally, Mark Keller cautions us that we should not downgrade the word drug or be frightened of using it correctly to describe alcohol. "The word drug itself should not be a pejorative word. Alcohol is a drug and penicillin is a drug. There is nothing inherently negative about something being a drug."

Research Finding 3.8

The final decision should be the rate of drinking.

> *The NIAAA has concentrated very heavily on the alcoholic and has lost sight of the fact that far more people are using alcohol moderately and sensibly without great harm, so that the two are blurred and distinctions are being lost.*
> **Interview with Thomas B.Turner, M.D.**
> Alcoholic Beverage Medical Research Foundation

After a moderate drinker understands how to compute BAC levels, determines the maximum number of drinks to be taken on any one occasion, decides on the drink type and potency, and arranges for sufficient food to accompany the beverages, a final determination remains. That is the rate of drinking.

The ultimate guideline for that decision should be to remain sober and in reasonable command of one's faculties. In this state, a person can drink without incurring excessive danger of accidents, in or apart from motor vehicles. That is reasonable drinking.

Since the most obvious public health problem derives from death and injuries involved in motor vehicles, I recommend that individuals and groups circulate the literature of the National Transportation Safety Board, the American Automobile Association

(AAA) and other dispassionate groups interested more in *safety* than in the demise of the alcoholic beverage business. The AAA has a dramatic slide/transparency presentation and a series of informative leaflets with all the pertinent facts on drinking and driving.

There is a safe target zone for drinking.

Vogler and Bartz in *The Better Way To Drink* suggest such a safe system "...to savor the good effects as your blood alcohol is rising up to a maximum of 55 and then quit drinking." Their goal of a BA of 55 (a BAC of .05) is achieved somewhere between the fourth and fifth drink for the average body size. With the addition of generous hors d'oeuvres to slow the absorption, five drinks spread over an evening would maintain a safe level of consumption.

The Vogler and Bartz safe drinking guideline demonstrates the oversimplification in DHHS Secretary Otis Bowen's statement that five drinks on any one occasion represent heavy, abusive drinking. For a person of 160 to 200 pounds, five drinks over an extended time period can represent a moderate, safe drinking target. The public needs a much more sophisticated standard.

For someone concerned about their own or a another family member's current drinking practices, Chafetz suggests the helpful technique of keeping a drinking diary (like a daily calorie diary) for a period of time for analytical purposes. "I suggest trying to keep this kind of daily record over a total of several weeks in your life. You may be quite surprised at the results. As you look them over, you might think about your priorities—what you want out of your own life. Is alcohol contributing to them? Is it enhancing your enjoyment of the situations you want to get the most out of?"

Research Finding 3.9

Moderate drinking is easily defined.

> *I think about keeping the amount on a regular*
> *daily basis at one ounce or a little bit more.*
> *That translates to two and maybe even three*
> *drinks. So, I'm satisfied if people say they*
> *have three portions of some kind of alcoholic*
> *beverage on a regular basis as being a safe level.*
> **Interview with Norman M. Kaplan, M.D.**
> University of Texas Medical School

This chapter promised both a definition of moderate drinking and a process of measuring it.

The medical citations, the information on blood alcohol and the physiology of alcohol presented in these opening chapters should be sufficient for anyone wishing to establish a safe drinking plan. They provide valuable perspectives for making moderate choices. It should be apparent that there are no absolute guidelines other than the reasonableness suggested by these many authorities. If you are in generally good health and commit to a prudent life style, alcoholic beverages can be an enriching, satisfying and, quite likely, healthy contribution.

However, if you have diabetes, suffer from a liver dysfunction, come from a family with a history of alcohol abuse, are currently pregnant, or suffer from chronic stomach unrest, don't drink. If you have any of these or other illnesses for which alcohol is often proscribed, consult your personal physician before determining what is reasonable drinking for you. Don't use this or any other book to gain permission to drink.

Use this book rather to dispel the systematic bastardization of the concept of responsible drinking emanating from current NIAAA officials. Recognize that this conservatism did not always exist within that important federal agency. Here is an excellent classification of the categories of drinking which appeared in the NIAAA's _Second Report to Congress on Alcohol and Health_ published in 1974.

These four logical drinking categories should be used to dispel the endemic confusion about drinking today. They define drinking in easy to understand, noncontroversial terms.

> **Moderate Occasional:** persons who drink any form of alcohol but only in small amounts at any one time, never enough to become intoxicated, and less frequent than daily.

> **Moderate Steady:** same as for Moderate Occasional except daily.

> **Heavy Occasional:** persons who get drunk occasionally with periods of either abstinence or moderate drinking.

> **Heavy:** persons who get drunk regularly and frequently.

Contrast these clean and precise definitions with the confusing concept of heavy drinking posed in the *Fifth Special Report to Congress on Alcohol and Health* published in 1983.

> Similarly, the term "heavy use" sometimes means that it is statistically more frequent than is true of American users generally. The heaviest using third of the population consume an average of 14 drinks per week at which pathological (or adverse behavioral) changes occur more frequently.

The *Sixth Special Report to Congress on Alcohol and Health* compounds the confusion by establishing an amorphous category called "heavier drinkers" including all of us who consume an average of one ounce of pure ethanol or two drinks daily. Gone by the boards is the Moderate Steady daily consumer despite the overwhelming evidence in medical literature that this is a harmless, healthy level.

The second report in 1974 had concluded:

> All in all, the data on general mortality suggest that for the amount of drinking, apparently unlike amount of smoking, there may be some kind of threshold below which mortality is little affected. In the absence of further evidence [the medical evidence since then has confirmed these findings], in fact, the classical "Anstie's limit" seems still to reflect the safe amount of drinking which does not substantially increase the risk of early death.

Most drinkers in America fit comfortably into the Moderate Occasional or Moderate Daily categories. The attempt at NIAAA to make daily drinking synonymous with heavy drinking is an outrage.

Finally, there are special circumstances and physical activities which demand particular caution and constraint in face of the tranquilizing and inhibitory effects of drinking. Boating, swimming and skiing, and other physical activities involve these special dangers. For example, a phenomenon known as boaters-hypnosis slows reaction time equal to the level of intoxication after four hours exposure to sun, wind, glare and water motion. Sun and snow can also induce a kind of trance-like hypnosis.

Alcohol intensifies the disorientation caused by swimming when water enters the inner ear. A drunk person will often swim down instead of upward seeking safety. Alcohol reduces the body's temperature and its natural protection system against cold water. The loss of motor skills and dexterity in the lower extremities from drinking also contributes to many a broken bone in skiing and other physical sports.

Research Finding 3.10

Public education should include
the values of moderate drinking

> Many prominent philosophers and other public figures have long extolled the virtues of moderation (Benjamin Franklin stands out as a prime example.) The middle way of moderation as an alternative to the extremes of excess and absolute restraint is also an important basic tenet of Buddhism, Taoism and other Eastern philosophies...many contemporary Western beliefs (e.g. Christian fundamentalism), on the other hand have adopted an absolute stance in which any use of taboo substances or activities (usually drugs and sexual behavior) is considered sinful...
> **G. Alan Marlatt, Ph.D. and Judith Gordon, Ph.D.**
> *Relapse Prevention*

I began this chapter with the suggestion that alcohol education should be required before the issuance of a driver's license, even though the majority of applicants would be under the legal drinking age of twenty-one.

Drinking should have just as demanding a learning curve as driving, typing or playing sports. Each endeavor requires a developing intellectual grasp of the fundamentals and physical dexterity that comes from years of practice, experience and exercise of good judgment.

When the Washington state legislature convened in January 1988, over 60 AIDS education bills were tossed in the hopper. It is appropriate that the political system come to grips with both drinking and AIDS, each of which constitutes a public health threat from the intemperate use of a good thing. It is critical that any AIDS curriculum distinguish between normal healthy sex and unorthodox practices which endanger human life and the well-being of society as a whole. Education about drinking should embody the same, dispassionate distinctions between normal and healthy practice and the wanton destructiveness in abuse.

Nations that inculcate drinking practices at an early age and associate drinking with food have less abuse among adults. That's a fact, though one which seems lost on most legislatures. Children in these early-drinking societies, for example those from Italy and Germany, enjoy a long and healthy drinking learning curve.

This does not mean that there are no alcoholics or drunk drivers in Italy and Germany, only that the population abuses less. It does mean that the established norm is moderate, nonabusive drinking in these societies. A consensus in American public education on moderate drinking could provide a dispassionate method of establishing such a norm for our young people. That education could recognize and support the alternative choice of abstinence while establishing moderate drinking as the acceptable norm for those who do drink.

We learn to drink in the same manner as we learn most everything else. By observation. Generally speaking, children in Irish, Russian and other northern European nations tend to overdrink because they imitate their parents. No matter what the nationality, children raised in moderate-drinking homes, tend to moderation.

The only way to break the cycle of abuse is to establish responsibility as a guiding norm. The current, publicly expressed attitude at NIAAA is that there _is_ no responsible drinking.

A positive attitude toward alcohol is important.

The problem with alcohol education in public schools today lies in our negative disposition toward alcohol. Many public school districts are now busily engaged in the Office Of Substance Abuse Prevention (OSAP) "War on Drugs" campaign which emphasizes the association of alcohol with street drugs. There is no distinction in the "Just Say No" literature between traditional cultural drinking practices and illegal underaged or abusive drinking.

Drinking education certainly will remain largely a family and peer group experience. We can act as if underage children will not experiment with alcohol but every study indicates that they will. We should demand from our state and federal officials fair and objective educational program materials. In a recent interview, psychologist Alan Marlatt suggested that moderation can be effectively taught, particularly at the college level. Marlatt said:

> What we are trying to do is to teach people moderation
> and the idea of will power control. We call it lifestyle
> balance. The notion of lifestyle balance requires the

individual to balance between the positive and negative
factors. Between what we call the wants and the
shoulds.

Our young learn how to drink by observation, just as they learn
eating and other behavior habits at the dinner table and in everyday
life situations. Often the wants overshadow the shoulds in these
learning experiences. Barnes, Farrel and Caine, in "Parental
Socialization Factors," place maximum responsibility on parents for
alcohol usage training:

> Socialization factors such as high parental and
> moderate parental control may have a significant effect
> in deterring the development of problem drinking in
> adolescents.

Youth should learn the dangers of drinking before driving.
The problems of youthful drunk driving will persist until we
determine that we must teach drinking as well as driving. That
pedagogy can be accomplished without the tasting, but it must not
be loaded with the pejoratives that now characterize the "Just Say
No" literature today.

A youngster does not automatically possess the skills for driving
an automobile by turning sixteen, nor does one acquire the skills and
restraint for moderate drinking by turning twenty-one. It is an
unfortunate fact that our current national consensus on alcohol use
maintains the age of majority must be twenty-one. Nineteen would be
a much more equitable age with high school behind and life
decisions ahead. Since Congress has now forced compliance from
all states, the legal age is not apt to change until a full scale
alcohol-use consensus has been achieved.

Yet, traffic experts and researchers are far from single-minded
on the age issue. A recent study of youth and driving by Asch and
Levy titled "The Minimum Legal Drinking Age and Traffic Fatalities"
suggests that we should teach the drinking skills before we allow
citizens to drive automobiles. The authors speculate:

> What we suggest as an appropriate view of the drinking-
> and-driving problem may in fact appear startling. The
> problem arises not because we permit people to drink
> when they are "too young"; but rather because we per-
> mit them to experience the novelty of "new drinking" at
> a time when they are legally able to drive. If drinking
> experience preceded legal driving, a potentially impor-
> tant lifesaving gain might follow. The suggestion that

people be permitted to drink before they are permitted to drive, is very likely impractical in social and political terms. But if saving lives is the objective, the data indicate that this type of policy change deserves more study.

Learning to drink, in a pedagogical sense, is as important as learning to drive. Given the hostile attitudes toward any drinking held by nearly one-third of the nation, it is vital that drinking education go through a public debate in the same manner as the AIDS controversy.

Summary of Chapter 3

When these warnings have been acknowledged, it finally devolves upon each of us to make the proper choices. Pace and Cross in *Guidelines To Safe Drinking* suggest the importance of using fact, rather than fancy, in public instruction:

> Studies bear this out, that people who know more about alcohol are less likely to fall under its spell...Strictly speaking, we should not consider alcohol an "enemy" of mankind. It's simply another one of the hundreds of drugs that may be put to good use or to bad use, depending upon a wide range of factors that include circumstances, experience, judgment and common sense. You will be more likely to drink moderately, or more safely, if you have a clear picture of what happens to ethanol from the moment the glass touches your lips, to the time it is absorbed into the bloodstream, and until much later when the alcohol content has been totally oxidized and eliminated from the body.

George Hacker, former alcohol policy director for the Center For Science In The Public Interest, often claimed in debates that "Moderation is almost never defined. Moderate drinking is a vague term that says very little and if we are really going to talk about moderation, we have to talk more about limitation. And these limitations would have to include abstinence."

This chapter has defined reasonable and healthy limits for moderate drinking using the latest scientific findings. It should provide for each reader a rational foundation for the development of a personal, finely-tuned drinking plan that will enhance and, perhaps, extend life. Moderation is truly the American way of drinking.

4

The Good and Bad News About Use and Abuse

*I think that most, perhaps all, drinkers
drink as a life-offering act—a quest for
love, a reaching-out toward one's fellow man,
a search for one's own better nature and for
the mysteries of life. That is the secret
the barroom banter tries to conceal.*
Junius Adams
Drink To Your Health

*Alcohol problems are permanent, because drinking
is an important and ineradicable part of
this society and culture. The possibilities for
reducing the problem by prevention measures are modest but
real and should increase with experience; they should not
be ignored because of ghosts of the past.*
Dean R. Gerstein
Preface in Alcohol In America

The statistics found in the media on drinking are nearly all misleading. In a nation of over 200 million, it is virtually impossible to know how many people drink, much less *how they drink.*

The best epidemiological data we have on drinking come from small group surveys. The best studies are those which gather individual diaries of drinking habits over extended periods of times. Examples of these are the twenty year Framingham, Massachusetts project, the Kaiser Permanente Hospital heart survey and the Chicago General Electric heart study, each cited in chapter 2.

Professor David Pittman of Washington University has studied alcoholism statistics for over three decades. Pittman in "Primary Prevention of Alcohol Abuse and Alcoholism," questions the validity of most of the available data for public policymaking:

Current measures of beverage alcohol consumption are
so beset with unresolved methodological and statistical

problems in the areas of production, sales, and per
capita consumption statistics that they should not be
used to set the social policy goals of any society in
reference to preventive programs for alcoholism and
alcohol-related problems.

Research Finding 4.1

Classic drinking definitions
include good and bad patterns.

> _We have the same problem that Russia has in that_
> _we are not an integrated society. I grew up in an_
> _ethnic home. I'm Dutch. I can't conceive of my_
> _parents' home not having alcohol in it. I can't_
> _conceive of anybody being drunk in my parents'_
> _home. It would have been sin._
> **Interview with Karst J. Besteman**
> Alcohol and Drug Policies Association

In a definitive study of drinking patterns titled _Drinking,
Community and Civilization_, Fallding describes the classical drinking
categories in terms of the reasons people drink:

Ornamental drinking symbolizes pre-existing community...The alcohol is not needed to generate any
relationship but to express this pre-existing solidarity
generated by trust.

Facilitation drinking is to ease a person's integration
into society, with which he still identifies.

In **assuagement drinking** alcoholization is made the
substitute for mutual trust and common purpose.

In **retaliation drinking** the person exploits the
incapacitating power of alcohol in order to make himself a passenger on the system. His drinking is to
protest his distrust against the community.

This classification shows ornamental and facilitation drinking as
perfectly proper, culturally rich practices. Assuagement drinking is
depicted as a device to help along many a shaky relationship. The
final category of retaliation not only leads to self destruction but
causes much of the social mayhem associated with alcohol.

The most significant of these classifications is facilitation drinking. This is one of the tools we use to get along with each other better as an organized society. The current thinking in anthropology is that alcohol helped precipitate the earliest of civilizations. If this theory is correct, alcohol may remain today one of the most important of social bonds.

Katz writing in the "The Evolution of Wine and Cuisine" proposes this theory that the discovery of alcohol was a civilizing human influence. He theorizes that the discovery that fruit and grain would ferment encouraged former hunter-gatherers to settle down. "My argument is that the initial discovery of a stable way to produce alcohol provided enormous motivation for continuing to go out and collect these seeds and to try to get them to do better."

So alcohol is both unifying and destructive, depending on its use by individuals.

Research Finding 4.2

Our legacy includes heavy, solitary drinking.

> *Alcohol was pervasive in American society.*
> *It crossed regional, social, racial and*
> *class lines. Americans drank at home, and*
> *abroad, alone and together, at work and*
> *at play, in fun and in earnest.*
> **William J. Rorabaugh, Ph.D.**
> *The Alcoholic Republic*

Colonial Americans developed three distinctive patterns of consumption. All remain as legacies from those founding times. The worst is solitary, abusive drinking, which is bad. The second is convivial, communal drinking, which, though heavily abused at times, is essentially good. The third is moderate drinking.

As an absolute rule, it is always best to drink with someone else. Drinking alone is bad business, always. But, families, groups and whole cultures have benefited from ornamental and facilitation drinking. However, colonial Americans took communal drinking to such extremes during the years surrounding and following the Revolutionary War that social gatherings often became stuporous, meaningless rituals.

The colonists and rum arrived in North America at about the same time. Columbus brought sugar cane to the Caribbean Islands from the Canary Islands on his second voyage in 1493 with the intent of creating sugar plantations for European commerce. Rum is a by-product of sugar processing called molasses. This dark brown, sugary fluid is fermented and then distilled into a fragrant and distinctive spirit.

Molasses and rum dominated colonial commerce.

With no other ready source of alcohol, early settlers fermented and distilled Caribbean molasses into a fiery alcohol which became a virtual staple in their lives. It was called "kill devil" and "rumbullion." American rum was first produced commercially in about 1650. Kellner in *Moonshine* tells of the fortuitous and enormously profitable triangle trade upon which America's first real fortunes were based:

> There was a market in the West Indies, however, which would pay cash for their goods and also offer them rum and molasses as trade items. Yankee merchants were unable to supply this market's most pressing need, slaves, but decided they could soon remedy this deficiency with a sort of trade triangle. So they brought molasses to New England to be made into rum, took the rum to Africa, traded it for slaves, took the slaves to Barbados, traded them for more molasses, took this molasses back to New England to be made into more rum which could be traded for more slaves, and so on for many years.

By 1750, Massachusetts had sixty-three working commercial distilleries. And the enormously profitable triangle trade endured until 1808 when President Jefferson officially outlawed it, more for trade protection than for humanitarian reasons. This slave trade was, no doubt, the most distasteful page, but one of the most profitable, in our social history.

Colonists quaffed rum as a daily routine, from infants to elders, in all possible ways. Kellner writes of this period, "Rum marched with the armies, fought against the Indians, sustained the explorer, and warmed the traveler. It comforted the lonely and ill and cheered the downhearted. It was used in medicine, in recipes, and many household remedies, including a cure for baldness."

Lender and Martin sum up this predisposition to heavy consumption in *Drinking In America* with, "All the drinks had their partisans, and drinking constituted a central facet of colonial life.

Indeed, two of the key characteristics of early drinking patterns were frequency and quantity. Simply stated, settlers drank often and abundantly."

To some degree, heavy drinking in the colonies reflected the ethnicity of the various European cultures. They drank heavily because their kinfolk drank heavily. Alcohol was considered not only a social verity but an essential contributor to health and well-being. That was the universal consensus on alcohol at the time. The first settlers were predominantly British and northern Europeans and no nation ever overdrank more profusely than the British. They were the pros in overdrinking.

Gradually, over the first century, American communal drinking patterns developed which reflected the truly severe conditions of life in the sparsely settled colonies. Alcohol abetted the need for unity in family and community affairs. Farmers rang a bells in the fields at ten in the morning and two in the afternoon so that the laborers might wipe the sweat of the brow and partake in a mighty draft of cider or rum.

The independent Ulstermen brought distilling skills.

In the early part of the eighteenth century, the Scotch-Irish of Ulster in North Ireland suffered abortive rents, failed promises from British kings and disastrous crop failures. They fled in great numbers to the promise of freedom, land and independence in America. These rugged farming folk maintained their distrust of British colonial authority. By the time of the revolution, nearly a quarter million of these truly independent, surly, hard-drinking, and, often, mean-spirited Celts had populated the wooded frontiers of America. They lived apart from the coastal settlements and the reach of the feared constabularies.

This was a different immigrant, one with deep-seated suspicion and distrust of others, and one who harbored a venomous hatred of anything British. Many historians describe these Presbyterian Ulstermen as the backbone of the independence movement. Dabney in _Mountain Spirits_ comments, "They were a new kind of settler, the real pioneer, who brought strong convictions to America, including a love of whiskey and a love of liberty."

Getz portrays their contribution in _Whiskey_, telling of the very substantial contributions of this new wave of immigrants to the freedom fight:

> The Scotch-Irish had made an important contribution
> to the history of whiskey. But, more than that, they had

become a distinctive ethnic group, intensely American, with a lasting effect upon the American character. Historians frequently mention the fact that while the English settlers in all the colonies were often divided in their allegiance at the time of the Revolution, the Scotch-Irish never wavered in their devotion to the cause of liberty. No individuals, no group endured the hardships and fought more bravely nor with greater distinction in the Revolutionary War than did the Scotch-Irish.

That was the good contribution of the huge wave of Scotch-Irish immigration. In retrospect, the Ulstermen took independence to the point of surliness or hostility. These simple people did not seek or find friendship and integration in the British-dominated Eastern seaboard societies. They headed for the hills or the vast expanses of western Pennsylvania which promised space to grow vegetables for survival and grain for whiskey. Whiskey was wealth in a barter economy.

When the Revolution had to be paid for, the new federal government adopted the century-old British excise tax on stills and their spirituous products. To escape such injustices, the Ulstermen had fled North Ireland and fought fiercely in the war. Angered and disappointed, the spirit-makers conducted a brief, ineffectual whiskey-rebellion in Pennsylvania and then fled in droves to the frontiers of Kentucky and Tennessee hoping to escape the revenuer.

This westward migration along the Cumberland Trail led a generation of skilled whiskey makers into a virtual promised land, the Kentucky Territory. There they found Indian corn and an endless supply of iron-free water. The entire state was on a limestone shelf which purified the whisky water. The combination of clean water and corn enabled the creation of Kentucky Bourbon, our nation's only native and thoroughly distinctive alcoholic beverage.

Solitary drinking and drinking to excess were traits that the Scotch Irish shared with many other frontier people. Thus did the bad habit of drinking-to-insensibility pass into the new American culture. It was also a consensus shared by a considerable part of the male population. Rorabaugh recounts many times in *The Alcoholic Republic* these two patterns of drinking among the colonists:

> In colonial days, there were two clearly differentiated patterns of drinking distilled spirits. One way was to drink small amounts with daily regularity, often alone

or in the family at home. Drams were taken upon rising, with meals, during mid-day breaks, and at bedtime. Americans who took their spirits in frequent but comparatively small doses did not become intoxicated; indeed, social scientists tell us that such drinking leads drinkers to develop a tolerance to alcohol's intoxicating effects. Coexisting with this pattern of drinking, but in sharp contrast to it, was the communal binge. This was a form of public drinking to intoxication that prevailed whenever groups of Americans gathered for elections, court sessions, militia musters, holiday celebrations, or neighborly festivities. Practically any gathering of three or more men, from the Mardi Gras to a public hanging, provided an occasion for drinking vast quantities of liquor, until the more prudent staggered home while the remainder quarreled and fought, or passed out. One observer estimated not long after the Revolution that a typical American indulged in such mass celebrations ten or fifteen times a year.

Rorabaugh clearly differentiates between the communal drinking behavior and the tendency among many in the society to wing it alone with alcohol. This is what we today call an alcohol binge:

What seems to have been essential to the would-be independent man was not the communal nature of the binge but the fact that it was episodic. Apparently he needed to punctuate his detached, rational independence with periods of frenzied, forgetful intoxication; to stupefy himself with liquor; to escape from himself.

In the early years of the nineteenth century, a distinct American pattern of solo-drinking emerged. It was born partly by the economic convolutions of the era, and partly by aspirations for a sense of personal independence from the tribe. Unfortunately, the culture of solitary drinking flourishes strongly today and it causes much of the abusive mischief of our times. There is a difference between communal drinking in a controlled setting with agreed-on upper limits and the type of unrestrained communal drinking engaged in by dissolutes in a skid road tavern. Not that friendly alcoholics are more admirable than solitary drunks, but history assures us that solo-drinking will never make the man, nor solve his problems.

Temperance, a fight against the overuse of spirits, gradually evolved over the nineteenth century into a socio-political phenomenon. The heavy drinking immigrant, often eastern or southern European and Roman Catholic, nearly always settled in the industrial and urban eastern cities. These strange, dark-skinned and papal-oriented newcomers represented perdition incarnate to the rural, land-bound Protestant and teetotaling farm society that evolved over the century. To this group, abstinence in alcohol eventually became almost a secondary issue to the protection of rural political power. Many small communities of America found the temperance movement an ideal device for keeping control away from the expanding metropolitan areas.

Temperance evolved into a major political movement.

Temperance ultimately became mindless zealotry, a path it seems again determined to travel in our own times. Lender and Martin write of this tendency in *Drinking In America*:

> Temperance workers were now more willing than ever before to impose their views on society for its own good, regardless of the opposition. In fact, the impulse to cleanse society as thoroughly as possible over-shadowed the battle against drinking itself. This trend probably reflected the success of the antebellum crusade in reducing alcohol consumption, for the dizzying levels of prewar drinking were gone (the high was about seven gallons of absolute alcohol per capita in 1830). By the 1850s, the drinking-age population was consuming only some two gallons per person annually, a figure close to modern consumption estimates.

But, by the end of the nineteenth century, while many were still drinking in a debauched manner, the majority in the society had developed moderate drinking habits very close to those that prevail today. From this viewpoint, old temperance and the stability of the industrial revolution had succeeded in stifling the worst of alcohol abuse. This was achieved long before the end of the last century, long before temperance evolved into anti-alcoholism.

Most drinkers were enjoying the benefits of alcohol-taking while a small percentage remained problem drinkers. The temperance workers of that 1890–1920 era chose to depict all drinking in pejorative terms, as an impermissible evil, just as the new temperance crusade does today. The Department of Health and Human Services describes all drinking as "risk" behavior.

Our history of drinking as a nation is not pretty (few are). But, against this backdrop of copious intake, our current drinking patterns are positive and moderate. Moderate drinking is the only acceptable goal for the future.

Research Finding 4.3

We learn to drink by observation
of adult and peer practices.

A young fellow came up to me and said. "You can't have any fun if you don't get drunk." The way I was raised, you can't have any fun if you do get drunk.
Interview with Mark Keller

Generally speaking, the observation can be made that where the act of drinking is well integrated into the culture—family use and daily use—when you are going to have less legal controls and also the lowest rate of alcoholism.
Interview with David J. Pittman, Ph.D.
Washington University

We perform, when drinking alcoholic beverages, according to a norm of expectation among our peers. Washburne in *Primitive Drinking* emphasized this truism through his research of the drinking practices of primitive peoples, particularly the surviving stone-age tribes:

Thus, by the time an individual starts drinking, he has a whole series of expectations in mind about his behavior when drinking, and his behavior while drunk will follow the pattern laid down in his society.

Another factor encourages aggression when drinking in many societies. A person is not punished as severely for doing forbidden things while drunk...In a sense, society is encouraging the discharge of aggression (another inhibited or suppressed behavior) when drinking, as the consequences will be less unpleasant.

Washburne reports on one surviving stone-culture tribe, the Tarahumara Indians of Central America. This group spends ten months each year preparing for a whopping tribal binge. The gala party lasts the remaining two months during which everyone, man, woman and child, gets roaring drunk and expresses communal love with everyone else. The Tarahumarans behave as they are expected to—expressing love, compassion and fraternal exultation.

Like the Tarahumarans, our behavior when drinking follows a predictable and expected pattern. Greeley, McCready and Thiesen explain in *Ethnic Drinking Subcultures* why the Irish often abuse alcohol more than Jews and Italians, even though they consume less alcohol:

> What is the common experience of those of, let us say Irish Catholic background, that leads them to vary from the national problem-drinking mean? We would suggest that it is the common experience of being raised Irish Catholic—in the sense that the interactions and expectations in some Irish Catholic families have a propensity to lead to higher levels of alcohol consumption (than in many Jewish families, by way of comparison) and greater tendencies toward alcohol problems.

Both the Soviet Union and the United States have major drinking problems, though ours pales by comparison to theirs. In both cultures, there is considerable solitary heavy drinking. In a penetrating new analysis of drinking cultures, Segal in *Russian Drinking* comes to these conclusions about how people act when drinking:

> All of the factors involved in causing different cultures to develop various ways of alcohol consumption fall into three major categories. The first category includes a group of variables related to the early history of a culture...The further social, economic and psychological development of a given culture, especially its most essential socializing institutions and child-rearing techniques which may or may not predispose to heavy drinking...The third category is connected with the ability (or inability) of society to develop mechanisms for controlling drunkenness, preventing antisocial manifestations of intoxication, and providing the individual with social support and an opportunity to reduce tension and achieve self-actualization without misusing alcohol.

Our way of teaching drinking to the young breeds misuse.

It's hard to imagine a more clumsy mechanism for the introduction of a lethal product to the young than ours. "You are twenty-one now, son, go forth and drink the dirtiest and most abused drug in America with prudence. Ignore all you have observed and learned about its vile nature (and that which you may have consumed illegally yourself) in your young lifetime." Unless there is a positive learning experience in the home, young people will continue to look at drinking as a forbidden fruit. Drinking seems an enticing, tantalizing practice, a rite of passage to the liberties and freedoms of adulthood. Robinson concurs in "Drinking Behavior in Alcoholism In Perspective:"

> Cultural expectations regulate the emotional consequences of drinking. Drinking in one society may regularly release demonstrations of affection; in another it may set off aggressive hostility.

That is what makes American drinking so profoundly difficult to analyze or to control. America is an amalgam of many different cultural heritages and geographic identities.

Greeley, McCready and Thiesen believe that, "Ethnic differences not only exist, then, they perdure." Their studies compared Irish, Italian and Jewish drinking habits. They found that distinctive patterns of drinking were internalized early in life and that they dictated lifetime habits for both sexes. The authors concluded, "It is not inconceivable that the basic reason for people of one ethnic group drinking more than the people of other ethnic groups is that their parents drank more...The Italians, unlike the Irish and like the Jews, have been able to integrate drinking into a stable life pattern."

Veteran psychologist James Royce, who taught the first college course in alcoholism at Seattle University over forty years ago, warns that these culturally induced drinking myths about drinking change very slowly, if at all. He writes in *Alcohol Problems And Alcoholism:*

> Have public attitudes changed? Very slowly. Ignorance, apathy, and downright hostility still pervade all levels, from the medical and other top professions down to the local tavern. Alcoholism in 1976 still got only 90 cents per victim in private support, in contrast to $197.52 per victim for muscular dystrophy, $180 per victim for hemophilia, $171.62 per victim for cystic fibrosis, and $87 per victim for cancer...

If drinking cultures do perdure through a lifetime, we can't be expected to do much to change adults. But, we surely should teach positive moderate drinking values in our youngsters because two-thirds of them will drink.

Research Finding 4.4

Youth will want to drink if alcohol remains a "forbidden fruit."

> *Additionally, moderate as well as abusive drinking by high school students is also on the downturn. This is because of two factors. One, there are fewer young people who place an inordinate mystique on drinking. Alcohol is no longer the "big deal" for them.The forbidden fruit syndrome has been diminished through positive education, not restrictive, negative controls.*
> **Interview with Augustus Hewlett**
> Alcohol Policy Council

In no other historical period have Americans placed so much importance and invested so much of their human and physical resources in their young. Often this overweening propensity to protect and support our "kids" fogs reason and good judgment. The fear of alcohol and drug involvement raises powerful passions and fears.

Secretary Bowen's assertion at the Department of Health and Human Services (DHHS) that three of ten young people "have problems with alcohol" may be correct, but that assertion requires some interpretation. If Bowen means simply that alcohol experimentation is going on among more than a third of youth, there is no dispute. Alcohol experimentation will continue until we do a better job of training the young to drink. The young always have experimented with alcohol and with the other adult amenities.

If the secretary means that alcohol is the cause of the many anti-social acts committed by youth from rape to suicide, we disagree. In *Monday Morning Report* newsletter, there is a list of problem conditions in American homes that are the underlying causes of youthful defiance and alcohol abuse. Taken from a St. Paul teenage treatment center registry, here are the home conditions reported by over sixty percent of troubled and misbehaving teens:

> Physical abuse...Sexual abuse...Learning disabilities...School suspension or expulsion...
> Arrests...Suicide...Poor self image...

We acquire most of our habits at home.

We acquire our habits at home and, secondarily, on the street from peer influences. Alcohol is consumed in two-thirds of American homes. In some homes, there is rampant adult alcoholism and drug abuse. In others, child molestation by drunken adults is a sad reality. These despicable acts are themselves a malignant learning experience for some children.

In other homes, alcohol is a civilizing, socializing resource and small, learning-doses of alcohol are given regularly to the youngest members.

Legions of poor inner-city and rich suburban youth grow up without positive male role-models. These youngsters observe that drinking and drugging on the streets offers instant profitability and financial independence. The fragmentation of the once strong family unit breeds heavy substance abuse. Cahalan and Cisin contend in *Social Aspects of Alcoholism*, "Anyone interested in assessing drinking practices and the epidemiology of drinking problems must take into account the values and attitudes prevailing among major subgroups in America, for such values and attitudes play a very large role in determining the direction and persistence of drinking behavior."

A recent *Time magazine article reporting on inner-city problems carried a dramatic report from the Fullerton, California police department. It compared the leading school disciplinary problems of today and forty years ago. Guess which list is for 1940:*

Talking	Drug abuse
Chewing gum	Alcohol abuse
Running in halls	Pregnancy
Getting out of line	Suicide
Improper clothing	Assault
Paper on floor	Rape
	Robbery
	Arson
	Bombings

The grinding poverty of six million female single-parented households, the 500,000 annual teenage pregnancies, the lack of goals of the underprivileged invite alcohol and drug abuse. A recent report about Washington state youth in the *Seattle Post Intelligencer* by Schnellinger opines, "Nearly 7 percent of children in Washington's public schools—about 50,000 of them—may be seriously emotionally disturbed, with problems such as violent tendencies, chemical abuse

or severe depression, according to a University of Washington
School of Medicine study." And this condition does not speak to the
thousands of youngsters who have dropped from the school system.
There are social conditions that are precursors of violence and
suicide. Alcohol does not cause any of these problems, but it
undoubtedly contributes in the sense that intoxicated youth take
dangerous chances.

Abuse habits in the home as depicted by Lang in *Alcohol:
Teenage Drinking* are far more important in predicting alcohol abuse
by the teenager:

> The parental characteristics and family factors
> associated with adolescent problem drinking include
> the following: (1) parents who are heavier drinkers
> themselves and who do not show much disapproval of
> drinking by their teenage children; (2) parents who
> show little involvement with their children, creating a
> family with little unity, affection, or general positive at-
> mosphere; and (3) parents whose standards for their
> children's behavior and discipline patterns are inade-
> quate or inconsistent, though not necessarily harsh.

One important aspect on teenage drinking is ignored by the
National Institute on Alcohol Abuse and Alcoholism (NIAAA). That is
communal family drinking. Most drinking families voluntarily give
controlled amounts of alcohol to their offspring in totally healthy
learning environments. The reports of youth drinking do not
distinguish between wholesome and illegal drinking. Why tell a
teenager to "Just Say No" when Uncle Mario pours the zinfandel in
full view of his own parents?

This is not to imply that the literature of "Just Say No" is all faulty
or even that it misses the mark. Many parts of that program are
inspiring, informative and helpful for young people. But the basic
attitude toward alcohol is repugnant to drinkers. It ignores the reality
of the adult world in which drinking is a common and benign
practice. The pamphlet *Be Smart: Don't Start Just Say No* published
by DHHS in 1987 is typical:

> Question: Is alcohol safer than other drugs?
> Answer: Many adults have an occasional drink of
> alcohol, but young people's bodies are still growing and
> forming. Even small amounts of alcohol can harm the
> brain and liver, and can affect your judgement and how

you move. In other words, you might fall off your
skateboard. Or even worse!

I know of no medical verification for the contention that small
amounts of alcohol can harm the brain or liver of growing children.
This is not picayune criticism. The federal government is projecting
false information and engendering hostile attitudes about alcohol as
a substance in its "Just Say No" crusade. The end doesn't justify the
means.

Reid in "Factors Associated with the Drug Use of Fifth Through
Eighth Grade Students" found that the students who were especially
vulnerable to adverse peer influence were those youngster who had
poor self-esteem:

> Peer influences are usually among the strongest predic-
> tors of adolescents' drug use. Peer influences are
> exerted in at least two ways— peer normative expecta-
> tions and peer use.

> Finally, drug users have been shown to have lower self-
> esteem than nonusers...Mitic even found regular users
> of alcohol to possess significantly HIGHER [their em-
> phasis] mean scores in overall esteem when compared
> to nonusers. This is consistent with the view that the
> standards and values of the predominant or salient
> culture or subculture must be taken into account when
> examining relationships of behavior and self esteem.
> These findings published in a 1987 *Journal of Drug
> Education*, demonstrate some important influences
> which entice youth to consume alcohol illegally and
> others to use street drugs. First, the "predominant or
> salient" culture of the adult majority in this country
> drinks moderately and therefore this practice provides
> a natural adult attraction to the majority of the young.
> Second, those who lack self-esteem, and those who are
> raised in the big cities where street drug cultures
> pertain, tend to utilize alcohol and street drugs to estab-
> lish and heighten their self-esteem.

Positive peer influences can help reduce illicit drinking.
Some studies confirm also that good peer attitudes can induce
positive practices. Brown and Skiffington in "Patterns of Marijuana
and Alcohol Use Attitudes for Pennsylvania 11th Graders" report, "A
new finding is that 11th graders' willingness to drink beer with their
friends has declined significantly, beginning in 1982, as has their

willingness to drink and drive, beginning in about 1981." Temple in "Trends in Collegiate Drinking in California, 1979–1984" assessing a six year survey of college students was able to report:

> The results suggest that the intensity of alcohol use –
> how often students drink, how much they drink and
> problems associated with their use of alcohol – has
> decreased. The results also indicated that commonly
> held beliefs regarding a contemporary rise in levels of
> both student drinking and alcohol-related problems
> among collegians are unwarranted.

Young people recognize that we live in a polydrug culture.

What do these contemporary studies confirm? That young people will continue to drink because that's what society expects them to do when they become adults. You could raise the age of drinking to thirty-four and teenagers would continue to experiment with this attractive adult behavior.

The extent of our polydrug culture is seen in a report by Williams et al. titled "Drugs in Fatally Injured Young Male Drivers" for the California Department of Health. It revealed that, in over four hundred highway fatalities over an eighteen month span, 25 separate drugs were found in the blood of these crash victims, aged fourteen to thirty-four. Alcohol predominated – present in 70 percent of the cases – with marijuana and cocaine in second and third place. Ponder for a moment a society which gives a five thousand pound weapon – in the form of an automobile – to youth who may be using an average of two or more drugs per day. Presumably, California highways today have similarly drugged drivers who simply don't care about themselves or others. They have unlimited access to lethal machines that hurtle along narrow strips of pavement at breathtaking speeds.

Alcohol and street drugs didn't cause those highway fatalities, although they undoubtedly dulled the reaction time of these uncaring young people. Mindless self-gratification, moral confusion, worship of speed and accidental happenchance combined to snuff out those young lives.

Zuker and Noll in "Precursors and Developmental Influences in Drinking and Alcoholism" point to environmental aspects in the society and conclude that:

> (1) longitudinal studies of problem drinkers, as
> children, show a lack of family cohesiveness, inconsis-
> tent parenting, and parental deviance...(2) ...that peer

influences become increasingly important as the individual grows older...(3)...early attitudes about alcohol
use and abuse appear to be influenced as much by cog-
nitive/developmental factors as they are by the content
of alcohol-related information...(4) changes in drinking
behavior to greater levels of consumption have been observed in transition periods of an individual's life, e.g.
high school to college, college to work, and these shifts
are accompanied by a change of friends, church attendance and interests.

Donovan et al. in "Problem Drinking in Adolescence and Young
Adulthood" summarize their study with, "Men and women classified
as problem drinkers while adolescents or college students
(1972–1973) tended to be nonproblem drinkers as young adults
(1979) although young men tended to be at greater risk than young.
women to maintain drinking problems."

Barnes et al. in "Parental Socialization Factors" stress the
positive values of high integration of interests between children and
parents. "Socialization factors such as high parental support and
moderate parental control may have a significant effect in deterring
the development of problem drinking, or other problem behavior in
adolescents."

Maus et al., in "The Problematic Prospects for Prevention in the
Classroom," find that straight pedagogy such as the "Just Say No"
variety do very little to prevent alcohol use or abuse by youth. But the
authors do point to a promising approach initiated in the Seattle
School District in which, "The focus is thus more on relationships
between children and their significant adults than on a given
curriculum dealing with drugs or alcohol." It is a sad commentary
that what at one time would have been "parents" must now be
changed to "significant adults" in this age of single parenting.

Parents know already that peer pressures are the single most
important influence outside the home. The behavior of most young
people depends on their friends. To an uncertain teenager, a
suggestion from a buddy carries the real weight. North and Orange in
Teenage Drinking see peer influence as the most important influence
in drinking decisions, along with the natural desire to do adult things:

For many teenagers, drinking and smoking represent
symbols of approaching adulthood. In much the same
way that many of us imitated our parents by dressing up

in their clothes, many teenagers begin to drink in order
to feel "grown up."

A great many studies have concluded that children of alcoholics
have a tendency to alcohol abuse, but those figures are often
exaggerated or misinterpreted. Harburg in "Parent and Offspring
Alcohol Use" reported that in some studies up to 50 percent of
alcoholics were children of alcoholic parents, but, "Although these
proportions are more than chance, they indicate that even alcoholic
parental drinking only weakly invites imitation by offspring."
Obviously, a great many alcoholics do not spring from alcoholic
backgrounds and a great many offspring of alcoholics do not abuse.

Blum in "Living Fast and Dying Young" warns:

> Over the past 30 years, adolescence is the only age
> group in the United States that has not enjoyed an im-
> proved health status...While death due to com-
> municable disease decreased appreciably, the rise in
> violent deaths among adolescents offsets any potential
> reduction.

Ummel provides the following discouraging statistics in "Teen
Pregnancy Facing the Challenge," a sad barometer of teen instability:

> In 1971, the annual expenditure (federal, state and
> local money) to fund family planning clinics and extend
> contraceptive services to teenage clients (about 300,000
> of them) was $11 million. By 1981 the annual national
> expenditure to serve 1.5 million teenagers had climbed
> to $442 million. In spite of the massive effort to reduce
> teen pregnancy, the results are disappointing. In 1972
> the pregnancy rate was 95 per thousand 15–19 year
> olds. In 1981 the pregnancy rate was up to 113 per
> thousand.

Underage drinking research paints a grim and sad portrait of the
pressures of teenage life today. Yet, as with adult abuse, it is a small
group that causes most of the problems. The recent allocations of
the Congressional War on Drug were announced by the Alcohol,
Drug and Mental Health Administration (ADAMHA). The war on drug
funds are administered by the Office of Substance Abuse Prevention.
Their allocations of funds accentuate the reality of pervasive social
unrest among "high risk" youth. These prevention, treatment and
rehabilitation projects are nearly all aimed at high-risk minorities and
center-city youth, not at the mainstream of American youth. High risk

youth from *ADAMHA News* in a story by Amatetti and Bass titled "Inner City Youth: A Challenge for Drug Prevention Efforts:

> High-risk youth are defined as anyone under 21 years of age who is at high risk of becoming a drug or alcohol abuser — for example, a child of a substance abuser, a victim of physical, sexual....abuse, a school dropout, a pregnant teenager, economically disadvantaged youth, one who has committed a violent or delinquent act, one who has experienced mental health problems, who has attempted suicide, or who is disabled by injuries.

Let us hope that these financial investments will work. Let us hope that high-risk youth can learn to join us in the mainstream. For the majority not at high risk, as Chafetz advises in *Young People And Alcohol*, we should provide training in moderate habits which youngsters can emulate. We teach other behaviors, why not moderate drinking? We can also show them how. "Through adult example," writes Chafetz, "youth can come to understand the importance of responsible drinking by those who make the personal, private decision to take alcohol...What we do, by and large, they will do."

Research Finding 4.5

There is a significant downward trend in the amount of drinking.

> *Some supporters of the NIAAA with primary research orientation would be relieved to see it become solely a research institute, with continuity of funding no longer jeopardized by involvement in controversial issues of alcohol control...But a number of constituency groups see that downsizing as a disaster.*
> **Donald Cahalan**
> *Understanding America's Drinking Problem*

The facts do not support the crisis atmosphere engendered at DHHS and the National Institute on Alcohol Abuse and Alcoholism (NIAAA.) Alcohol use is trending down. Classic control of availability theory holds that down trends in usage bring less abuse. Why, then, the dire predictions from NIAAA and DHHS?

In September 1987, the DHHS publication *Surveillance Report No. 7*, titled "Apparent Per Capita Alcohol Consumption" includes this finding:

> Overall, per capita consumption increased annually from 1977 to 1980, reached a plateau in 1980 and 1981, and then began an annual decline until its level in 1985 was slightly below the 1977 level.

Here are figures from that DHHS report showing the soundly established downtrends. Figure 1 demonstrates the per capita uptrend for all three alcoholic beverages types from 1950 to the mid-1980s. Figure 2 shows a distinct downtrend from 1982 onward in per capita consumption of alcohol. In this graph, the top line represents the total per capita consumption during the test period. The report text says that there was a small increase of consumption during the 1950s, a rapid (21.3 percent) increase during the 1960s and a moderate (9.1 percent) increase during the 1970s.

The unbroken line running through Figure 2 illustrates how drinking increased annually from 1977, peaking in 1981. When adjusted for the popular low alcohol products such as coolers, the consumption in 1985 was virtually the same as in 1969. Almost one hundred million low alcohol wine coolers (two percent of the total market) and thousands of cases of lower alcohol spirits, like schnapps and spirit based coolers are counted as 12 percent table wine and high proof spirits in the DHHS publication. Don't ask why.

Their own figures dispute the present crisis atmosphere. Americans have cut back on their drinking steadily during a period in which economic barometers were still rising. Over the past three decades, there has been a loosening of liquor laws around the country along with an expanding availability of all alcoholic beverages. This down trend runs counter to control of availability theory. A May 1985 Yankelovitch poll reported that 33 percent of respondents were drinking less while only 6 percent said they were drinking more.

NIAAA epidemiologists confirm the downward trend by Williams et al. in "Epidemiologic Bulletin No. 15" as reported in the Spring 1987 issue of *Alcohol Health & Research World*. These scientists project that there won't be much change over the next decade. They report that from 1985 to 1995, the number of alcohol abusers will remain stable while the number of alcoholics will increase slightly. These NIAAA and DHHS figures reflect the established downward trend in drinking. The slight changes in abuse patterns are due more

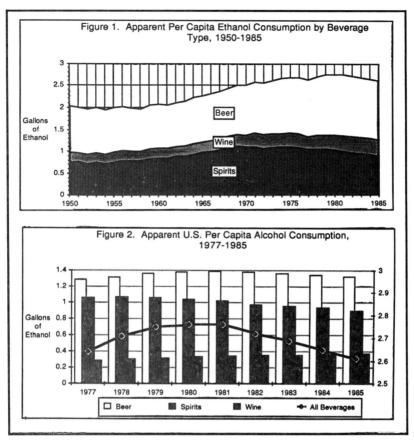

Figure 1. Apparent Per Capita Ethanol Consumption by Beverage Type, 1950-1985

Figure 2. Apparent U.S. Per Capita Alcohol Consumption, 1977-1985

to changes in the sex and age distributions of the population than to any new crisis in abuse. By 1995, the number of men aged 18 and older will rise by about 6 percent. The percentage of abusers will increase with this young male population.

Bureaucrats widen the definition of problem drinking.

To establish the crisis, planners broaden the category of "problem drinkers." The NIAAA has established a set of criteria called Alcohol Dependence Symptoms which incorporate a wide roster of human actions. The 1987 spring issue of *Alcohol Health & Research World* cites the various qualifying conditions for problem ingestion: "My drinking sometimes makes me bad tempered or hard to get along with" or "I spent too much money on drinks, or after drinking," and "I sometimes kept drinking after I promised myself not to." If the net is large enough, eventually, it will catch us all as abusers.

Industry prognosticators see no great increases in drinking on the horizon. *ADWEEK*, the advertising bible, projects a negative growth of 0.1 percent for the consumption of all alcoholic beverages extended to the year 2000. That hardly seems a danger. At the most recent wine and spirits wholesalers' conclave, industry consultant Marvin Shaken delivered similar predictions. Shanken said that spirits will continue their downward trend, dropping as much as another 9 percent. Wine, according to Shanken, will grow a scant 1 percent by the close of the century. The continuing downtrend in consumption and the uptrend to pricey, food-oriented beverages deny Bowen's predictions of vastly increasing alcohol abuse problems and costs. Americans are drinking less, and more selectively.

The nation is moderate in drinking by world standards.

The United States now ranks about 12th in per capita consumption among the industrialized nations, holding down 10th place in distilled spirits (distilled spirit consumption has dropped each of the past ten years), 12th in beer and a lowly 30th in annual wine quaffing. That is not to say that our current consumption levels have any intrinsic merits or demerits, but that we definitely fit in the moderate mold when compared to many other nations. No doubt, the large nondrinking minority skews our per capita figures. *Monday Morning Report* for January 18, 1988 provides statistics from the Business Consumer Expenditure Survey. They report that average weekly grocery expenditures for wine, spirits and beer constitute $3.87 cents, or 7 percent, of the average $58.85 budget. This seems to be a wholly reasonable expenditure for a product that gives such pleasure, nutrition and tranquilization.

Finally, alcoholism epidemiologists have been using cirrhosis deaths for decades as a surrogate measurement for the incidence of alcoholism. That index has dropped over 30 percent in the past two decades. Pittman warns against its accuracy as an alcoholism gauge, "Liver cirrhosis can be caused by more than alcohol abuse, e.g., chronic hepatitis, noxious chemicals, nutritional deficiencies and so forth."

Research Finding 4.6

A definition is needed between
daily drinking and heavy drinking.

I find the vast majority employ moderation most of the time. Only a steady minority, about 10 percent, abuse a substance or activity, making it the focus of their lives. It almost doesn't matter whether the substance is alcohol, cocaine, heroin, jogging, sex, tranquilizers, food..."
Stanton Peele
The Washington Post

If alcoholism research would expand its horizons and look for the reasons and influences that make a person moderate, in alcohol and every other type of consumptive pattern, we could develop new, positive behaviors to emulate. We could set objectives for adults and better educate our offspring. We could get off the hobby horse of blaming alcohol for our own failings.

This blurring of heavy drinking with regular daily drinking also skews the statistics, confuses the public and discourages healthy levels of drinking. The words "heavy drinking" really have only one connotation. To most of us, it means problem drinking. The NIAAA does nothing to discourage the worry of moderate drinkers that their habits may lead to alcohol addiction. Peele in "The Pleasure Principle in Addiction" defines an addiction as requiring an existing condition. It is not picked up like a flu bug. There is will power and decision making involved in addiction. A person does not become addicted involuntarily:

> The term addiction is often used as a tautology. Thus people are said to engage in an activity which harms them — like cigarette smoking — because they are "addicted" to it...Drug and other addiction is not pleasurable, and the cure for addiction — like the cure for inadequate theorizing about addiction — is an awareness of how the addict is unable to extract genuine pleasure and satisfaction from life experience.

Those of us who find pleasure in a "life experience" which includes modest amounts of alcohol are not at risk of addiction. That is why there is great mischief in the current NIAAA description of daily drinking as "heavier drinking."

Bureaucracy radicals are confusing use and addiction.

Surgeon General Koop is now comparing nicotine addiction to cocaine and heroin addictions. Chocolate may soon be added to the list. We can expect that new temperance advocates will increase their linkage of "alcohol and other drugs." We can anticipate DHHS will be comparing the addictive dangers of alcohol to those of tobacco and cocaine.

But the media is finally beginning to question some of this impassioned public health radicalism. Fingarette's thoughtful *Heavy Drinking* is getting a favorable hearing. Trebach's insistent questioning of our attitudes toward drugs in *The Great Drug War* is having an impact. Kaplan's *The Hardest Drug* raises more questions about our misunderstanding of addiction. Peele, Siegel and Zinberg have added more insights to the addiction argument as cited elsewhere in this text. This professional research and argumentation is finally raising red flags. In the last month, I received clippings from the *San Francisco Chronicle*, the *Cedar Rapids Gazette* and the *New York Times* calling for a study of decriminalizing drugs. These hard questions should be asked about the direction and purposes of the great War on Drugs (including alcohol).

Charen in "Surgeon General Invites Smokers to Feel Helpless" pointed to Kaplan's arguments in challenging Surgeon General Koop's most recent easy use of the term addiction. "When asked to explain his equation of tobacco with heroin and cocaine, he replied: 'Nicotine satisfies the criteria for addiction.'" Koop then cited the compulsive behavior, the psychoactive effects and the rewards of persisting in the habit. These factors, in his judgment, make smoking akin to heroin abuse. Those same standards can apply to nearly everything we classify as a pleasurable food. They eliminate any sense of personal responsibility and make the drug itself the offender. Charen writes "Koop is inviting the 51.1 million people who smoke to feel helpless in face of their habit."

Charen continues citing Kaplan's arguments, "Actually heroin withdrawal is similar to a bout with the flu, nothing more. When the price of heroin rises, many junkies voluntarily undergo withdrawal so they can make do with less." This is not to say tobacco, heroin or alcohol addictions are to be slighted. But it is to say the normal drinking habits of people in this nation are nothing akin to these addictions, no matter how loosely you use the term. Koop says the fifty million smokers can't quit. How about the fifty million former-smokers who already have quit? How about the millions of former alcoholics who don't drink any more? Most of the smokers quit cold turkey without help. Many former alcoholics have as well. As long as no one challenges these federal propagandists, they will continue to use grandiose and frightening terms which have little meaning in the real world.

I have deliberately steered this book from overinvolvement with emotional arguments surrounding alcoholics or drug addicts. It is written for people who are neither. But you cannot get moderates to recognize values in their drinking if they are being constantly harangued that they are endangered by the most frightening of all deficits—the clutches of unrelenting, overpowering addiction.

Daily drinking is cast as a health hazard.

Here is another example of deliberate confusion in terms by a government agency. The result was to cast harmless daily drinking as a danger to health. The Centers for Disease Control (CDC) in Atlanta has monitored alcohol data in a number of states since 1984. In their publication *Morbidity And Mortality Weekly Report* on February 13, 1987, the editors stated, "In this analysis, the prevalence of heavier drinking was based on the percentage of persons who reported regularly having an average of two or more drinks (beer, wine, liquor) every day. This cut-off is not intended to identify alcohol abusers, but rather individuals who were consuming alcohol with regularity at the time of the surveys." A footnote refers the reader to the NIAAA reports to Congress for the establishment of the heavier drinking cut-off.

It is good that the report makes the a distinction between daily and heavy drinking, but there is how an official of CDC used the report with the media across the land. It was used to propagandize that two drinks a day constitutes abusive behavior.

The survey reached "A total of 25,221 persons by telephone in the 22 states in 1985. In this group only 7 percent reported regularly having two or more drinks per day." The report also editorialized that "intakes at or above this cut-off level contribute a disproportionate share of alcohol-related morbidity and mortality."

The "intakes at or above this cut–off level" shows the mischief of confusing daily with heavy. Of course, alcoholics and problem drinkers are included in the two drink daily level. But, there is no logic for including daily moderate drinkers in the heavier drinking abuse category simply because they also take two drinks a day. Note that there is no mention of lessened morbidity and greater health benefits from moderate intake. Dozens of research projects show health advantages among drinkers at that cut-off level and even up to three or four drinks per day.

The *Seattle Times* headline was typical in its misinterpretation. "Survey Shows Heavy Drinking Varies Widely from State to State." The article compared a number of states and quoted Centers for

Disease Control epidemiologist David Williamson that, "It's not clear which is more harmful, 60 drinks in a month on three days or... consuming every day."

There is clearly a vast difference to health between consuming 60 drinks in three days and the same amount over 30 days. But the federal agency that fights major diseases tells the nation in a news release that two drinks a day may be heavy, harmful drinking. And no one disputes this gross inaccuracy.

The validity of the CDC survey findings are not in dispute. That only 7 percent drank two or more drinks a day is consistent with other surveys. It's the categories themselves that are nonsensical. Two drinks a day does not constitute heavy drinking for the normally healthy adult.

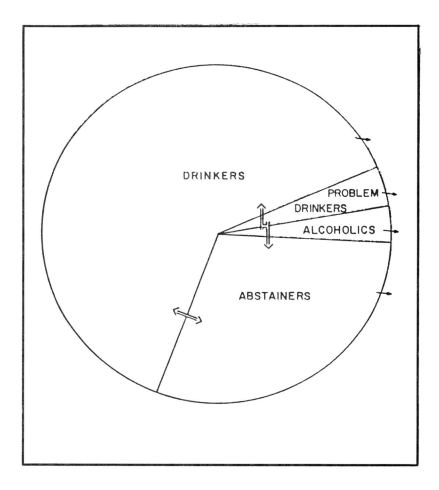

Problem drinkers form a large minority in society.

Researchers estimate between 5 and 7 percent of the total drinking population are alcoholics. See pie chart below. Another 5 percent of drinkers fall into the problem or abusive drinking category. Together, they form a significant abusing minority.

There is no precision in alcohol abuse numbers. George Gallup does a lot of polling in alcohol matters and is active in the National Council on Alcoholism. Gallup once said that he concurs with Mark Keller's estimate that there are 5 million or less true alcoholics. Another famous numbers man recently made a sensational, outlandish estimate of the nation's alcoholics. Louis Harris, one of America's most widely respected pollsters, makes the following statement in his new book, *Inside America:*

> The significant fact is that 32% of the nation's households have someone at home with a drinking problem. This comes to 28 million homes where drinking problems exist with at least one alcoholic person in the family.

Such gross misrepresentation by a famous public pollster would be laughable in any other field but alcohol. With alcohol it is accepted. Whatever the true problem-drinking number, it changes daily as some enter periods of abstention while others fall off the wagon.

Seven percent of 127,697,000 (NIAAA estimates) drinkers equals 8,938,790 suffering people. Of course that leaves the remaining 118,758,210 of us, many at the two to three drink per day level, who are temperate drinkers and not druggers. For the majority, alcohol is a beverage, quite often a food, and, on occasion, the impetus for truly aesthetic experiences.

This following pie-chart was devised by Mark Keller in an article titled "Problems of Epidemiology in Alcohol Problems" written in the 1970s. Though the population figures have changed dramatically in the interim, it is doubtful if the percentages of alcoholics and abusers have varied much over the intervening years. Keller pegged adult drinkers at 70 percent while contemporary pollsters place the number closer to 65 percent. Keller estimated alcoholics and problem drinkers at 5.2 percent each of the total drinking population.

An editorial in recent issue of *Bottom Line* stated, "If all those in the heavy drinking category could be persuaded to limit their alcohol consumption to 2 standard drinks per day, that would reduce the sales of beer, wine and distilled spirits (at the 1985 level) by 55%."

True enough, if the objective is a simple reduction in per capita drinking. But it is also obvious that if the 119 million light and moderate drinkers were to increase consumption to up to two drinks daily, it would overburden the present supply system, spawn a massive new beverage industry and, quite possibly, produce a healthier population.

Research Finding 4.7

Problem drinking statistics are
based on flawed assumptions.

> *There are vested economic interests that*
> *are trying to expand the definition of alcoholism*
> *problems to benefit the treatment industry which*
> *has emerged over the last two decades.*
> **Interview with David J. Pittman, Ph.D.**
> Washington University

As reported by Gross in *How Much Is Too Much,* the original estimate of American alcoholics and abusers (the 9 million figure) was unscientific. That number comes from the work done by Cahalan in *American Drinking Practices.* Gross reports:

> In the book, Cahalan conjectured that 9 percent of the adult population of the United States could have drinking problems — a conclusion based on survey results of a representative sample of adult Americans twenty-one years of age and over. Because the census figures in use at the time indicated that there were 100 million Americans twenty-one and older, the NIAAA researcher wondered if one could say that the "alcoholic" population numbered 9 million — 9 percent of the total.

According to Gross, Cahalan protested that the "9 percent" in his samples weren't only alcoholics but included light, medium and heavy drinkers. Despite this disclaimer, NIAAA presented the 9 million estimate to Congress. Time passed. Congress and the public became accustomed to hearing about 9 million alcoholics. That number was then arbitrarily and capriciously rounded to an even 10 million. It's remained the base for all computations since.

Josephson, of the Columbia University School of Public Health, criticized the paucity of evidence for the estimate in "An Assessment of Statistics on Alcohol-Related Problems:"

> An objective assessment of government statistics on alcohol-related problems, many of them compiled in the *Third Report to the U.S. Congress on Alcohol and Health* in 1978, indicates that there is little sound basis for claims that there are upwards of 10 million problem drinkers (including alcoholics) in the adult population and that their number is increasing; that there are 1.5 to 2.25 million problem drinkers among women; that there are over 3 million problem drinkers among youth; that the heavy consumption of alcohol by pregnant women leads consistently to a cluster of birth defects—the so-called Fetal Alcohol Syndrome; that half of all motor vehicles accident fatalities are alcohol-related; and that the cost of alcohol abuse in 1975 was $43 billion. These and other claims about the extent and consequences of alcohol use and abuse—some of them fanciful, others as yet to be supported by research—are part of the "numbers game" which besets discussion of alcohol-related problems and policy.

Gusfield in *The Culture Of Public Problems* also repudiates as fiction the original 9 million figure:

> First, one category of analysis was substituted for another. The major thrust of the ADP (American Drinking Practices) surveys of drinking problems was to shift attention from chronic alcoholism with a pattern of addiction, ...to a more diffuse and differentiated concept of "problem drinking"...A second source of the fictional character of public fact, the as is quality of certitude and authority, stems from using the material of these sample surveys as sources of conclusions on prevalence rates...Further, as is often the case in panel studies, the sample actually used was not a good one from which to make projections to the total national population.

These are heavy-weight criticisms from highly qualified academicians. Josephson stressed its shallow base more than the invalidity of its findings. "The surveys on which they are based vary in definitions and in methods of collection; there is the possibility, not necessarily equal, of over—as well as under—reporting in such surveys; and few surveys take into account the reversibility of drinking problems. For these and other reasons, there are neither reliable nor valid data on the national prevalence of trends in problem drinking."

Cahalan et al. in *American Drinking Practices*, the bedrock work upon which all the confusion rests, also found a strong age-relation pattern in drinking problems. This means today's problems could be lessened tomorrow simply by the aging of the abusing population:

> All surveys show clear relationships between age and amount of drinking..the survey confirmed that the use of alcohol is typical rather than unusual behavior for both men and women in the United States.

Cahalan and Cisin concur that we are not dealing with a single, quantifiable group but a shifting population in "Drinking Behavior and Drinking Problems" *from Social Aspects Of Alcoholism*:

> There is a fairly high turnover in the problem drinking of many individuals, in addition to a general tendency for older persons to drop out of the drinking and problem drinking classes. The implications are that the average problem drinker frequently presents opportunities to help him to mobilize his resources to bring his drinking under better control.

The graying of America means that we will probably have fewer problem drinkers in the years ahead, not more. Cirrhosis deaths are down by nearly one-third. Drinking among teenagers is down. At his national conference, Bowen of DHHS claimed up to 18 million abusers or alcoholics over the age of 18 and 3 of 10 adolescents with problem drinking (ADAMHA News November 1987). These spurious claims permit Bowen to project the costs of alcohol abuse to $136 billion in 1990 and $150 billion in 1995. On phantom figures.

Research Finding 4.8

Alcohol is unfairly cast as a gateway drug.

> *On the streets of New York, violence is so common that some kids believe a sexual attack is considered rape only if it is committed by a stranger...worldwide 100 million children are*

*without a home. Estimates in the United States
range from 250,000 to 400,000 homeless kids.*
Caroline Young
The Seattle Post Intelligencer

This has been a difficult and, no doubt, controversial chapter. Statistics are always a pain. But, the world runs on numbers and a correct understanding of drinking numbers is essential to the debate on alcohol controls. Mendelson and Mello state the obvious in *Alcohol Use And Abuse In America* :

> Numbers are the standard by which the seriousness of a problem is measured, the cudgel by which the political process is pushed and shoved, and the ultimate criterion for some. Yet the extent that numbers are sanctified as absolute truth, they may be dangerously misleading.

Secretary Bowen, in his speech to the National Convention on Alcohol Abuse and Alcoholism in November 1987, characterized alcohol as a "gateway drug" for children. "It's especially disturbing to me that alcohol use by young people increased the chances that these young people will use other drugs — it's the gateway theory at work."

Donald Ian Macdonald, administrator of ADAMHA and drug advisor to the White House, echoed the gateway charge at the same conference. In the January ADAMHA newsletter, "Macdonald reminded the audience that his experience as a pediatrician and a father has made him aware of alcohol's potential to be a 'gateway drug' preceding other forms of teenage drug abuse."

While I respect the personal opinions of Bowen and Macdonald, neither presents research evidencing the gateway theory. Yet they use the power and prestige of the White House and DHHS to convey this personal opinion to a society confused and frightened by the drug menace. Macdonald quotes Nancy Reagan in the same speech as saying, "Clearly, alcohol is a drug." Without question, the intent of these administrators is a linkage of drinking to the potential of drug addiction.

Kaufman addresses this issue in "The Relationship of Alcoholism and Alcohol Abuse in the Abuse of Other Drugs" and he notes that the gateway theory is unproven:

> The steppingstone hypothesis was controversially presented as a primary danger of marijuana in that it

led to the use of "hard" drugs, particularly heroin. A major refutation of this theory has been that alcohol is a more common precursor and therefore a step-pingstone to heroin dependence. Schut et al. showed that 97 of 100 heroin addicts reported using alcohol prior to illicit drugs...We propose that neither alcohol nor marijuana are truly steppingstones in that they seduce a nonpredisposed individual down the path to "hard" drugs. Rather, they are both very commonly used in our society and are used and abused more frequently by those who eventually go on to "harder" drugs. However, the gateway hypothesis is presented as dramatic fact when it is an untested hypothesis which is extremely difficult to support or refute.

To say that youngsters who are already at high risk of drug abuse frequently use alcohol is one thing. To say that an inordinate number of young people experiment with alcohol with tragic results is one thing. To say that we should do everything in our power to discourage this activity and to train young people to abstain until legal age is one thing. To say that alcohol is a steppingstone drug that leads to the use of street drugs is childish. The Drug Abuse Council in its persuasive book *The Facts About Drug Abuse* provided a thorough review of drug usage in America in 1980. Surely this work is known to Dr. Bowen and his associates at DHHS and NIAAA. Some of its salient findings are:

1. Psychoactive substances have been available for use since the beginning of recorded time and will predictably remain so.
2. While the use of psychoactive drugs is pervasive, misuse is much less frequent.
3. While not enough is known about why certain individuals misuse drugs, it is known that there is a definite correlation between pervasive society ills — such as poverty, unemployment, and racial discrimination — and drug misuse.
5. Drug-related laws and policies center too often on the drugs themselves and not often enough on the problems of people misusing them.

It's time for to us to look for answers in the society and not in the substances that society members abuse.

Research Finding 4.9

Alcoholism is called a disease,
though it lacks a pathogen.

> *Alcoholism and drug abuse are diseases
> in much the same sense as tuberculosis
> is a disease. The tubercle bacillus and alcohol
> bring about a negative reaction in humans.*
> **Donald Ian Macdonald, M.D.**
> *Drugs, Drinking and Adolescents*

> *Particularly in such an emotionally laden area as
> alcohol problems, epidemiologists and behavioral
> scientists must be particularly cautious lest they fall
> into ways of thinking that are influenced more by
> ideological commitments than by the facts.*
> **Don Cahalan and Ira Cisin**
> *Social Aspects of Alcoholism*

Cahalan and Room in *Problem Drinking among American Men* identify the natural tendency to speak of alcoholism only in general terms, "There is a strong tendency for adherents of each [alcoholism] model to claim for it the entire territory of drinking problems." Many professionals dispute the disease appellation. In 1957, the American Medical Association combined several articles that had been previously published in their journal into a pamphlet titled *Manual on Alcoholism.* This manual adopted the World Health Organization (WHO) position that alcoholism was a "specific disease entity" and a "highly complex Illness." The definition of the disease stated:

> Alcoholism is an illness characterized by preoccupation with alcohol and loss of control over its consumption such as to lead usually to intoxication if drinking is begun; by chronicity; by progression; and by tendency toward relapse.

Since its adoption, the disease construct has been under constant attack. It can mean many things to many people. The World Health Organization's interpretation is very broad:

> Any form of drinking which in extent goes beyond the traditional and customary "dietary" use, or the ordinary compliance with the social drinking customs of the community.

Public acceptance of this disease concept has been a signal accomplishment according to the opinion of many prevention and treatment specialists. It brought the alcoholic out of the closet of moral shame and into the treatment system. Today there are as many theories of disease and addiction as there are treaters. Dr. Joseph Pursch summarized the many points of view in a newspaper column titled "Genetics and environment play a part in alcoholism but the result is the same:"

> The present state of knowledge about alcoholism suggests that alcoholism results from a combination of genetic, familial, cultural and psychological factors. One or more may be present.

There is an enormous range for interpretation and many points of view of what the term "alcoholism disease" means. We have seen earlier in this chapter that the NIAAA and the Centers for Disease Control characterize 14 drinks per week as heavy drinking. Is two drinks a day a form of alcoholism?

In another of his syndicated columns titled "Few Doctors Understand Alcoholism," Dr. Joseph Pursch tells about a poll which distinguished between the public belief of alcoholism as disease and the belief of the average physician:

> One of the polls (Gallup in 1982) shows that 79 percent of the lay public feels that "alcoholism is a disease and should be treated as such in a hospital." In contrast, a recent poll of physicians done by the American Medical Association's Center for Health Policy Research shows that only 21 percent of the physicians polled think alcoholism is a disease, while 57 percent see it as a "combination of a disease and symptomatic of a psychiatric disorder."

Fingarette in *Heavy Drinking* questions the need for expensive rehabilitation treatment programs:

> The aim of treatment programs based upon the classic disease concept is to bring the alcoholic to a complete, permanent abstinence from alcohol...one must ask the proponents of the disease theory to explain why elaborate treatment programs are needed to enable or teach alcoholics to abstain from the first drink. Why, once sober, would an alcoholic take a drink?

Fingarette calls the disease concept a great myth and points to the internecine warfare "between experimental and scientific approaches" singling out the predominance of paraprofessionals in the field who often are recovering alcoholics. So, says Fingarette, they have a "...stake in persuading government, private funders, and potential clients and families of the truth of their organizational doctrine."

Alcohol is not addicting to millions who use it daily.

In another vein of criticism, Stanton Peele raises the fundamental question about addiction itself in "The Limitations of Control-of-Supply Models." Peele observes that millions of people take hundreds of millions of drinks on a regular basis and never become addicted.

> Why is this addicting substance used so nonaddictively:
> 25 billion individual occasions in a year when
> Americans drink alcohol, only a minute percentage
> lead — even among those designated as problem
> drinkers — to uncontrolled behavior.

Despite these many criticisms and the promotion excesses of some aggressive care-deliverers, the disease idea works in releasing insurance and government support for people in need. It has a practicality to it even though it lacks a scientific basis. The argument made by Mendelson and Mello in *Alcohol Use and Abuse in America.* shows that the disease concept has some very practical advantages:

> In 1970, Congress passed new legislation establishing a
> larger bureaucracy...Once resources became available,
> scientists began to study alcoholism as a biomedical
> disorder, and what might justifiably be called the dark
> ages of alcoholism came to an end. In very practical
> terms, that's what we have wrought by designating
> alcoholism as a *bona fide* disease instead of a moral
> aberration. We can get at it with public and private
> funds and look for its root causes including genetics.
> But that neat classification does not totally eliminate
> personal volition and responsibility.

Vatz and Weinberg in "Disease Idea is and Obstacle" emphasize the need to keep a balanced perspective, however, when naming behavioral patterns as disease:

> Today many, if not most, of those in the mental health
> professions are willing to call virtually any deviant or ex-
> cessive behavior an "illness" or an "addiction" — includ-

ing violent crime, gambling, jogging, sex, work, eating
and, especially, alcohol.

So, the general public has adopted the disease concept. Others,
in and out of the alcoholism treatment profession, believe that the
present consensus on disease will evolve into a broader
understanding of the many factors that impel abuse. In "An Adoption
Study of Genetic and Environmental Factors in Drug Abuse," Cadoret
et al. caution that environment is still a major factor in that choice:

> Thus, the temporal order of the environmental events
> preceding the outcome suggests that the direction of
> causation is primarily from environmental event to
> outcome...most of these drug abusers also had adoles-
> cent antisocial behaviors, which usually preceded the
> drug abuse.

We won't get our kids (or our adults) to "Just Say No" until we
ourselves "Just Say Why" to the miserable, dead-end environments
for many in our society.

Summary of Chapter 4

Only reluctantly have I included this discussion of the highly
controversial topic of alcoholism as disease. However, the disease
rationale lets the public off the hook. By so thoroughly embracing the
disease concept, we have sloughed off the larger problem of defining
our own moderate drinking habits. We can and do say that *others*
have problems with alcohol, not us. But moderates do have a
massive problem. That is the lack of agreement on what constitutes
responsible drinking.

In a paper titled "Attitudes About Alcohol: A General Review,"
Crawford studied 266 articles relating what people think about
alcohol use and misuse. He concluded, "...adults typically regard
themselves as moderate drinking but disapprove of excessive
drinking by others." It's the other fellow's problem. Not ours.

The more I study alcohol usage, the more I am convinced it is a
problem of doublethink—and the more impressed I am with what
anthropologists call *cross-cultural considerations. Mac Marshal I in
Beliefs, Behaviors & Alcoholic Beverages* summarizes relevant
conclusions which could provide the basis for a workable American
alcohol consensus. Here are several of his numbered findings:

> 1. Solitary, addictive, pathological drinking behavior
> does not occur to any significant degree in small-scale
> traditional pre-industrial societies; such behavior

appears to be a concomitant of complex, modern, industrialized societies.

2. Beverage alcohol is usually not a problem in society unless and until it's defined as such.

3. When members of a society have had sufficient time to develop a widely shared set of beliefs and values pertaining to drinking and drunkenness, the consequences of alcohol consumption are not usually disruptive for most persons in that society.

4. The amount of pure ethanol in the beverage consumed bears little or no direct relationship to the kind of drunken comportment that results.

14. When alcoholic beverages are defined culturally as food and/or medicine, drunkenness seldom is disruptive or anti-social.

16. Once alcoholic beverages have become available in a society, attempts to establish legal prohibition have never been proven completely successful.

These findings are diametrically opposed to the control of availability theory of new temperance. The amount we are drinking is dropping and the problems apparently are remaining about the same. The arguments presented here suggest that the best way to reduce the problem of drunkenness is to define an acceptable role for alcohol and to teach the young to drink. Since people are going to drink anyway, these arguments makes common as well as scientific sense. But it is also obvious that the one-third that does not drink — for whatever reason — is not likely to forge a new moderate consensus or to educate their offspring to drink.

That places the burden of straightening out this enduring mess on the moderate drinker. That's the objective of this book.

Alcohol problems are endemic, not epidemic.

This chapter has placed the numbers game into better focus. In reading all these many statistics, I have been struck by the comparatively small size of the abusing population through many generations. There is an important difference between an endemic problem that seems to come with the territory and the crisis atmosphere that surrounds an epidemic. Without question, the federal government and many in public health are crying fire when there are only controlled embers. There is a fire but no apparent contagion. If history shows us anything, it is that about five percent of the drinkers in the year 2000 will be struggling with the terrors of alcoholism. Another five percent of criminals and incorrigibles will be abusing alcohol and endangering the roadways.

I wish to could be more optimistic but the figures don't work out any other way. We have made substantial progress in reducing highway deaths in general but they persist, as do those related to alcohol use.

Most Americans drinkers are not now and never have been in danger of the "disease" of alcoholism. That is because the most people do not have the genetic markers or suffer the environmental conditions conducive to abuse. Even when people have both predisposing conditions—genetic weakness and a distressful lifestyle—there still is no assurance that the disease will strike. Alcoholism is apparently highly selective and the victim is very much involved in the progression of the disease.

As example, I was amazed to learn how few of the homeless in our nation are alcoholics or alcohol abusers. If there ever was a population primed for alcohol abuse, the homeless is it. I had made the mistake of thinking of these drifting, aimless souls as overwhelmingly inebriates. Not so.

The Spring 1987 issue of *Alcohol Health & Research World* featured the homeless. It reported that for the past century the percentage of alcoholics among the homeless has remained at 30 percent. More than any other single statistic in this study, this finding sticks in my mind. It illustrates the fallacy of the Noble theory that anyone can be locked in a room and made an alcoholic. The fact that alcoholism among the homeless remains at 30 percent is puzzling. It suggests that there are many reasons for being on the streets aside from alcoholism.

This chapter has demonstrated that, in a comparative sense, Americans are not massive alcohol consumers. It has shown, however, that a small minority of drinkers does abuse heavily. The problem with new temperance is that it ignores reality and the profuse lessons of history, anthropology and medical science. In their place, it offers "Just Say No" for those seeking to understand alcohol use in adult life, and "Just Say Less" for those who are grown up.

5

Costs and Benefits:
Balancing the Ledger

*Alcoholism is a disorder of great
destructive power. Depending upon how
one defines alcoholism, it will afflict,
at some time in their lives, between
3 and 10 percent of all Americans.*
George Vaillant
The Natural History Of Alcoholism

*I have taken more out of alcohol
than alcohol has taken out of me.*
Winston Churchill

*Alcoholism treatment is under-funded
at the present time. It—and the people
affected by it—should not be held liable
or share a disproportionate burden for
the financial ills...*
Rashi Fein, Ph.D.
Alcohol In America: The Price We Pay

In the previous chapters, we have evaluated briefly the health
and social values in moderate drinking. There are many social,
culinary, ritualistic, business, religious and hedonistic reasons why
people drink in a nonabusive manner. But every human function has
its economic consequences. Here is an evaluation of some of the
monetary effects of legal alcohol usage.

If Professor Solomon Katz is correct in his theory, nomadic
tribes civilized in order to obtain a continuing supply of beer. In that
primeval moment of tribal decision-making, alcohol gained a lasting
economic status. When the wandering horde decided to settle near
the banks of the Tigris to cultivate wild barley for brewing, alcoholic
beverages gained an economic importance in the affairs of men.
From that time, the benefits and liabilities in drinking had to be

measured in dollars and cents. The production of beer required the allocation of land, labor, production, distribution and, of course, consumption, as it does today. Through the intervening centuries, tribal leaders, kings and presidents exercised tight control over alcohol. Not only did its unbridled use invite mayhem, but alcohol production could always be depended on to provide a steady source of governmental revenue. The supply of alcoholic beverages was used by governments to control the crowds and provision its standing armies. Alcohol abuse caused problems, but alcohol production employed people, enriched the treasury and made people happy. It does so today.

Only one side of the ledger is drawn by current administrators.

During this century, we have had a protracted war with ourselves on how to treat alcohol. Mostly we have come down harshly on the evils of drinking. It is not that our government alone ignores the benefits. To some degree, we all do. But the Department of Health and Humans Services (DHHS) approach today deliberately subverts those benefits when it shows only one side of the economic equation. The cost statistics include only the deficits. It's as if there were no measurable values, no positive commercial attributes in alcohol production and no human merit in its consumption.

Were we to judge motor vehicles on their deficits alone, we would undoubtedly return to real horse power. We integrate the automobile into society and accept its consequences. Alcohol has not achieved that integration and acceptance in our society today.

The society absolutely needs vehicular transportation, so we accept the costs of motor vehicular use as essential to our way of life. We revel in its advantages and try our best to keep down the costs. Remember that well over half the deaths each year on the highway involve sober drivers.

While it isn't an exact parallel – since we don't *need to drink* in the same manner that we need motor vehicle transportation – the majority in society deplore the lives lost and ruined, on and off the highways and forget that alcohol has a two sided ledger just like the automobile. It has its pluses as well as its minuses. That's the point of this chapter. This is a look at the *total* economics of alcohol.

If and when the media and the general public take a closer look at those economics – the growing, making, distributing, retailing and consuming of alcoholic beverages – the new temperance balloon will likely burst. Control of availability will be exposed for what it is, counterproductive and antisocial.

Research Finding 5.1

NIAAA cost estimates are flawed.

*Projections of the 1980 estimate to
future years, adjusting only for inflation,
indicate that in 1983, alcohol abuse
cost the United States almost $117 billion.
Of this amount, nearly $71 billion is
attributed to lost employment and reduced
productivity...*
Sixth Report to Congress on Alcohol and Health

*Unfortunately, if history is a reliable guide,
the billion dollar cost estimates will be trotted
out for their scare value, loaded with the
insinuation that an active anti-alcohol policy
now will save these wasted billions.*
Thomas McGuire, Ph. D.
"Assessments on Statistics of Alcohol-Related Problems"

The cost figures for alcohol abuse published by the National
Institute on Alcohol Abuse and Alcoholism (NIAAA) are based upon a
formula developed in 1980 by the Research Triangle Institute (RTI).

A report in the Winter 1984–85 issue of *Alcohol Health &
Research World* titled "RTI: Economic Costs of Alcohol Abuse and
Alcoholism" estimated "...the economic costs of alcohol abuse and
alcoholism in 1980 to be $89 billion. The projected costs of
alcoholism and alcohol abuse in 1985 were $116.7 billion." Each year
NIAAA adds more dollars for inflation and builds its house of
economic cards on this RTI base. As we have seen previously,
Department of Health and Human Services (DHHS) Secretary Otis
Bowen now projects that abuse costs will increase to $136 billion in
1990 and to $150 billion in 1995.

In the article, the NIAAA explained how they arrived at these
combined costs of alcohol abuse and alcoholism. A key assumption
in the RTI computations is that "...problem drinkers are 21 percent
less productive when compared to otherwise similar persons
accounting for $49.8 billion in reduced productivity." We will come
back to this essential assumption several times because it represents
over *half* of their entire cost estimate.

The article noted — but did not justify in any tangible manner — a
prodigious jump in these annual costs from $49.4 billion in 1977 to

$89.5 billion in 1980. This quantum leap was attributed to inflation and changes in *methodology* for estimating the effects of alcohol abuse in the workplace. Inflation accounted for $15.3 billion of the total increase, or 38.1 percent. That's a lot of inflation in three years.

A "Highlights" section of the NIAAA article explained various parts of the cost estimates and related specific items as percentages of the Gross National Product (GNP). Here are some of those highlights:

> Losses of potential productivity (indirect costs) due to alcohol abuse and alcoholism were equal to approximately 2.7 percent of the $2,632 billion Gross National Product in 1980.

> Real goods and services (direct costs) used to fight alcohol abuse were about 0.7 percent of the GNP in 1980.

Table 1. Estimated and Projected Costs of Alcohol Abuse and Alcoholism 1980-1983 ($ in billions)

Cost category	Estimated Costs 1980	Projected costs 1981	1982	1983
Direct costs	**$18.0**	**$20.3**	**$22.3**	**$23.9**
Treatment and Support	10.5	12.1	13.6	14.9
Support	(1.0)	—	—	—
Treatment	(9.5)	—	—	—
Crime	2.3	2.5	2.6	2.6
Public	(2.1)	—	—	—
Private	(0.3)	—	—	—
Property loss/Damage	(*)	—	—	—
Motor vehicle. crashes	2.2	2.4	2.6	2.7
Social welfare programs	*	*		
Other	2.9	3.2	3.5	3.7
Indirect costs	**$71.6**	**$79.7**	**$87.1**	**$92.8**
Morbidity	54.7	60.9	66.6	70.9
Reduced productivity (in workforce and household)	(50.6)	(56.4)	(61.6)	(65.6)
Lost employment (in longterm treatment)	(4.1)	(4.6)	(5.0)	(5.3)
Mortality	14.5	15.8	17.1	18.2
Incarceration	1.8	2.2	2.7	3.0
Motor vehicle crashes	0.5	0.5	0.6	0.6
Victims of crime	0.2	0.2	0.2	0.2
Total	**$89.5**	**$100.0**	**$109.4**	**$116.7**

> The largest single economic consequence ($50.6 billion in 1980) was reduced productivity in the workforce and the household.
>
> About 10 percent of our nation's workforce is impaired by alcohol abuse accounting for a cost equal to 1.9 percent of the GNP in 1980.
>
> There were 69,000 premature deaths in 1980 due to alcohol abuse accounting for costs totaling $14.5 billion.
>
> The $3.2 billion costs of fetal alcohol syndrome (FAS) included treatment costs of $0.7 billion, special education and other services of $1.7 billion, and lost and reduced productivity of $0.8 billion.

The total cost estimates for four years are shown in the box above. It is reproduced from the Winter 1984–1985 issue of *Alcohol Health & Research World*. Note that crime and indirect costs constitute major line items. As example, for 1983, crime and indirect cost came to $95.4 billion or over 80 percent of the total estimate of costs of alcohol abuse and alcoholism.

In this chapter, scholars and treatment authorities will argue that the NIAAA estimates are not based on sound accounting. NIAAA assumes there is a population of abusers that is affected by alcohol and alcohol alone. They assume that, in the absence of alcohol, this population would become fully productive citizens. They thus include millions of dollars in lost productivity and wages for a segment of society that has dropped out. Some people in our society are not productive because they choose not to be. To assume that all current abusers would want to become productive is simplistic. To assume that all alcohol abuse can be eliminated from society is unrealistic in terms of known history. As with the automobile, there is an ineradicable level of costs. There will remain a certain number of abusers in society simple because of the existence of alcohol. To imply otherwise is deceptive. It is important in the evaluation of the economic costs and benefits that the basic assumptions be realistic.

Let us take a realistic look at these costs and benefits.

Research Finding 5.2

Scholars raise questions
about cost methodology.

> *Estimates of the cost of abusive behavior*
> *are not, have not been, and generally cannot be compared*
> *with the benefits of nonabusive consumption*
> *of alcoholic beverages.*
> **Research Triangle Institute Report, 1977**

> *In the heroic ages our forefathers*
> *invented self government, the Constitution*
> *and bourbon., and on the way to them*
> *they invented rye. Our political*
> *institutions were shaped by our*
> *whiskeys, would be inconceivable*
> *without them. They are distilled not only*
> *with our native grains, but from our native*
> *vigor, suavity, generosity, peacefulness*
> *and love accord.*
> **Bernard De Voto**

The Research Triangle Institute (RTI) report was hefty even for a government document. It consisted of 400 pages of discussions, tables, arguments and documentation, bibliographies and indices. Yet, the quotation above questions the reliability of the entire instrument. How could a sophisticated study of a multi-billion dollar commodity completely ignore the benefits side? Only with alcohol could this be permitted.

In searching for an answer, I was given a critique of the RTI report by the Beer Institute consisting of an exchange of memos between Henry B. King of the U.S. Brewers Association and DHHS in 1981. A principle author of that critique was R. S. Weinberg, economic consultant to the beer industry and professor of marketing at Washington University in St. Louis.

The first thing to note is that RTI was not asked by DHHS to develop new cost estimates, or to criticize those in use at NIAAA. The RTI organization was directed to develop a methodology for "...taking existing data from many different sources, principally existing HEW [Health Education and Welfare] and DHHS sponsored studies and reports, and recombining these estimates in such a fashion as to produce a set of estimates for each of the three problem areas (alcohol abuse, drug abuse and mental illness) that are more directly comparable, i.e., consistent, with each other than the estimates published in the original reports."

This initial intent should be noted because the contracting agency specifically eliminated from RTI's agenda any criticism of the original cost estimates. Flawed or accurate. It asked RTI to develop a system to integrate "original reports." As we shall see later in this chapter, many of these original reports are built on sand.

Another necessary distinction has to do with alcohol as a legal food and beverage. Merging the costs of alcohol, mental health and drug abuse goes to the heart of the argument of this book. Perhaps we can someday eliminate drug abuse and mental illness. The eradication of drinking is neither feasible nor desirable, only the lessening of its abuse. Unless the distinction between abusive and proper usage is made at the very beginning of any study, the results will lack reason and balance. Since there is no recognition of the benefits of drinking — no balance of accounts — the NIAAA cost estimates are fundamentally flawed.

Lost productivity estimates contain potential errors.

The most intriguing element in the memo from the U.S. Brewers Association to DHHS was the argument advanced by economist Weinberg that the potential error in the RTI assumptions was so gross as to render the final estimates useless. "Any attempt to develop a set of comprehensive global cost estimates requires the use of many different assumptions and component estimates. Each of these assumptions and estimates may be subject to some error." As we have seen above, RTI was not to question the assumptive figures. As we shall see later in this chapter, those figures are shot through with academic errors. Weinberg concluded:

> The possible low value is almost 41.0 percent lower than the value we used and the possible high is 61.1 percenthigher. The possible high value is 2.7 times greater than the possible low value...For the reasons discussed above, we have serious doubts about the accuracy of the estimates shown on Table 5-1.

To prove this point, Weinberg took the largest component in the cost estimates — lost productivity of 18.4 percent by 9.03 percent of the labor force — and compared those presumed losses against the then current Bureau of Economic Analysis (BEA) figures on the total compensation of employees. Weinberg found that, "The RTI estimate is 61.3 percent larger than the reported BEA estimate...we would estimate a cost of reduced productivity...38.0 percent less than the RTI estimate. This difference is too large to be explained by methodological differences alone and lead us to question the RTI assumptions."

That's a significant difference. There could be a variance as high as 38 percent in the figure which constitutes 54 percent of the total costs. What kind of cost estimates are these?

The point of this exercise is not to win some mythical cost/benefit battle with the federal authorities. This book does not have the space nor do I have the expertise in economics to explore the riddle of faulty assumptions. No one wishes to deny the real costs to individuals and to society in alcohol abuse. But public policy should be based on something more substantial than estimates that can be off mark by nearly 40 percent. No one seems to be watching the store. There is no congressional or administrative overseeing of these estimates. They are simply placed before the public as fact.

The methodology in the NIAAA cost estimates is simplistic. It should be abandoned in favor of new, completely objective analyses of the costs and benefits of drinking. This next cost accounting of alcoholism should be performed by a prestigious accounting firm with no ties to NIAAA or DHHS.

Weinberg sent me a short quote from the late English economist E. F. Schumacher which questions all economic estimates:

> It is fashionable today to assume that any figures about the future are better than none. To produce figures about the unknown, the current method is to make a guess about something or other — called an "assumption" — and to derive an estimate from it by subtle calculation. The estimate then is presented as the result of scientific reasoning, something far superior to mere guesswork. This is a pernicious practice which can only lead to the most colossal planning errors, because it offers a bogus answer where, in fact, an entrepreneurial judgment is required.

The rights of nonabusers are totally ignored.

Those questionable NIAAA estimates involve not only the lives of millions of problem drinkers. They impact millions of others who have invested their lives, skills, financial resources and careers in producing and selling legal alcoholic beverages. Involved also are the health and well-being of 130 million citizens who have chosen to consume these legal products.

It is untenable for federal authorities to ignore the rights of alcohol producers and the rights of the nonabusing drinking public. RTI's memo did recognize the existence of alcohol benefits but disclaimed any responsibility to identify them. "All discussants emphasized that this type of study focuses only on abusive use of alcoholic beverages. These abuses are distinct from the benefits to society of nonabusive consumption of alcoholic beverages, benefits which are very real and tangible." I suggest that we get some new discussants.

The costs of alcohol abuse can never be totally eliminated in society any more than the nation can eliminate the costs of reckless automobile usage. In both cases, we should continue fighting to reduce those costs without sinking to the use of fraudulent propaganda.

Research Finding 5.3

Moderate drinkers' gains in
productivity offset costs.

> *Examination of the use of alcohol in traditional*
> *agrarian society reveals that drinking and the drinking*
> *context is for the most part integrative, conflict-*
> *reducing, and reinforcing of corporate identity.*
> **Andrew Gordon**
> *Alcohol Use in the Perspective of Cultural Ecology*

Moderate drinking has cultural, esthetic, therapeutic and culinary benefits. Alcohol obviously plays an economic role in the lives of its users. The lives and affairs of over 100 million nonabusers are directly impacted by alcohol's pricing and availability. Alcohol expands and enlivens these people, making them more productive just as abusers become less so.

The RTI economists say that the costs and benefits cannot be compared but they agreed that such benefits did exist. If one accepts the RTI estimate that society loses 21 percent of its productivity among the abusing population, there must be a compensatory increase or maintenance of productivity among the 90 percent of drinkers who do not abuse.

In searching for such an estimate, I interviewed Professor Robert Weinberg. To my surprise, Weinberg said that there was no need to construct an elaborate, item-by-item list of direct and indirect costs such as found in the RTI–NIAAA figures. Such a table would

BALANCING THE LEDGER ON ALCOHOL COSTS AND BENEFITS

Types of Costs	Costs In Millions		Benefits In Millions
Core Costs			
Direct			
Treatment	$ 13,457		
Health Support Serv.	1,549		
Indirect			
Mortality	18,151		
Reduced Productivity	65,582	Increased Productivity	$116,900
Lost Employment	5,323	(Moderate Drinkers at	
Other Related Costs		1.2 percent of total	
Direct		business activity)	
Motor Vehicle Crashes	2,697		
Crime	2,631		
Social Welfare Admin.	49		
Other	3,673		
Indirect			
Victims of Crime	194		
Incarceration	2,979		
Motor Vehicle Crashes	590		
Total	$116,875	Total	$116,900

look good on paper, but it would be subject to the same errors as the NIAAA figures.

As an alternative, he suggested a single assumption be made about the largest and most important single item in the NIAAA cost figures — reduced productivity. On the basis of that assumption, here is Weinberg's comparative analysis of costs and benefits compared with the NIAAA estimates.

Errors are easily multiplied in cost estimate models.

Weinberg's comparative chart including the benefits of increased productivity for nonabusing drinkers is shown above. It is reproduced from an article in the September–October 1987 issue of the *Moderate Drinking Journal* titled "Benefits of Alcohol Use Wash Out the Costs of Use Says Noted Economist." Here are excerpts from that extensive interview with Weinberg:

> Any time a person attempts to estimate the overall cost of alcoholism, or the costs of snow storms for that matter, they run into technical difficulties. If you have a number of factors, and the model is multiplicative, you inevitably end up multiplying the errors. Any time you have a long chain of events, as all of these gross estimates are, relatively small errors crop up in each estimate.

> When we look at the real world, and that is the only
> world, everything depends upon everything else. As an
> economist, I call these assumptions black boxes. You
> tell me that you have gone through a very complicated
> procedure and that you have estimated the adverse
> effects of alcohol abuse to total $117 billion. I will then
> use the Gross National Product as my relative scale
> simply because most everyone is familiar with it.

By comparing the benefits to the GNP, Weinberg was utilizing
the same frame of reference employed by NIAAA in their 1985
highlights. He then went on to make estimates of how much
nonabusers' productivity would need to be increased — by virtue of
the jobs that they maintained or their increased earnings and
production of goods.

> Yes, I have made the observation that many people
> lead a fuller, richer life because they drink moderate-
> ly...Well, if I calculated that there had to be a produc-
> tivity increase among moderates of say, 82 percent, no
> one would believe my assumption. But, there is a believ-
> able level of increased productivity which the unbiased
> person could accept.

Weinberg then calculated the total business activity for the year
1986 which he found to be a figure which was 2.3 times the Gross
National Product or a total of $9.7 trillion.

> Now, that NIAAA cost figure of $116.8 billion is actual-
> ly 1.2 percent of the total $9.7 trillion receipts of all
> business. Therefore, I am making the assumption — my
> black box if you will — that the over one hundred million
> moderate drinkers enjoyed an increase in productivity
> equal to 1.2 percent of all business receipts.

The NIAAA projects a "loss of productivity" among their
estimated 18 million alcohol-impaired equal to 2I percent of
production. This figure amounts to $65.8 billion, over half of their total
cost projection of $116.8 billion for alcohol abuse. Weinberg
suggests that the 115 million light-to-moderate drinkers realize a 1.2
percent gain in productivity which totals $116.9 billion, washing out,
in an economic sense, the purported costs of abuse.

> Philosophically I am on solid ground because I am
> letting them write the ground rules. I am accepting
> their definitions of cost categories and simply looking

for benefits in one or all of these categories. Now, I cannot tell you without doing extensive research what the exact benefits are, but I can use the principle of inversion. I can ask the question, "What has to happen in order for the benefits to cancel out the costs?" I calculate then that what has to happen is so modest that it is reasonable that the two wash out.

So, Weinberg balances the cost ledger with a single line item of benefits by quantifying increased productivity. The primary assumption is that there is some quantifiable level of improved productivity among the 115 million nonabusive drinkers. That is a more reasonable likelihood than the assumption that all abusers would return to productivity if they simply stopped drinking.

Obviously, were he to spend the hundreds of hours of cost accounting — using the same techniques that RTI devised to estimate lost hours of productivity, percentage of costs for crimes and arsons, premature deaths, alcoholism care, hospitalizations, etc., — the benefits would far eclipse the costs. There is a ten to one ratio of moderates to abusers. But that was not Weinberg's point. It is enough in his judgment to prove the existence of real economic benefits. NIAAA should be required to incorporate these benefits into their future computations.

Research Finding 5.4

The economy of alcohol is
vital to many states.

> *First, there is the problem of constructing valid quality-of-life indicators and relating them to measures of health status. Second, there is the difficult task of integrating nonmonetary information on quality of life with the dollar magnitudes estimated for direct and indirect economic costs.*
> **Thomas Hodgson and Mark Meiners**
> "Cost-of-Illness Methodology"

America today is not a large consumer of alcoholic beverages in comparison to other Western nations but these beverages play a very large economic role in many regions and communities. Our country ranks 9th in spirit intake, 12th in the amount of beer per person, and a distant 30th in wine consumption when compared to per capita intake in other industrial nations.

ECONOMIC ACTIVITY OF BEER

Industry Sector	Economic Activity
Agriculture	$5,192,747,000
Construction	1,131,421,000
Transportation/Warehouse	5,128,529,000
Food Processing	20,168,417,000
Wholesaling	10,407,915,000
Retailing	8,183,588,000
On-premise Sales	16,537,821,000
Financial	6,803,220,000
Business & Personal Services	9,943,133,000
Other	31,094,561,000
Total Activity	**$114,142,352,000**

JOBS GENERATED BY BEER

Industry Sector	Employment
Agriculture	91,014
Construction	7,075
Transportation/Warehouse	70,378
Food Processing	85,772
Wholesaling	170,668
Retailing	307,294
On-premise Sales	616,870
Financial	94,223
Business & Personal Services	297,542
Other	227,065
Total Employment	**1,967,911**

Yet, we consumed an impressive total of 6.6 billion gallons of alcoholic beverages in 1986. As was shown earlier, we have been, for nearly a decade, on a downward trend in spirituous liquor drinking, and only wine, among the beverage types, has shown any kind of steady increase over recent years. Wine coolers vaulted from a nonexistent market several years ago to comprise over two percent of the total alcoholic beverage trade in 1987.

It is difficult to compile an economic composite of the alcoholic beverage trade from existing data. The most sophisticated economic study I know of is titled "The Economic Contribution of the Beer Industry to the States" prepared by Steve L. Barsby & Associates. Since beer consumption is four times that of wine and spirits combined, these Barsby figures represent about three-fourths of the entire trade.

More than four million acres of farmland are required to produce the barley and rice in an annual beer harvest that exceeds $860 million in value. Those dollars are dispersed through small towns in America, whether the population drinks or not. Think of the 16 billion glass bottles and the 35 billion steel cans required for the beer trade alone. Many cities and towns benefit from this extensive production.

Alcohol is a significant source of state and federal taxes.

In addition to producing nearly a million basic jobs and employing legions of productive workers in associated service industries, the alcoholic beverage trade is a major tax generator. Every barrel of beer sold provides the federal treasury with another $16 dollars. The "Annual Statistical Review 1984–85," published by the Distilled Spirits Council of the United States (DISCUS), contains these impressive figures:

> Production and marketing of alcoholic beverages provide employment for 784,000 people. Payrolls exceed $18 billion, and retail sales $66 billion. In addition, considerable employment and incomes are generated by the materials and services of other sectors of the U.S. economy needed for producing and marketing spirits — the grain and fruit used in distillation, the bottles, the containers, printing, advertising, and transportation among others. And of major importance, federal, state and local governments obtained revenues of $12.5 billion dollars in 1984 from taxes on spirits, beer, and wine, revenues essential to finance a number of basic government functions. The distilled

spirits industry alone raised $6.9 billion of such
revenues from taxes on its products.

The DISCUS and Barsby reports place in perspective the
economics involved in the growing, manufacturing and retailing of
beer. Ironically, Barsby's total of $114 billions in annual economic
benefits from beer alone is nearly equal to the NIAAA projection of
alcohol abuse costs.

It is puzzling that the political and economic leaders in the
affected states do not rise up in righteous anger at the DHHS
temperance programs. Public health officials continue to demean a
major, legal industry with very little response from those affected.
One reason for this may be that the industry and its many suppliers
suffer the same ambivalence as the public at large. There are no
support coalitions for alcoholic beverages as there are for beef, milk
or other commodities.

Citizens for Moderate drinking will be campaigning in 15 states
during the 1988 presidential campaign. These states produce the
bulk of the alcoholic beverages which we consume. Politicians from
these areas should demand better treatment from federal officers
who operate in the public health arena. These 15 alcohol-producing
states comprise over fifty percent of the national Congress.

I agree with Weinberg when he warns that economic interests
alone should never be used to justify drinking. But, given the benefits
in health, productivity and general well-being already described,
these economic arguments take on much greater significance. There
is nothing wrong, either, with basic economic interests.

Research Finding 5.5

NIAAA cost assumptions are
disputed in research papers.

> *It was not until recently that America began
> in a concentrated and comprehensive way to
> address the other two factors in the Public Health
> Model. By far, the lion's share of attention has
> been devoted to alcohol, and the more restrictive
> the controls, and the more people covered, the
> more profound have been their failures.*
> **Augustus Hewlett**
> *Public Policies for Problems of Alcohol Abuse*

A critique of these RTI cost computations and of other alcohol-related data was prepared in 1980 by seven academicians under the direction of Professor Eric Josephson of the Columbia University Department of Public Health. In the chapter titled "Assessment of Statistics on Alcohol-Related Problems," Josephson states his reservations about the NIAAA figures:

> An authoritative economic study, commissioned by NIAAA, has it that alcohol abuse, which of course lends itself to various definitions, cost the U.S. $43 billion in 1975; like the estimated number of alcoholics in the population, this figure keeps rising in official statements regarding the issue. A critical review of the study from which this estimate is derived suggests that it may have overstated some of the costs (because of limitations in the data on the estimated number of alcohol abusers on which it is based, because it failed to include some of the benefits of alcohol consumption, and because certain costs associated with alcohol abuse are interpreted as due solely or primarily to such abuse). However, the study may also have understated some of the costs because of an incomplete accounting of all items which could conceivably be associated with alcohol abuse.

Another contributor to the critique of NIAAA statistics, Dr. Thomas McGuire of Boston University presents a number of philosophical as well as tactical deficiencies in the original NIAAA estimates. The original documentation was done by Berry and Boland as reported in "The Economic Cost of Alcohol Abuse." These authors established the original $42.75 billions in costs on which the later RTI projections were based. It is important here to recall that RTI was not charged with making new estimates but in blending together the existing cost figures. In the above paper, Professor McGuire raised the following objections to this original data:

> Berry and Boland minimize the scope for intelligent consumer decision-making in alcohol purchase by assuming no adverse effects are foreseen and taken into account by users.

> Berry and Boland consistently interpret a statistical association between alcohol and social costs, such as the use of health resources, as indicating a causal relation.

The costs and benefits of alcohol consumption go partly to the direct user and partly to others in the society...These private benefits and costs are completely analogous to the benefits and costs from any other commodity in the economy — soft drinks, shirts, washing machines, and so on. Berry and Boland are not concerned with these.

This argument would most convincingly apply to the majority of drinkers who are not alcoholic and for whom drinking represents a free choice...drinking that affects the drinker would be more than balanced off by the private benefits of drinking.

In a typical simple comparison of alcohol abusers and non-abusers, the abuser population has more problems...to say that the abuser population would be the same as the non-abuser population if only they wouldn't drink so much, is to overstate the importance of alcohol.

A major problem in this section, tending to overstate costs of alcohol abuse, is the disregard of other factors, such as mental illness and disorder, which are positively associated with alcohol abuse and may also be the cause of extra health costs.

In spite of this statement, Berry and Boland make no attempt to correct for the influences of age, experience, time of day, personal recklessness or other factors in accidents, nor do they recognize that omitting these factors (which is necessary in the absence of data) is likely to lead to an overstatement of the effect of alcohol on accidents.

Experts at alcoholism treatment centers may tend to overstate use of health services by alcoholics.

The lost productivity concept is questioned.

The most arguable assumption in the $117 billion cost estimate is the one attributed to productivity — and that single item accounts for 54 percent of the total costs. Henry B. King, then president of the United States Brewers Association, sent an analysis of the RTI figures to the Alcohol, Drug and Mental Health Administration (ADAMHA) on July 1, 1981. The memo cited inconsistencies in Berry and Boland because, "...they force us to question the validity and accuracy of the methodology and intent of the report. Overstating or understating the economic cost of a particular social problem is not desirable but difficult to avoid." King wrote:

> To the extent that alcohol abuse by some individuals is symptomatic of other problems, the associated morbidity and productivity losses are mislabeled when allocated to alcohol abuse. There is a strong likelihood that future studies will determine that some proportion of the lost and reduced productivity associated with alcohol abuse may be more properly labeled as due to mental health...Apparently it does not matter to the authors of the RTI study whether productivity losses are due to alcohol abuse, drug abuse or mental illness.

In an inconclusive response to this question of causality, the RTI writer admitted "...there is little evidence to show how alcohol causes property crime. We assume that only 10 percent of alcohol present offenses were caused by alcohol consumption." How can professional statisticians assign 10 percent of the costs of crime or anything else "just because," while admitting that they have no real evidence for that causal effect?

The brewers' memo asks, "If RTI does not know what the relationship is, why assign the figure of 10% — why not 1% or 90%?" The RTI authors then cited weak and contradictory evidence "...we are reluctant to ascribe a causal relationship between drug abuse and violent crime." It nearly surpasses belief that NIAAA's recent report to Congress has escalated the questionable RTI estimates of 10 percent to a preposterous 40 percent. The sixth report states blithely, "There was somewhat less alcohol involvement in cases of property crime (40 percent) and drug offenses had at least alcohol involvement (29 percent)."

Is this the real economic world or never-never land? Are we being led down a primrose path deliberately strewn with fabricated statistical information?

Researchers distinguish between cause and relationship.

In criticizing these cost estimates for crime, suicide, motor vehicle crashes and incarceration, it is necessary to distinguish between *causal reasons* — being a true cause of — and casual relationships. Light in the "Costs and Benefits of Alcohol Consumption" questioned NIAAA use of indirect costs:

> The first may be termed the problem of causation versus correlation. As any social scientist knows, it is one thing to say that event A (alcohol abuse) is often associated with event B (motor vehicle accidents), but quite a different thing to say that event A causes event B. A second major difficulty is the failure to adequately assess the economic benefits of use. Granted that the purpose was to measure costs; intelligent public discourse and decisions must be based upon some sort of cost-benefits analysis, however crude.

How far does NIAAA go in attributing responsibility for human physical problems to alcohol usage? In an article in *Science,* Director Enoch Gordis of NIAAA is quoted as estimating that 25 to 40 percent of people in general hospital beds are being treated for the complications of alcoholism. "Thus, the disorder, (and to a lesser extent, drug addiction) operates anonymously to swell the ranks of patient population, its consequences being treated under an almost limitless number of headings including liver disease, gastrointestinal disorders, heart disease, and psychiatric problems."

Drunk driving statistics are challenged for accuracy.

Perhaps the most emotional of all issues related to alcohol use is drunk driving. Everyone has known the tragedy of maimed or shortened lives because of accidents involving alcohol. The media constantly repeats the "fact" that fifty percent of all highway fatalities are alcohol-caused. That figure is untrue, as all traffic authorities know. Yet it predominates. Here is comment on its validity by Lawrence Sherman in a Crime Control Institute Report "Drunk Driving Tests In Fatal Accidents:"

> Until 1985, the FARS (Federal Accident Reporting System) estimates were based upon tests of deceased drivers in only 15 states...The most striking fact about the 1983 data on testing of fatally injured drivers is that 40 states failed to comply with their own laws requiring such tests...The FARS data is only as good as what the states supply. With "garbage data" from states on

alcohol tests, only "garbage" national estimates of
drunk driving can result.

Regardless of the flaky data, is alcohol causing or related-to fifty
percent of all highway fatalities? Secretary Bowen's *Sixth Special
Report to Congress on Alcohol and Health* found, "The proportion of
fatally injured drivers who were legally intoxicated dropped from 50
percent in 1980 to 43 percent in 1984 [see table 5 and figure 4 below
from the Sixth Special Report to Congress on Alcohol and Health]."

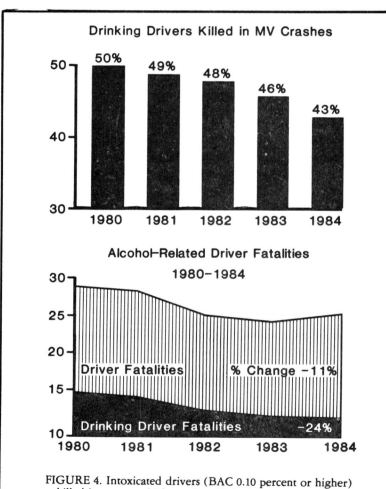

FIGURE 4. Intoxicated drivers (BAC 0.10 percent or higher)
killed in motor vehicle crashes, United States, 1980–1984.

SOURCE: NIAAA 1986b.

Sociologist and traffic expert, Laurence Ross, University of New Mexico, and York University law professor, Graham Hughes said this about the purported 50 percent alcohol-involved fatality statistic in "Drunk Driving: What Not To Do:"

> It is frequently stated that alcohol is responsible for 50 percent of U.S. traffic fatalities, but the statistic has no solid foundation. The figure includes all traffic deaths in which anyone directly involved has consumed any alcohol...Perhaps the most accurate estimate, from the National Academy of Sciences, attributes roughly 25 percent of fatal accidents to intoxication.

Traffic safety experts say that statistics are inflated.

One would expect the executive of the Insurance Institute for Highway Safety to be as conservative as possible when discussing alcohol and driving. In the Institute's publication *Status Reports*, President Brian O'Neill says:

> ....an estimated 25,000 lives lost each year to drunk drivers is wrong...In 1984, there were about 25,000 fatal crashes...then about 12,000 to 13,000 deaths could be attributed to drivers with BAC's of 0.10 or higher.

Traffic safety expert C. F. Livingston reported in *Straight Talk About The Drunk Driving Problem* that 83 percent of the reported fatalities consisted of the intoxicated drivers, passengers who chose to ride with them, or intoxicated pedestrians. The fact that the intoxicated people are killing mostly themselves does not make those fatalities any less tragic, but it does place the danger to society in a clearer light.

Alcohol as causal agent in crime is disputed.

Table 10 in the sixth report lists 132,620 convictions for crimes by type and compares it to the number "of convicted persons who used alcohol" and then reports that "...64 percent of inmates convicted of public-order offenses had used alcohol just before the offense." It is obvious that this juxtaposition implies a causal relationship between drinking and the crimes.

The Justice Department, *Bureau of Justice Bulletin*, published in January 1983, reported "About 1 in 4 inmates convicted of violent offenses, especially robbery (32%) and murder/attempted murder (30%), roughly 1 in 10 convicted of public-order offenses, mainly weapons offenses (21%), had used drugs just prior to the offenses for which they were currently incarcerated."

Does this polydrug use by criminals in some manner establish a "causal" responsibility for the crimes committed? Justice department officials say no. A special bulletin titled "Prisoners and Alcohol" argues against any causal relationship between alcohol and crime:

> The relationship between alcohol consumption just prior to the crime and the crime itself has not been sufficiently explored by these data. It is tempting to point to the very heavy drinking (again, the equivalent of at least 8 cans of beer, 7 glasses of wine or nearly 9 ounces of 80 proof liquor) as the proximate cause of many crimes, since 30% of the offenders admitted to such large consumptions just prior to their offense. The survey strongly suggests however, that for many offenders these are typical daily drinking levels.

Summary of Chapter 5

The NIAAA is using their widely publicized estimates of alcohol abuse to justify the imposition of new controls on alcoholic beverages. Alcohol abuse is costly enough without any embellishment. Whatever the accurate dollar total might be, alcohol abuse is an appalling, tragic testimony to man's inhumanity to himself.

These deceptions would be of minor consequence if they were not so cleverly associated with the control of availability political agenda. The raising of the minimum drinking age age to twenty-one can be attributed in part to these obfuscations. In the same light, the other objectives of increased taxation, pejorative product labeling, planned limitations on retail availability and general demeaning of alcohol as a street drug need this backdrop of prevarication to sustain the crisis atmosphere.

With little overseeing by Congress or questioning by the media or the academic and scientific communities, DHHS has been able to establish a crisis atmosphere where none truly exists. We must come to recognize publicly that some of our numbers are not going to follow the rules of decency and restraint. We will have our ne'er-do-wells and criminals who are going to abuse alcohol no matter what we do.

Chapters 4 and 5 have been highly critical of the statistical games being played with the numbers of problem drinkers and the costs that this abusing segment incurs. The process of consensus cannot take place in an atmosphere of hype and propaganda.

We have to balance the ledger.

Part 2

THE PROHIBITION MENTALITY

How Alcohol Radicalism Dominates In Public Health

6

New Temperance
And What it Means

> *Oh God! That men should put an*
> *enemy in their mouths to*
> *steal away their brains.*
> **William Shakespeare**

> *Drink is in itself a good creature of God,*
> *and is to be received with thankfulness,*
> *but the abuse of drink is from Satan;*
> *the wine is from God,*
> *but the Drunkard is from the Devil.*
> **Increase Mather, 1673**

> *Alcohol is the dirtiest drug we have. It*
> *permeates and damages all tissue. No*
> *other drug can cause the same degree*
> *of harm that it does.*
> **Dr. Ernest Noble**

No one needs to drink alcohol. To stay alive. But Americans always have in large numbers, and probably always will. Just as likely, a minority will continue to abuse this substance to their own detriment and to the endangerment of others in the society.

Drinking calls for caution. There are obvious dangers. Even so, there is enhanced health in moderate lifetyles which include daily drinking. This is all but irrefutable. Daily moderate drinking does no apparent harm, and this is an important finding. Since more than nine of ten drinkers don't abuse, the accumulation of personal and economic benefits among nondrinkers outweighs the indisputable costs of those who misbehave. This being true, why don't moderate-drinking Americans feel more comfortable about their drinking habits?

Drinkers are ambivalent because they have been bamboozled by two hundred years of anti-alcohol propaganda from government, and a studied indifference from the media and medical fraternity. This won't change until the drinking majority insists on a new consensus on drinking. Pejorative words and phrases like "booze" and "the most abused drug in America" will have to be excised from public proclamations. Words like moderation and responsibility must replace them.

Americans often think in extremes about drinking.

Gilbert Chesterton, the British writer and philosopher, once remarked that no one wants to talk about religion and politics and they are the only two things worth talking about. I wonder whether he wouldn't now add drinking to that list. Regarding the American ambivalence on drinking, Chesterton once commented:

> The dipsomaniac and the abstainer are not only both mistaken, but they both make the same mistake. They both regard wine as a drug and not a drink.

This book is designed to rattle the cages. It asks moderate drinking Americans (by far the majority) and those who share in legal and moral benefits from the commerce of alcoholic beverages to get off the sidelines. The political system should debate new temperance before it is too late.

The political propaganda from the Department of Health and Human Services (DHHS) and the National Institute on Alcohol Abuse and Alcoholism (NIAAA) needs public refutation. At the end of the First World War, prohibition swept through Congress and the legislatures of America like a runaway train. During the past two years, it has been chilling to watch how easily the Congress and the state legislatures capitulated on raising the age of drinking to twenty-one.

Many of these states had already been evaluating the drinking age levels from 18 to 19 and discriminating as to alcohol content allowable at the younger ages. All those important local determinations have been swept aside by the arbitrary blackmail scheme set up by the pressures of new temperance on a jittery Congress. Raise the age or lose highway funds.

Federal alcohol controls won't work.

A major finding of this book is that alcohol control works best on the local level. The culture of drinking in Salt Lake City differs from the drinking habits in the bayous of southern Louisiana. No law on drinking made in Washington D.C. is going to have the same meaning and effect in Memphis as in Butte. The massive disrespect for law and order occasioned by prohibition, amply demonstrated the incapacity of law alone to structure moral order. The only good consequence of prohibition was the Twenty-first Amendment's placing of alcohol control laws at the state level. Many states went one step further by placing alcohol control local options within county and city jurisdictions.

Social issues do not yield to political quick fixes. We need debate, argumentation and thoughtful decision-making.

Research Finding 6.1

There was ample cause for original temperance.

> *Carpenter Thomas Green was promised by contract, "Four dollars at Christmas with which he may be drunk for four days and nights; two dollars at Easter to effect the same purpose; two dollars at Whitsuntide to be drunk two days; a dram in the morning and a drink at noon."*
> **George Washington at Mount Vernon**

Drinkers abuse alcohol and other drugs in times of stress. The years between the calamitous break from England, in 1776 till 1830, were among the most stressful in the life of this nation. During this period, religious, medical and social leaders formed the first of our three great waves of temperance.

Another more politically inspired temperance movement developed in the late 1890s and it ultimately led to prohibition. We are in the third major anti-alcohol social convolution at this present time. The first temperance drive was an attempt to stem the drinking excesses resulting from the social, political and cultural revolutions of the late eighteenth and early nineteenth centuries. Originally, temperance meant just what the word implies. To drink less voluminously. To drink only in moderation. By 1820, endemic heavy drinking had begun to threaten the stability of family life. Traditional European ways of imbibing gave way to wanton and sustained drinking. The very economy of the new nation was endangered by drink.

Heavy drinking periods are often tied to stress.

Much of the population was confused and uneasy with the machinery and work skills necessitated by the industrial and agricultural revolutions. The old ways of life were crumbling. When social organizations fail to cope with rapid change, substance abuse erupts almost as a human safety valve.

In *The Alcoholic Republic,* William Rorabaugh explains how these periods of heavy alcohol abuse correspond with unsettled economic times:

> Social scientists have thus far suggested that drinking is a function of a culture's social organization. When social systems fail to meet individual needs, a high intake of alcohol and drinking to excess may occur. In particular, a high level of drunkenness is likely in cultures that are anxiety-ridden, structurally disintegrating, or incompetent in providing individuals with a sense of effectiveness.

There are parallels between those uncertain days for the nation and the problems of the unemployed in our large industrial centers today. Anxiety, disintegration of the social order, licentiousness and lack of hope for an economic future are the hallmark problems of many central cities in America today. Substance abuse today has strong roots in social dislocation and unemployment as it did in 1820.

Americans developed the habit of drinking alone.

In developing a new consensus on drinking, we cannot deny that overdrinking was a public nuisance in our past and that it remains so yet today. Lender and Martin in *Drinking In America* identify the common early American drinking patterns which eventually developed into the inane myth of the macho drinking man:

> Relatively heavy and frequent drinking, with the very American preference for hard liquor, had become common throughout the nation. In fact, the period from 1790s to the early 1830s was probably the heaviest drinking era in the nation's history. Consumption estimates tell the story dramatically. From an annual average of 5.8 gallons of absolute alcohol per capita (for people 15 years and older) in 1790, mean absolute alcohol intake rose to 7.1 gallons a year by 1810 and, with minor fluctuations, remained at about that level until at least 1830.

Historian Rorabaugh tells how alcohol played a prominent, even essential, role in the grim colonial diet:

> Cider and whiskey were America's most popular drinks. Both were cheap and plentiful where available and, because they were processed in the United States from home-grown products, both benefited from

nationalistic sentiment. The taste for strong drink was no doubt enhanced by the monotony of the American diet, which was dominated by corn.

The thousands of Scotch-Irish immigrant distillers and the abundant fields of rye combined to provide whiskey to metropolitan Philadelphians at 25 cents a gallon in 1830. Good whiskey was cheaper than milk, coffee or tea. Alcohol was both a medicine and the carrier of dozens of commonplace herbal nostrums. Alcohol remains to this day the base for most patent medicines, and its tranquilizing dimension provides most of their therapy. In 1830, alcohol was considered good for whatever ailed you, from childbirth to snakebite.

The serious consequence of this abusive period was the development of solitary, rapacious drinking. While drunkenness was common to many northern European cultures, drinking was most often a communal affair. People got drunk together in some minimal state of social harmony, at least at the beginning of the bouts. The ingrained American habit of drinking alone and to excess stands in vivid contrast with the more gracious, socially integrated Latin and Jewish drinking cultures.

Kobler in *Ardent Spirits* demonstrates how liquor was truly a ubiquitous daily companion of our founding fathers, a component in every social and business procedure, large or small. Alcohol was not something to be considered only as the sun passed the yardarm or the clock announced a five o'clock cocktail hour:

> So highly did the colonies prize booze that their statutes regulating its sale spoke of it as "one of the good creatures of God, to be received with thanksgiving." In some communities it was traditional to seal a bottle of whiskey in the cornerstone of a new church or public building. Taverns were not only licensed to sell liquor, but required by law to keep sufficient supplies on tap. Few business transactions were consummated, few births, christenings, graduations, marriages or investitures were celebrated without torrential libations... Workmen received part of their pay in rum...Hard liquor had the endorsement of doctors...A life insurance company increased its premiums by 10 percent for the abstainer, whom it considered "thin and watery, and as mentally cranked, in that he repudiated the good creatures of God as found in alcoholic drinks."

That was the real world in which the first president of the United States, himself a profitable commercial distiller (a fact carefully scrubbed from most history books) engaged his carpenter Thomas Green with the promise of "...four dollars at Christmas with which he may be drunk for four days and nights; two dollars at Easter to effect the same purpose..."

Colonists shared a consensus on alcohol's proper role.

There was a consensus that alcohol belonged. It was part of colonial life. Alcohol was thoroughly integrated into the fabric of everyday life. Benjamin Franklin expressed the common wisdom of the times when he wrote, "Wine is constant proof that God loves us, and loves to see us happy." Generally, men, women and children had easier lives because wine, beer, cider and spirits relieved the daily grind. And that was no small accomplishment in those rigorous days.

Overdrinking is overdrinking, no matter the historical context. But, regular drinking and moderate regular drinking do not constitute overdrinking or "risk behavior" to the judicious person.

Adams in *Drink To Your Health* expresses the need to capitalize on these trends and to broaden our research horizons to study not only the alcoholics and their offspring, who also tend to addiction, but the offspring of alcoholics who *do not* become addicted, and those of us who maintain sobriety in a lifetime of daily drinking:

> Although many meticulously-performed experiments have come out for the alcohol research movement, one can criticize it on the whole for: 1. Exaggerating its constituency and thus not pinpointing those persons most in need of medical help. 2. Concentrating its experiments...on studies calculated to demonstrate the noxious effects of alcohol. 3. Failing to pursue promising lines of inquiry or do follow-up research studies that might prove helpful to the drinking population.

The newfound and heightened association of wine and other alcoholic drinks with food is illustrative of the trend to real temperance. Lolli et al. in *Alcohol In Italian Culture* sums up this crucial relationship:

> If what has been learned thus far were to be summarized in a few words, it could be said that for the Italians drinking is a part of eating, even a form of eating, for wine is a food; that to the extent that the descendants of Italians in America retain ancestral cul-

tural traditions, they drink with the same attitudes and in the same ways; and that the set of attitudes which does not separate drink from food is at least partly responsible for the relative sobriety of Italian drinking.

Research Finding 6.2

Availability controls won't work in our diverse culture.

> *In the Nordic countries — Finland, Sweden, Norway, Iceland — they probably have a great degree of empathy for that point of view. In eastern European countries there is a lot of empathy for it. The Soviet Union emphasizes control of consumption...In southern Europe, their drinking is well integrated into family mealtime ritual; you have very few individuals with alcohol problems in these countries. For example, in Portugal, I don't think there is even any drunk driving statutes or legal age for the purchase of alcohol.*
> **Interview with David J. Pittman, Ph.D.**
> Washington University

The political systems for controlling alcohol have once again become the targets of dedicated political activists. The World Health Organization promotes the idea of lowering total per capita drinking across the globe, without reference to levels of use or abuse. Italians drink four times the alcohol of Americans and have one seventh the problems. No matter. The objective is to lower the drinking levels. In America, an openly anti-alcohol coalition of governmental and private agencies has devised a detailed set of political controls that presage a return to a new kind of prohibition.The Supreme Court has given Congress vast new authority to withhold federal funds from the states that do not meet a congressional standard of public health.

Dole v. South Dakota was a benchmark alcohol case.

A key court decision was South Dakota against Dole which held that Congress could withhold federal highway funds from states that did not impose age twenty-one for drinking. This changes the alcohol control ball game dramatically since alcohol control could theoretically shift from the states to the federal congress. A simple majority in Congress now can resolve major national controversies, such as health warning product labels, by threatening any recalcitrant state to withdraw vitally needed highway or social program funding.

Our federal government's leadership apparently does not believe in moderate drinking. Loren Archer, the permanent deputy director of the National Institute on Alcohol Abuse and Alcoholism (NIAAA) publicly stated that there is no such thing as responsible drinking. Dr. Otis Bowen convened an Alcohol Abuse and Alcoholism convention in Washington, D.C. at which he announced the creation of a privately-run citizens organization designed "to promote community awareness of alcohol abuse." This awareness would presumably be guided by the control of availability doctrine. Of even greater concern, Dr. Bowen instructed all agencies under his direction to drop the phrase "substance abuse" in favor of "alcohol and other drug abuse."

We regularly consume safe dosages of all types of legal drugs. But what is a correct and healthy dosage for the alcohol found in wine, beer and spirits? Dr. Thomas Turner, director of the Alcoholic Beverage Medical Research Foundation, says that NIAAA distorts the issue by omitting any reference to dosage. In an interview in the _Moderate Drinking Journal,_ Turner said:

> The totality of the NIAAA approach is that they inadvertently, or purposely, downgrade the question of quantity in drinking. This is the one drug that has an enormous spectrum of activity. More than almost any drug that is familiar and that is used medically or socially. There is just no relation to what happens at totally different levels. I can't help but feel that this one key thing is purposely ignored in the whole NIAAA approach.

Dr. David Musto, Yale Medical School psychiatrist and historian of narcotic use in United States, made the following comment in an interview in _Wine East_ about this engineering of science:

> In a way, then, there is a battle going on between researchers that indicates that the key issue at present is not a moral one. It's coming down to science; and if science seems to say that any amount of alcohol is bad, then I would say that those who produce alcoholic products would have a difficult time. But the battle, as I've said, is being fought more often now in laboratories or in research results or in the interpretation of

> research results by interested groups than it is in the
> churches.

Mark Keller, editor of the *Journal of Studies on Alcohol* labels
this kind of thinking as New Academic Inhibition:

> They see alcohol as the cause of the problem and I see
> people as the cause. The Inhibitionists imply that the
> bottle is chasing the man. It is true that if you have
> more people who are drinking too much, you will have
> increased alcohol consumption and increased
> problems. But if you make drinking inconvenient, it is
> the moderate drinker who will drink less.

So, new temperance has virtually pre-empted the federal
machinery for alcohol and health and operates under a virulently
anti-alcohol philosophy. That should be of concern to every
moderate drinker.

Research Finding 6.3

Leadership is ignoring the new temperance issue.

> *I think the control advocates are*
> *a minority among those in public health,*
> *but they have been muted in the same way that*
> *the ultra-drys were muted when Morris Chafetz*
> *was director of NIAAA.*
> **Interview with Augustus Hewlett**
> Alcohol Policy Council

Over one hundred and thirty million Americans drink with some
degree of regularity. Apparently they harbor some pretty strong
misgivings and uncertainty about the practice. How else does one
explain the findings of the Gallup public opinion organization printed
in the January-February edition of *Alcoholism and Addiction:*

> Eight in 10 (79%) would like to see a federal law that
> would require health and safety warning labels...Three
> in four (75%) favor a federal law that would require
> TV and radio stations carrying beer and wine commer-
> cials to provide equal time for health and safety warn-
> ings...Two in three (66%) favor a proposal to double
> the federal excise taxes on alcoholic beverages...

These contradictory sentiments — of drinking but saying that the practice is unhealthy — are typical of our public apprehensions.

This is a remarkable national attitude toward a substance that research says can help lessen the incidence of heart attacks by fifty percent. Alcohol could be a factor in reducing premature deaths from all causes by eleven percent. Something is radically wrong in a population that drinks regularly but covertly believes that health and warning labels are necessary.

The good news of moderation is not reaching the public.

There is a powerful, persuasive but neglected story on health and drinking in the medical journals. But we have ritualistically stood in stern judgment of any drinking for so long that the academic, political, medical and information professions have virtually abandoned public discussion of its merits. The prohibitionists have no sustained opposition. There is an occasional article in a national newspaper warning of the social peril in new temperance but there is no sustained opposition to the propaganda of NIAAA. The thought leaders we look to for wisdom and counsel on social issues cut and run when it comes to alcohol.

In another poll commissioned by the Distilled Spirits Council of the United States, George Gallup found evidence of this monumental ambivalence among our brightest and best. He reported that over 80 percent of thought leaders were aware of the reports of medical benefits in moderate drinking, but that a startling fifty percent of those _cognoscenti_ discounted the evidence.

I was encouraged to read the recent speech of Dr. David Whitten, assistant professor of physiology to a meeting of the Society of Medical Friends Wine. Whitten urged the doctors in attendance to exercise leadership on the issue:

> I sometimes feel very lonely when I speak to various gatherings regarding the good things about wine. An important wine writer for the _New York Times_ last spring asked me why there were not more physicians willing to speak up and assert that wine is good and good for you. I would like to see the medical fraternity join me in a strong effort to reverse the steadily mounting rush toward prohibition.

Even more than physicians, the producing industry needs to heed Dr. Whitten's plea. John De Luca, president of the Wine Institute explains how these factors impact industry decision makers:

> These last months have been almost traumatic on the industry with the introduction of the liability lawsuits. Now executives are faced with the prospect of the witness stand. Statements they make in public can be used against them by plaintiff attorneys. This has never happened before and so lawyers have been very strong in advising caution.

The fact is that alcoholic beverages are used in a responsible manner by almost all drinkers, and are abused at times by a minority of drinkers. Rational distinctions may be sustained at marketing levels between wine, beer and spirits but not in the alcoholism and abuse fields. To the addicted and the abuser, the source is irrelevant.

Recent interviews with industry leaders lead me to expect that the industry will soon confront new temperance. They should apply political pressure on the federal agencies because they are the primary propaganda outlets for new temperance. Coalitions of commercial interests, as recommended in chapter 12, could be effective in this effort. The federal government should be prevented from fostering programs which will curtail or destroy major commercial interests which are integral to the economies of many states.

Balancing the political equation alone will not stop new temperance. It is firmly entrenched in these federal and state bureaucracies and in a few, prestigious and well-funded private agencies. Beverage industry lobbyists have an excellent track record in protecting their interests in legislative halls. But this battle is for the public mind and it will require a longer, more sustained and purposeful projection of the values and benefits of moderate drinking to the society. This requires inventive action, not reaction.

Beverage alcohol producers operate under very restrictive advertising rules administered by the Bureau of Alcohol, Tobacco and Firearms (BATF). These rules forbid the producers from claiming caloric and therapeutic values in their products. In a period of developing scientific evidence about moderate drinking and health, these archaic, post-repeal, temperance restrictions should be examined again. A method should be worked out whereby legitimate data can be communicated to the public without false claims.

A major winery executive has decided to speak out.

One winery leader, Robert Mondavi, has committed his entire marketing and sales staff to a public confrontation of these issues. Mondavi justifiably resents and rejects the categorization of his wines as abused drugs and the association of any wines with cocaine and crack. He intends to reach the public with evidences of the healthy aspects of wine drinking. Mondavi declares with indignation:

> They are equating wine with heroin and crack. They are saying that moderate use of wine is not different from moderate use of narcotics. That certainly is not the message our children should be getting. There is no such thing as a moderate use of heroin or crack.

This kind of forthright counter-offensive in the public arena is the only sensible approach for a beleaguered industry which has too long accepted a demeaning public status for its products. If other leaders of wine, beer and spirit companies would join Mondavi, America would have a rare, historic opportunity to throw off the long-held yoke of alcohol ambivalence.

In the early 1970s, many national alcoholism leaders did undertake that difficult process of hammering out the language and the mechanism of a provident consensus on drinking. A consensus would benefit everyone—the abstainer, the moderate drinker and the abuser. A resurgence of temperance thinking, fostered during the Ernest Noble era at NIAAA, effectively sidetracked those efforts. Chapter 13 outlines the groundwork for consensus as developed by these blue ribbon committees. What is needed today is the courage and commitment to begin that task again.

Research Finding 6.4

Alcoholism professionals disapprove
of control radicalism.

> *I don't think the service constituency, the people who deal with the problems in the treatment systems, have a great passion for the control issues.*
> **Interview with Karst Besteman**
> Alcohol and Drug Problems Association

New temperance leaders are few in number but powerful in influence. The same names appear over and over again in the literature and on the public platforms. There is no ground swell of community support as there was in 1919. In its place is an articulate, committed minority of public health professionals and organizations dominated by recovering alcoholics. It is important for moderates to understand that these radicals do not speak for the entire treatment and care profession.

The post-World War II era was a period of progress and tentative cooperation in the abuse-treatment and prevention fields. The hardliners and liberals worked together in cooperative organizations. Nearly everyone agreed there was need for a federal presence in alcoholism beyond the minor desk it held at the National Institutes of Mental Health.

This period of cooperation helped create the National Institute on Alcohol Abuse and Alcoholism (NIAAA). Following repeal, the federal government had no specific role in alcohol matters. The Twenty-first Amendment placed control responsibilities, prevention and care programs — at the state level.

The first director of NIAAA, Harvard psychiatrist Dr. Morris Chafetz, represented the liberal end of the alcohol problems coalition. The second director, Dr. Ernest Noble, represented the conservative, alcohol-hating end. He still holds this view today as the Thomas P. & Katherine K. Pike Professor of Alcohol Studies at the University of California in Los Angeles. Most of Noble's successors have hewed to his narrow vision of drinking as evil.

Post -World War II cooperative era ended by new temperance.

The clash between these two public philosophies eventually retrogressed into the internecine warfare that has characterized the field since its inception. Michael Q. Ford, director of the National Association of Alcoholism Treatment Programs, was a staff officer at the National Council on Alcoholism (NCA) when the major shift to hardline, anti-alcohol programming occurred. The NCA drummed off its board all those who represented the generally moderate views of NCA's founder Marty Mann. Ford writes in _Private Sector_ about this deep division between the wets and the drys in the professional treatment and care fields:

> The wet-dry issue is one that has been in this field for
> the breadth of its history and will surely remain.
> However, the pinnacle of its attendant debate was, in
> my view, the ill-fated alcoholic beverage warning label
> amendment to the NIAAA reauthorization bill in 1979.
> That amendment rended deep personal, professional,
> and organizational wounds that today, six years later,
> are yet unsalved, much less healed. It was the beginning
> of an era of mistrust and disarray in the field, with
> emotionality supplanting worthy debate and effective

public policy. It brought about the dismantling of a
coalition of some 30 organizations which, at least, had
served as a forum for debate and consensus.

Wiener in *The Politics of Alcoholism* discusses Dr. Chafetz's
well-known reputation as a proponent of responsible drinking:

> Dissemination of the Room-Day findings: That the
> mortality rate for abstainers was higher than for
> moderate drinkers, was given a giant boost by NIAAA
> Director Chafetz, who was then championing his con-
> cept of "responsible drinking." Chafetz's views on the
> appropriate use of alcohol had been summed up five
> years before his appointment in his *Liquor: The Servant
> of Man*, to wit: alcoholism is a major public problem,
> liquor is not. His position on the safe drinking of
> alcohol had been a factor in Chafetz's appointment,
> where it was expected he would place an emphasis not
> only on treatment but on education and prevention.

This point of view sought to meet the needs of all users,
moderates and abusers. Lewis has an account of the radical beliefs
of Ernest Noble as reported in *The Journal of Studies on Alcohol:*

> In a relatively brief period, Dr. Ernest P. Noble, who on
> 1 February 1976 formally took office as director of the
> National Institute on Alcohol Abuse and Alcoholism
> (NIAAA), has set a new tone and pace for the federal
> alcoholism effort. Question: [to Noble] Following up on
> this, do you see a correlation between consumption and
> the size of the problem? Noble:...In my estimation, we
> could assemble a roomful of people, lock the door, and
> if I keep pouring enough alcohol into those people over
> a lengthy period of time, I can make every one of them
> an alcoholic.

A recent study on drinking patterns in the United States by
Hilton and Clark titled "Changes In American Drinking Patterns and
Problems, 1967–1984" demonstrates little change in the number of
alcoholics and abusers during a recent period of increasing
consumption. "There were few significant differences in drinking
patterns with the exception of a small increase in the percentage of
men who were abstainers in 1984." There is evidence that attacking
the product will waste time and effort that should be better expended
on learning more about the causes of abuse and addiction. There are
no simple solutions to very complex human problems.

Research Finding 6.5

New temperance seeks to lower per capita consumption.

We opened up the avenues of treatment and we saw a lessening of the punitive attitudes toward alcohol itself. People began to realize that there is nothing wrong with drinking. That attitude carried through the 1970s until Strom Thurmond and others adopted the Ernest Noble theory that we've got to get tough and cut down the per capita consumption.
Interview with Augustus Hewlett
Alcohol Policy Council

The only rationale for lowering consumption is the assumption that any drinking inevitably leads to abuse. There is no meaningful authority in the scientific literature for such a harsh characterization of drinking. This is the major tenet of the international movement called the control of availability, a theory developed first by the French alcoholism researcher Ledermann. Bruun et al. in "Alcohol Control Policies" sum up the movement's essential credo:

> If a government aims at reducing the number of heavy consumers, this goal is likely to be attained if the government succeeds in lowering the total consumption of alcohol. The greater the amount by which the total consumption is lowered, the more confident the government can be that the prevalence of heavy use is in fact being reduced.

So much for logic. Applying the same reasoning, perhaps the government can reduce wife-beatings by limiting the number of marriage licenses processed. Supply control failed spectacularly in prohibition since the per capita consumption had returned, in the early 1930s, to about the same level of 1919 when abstinence was imposed by law. It is failing just as spectacularly today in Russia under strict control of availability measures imposed by the Gorbachev regime. Moonshining and bootlegging are returning with a vengeance under the three-year old Soviet new temperance control of availability campaign.

Research Finding 6.6

Alcoholic beverages should not be equated with street drugs.

*The moderate drinker not only represents the
fear that his example may be catching. His prestige
and his behavior are actually diminishing the
value of abstinence in the hierarchy of actions
by which prestige can be increased.*
Joseph Gusfield
Symbolic Crusade

New temperance fears most the concept of moderate drinking.

Public health officials must be told by their political superiors to
stop calling alcohol the most abused drug in America. The statement
is factually incorrect. Tobacco, marijuana and prescription drugs are
more abused than alcohol. So is sugar if you accept it as a drug.
Koch in "Alcohol: Gift of God" writes, "Drugs can be beneficial,
nonconsequential or dangerous. Aspirin is a drug. Tea contains two
drugs, caffeine and theophylline. Chocolate, salt and powdered sugar
can, in a larger sense, be classified as drugs as can vitamins. In a
sense, the body even manufactures its own drugs, as with
endorphins or as with enzymes which initiate and facilitate the
chemical reactions so necessary to its metabolism."

Drugs are not intrinsically bad. Drugs permeate our existence.
Drugs save lives and ease our pains. There is a drug store in every
neighborhood. Coffee, chocolate and processed sugar are drugs in
the sense that fructose gives a momentary lift.

The debasing of alcoholic beverages has always been a primary
goal of hard-line temperance. Drinking, for temperance advocates,
constitutes an intolerable malignancy. Erickson writes in *Wayward
Puritans: A Study in the Sociology of Deviance* about the self-fulfilling
prophecies of those who seek more government control:

> It is not surprising that deviant behavior should appear
> in a community at exactly those points where it is most
> feared. Men who fear witches soon find themselves sur-
> rounded by them...The results of the present study sug-
> gest a parallel conclusion, namely, that societies that
> fear alcohol soon encounter problems with disruptive
> alcoholics.

This bedeviled witch-hunting creates an aura of danger and
mischief for alcohol far beyond any reality of its present dangers.

Research Finding 6.7

The intent is to destroy the economy of alcohol.

> *When MADD [Mothers Against Drunk Driving]*
> *began its national campaign, it*
> *attracted elements which, in my view, have as*
> *much interest in doing damage to a major*
> *American industry as in reducing alcohol abuse.*
> **Interview with Augustus Hewlett**
> Alcohol Policy Council

True control of availability would require a pervasive network of economic regulations. But the primary mechanism of new temperance is price control. Advocates want to raise the cost of drinking to the point that it discourages its practice. Other punitive measures include regressive and high taxation, the elimination of normal advertising and marketing rights, reduced hours of sale and fewer retail outlets.

These proposed controls would surely limit the supply of alcohol — at least legal alcohol — by indiscriminately impacting moderate and light drinkers in an effort to get at the abusers. The monumental effrontery of these proposals would be laughable were they not taken so seriously in state and national legislatures. All sorts of measures have already been achieved — from the elimination of happy hours to the posting of fetal warning posters. And the control advocates haven't any scruples when it comes to laying the financial burdens of abuse on the nonabusing majority.

What is to be said for those Americans who have invested their careers, skills and financial resources in the growing, producing and merchandising of wines, beers and spirits? In my state of Washington alone, hundreds of citizens have invested millions in private capital in the construction of nearly seventy wineries over the last decade. These wineries have become a popular new tourist attraction and grapes are the hottest commodity in the agriculture of Eastern Washington.

Price control is the key tool of control advocates.

Ewing and Rouse in *Drinking* generalize on the control of availability economic theory:

> Our general conclusion is that in the manipulation of
> the relative price of alcohol, governments would have

at their disposal a powerful instrument to control the
prevalence of hazardous drinking including alcoholism.

Dr. David Pittman, professor of sociology at Washington
University, has studied temperance movements for over thirty-five
years. Pittman describes the following as items on control of
availability agenda as it has emerged in the United States.:

1. Raising the majority to twenty-one
2. Restricting or curtailing advertising
3. Curtailing hours and convenience of
availability at retail
4. Enforcing mandatory price increases
5. Imposing health warning labels
6. Disallowing normal business deductions
7. Counter-advertising warning of health
dangers in consumption
8. Earmarking funds from taxes to rehabilitation
9. Tying retail prices to the consumer
price index
10. Mandatory provision of public health information
11. Raising excise taxes and equalizing them among
beverage types

No matter what business you are in, consider the chaos that
would be occasioned by this panoply of economic controls. Then
consider that Number 1 already has been accomplished. Numbers 2,
5 and 7 are under consideration by Congress. A congressional
budget office has just recommended consideration of 9 and 11. A bill
in the House would accomplish Number 6. A prestigious business
coalition established by the Center for Science in the Public Interest
supports Number 11. And that's just in the national Congress. Many
similar bills are pending in the state houses.

Research Finding 6.8

Moderate drinkers need to come out of
their closets of ambivalence.

> *This is where we stand. Fifty years after the end
> of Prohibition, we are being advised to enact inhibition.
> Along with the scientists, the alcoholismists—with still
> mainly alcoholics in their ranks and leadership—are
> in full cry against alcohol. I have heard the foremost*

*leader among them say, "If it hadn't been for alcohol,
I would never have become an alcoholic." What he meant
to say was alcohol is the cause of alcoholism. And
that is what many alcoholics would like to believe.*
Mark Keller
Law, Alcohol and Order

Drinking is an important social concern. Alcohol misuse has taken more lives and caused more misery than atomic energy, AIDS and the ozone layer combined. Like the common cold, alcohol abuse is the great equalizer. No segment of society is immune to its ravages. It's too important to leave the decisions about our alcohol future to the cadre of alcohol-haters now in control of the public health machinery.

Augustus Hewlett, veteran of more than a quarter century in the alcoholism field and currently president of the Alcohol Policy Council says, with the authority of experience, that we have made tremendous strides over the past two decades in the alcohol abuse field. Hewlett cites the following:

1. The acceptance of the disease concept of alcoholism
2. The downward trend of youth drinking
3. The elimination of the drunk as a comic in the entertainment media
4. The placement of alcoholism in private and corporate insurance coverages
5. The vast network of treatment centers
6. The acceptance of personal responsibility for health and moderation among our people
7. Corporate alcoholism programs in many major industries
8. College and university alcohol moderation programs
9. The elimination of the alcoholism stigma

Hewlett says that the NIAAA is creating false epidemics where none truly exist. "In the United States today, those calling for more restrictions on alcoholic beverages and sending negative messages about these products are creating a growing illusion that alcohol-related problems are of runaway proportions and getting worse. Such illusions breed bad laws. Even the nation's news media are now helping to promote this illusion under the tutelage of the control advocates."

Summary of Chapter 6

One of the monumental studies on alcoholism, representing a collaborative effort of dozens of researchers over forty-five years, found a need for this nation to replicate the European system of training the very young in proper drinking habits. In the recently published report on this study titled *The Natural History of Alcoholism*, George Vaillant suggests a course of action infinitely more logical and promising than the punitive controls on availability:

> A second conclusion is that if culture does play such an important role in the genesis of alcoholism, we must try to uncover ways of socializing healthy drinking practices, so that such practices will remain for a lifetime under an individual's conscious choice. Introducing children to the ceremonial and sanctioned use of low-proof alcoholic beverages taken with meals in the presence of others, coupled with social sanctions against drunkenness and against drinking at unspecified times, would appear to provide the best protection against future alcohol abuse.

There is no other logical approach for a nation in which two-thirds of its adults drink in moderation. A family cannot hand down healthy social family drinking practices when alcohol is portrayed as a dirty substance, drinking as unreasonable behavior and alcohol the most abused drug in America. The federal government, and many of the state and private alcoholism agencies, are preaching radicalism in alcohol control that flies in the face of history, experience and academic research. Families that do drink (the majority) should be encouraged to introduce alcohol at an early age and in controlled circumstances, without guilt or apprehension.

Cahalan, Cisin and Crossley, in *American Drinking Practices* are quite explicit about the problems inherent in a negative approach to alcohol, as personified in the "Just Say No" campaign:

> On the other hand, when we look at the other kind of dangerous activities, exemplified by drinking and sex, we seem to know only one word: "Don't!" We do not bother to say that there is a right way and there is a wrong way: we just say "Don't!" In spite of the fact that our society fails to make abstainers out of our children, we continue to say "Don't!" We do not really want to produce abstainers: we have the illusion that they will follow our advice and be abstainers (in the case of sex, until marriage; and in the case of alcohol, until

maturity) until they reach the magic age at which they can handle these activities...Now this is sheer hypocrisy...We should be brave enough to tell the truth; that drinking is normal behavior in the society, that moderate drinking need not lead to abuse; that drinking can be done in an appropriate civilized way without shame or guilt.

Moderates need to come out of their own closets of shame and ambivalence to capitalize on the already established trends toward moderation in drinking. This is truly the new American way.

7

A Mini-History of
Prohibition and Repeal

> *Mother makes brandy from cherries;*
> *Pop distills whiskey and gin:*
> *Sister sells wine from grapes on our vine,*
> *Good grief, how the money rolls in!*
> **Anonymous**

> *I make my money by supplying a public demand, If*
> *I break the law, my customers, who number hundreds of*
> *the best people in Chicago, are as guilty as I am. The*
> *only difference between us is that I sell and they buy.*
> *Everybody calls me a racketeer. I call myself a businessman.*
> **Al Capone**

> *Prohibition's better than no whiskey at all.*
> **Will Rogers**

> *Prohibition's an awful flop.*
> *We like it.*
> *It can't stop what it's meant to stop.*
> *We like it.*
> *It's filled our land with vice and crime;*
> *It don't prohibit worth a dime.*
> *It's left a trail of graft and slime.*
> *Nevertheless, we're for it.*
> **Franklin P. Adams**

Prohibition was a flop.

Here are some details about its failure to prohibit and the moral revulsion the led to its repeal. Prohibition arose from very strong and legitimate concerns. It reflected widespread fear and disillusion with major changes in the nation's social and economic structures.

Research Finding 7.1

Prohibition didn't prohibit drinking.

> *The amount of money spent on bootleg liquor*
> *in this period (1927–1930), however, was between*
> *four and five billion dollars a year, exactly*
> *equivalent to the amount which would have been*
> *spent if legal liquor had been sold...*
> **Andrew Sinclair**
> *Era of Excess*

Wayne Wheeler of the Anti-Saloon League drafted the Eighteenth Amendment. It was concise and to the point. The first article stated the following:

> After one year from the ratification of this article the manufacture, sale or transportation of intoxicating liquors within, the importation thereof into, or the exportation thereof from the United States and all territory subject to the jurisdiction thereof for beverage purposes is hereby prohibited.

In December 1917, the measure passed both houses of Congress and, within a calendar year, had cleared thirty-three states for ratification. Eventually, only Connecticut and Rhode Island resisted passage of the foolish, doomed social venture. On midnight January 16, 1920, prohibition became law. In the thirteen years of its turgid existence, enforcement officers arrested over 517,000 liquor purveyors, seized 1,600,000 stills, captured over 9 million gallons of illegal booze and confiscated more than 45,000 automobiles and 1,300 boats. All these convictions and confiscations were but a pittance against the flourishing trade in alcoholic beverages. Prohibition clogged our courts (as the War on Drugs is doing today), filled our jails, and, meanwhile, the people continued to drink at the same pace as before. Getz in *Whiskey* wonders what prohibition meant to the nation's economic decline:

> No one knows whether the stock market crash of 1929 can be charged to the unemployment caused by Prohibition. There were, undoubtedly, many causes, including the unbridled rush to buy stocks by millions of people who knew little or nothing about the stock market, and by those who did know, a total disregard of the danger signs. What we do know is that, for the first time in U.S.

history, an entire American industry was wiped out by
government fiat.

Research Finding 7.2

Prohibition leaders were master politicians.

> *In those states which refused to do the bidding*
> *of the "Drys" to adopt laws prohibiting the sale*
> *of alcoholic beverages, the so-called Temperance*
> *organizations and the Anti-Saloon League pursued*
> *a relentless, and even wrathful, effort to*
> *transform the social and drinking habits of the*
> *people in cities, towns, villages, counties,*
> *precincts and even single blocks...*
> **Oscar Getz**
> *Whiskey*

By 1850, thirteen states had passed various prohibitionary dry
laws. The national political potential was evident. To fill the void,
along came Frances Willard as president of the Women's Christian
Temperance Union (WCTU). Willard set out to organize every city
over 10,000 people in the United States, a remarkable objective
which she virtually accomplished. Never before or after has a female
on the American political scene accomplished such an impressive
organizational scheme. Her legacy is the feminist movement of our
times.

Carry Nation, another temperance sparkplug, was an odd and
charismatic character. Nation personified the anger and passion of
the drys through her hatchet attacks on tavern back-bars. She was
the populizer of prohibition.

Wayne Wheeler was the crafty organizer and lobbyist. By force
of his personality—and the millions of votes he commanded through
conservative churches—Wheeler held prohibition together as a
political force long past the time of its public acceptance. Churches
in America tendered contributions of over $2 million annually to his
Anti-Saloon League, an enormous political slush fund at the time.

This triumvirate organized American like no time before or since.
They were masters at the political game. By 1902, every school in the
nation offered a course in temperance, which was tantamount to
teaching total abstinence of alcohol. Abstinence is the objective of
the "Just Say No" campaign currently being sponsored by DHHS.

Prohibition was a cumulative political movement. Politicians responded to the continuing, unrelenting pressures. Twenty-six states by 1917 voted some kind of dry laws. Kerr in *Organized for Prohibition* outlines the genius of Frances Willard. She realized that the power of organized voters could be manipulated to achieve other objectives beyond a single issue of alcohol control:

> The WCTU and Frances Willard were in the thick of these events. Willard believed that a partisan strategy was not simply the best vehicle for achieving Prohibition, but a desirable means of promoting other social reforms as well.

Pragmatic and visionary, Frances Willard was brighter than all the impassioned ministers and bellicose politicians who carried the public banners of prohibition. Willard connived to create a Home Party, a third force in American politics, that would have undoubtedly precipitated womens' rights and many other social issues years earlier. Aaron and Musto, in the chapter "Temperance and Prohibition in America," from *Alcohol and Public Policy: Beyond the Shadow of Prohibition* warn of the danger of portraying this galvanic social movement only in terms of the alcohol issue:

> Detached and abstracted from their historically specific contexts and presented as a single crusade around which cranks and fanatics have clustered for 150 years, temperance and prohibition have been portrayed as touchstones of bigotry. The record of efforts to restrict drinking is, of course, far too complicated to warrant such axiomatic disparagement.

Mendelson and Mello in *Alcohol Use and Abuse in America* concur that such movements have deep and complex roots:

> The perennial seekers of simple solutions to complex problems did not appreciate that foreign immigration, westward migration, industrial expansion and urban growth were as much a part of this process as the saloon.

It was the organization and leadership genius of Wheeler and Willard that pulled together these random, fitful national sentiments and molded them into a powerful political machine. A similar process of political organizing is unfolding today under new temperance but there is a critical difference. New temperance lacks the organizational grass roots that meant vast political power. Sinclair in *Era of Excess* explains how tightly organized was this political machine:

Without an organized voting group behind it, the [Anti-Saloon] League would not have been able to apply political pressure on the legislatures of the states and on Congress. With the menace of thousands of votes at the next election... the League could make the representatives of the people vote against their personal wet convictions.

Research Finding 7.3

Governmental moral interference never works.

The prohibition cases brought into federal court most certainly represented only a fraction of the actual offenses...In 1920, 5,095 of the 34,230 cases involved prohibition violations; during 1929 75,000 cases were concluded.
David Kyvig
Repealing National Prohibition

Prohibition was an unenforceable legal nightmare. Legislatures can pass laws, but the people decide whether they are going to be obeyed. With only a handful of peace officers supervising over 100 million people, and such other matters as crime and traffic to attend to, no one ever expected rigid enforcement of the liquor laws. In the passion of the moment, many states wrote strong enforcement laws incorporating the objectives of the Volstead Act (the Eighteenth Amendment). Sinclair in *Era of Excess* reports on New York State's alcohol enforcement legislation:

Within a week, the courts of the state were clogged up with liquor cases. Nearly 90 percent of the accused were dismissed by the courts; 7 percent pleaded guilty; only 20 cases out of nearly 7,000 resulted in a trial by jury, conviction and jail sentence. When Alfred E. Smith signed the repeal of the law in 1923, making New York the first state to confess to the utter failure of state prohibition enforcement, the impossibility of the job had already been demonstrated.

The most ironic contribution of the prohibition years was the return of distilled spirits, the target of old temperance, as the beverage of preference. Lender and Martin explain this anomaly in *Drinking In America*:

The high cost of illicit drink also had an impact on consumption patterns by type of product. By the 1890s, annual per capita absolute alcohol consumption was fairly evenly balanced between beer (45 percent) and spirits (47 percent), with wine a distant third place (7 percent). By 1919, the figures read 55 percent for beer and only 37 percent for spirits—the beer invasion had obviously succeeded. But prohibition altered the situation, raising the relative proportion of distilled beverage consumption. Estimates from Warburton's calculations indicate that of all absolute alcohol consumed in the Volstead years, roughly 75 percent came in the form of whiskey, gin, scotch, or other spirits, with some 15 percent in beer.

An unintended, wholly deplorable, but inevitable consequence of prohibition was that drinking became synonymous with drunkenness. During prohibition, when one drank it was for the express purpose of getting drunk. It was truly "risk" behavior. Many young people between the ages of nineteen and twenty-one today are experiencing this same confusion of purposes. Mendelson and Mello in *The Diagnosis and Treatment of Alcoholism* spoke to this often ignored reality:

Certainly the years between 1920 and 1933 provided little opportunity for the development of control-oriented drinking customs. In the speakeasy, perhaps even more than in the old-fashioned saloon, the first standard of control was absent. Drinking was not clearly differentiated from drunkenness, nor, obviously, was it associated with ritualistic or religious celebrations. People did not take the trouble to go to a speakeasy, present the password, and pay high prices for very poor quality alcohol simply to have a beer. When people went to speakeasies, they went to get drunk.

Prohibition destroyed the growing wine culture.

Muscatine in "The Maturing Of Wine-Related Culture in the United States," an article in the *Bulletin of the Medical Friends of Wine*, outlines the decimation of what was then a flourishing and growing wine culture in the nation.

Prohibition effectively destroyed what was developing as a traditional wine culture...Of the 700 pre-Prohibition California wineries, 130 stayed alive by making sacramental and medicinal wine, and growers even

> prospered by supplying grapes to home winemakers...
> By the end of Prohibition in 1933, most of the fine wine
> grapes had been planted over to vineyards of Alicante
> and our palates had forgotten how a good wine tasted.
> A whole generation, in fact, had never tasted a decent
> wine.

It is, of course, difficult to reconstruct with any accuracy how much alcohol was consumed in this fruitless thirteen year span. One authoritative source, Columbia University professor Clark Warburton, reported on the financial ramifications of prohibition in 1932 in *The Economic Results of Prohibition*. Warburton estimates that the illegal beverage production jumped from 33 million proof gallons in 1921 to a high of 225 million gallons in 1929, with another 4 million gallons imported. Warburton computed his data on analysis of three factors; materials purchased to make alcoholic beverages, from death rates associated with alcohol and from police records of arrests involving liquor.

The nonabusing consumer got soaked in the pocketbook.

Temperance advocates today don't care about the average consumer. Their new tactics will work to soak the consumer just as formal prohibition did. Cashman in *Prohibition: The Law of the Land*, reports on the other side of alcohol economics, the cost to the consumer, as portrayed in a 1926 pamphlet published by the Association Against the Prohibition Amendment. This treatise reported that legal pre-prohibition spirits during 1910 to 1917 averaged 142 million gallons per year at $5 per gallon for a total retail cost in excess of $710 million. Cashman estimates that by 1926, spirits averaged $24 per gallon. Obviously, the drinker got soaked heavily in the pocketbook as a tribute to organized crime.

Whatever else prohibition did, it didn't stop the flow of wine, beer or spirits. It only increased the costs and the human indignities to their consumers. Deaths from cirrhosis steadily increased during the decade. And many American homes turned to making their own, as in colonial times. Kobler in *Ardent Spirits* cites the massive movement in home brewing:

> In New York City alone, more than 500 malt and hops
> shops flourished with almost 100,000 dispersed
> throughout the country, plus 25,000 outlets for assorted
> home brewing apparatus. The national production of
> malt syrup in 1926 and 1927 came close to 888,000,000
> pounds. Allowing a normal 10 percent for nonbrewing
> uses, enough remained for 6.5 billion pints of beer.

So, aside from the social confusion, the demeaning of common law, the bribery and skulduggery in law enforcement, the destruction of an industry, the loss of proper avenues for inculcating sane drinking habits in the young, the buttressing of an already healthy crime network, the impacting of the farm economy which undoubtedly contributed to the onset of the Great Depression, and the loss of millions in state and federal tax revenues, prohibition was probably a good thing. At least, as Will Rogers remarked, prohibition was better than no whiskey at all.

Many mini-prohibitions prevail in several states to this day contributing to overdrinking and rampant abuse, as was shown in earlier research. Linsky et al. in "Drinking Norms and Alcohol-Related Problems in the United States" show that the worst problems today with alcohol are in those states still clinging to prohibitionary laws— Mississippi, Utah, Kentucky, Georgia, Tennessee, Alabama, South Carolina, Oklahoma, Arkansas, and Idaho. Yet new temperance blindly looks to more government controls.

Despite the passage of sixty progressive years since repeal, Americans still seem divided and confused about alcohol control. In this uncertain atmosphere, the panaceas proposed by the Center for Science in the Public Interest and the National Council on Alcoholism win the backing of the Department of Health and Humans Services.

Deja vu.

Research Finding 7.4

Repeal was inevitable but slow in coming.

> _Of 922, 383 readers polled by the Literary Digest_
> _in 1922, 40 percent favored modification of the_
> _Volstead Act, and 20 percent repeal of the Eighteenth_
> _Amendment...four years later, 81 percent_
> _were for modification._
> **John Kobler**
> _Ardent Spirits_

Laws on the books have a way of lasting beyond their useful years. This maxim is even more true in the case of laws involving moral turpitude and social mores. That's the scary thing about the present regrouping of new temperance around the passage of laws raising the age of drinking to twenty-one, lowering the availability of the product in terms of hours and the number of retail sites, the loss of advertising privileges and the labeling of alcoholic beverages as toxic or hazardous to health.

Repeal forces were not effective until nearly the end of the 1920s. Kyvig, in *Repealing National Prohibition*, quotes Senator James Wadsworth of New York in 1926, "This Prohibition thing is getting worse every day. It cannot go on this way or the whole government will be disgraced." Yet, it did go on for another seven years and the entire nation was thoroughly disgraced in the interim. Though drug, traffic and public health authorities have already discovered that upper teens are continuing to drink despite the new laws. The laws will probably hang on in many states for years.

Repeal of the Eighteenth Amendment became a driving issue in both parties in the presidential campaign of 1928. The Republican structure remained for prohibition while key elements in the Democratic party stood for repeal. Kyvig comments, "At their 1932 conventions, however, Democrats and Republicans produced sharply contrasting planks on the liquor ban, tying the law's fate thereafter to partisan fortunes."

Repeal politics involved the entire social spectrum.

What had happened between the 1928 and 1932 national elections was a significant coalescing of many diverse forces for the logic of repeal. One of the most effective organizational voices was the Association Against the Prohibition Amendment (AAPA). Pauline Sabine, a member of the National Republican Committee, assembled the Women's Organization for National Prohibition Reform (WONPR). Another effective group was the Voluntary Committee of Lawyers. Sabine, a remarkable woman of equal stature with Frances Willard, resigned her seat on the National Republican Party to organize the women's crusade for repeal.

These independent groups and individuals had for several years been exploring ways to challenge the legality of the amendment. A key in this strategy was the fact that there had never been a plebiscite. American citizens had never voted on the issue. Finally, in 1931, Congress authorized the Wickersham Commission. It produced a report which held that the amendment process itself was unconstitutional. It faulted the Eighteenth Amendment for bypassing the individual voter. Their report states, "In many instances, as a result of old systems of apportionment, these legislative bodies were not regarded as truly representative of all elements in the community.

The tide turned when many well known conservatives publicly admitted the failure of prohibition. Arch-conservative Congressman James Beck is reported by Kyvig as saying, "No amendment has more vitally affected the basic principle of the Constitution *viz.* Home Rule. That the federal government should prescribe to the peoples of the States what they should drink would have been unthinkable to the framers of the Constitution." The crucial turnabout came when John D. Rockefeller, Jr., a personal contributor of over $350,000 to the Anti-Saloon League, wrote the following apologia as reported by Kyvig:

> When the Eighteenth Amendment was passed, I earnestly hoped—with a host of advocates of temperance—that it would be generally supported by public opinion...That this has not been the result, but rather that drinking has generally increased; that the speakeasy has replaced the saloon, not only unit for unit, but probably two-fold if not three fold...that crime has increased to an unprecedented degree—I have slowly and reluctantly come to believe.

Kyvig points to the overwhelming election of Roosevelt, the grinding impact of the late depression years. There was a desperate need for more governmental revenue. In this atmosphere, there was the rapid passage in the 1932 Congress of the repeal amendment and its equally rapid approval by state legislatures. Still the drys clung to their fanciful image of an idyllic, alcohol-free world. As they do today.

Research Finding 7.5

New temperance generates false hopes.

> *Prohibition will certainly never return...But while extreme forms of controlling consumption of alcohol are utterly lacking in feasibility, there is a chance that state policy may once again assume a more interventionist role.*
> **Paul Aaron and David Musto**
> *Temperance and Prohibition in America*

There are some fearful warnings to be found in this review of our national trauma of prohibition. We learned over the first three decades that emotionalism can easily manipulate the political system into extremes beyond the pale of logic and common sense.

A study published by the Distilled Spirits Council in 1984, "Moderation Is In the Public Interest" raises the pertinent question whether emotionalism is being used once again to mask reality:

> Yet just as 50 years ago the saloon symbolically repre-
> sented everything everybody ever disliked about
> alcohol, the war against drunk driving has similarly
> allowed every modern-day group with a complaint
> against drinking — legitimate and otherwise — to further
> its agenda within the heightened media, legislative and
> judicial awareness. Accompanying this more con-
> centrated attention to the problem of the drunk driver,
> is a shift to alcohol, not just the drunk driver as the
> villain. Increasingly, the debate is focusing not just on
> the minority of consumers who abuse beer, wine or
> liquor, but on drinking *per se* and all drinkers as the
> problem...Raise the drinking age. Increase alcohol
> taxes. Ban alcohol advertising. Close down the bars.
> Pass dram shops and sue the alcohol server if you're
> injured by a drunk. Is this what we've learned from
> years of dealing with the good and bad of drinking?
> Have we forgotten the lessons of Prohibition? Do these
> measures offer any route to further progress? Is there
> an alternative to a control-of-availability response to
> alcohol abuse problems?

Summary of Chapter 7

Not much has changed. History has a dogged way of repeating itself. Kerr in *Organized For Prohibition* points to the prime target of the "still twitching" prohibitionary movement as "The Business Of Drink:"

> The prohibition movement of the late nineteenth and
> early twentieth centuries was convinced that it was fight-
> ing the liquor trust...It was the business system that
> prohibitionists sought to destroy...Long before the Anti-
> Saloon League was organized or became a powerful
> political force, dry reformers were convinced that the
> permanent improvement of the American society
> required extinction of the liquor traffic...Once the
> traffic's practices were brought to light, the reformers
> were convinced, an indignant public would insist on
> prohibition.

8

Control of Availability:
An Economic Prohibition

*In short, again, the emphasis is on the agent,
alcohol, as the best variable to control ...
When all the trimmings are removed from the
control of consumption policy, it still remains,
prohibitionistic orientation to the problem of alcoholism.*
David J. Pittman, Ph.D.
Primary Prevention of Alcohol Abuse and Alcoholism

*Thus, implicit in this model, was not only
reducing the demand for alcohol, but also
its supply....one aspect of the plan dealt
with the control of availability of the agent.*
Ernest P. Noble, M.D.
Sixth World Prevention Conference

*I believe that addiction is the central theme our
culture uses to explain and attack drug use of
which it disapproves, and that the promotion of
addictive imagery has major consequences for
amount, style and results of drug use.*
Stanton Peele, Ph.D.
"What Does Addiction Have to Do
With Level of Consumption?"

Alcohol control is essential. In the interest of order, health and
well-being, societies must manage the supply of alcoholic beverages,
just as they must control vehicular traffic. The dividing question is
whether alcohol has an important, unifying role in society in the same
manner as the automobile. Both are the proximate causes of death
and suffering. The automobile is praised by the government for its
utility. Alcohol is treated only in its debilitating conditions.

The control of availability theory mandates hostility.

A generalized animosity toward alcohol becomes the rationale for the broad scope of market interference programs. Control of availability travels under other names in the world of research. It was developed originally as the "distribution of consumption model" and is now found in the literature as the "control of consumption", the "control of supply," and so on. The terms all mean the same thing. Curtailment of market supply by government interference.

Anyone who has read the history of prohibition must wonder at the depth of naivete of this doctrine. It contends that government intervention in the free market will eliminate the enticements and impulses to overdrink. Nowhere in the long history of alcohol control has this theory worked. It is paternalism at its worst and socialism at its best. Alcohol controls have worked best on a local level where the majority accepts them. They have been more effective in small, culturally or religiously unified, socialistic or paternalistic countries and they have been less effective in the larger, democratic and pluralistic environments.

Research Finding 8.1

Control of availability is
built as a house of cards.

> *There's been a careful selection of NIAAA*
> *[National Institute on Alcohol Abuse and Alcoholism]*
> *leadership in the political arena for the last several years.*
> *There's no reason why these people shouldn't be put on notice.*
> *Because if you remain silent, the people we are talking*
> *about are not going to remain silent.*
> **Interview with Karst J. Besteman**
> Alcohol and Drug Policy Association

The control of availability demands massive government intervention in the marketplace of alcoholic beverages. This intrusion relies upon some assumptions and computations developed by the French researcher Ledermann in the 1950s. A model system that Ledermann developed argues that the mean consumption level of alcohol in a society determines the overall consumption levels at each end of the consuming spectrum from light to heavy. These theories were amplified by Bruun, Schmidt, de Lint, Popham, Room and others in the professional research literature. David Pittman in *Primary Prevention of Alcohol Abuse and Alcoholism* identifies the faulty Ledermann statistical evaluations as the real foundation for the current drive to reduce consumption:

> Therefore, it is assumed that one has to know only one parameter of the distribution, the mean consumption, to predict the other parameter of the curve, the percentage of drinkers in the heavy consumption category.

The theory built upon this questionable statistical base was outlined by authors from several countries by Bruun et al. in *Alcohol Control Policies,* a publication of the Finnish Foundation For Alcohol Studies in 1975. In the paper, the authors took note of the questionable statistical basis of the theory. "Not every increase in the general level of consumption would, of course, be expected to entail exactly the increase in prevalence of heavy use to be predicted from the statistical model." Human beings, after all, are capable of exercising freedom of choice. Yet, the paper went on to conclude:

> 1. A substantial increase in mean consumption is very likely to be accompanied by an increased prevalence of heavy users.
> 2. If a government aims at reducing the number of heavy consumers, this goal is likely to be attained if the government succeeds in lowering the total consumption of alcohol.

Following a thorough outline of the statistical foundation of control theory, Pittman finds, "...the conclusion must be drawn that this premise is statistically fallacious." Pittman also attributes reservations to others in the scientific community:

> The control of consumption model has been severely criticized by scholars such as Parker and Harman, Lauderdale, Miller and Agnew, Duffy and Cohen and Singh among others. They have raised valid questions concerning the control model, especially the assumption that there is a constant relationship between mean alcohol consumption in a population and the prevalence of heavy consumers and that the dispersion of consumption is a constant regardless of the population studied...Furthermore control theorists do not discuss variations in patterns of consumption between societies and over time periods.

So much for the scholarly base of the control of availability model. Garbage in — garbage out.

Research Finding 8.2

Control of availability implies
everyone is in danger.

> *Likewise, this view would hold that the control of
> substance availability should have a decisive impact
> on a society's substance abuse problems. The evidence
> arrayed against this synthesis is considerable, however.
> In the case of illicit drugs, substance control
> policies have been a notorious failure.*
> **Stanton Peele, Ph.D.**
> "The Limitation of Control-of-Supply Models"

An important exchange took place between Stanton Peele and
Robin Room in the *Journal of Studies on Alcohol* in mid–1987. Peele,
in "What Does Addiction Have to do with Level of Consumption? A
Response to R. Room," holds that "...control policies are based on
the negative images that societies hold of substances of which they
disapprove, and in modern medico-technological societies these
images mainly concern a substance's addictiveness."

In "Alcohol Control, Addiction and Processes of Change:
Comment on "The Limitations of Control-of-Supply Models for
Explaining and Preventing Alcoholism and Drug Addiction," Room
pointed to the blurring of dependency with simple heavy alcohol use:

> On the other hand, "addiction" as it is used in the
> wider society, is much more focused on what used to be
> called psychological dependence, and in particular on
> the experience of loss of control over one's drinking
> and thus over one's life – an experience that may not be
> very closely linked to particular patterns of heavy
> alcohol use.

Though Room notes that prohibition made a "wonderful medium
for the generational revolt of middle-class youth" and that the current
21 year mandate "offers a tempting arena for future generational
revolt," he still argues, "In my view, controls on availability are a
potentially useful part of an overall societal policy on alcohol,
tobacco or other drugs."

Researcher questions the popular concept of addiction.
Peele says that many in public health leadership today are
insistent on identifying alcohol with other drugs, namely cocaine,

which is firmly fixed in the public mind as a powerfully addictive substance. Peele quotes a National Institute on Drug Abuse (NIDA) definition of cocaine which is widely accepted in society:

> If we were to design deliberately a chemical that would lock people into perpetual usage, it would probably resemble the neuropsychological properties of cocaine....It is likely that anyone with access to cocaine in quantity is at risk.

Peele points to two studies concerned with the differences between addiction and situational use. In one, Siegel reports on a nine-year follow-up of college cocaine users who remained moderate users without addiction as adults. In the other, Zinberg reported on hundreds of thousands of returning Viet Nam war veterans who voluntarily kicked their habits. Peele maintains that a high degree of volition and environment is involved in addiction:

> There is a firm empirical basis for conceiving that the severity of alcohol withdrawal, up to and including death, is a function of expectation, setting and culture.

Peele cites the fact that nearly 90 percent of the 30 million Americans who have stopped smoking did so on their own, without addiction intervention. Zinberg in *Drug Set and Setting* sets forth the development of the addiction philosophy at the World Health Organization:

> Researchers in the field of drug use tended initially to look at all styles of drug taking as drug abuse, that is, as physiologically addictive. Later, when it became apparent that not all substances were physically addictive, they turned to a new concept, that of psychological habituation.

Zinberg's arguments against massive controls are based on the reality that "...others may benefit from regular, controlled use because it brings them relaxation and sense of freedom from inhibition." He concludes:

> First, the prohibition mentality directly opposes the interests of most users, who place intoxicants near the top of their hierarchy of values...It is undoubtedly true that our commitment to work and thus to self-esteem and our relationships with others are our overriding daily concerns...Religion used to be considered the third most important interest; but now the interest in intoxicants and food has begun to claim that position.

Peele's basic argument is that *people* become addicted, not that alcohol or cocaine are necessarily and intrinsically addictive. This is the logic in Peele's closing argument:

> An alternative prevention model (to that of portraying a drug's overwhelming power and appeal) approaches people's use of a drug—including whether they use it at all, use it regularly, become addicted to it and quit use after addiction—as being determined by the values they place on the other choices open to them.

> We might even say that we encourage the kind of mind-lessness that may be a part of seeking drug unconsciousness when we blur the moral, intellectual and scientific distinctions that surround the unhealthy cultural and individual use of drugs.

Research Finding 8.3

Control advocates have made
a major shift in U. S. policy.

> *There is no question that the case of South Dakota v. Dole opens the door to increasing regulations on alcoholic beverages, and that's probably the goal of the new temperance movement— to have uniformity throughout the 50 states.*
> **Interview with David J. Pittman, Ph.D.**
> Washington University

During the Reagan administration, a climactic shift has occurred in public policy on alcohol control. Federal officials have adopted the philosophy of the control of availability. It is important for moderate drinkers and alcoholic beverage industry workers to understand this major shift.

The guiding philosophy of control of availability was established in *Problems Related to Alcohol Consumption* produced by the World Health Organization in 1980. Public health is now the umbrella and governmental intervention is the device. Dr. Ernest Noble, the former director of NIAAA who first introduced the concept of reduced consumption in the United States, told the Sixth International

Commission for the Prevention of Alcoholism and Drug Dependency how his pioneering work brought results:

> Over time, however, considerable support has been obtained for NIAAA's [National Institute on Alcohol Abuse and Alcoholism] prevention approach...The National Council on Alcoholism, the largest and most powerful of the U.S. voluntary organizations originally took no position on the NIAAA's "Prevention Statement" but came forth in 1982...The World Health Organization, in numerous past and recent reports prepared by panels of international experts, provides evidence for the importance and effectiveness of control measures in the prevention of alcohol problems.

At a recent annual meeting, the American Public Health Association (APHA), which represents a membership of 50,000 professionals, adopted a position paper titled "Alcohol Tax Policy Reform." The paper argues a decidedly radical political approach for the American society which is quite in line with the international connivance of control. Included are their recommended objectives:

> 1. a substantial rise in the federal alcohol excise tax rate, to at least the level, in real dollar terms, of that of 1972,
> 2. the equalization of excise taxes by alcohol content for all three types of alcoholic beverages...
> 2. the indexing of the alcohol tax rates to inflation; and
> 4. the discontinuation of tax deductions for the use of alcoholic beverages.

That's quite a revolution that Ernest Noble's new temperance has wrought. Our largest body of public health practitioners vote to destroy free enterprise in a major industry. That's what those four recommendations would beget.

In the *Moderate Drinking Journal*, Augustus Hewlett recalls when Ernest Noble first came to a meeting of the Alcohol and Drug Problems Association of North America (ADPA) with the per capita reduction policy paper. Hewlett was then executive director of ADPA which acts as a clearinghouse for policy and action by a range of participating agencies:

> In 1977, Ernest Noble, director of NIAAA, came to our coalition meeting of 25 or so agencies, about everyone who had an interest in the field, with a proposal that national policy focus on stabilization of per capita con-

sumption based upon the hotly contested Ledermann
hypothesis otherwise known as the Distribution of Consumption. We turned him down. Most of us felt that it
was irrelevant whether consumption was up or down.
We wanted those who needed help to seek it. That was
the objective.

The Education Commission recommended a consensus.

Two years earlier, the Education Commission of the States' Task
Force On Responsible Decisions About Alcohol, chaired by former
West Virginia governor John West, had completed a widely
representative study. This important document became the national
policy on alcohol in the Carter administration. It includes the
following:

> Up to now our society has not developed a national set
> of guidelines as to what actually constitutes the respon-
> sible use and responsible nonuse of alcohol. Generally
> speaking people want and need to know specifically
> what is expected of them when they receive a message
> that suggests either developing new behaviors or chang-
> ing current behaviors.

The task force called for an educational system in which
individuals would make free choices. Alcohol was not treated as a
societal evil, but the choice of use was associated with the exercise
of personal responsibilities. That was, in effect, support of
responsible drinking. New temperance advocates interposed the
current defamation of alcohol as a substance. Psychiatrist and
temperance writer David Musto in "Understanding Today's
Temperance Movement" comments on the minimum age-to-drink
issue. He finds this issue an important step toward the control of
availability agenda:

> From my point of view, as someone who is interested in
> analyzing these shifts of attitudes and movements, there
> has been nothing like this by the federal government
> since Prohibition. It was an issue on which the Reagan
> administration publicly changed its mind. The
> advisability of taking this action nationally, as opposed
> to doing it within the states, went against the
> president's basic philosophy...This change in attitude,
> coming about 10 years after the drinking age in many
> states had been lowered to 18, is a remarkable shift in
> public attitude and in the political response...Events
> like these are milestones in the change of perception of

alcohol from being one kind of thing to being another kind of thing.

Zinberg concludes in _Drug Set and Setting,_ with a nod to fellow researcher George Vaillant and his profound and informative _Natural History of Alcoholism,_ the importance of family and friendships in maintaining moderate habits:

> On measures such as capacity to relate to others, to maintain close friendships and family ties, and to continue in good physical and mental health, the abstinent or near-abstinent score as poorly as the serious problem drinkers or the alcoholics. Statistically, moderate drinkers score significantly higher on each item. Vaillant says, only partially in jest, that his "findings have caused me to increase my drinking."

Research Finding 8.4

Control programs fails to achieve lowered abuse.

> _When the rules were coming down from the state levels, or during Prohibition from the federal level down, the attitudes were not consistent. If you want really good control or prevention policy, then establish it at the county level, close to a reflection of the lifestyle of the residents._
> **Interview with Karst J. Besteman**
> Alcohol and Drug Problems Association

The final question should be, "Does it work?" The answer is no.

Hilton and Clark in "Changes in American Drinking Patterns and Problems, 1967–1984" provide current evidence of failure of control of availability. This article is about a population survey of drinking practices taken over a seven year period. The authors cite the Ledermann thesis as an important question in their research and they conclude:

> Finally, we must comment on the status of these findings as evidence for or against the single distribution theory. On the basis of that theory, increases of greater than 11.8% would have been expected in the prevalence of heavy drinking. Our finding was that there was not a significant increase in the prevalence of

heavy drinking between 1967 and 1984...This increase
may have failed to be significant only because the
sample sizes employed were insufficiently large.

Failure seen in basic premises of control systems.

The failure of control of availability lies not only in poor study
samples but in its basic premises. It has failed to function because
Ledermann's original samples were too small to form a realistic base
and because it presumes only one relationship in a field in which
many factors interplay. There is, for example, no interest in what role
other "addictive" substances may have had in the lives of the study
group. Grant and Gwinner in *Alcoholism In Perspective* raise this
pertinent issue:

> To ban alcohol or to increase taxation to prohibitive
> levels does not reduce human suffering in any real
> sense. It may and even this is doubtful, given the in-
> crease in illicit production which would ensue, with no
> quality controls and thus with higher toxicity) reduce
> liver cirrhosis, but the increase in crime, black-
> marketeering and associated activities will more than
> compensate for any modest advances. In addition, all
> those who have been quietly using alcohol as a simple,
> cost-effective tranquillizer will start turning elsewhere
> for their self-medication, probably with far more
> damaging and costly (in health terms) consequences.

This is a question that the single-minded fanatics of control
refuse to entertain. What do moderate drinkers turn to effect the
tranquilization of an occasional beer or glass of wine. Light in "Costs
and Benefits of Alcohol Consumption" raises this specter:

> When one considers the impressive statistics that 57
> percent of all adult Americans drink at least once a
> month; that 29 percent of all prescription drugs in the
> United States are for psychotropic drugs; the amounts
> of illicit drugs including amphetamines and bar-
> biturates; and the consumption of nicotine and caf-
> feine, one begins to suspect that a major source of
> social and economic cohesion in this country is the
> ubiquitous use of mood-altering substances. It is inter-
> esting to speculate on the effects of a complete elimina-
> tion of alcohol abuse: what would be the economic cost
> of the consumption of alternative substances and/or of
> the antisocial behavior which would occur.

Control of availability could actually increase problems.

Dull and Giacopassi,in "An Assessment of the Effects of Alcohol Ordinances on Selected Behaviors and Conditions," evaluated city and county ordinances and five socio-demographic variables in the state of Tennessee. In this state, alcohol control is a local city option. Therefore, Tennessee serves as a laboratory showing the impact of various degrees of control from city to city.

The control of availability theory is a bummer in Tennessee. The authors say in their abstract that, "The findings indicate that alcohol availability measures are almost uniformly negatively correlated with the dependent variables." The "forbidden fruit" concept was advanced to explain these findings in which the tougher the control, the greater the abuse. Tennesseeans presumably are a relatively homogenous population in comparing the reports city to city. Uniformly, there are more suicides, homicides, motor vehicle fatalities and liver mortality in the cities in which their alcohol laws are more strict. This stunning refutation of the control of availability theory appeared in the *Journal of Drug Issues* in 1986. Naturally there is no mention of its arguments in any NIAAA or Department of Health and Human Resources publications.

The study examined all cities in Tennessee with populations of over 10,000 residents. Thirty-seven cities met this requirement, so the study was broadly based. The authors conclude:

> From the correlation matrix, we found that type of alcohol ordinance is significantly and inversely related to liver mortality and suicide rates. However, stronger correlations were found between the deleterious behaviors and conditions and the socio-economic variables.... Our data give support to the "forbidden fruit" hypothesis whereby stricter ordinances actually lead to an increase in socially undesirable alcohol-related phenomena. On the basis of our data, it appears doubtful that tighter restrictions on availability will alleviate these problems.

Another 1980 study by Ornstein, "Control of Alcohol Consumption Through Price Increases," also denies the central premise of the controllers:

> There is no support for Parker and Harman's conclusion that income effects dominate price effects, nor is there evidence of inelastic demand for distilled spirits in the U.S. Schmidt and Popham's conviction

that consumption is sensitive to price changes is supported, but that sensitivity varies across beverages, and how effective price changes would be in reducing heavy drinking remains untested.

How much proof do these social tinkerers need? Heien and Pompelli, in "Stress, Ethnic and Distribution Factors in a Dichotomous Response Model of Alcohol Abuse," find:

> The empirical results based on data from Canada and the United States indicate that ethnic and stress factors strongly influence alcohol abuse. The stress variables include the rates of unemployment and divorce. The ethnic variables are the percentages of population that are African, French, Italian and Mexican ancestry. Distribution factors such as price, income and control measures were generally less important.

Finally, Smith, in "The Wrath of Grapes: the Health-related Implications of Changing American Drinking Practices," demonstrates that control of availability theories simply are not working:

> A detailed investigation shows that four of these "drier" states are in the top twenty in terms of their death rates: North Carolina, West Virginia, Oklahoma and Tennessee...it appears that alcohol-related mortality is not related in a linear fashion to the mean level of consumption, or to increases in the consumption of alcohol.

Research Finding 8.5

The alternative Is a moderate consensus.

> *In South Dakota, we have no problem. The testimony before our legislature was that the 21-year old drinking law will increase young people's drinking and driving. Now they can go to our 3.2 [3.2 beer] bars. They go there because it's a social meeting place; it's not just a place to go drinking.*
> **Mark Meierhenry**
> Attorney General of South Dakota

If tighter controls do not work, what is the alternative?

Hewlett, in "Public Policies for Alcohol Related Problems," opts for a responsible drinking level to be obtained through a national educational approach, the conclusion of the Education Commission of the States task force cited above. Hewlett recommends:

> The goal of the proponents of the educational approach to the reduction of alcohol related problems in American society is the development of a healthy national atmosphere which will be conducive for those who can drink and who choose to drink, to do so responsibly, in moderation and without guilt; and for those who, for whatever reason, develop a problem with alcohol to recognize that problem at the earliest possible stage and to seek appropriate help.

Hewlett cited the substantial progress made toward moderation and the placement of the problem on the host abuser instead of on the agent alcohol. This approach holds each individual as responsible for his or her own drinking. The development of the Alcoholics Anonymous movement in 1935 and the disease concept of alcoholism, as pioneered by Jellinek in 1960, helped to emphasize the individual's role and responsibility to fight alcoholism. The disease concept also helped to eliminate the shame factor and the implication of moral turpitude. This encouraged individuals to come forward for treatment. This concept now is being used to blame alcohol to the degree that the individuals hold little or no responsibility for their actions.

Also over the past thirty years, many institutional advances have been made in the prevention and treatment fields. In 1967, the report of the Cooperative Commission on the Study of Alcoholism sought a public consensus on moderate drinking. In 1968, Methodist leadership declared that abstinence was no longer a tenet of faith. In 1972, the first administration at NIAAA worked to support responsible drinking as well as care of the alcoholic. The formation of the National Coalition for Adequate Alcoholism Programs (NCAA) in 1975 and formation of dozens of state and private agencies have made an encompassing institutional framework to assist the individual in prevention and care.

The alcoholism field has been fraught with endless and sophisticated controversies, but there has been remarkable progress and effective institutional delivery of care. New temperance threatens much of that progress by bringing back the stigma of alcohol-as-evil and the clumsy, unworkable intervention of government. The principle failing of new temperance is its lack of faith in the people it seeks to serve.

Summary of Chapter 8

The capitulation of the White House to support of the age twenty-one movement was a signal victory for the control of availability advocates. The decision by the Supreme Court to uphold the congressional blackmail could mean a return to the alcohol dark ages. Congress can now spend its money any way it wants in pursuit of the national public health. Control advocates are pushing Congress hard on labeling and other repressive measures.

Smith and Harham in *Alcohol Abuse: Geographical Perspectives* summarize why the argument for greater federal control can be tempting to legislators. The drys point to the inconsistencies which might be harming the national public health. However, the authors also point to the fact that those states with the fewest controls have the fewest problems, a fact ignored by control advocates:

> Because each state in the United States has its own laws to govern the availability of alcohol, the net effect is a hodgepodge of often contradictory regulations. Where alcohol is not easily available, it may become a more prized possession, bought in larger quantities, and consumed more rapidly and secretly. As we shall see later, there is evidence to suggest that alcohol-related problems are greater in the "drier" states where alcohol is less available than in wetter states.

I close with an argument from the National Institute for Mental Health publication titled *Alcohol and Alcoholism*, prepared in 1967, before the onslaught of control advocacy:

> The most complete prevention of excessive drinking would be provided by the most complete prevention of all drinking...This has been attempted many times in various parts of the world — most recently in Finland and the U.S. — and the penalties for violation have ranged from fine and imprisonment or death...no country in Europe or the Americas has yet succeeded in eliminating the use of alcohol by legislative means.

Amen.

9

The Prohibition Coalition
is Three Sheets to the Wind

> *The moderate drinker not only represents the*
> *fear that his example may be catching. His prestige*
> *and his behavior are actually diminishing the value*
> *of abstinence in the hierarchy of actions by*
> *which prestige can be increased.*
> **Joseph Gusfield, Ph.D.**
> *Symbolic Crusade*

> *I believe it's a cop-out to say that it's the*
> *person and not the bottle.*
> **Ernest Noble, M.D.**
> University of California

> *The alcoholic beverage industry is doing everything*
> *it possibly can to maximize sales and maximize*
> *drinking by the American public.*
> **Michael Jacobson, Ph.D.**
> Center For Science In The Public Interest

The first written legal code, on alcohol control, *The Code of Hammurabi, King of Babylon,* written circa 2250 B.C. had more rules for drinking than for any other civic activity of that era.

Government control must be maintained over alcohol today as it was in those ancient days. Governments must play the key role since they act in behalf of the entire body politic. But being in control does not require the government to be *against* alcohol.

Alcohol control is most effective at the state level.

The Twenty–first Amendment placed alcohol control at the state level in the United States where it could more properly reflect the many regional differences in drinking practices. That's where it still belongs in our nation, not in some distant federal bureaucracy where moral rights and wrongs can be judged from afar. Sinclair in *Era of Excess: A Social History of the Prohibition Movement* identified the reformist tendencies which are implicit in every piece of new temperance legislation proposed today:

> Prohibition sought to regulate human morality and human habits. But the trouble with moral legislation is that it does not keep to the limits set by reasonable and respectable men....The lessons of prohibition are plain. The fine frenzy of a minority, a long period of indoctrination, a powerful pressure group, and a state of national fear can cause the adoption of an ill-considered reform. But the success of an unpopular reform is illusory, a mere string of words on a document.

The United States needs to work out some kind of new alcohol-use consensus. In our interview, sociologist David Pittman warned of the strength and determination of new temperance advocates. "To understand the hostility and negativism toward alcoholic beverages in American society, you must understand the whole spectrum of vested interests that are actively engaged in socially constructing alcohol problems and alcoholism." The forces driving for a return to semi-prohibition are far from illusory.

Research Finding 9.1

New temperance depends
on the public health bureaucracy.

> *The New Temperance Movement ...*
> *seems to have no corporate charter,*
> *no headquarters, no annual report, no*
> *board of directors, no visible sources of*
> *prime financial support. So, are we*
> *wrestling with an illusion?*
> **Paul Gavaghan**
> Distilled Spirits Council

The prohibition coalition, like Gaul, is divided into three parts. Its three major constituencies include the professional bureaucrats, the traditional religious drys and the moral entrepreneurs, a term coined by David Pittman. Of these three parts, the bureaucracy is, by far, the most important.

Funding for any social program involves the creation of a bureaucracy. Someone has to be hired to allocate and manage the funds on the government level. These civil servants interface with the care or service deliverer and that's how an interlocking bureaucracy, public and private, is formed. It is inevitable in any form of government, and it is not necessarily a bad thing.

The largest component in the new temperance, is this bureaucratic coalition of interests between governments with money and others who vie for the privilege of spending it. This segment includes the academics, the federal and state alcohol and drug administrations, many private treatment corporations, and a host of public health entities ranging from the National Council on Alcoholism to the American Public Health Association.

The bureaucrats of therapy are generally articulate, organized, passionately committed and highly active in the cause. They understand and adroitly employ the mechanics of a pressure-group society. From the professional, tenured bureaucrats who staff National Institute on Alcohol Abuse and Alcoholism (NIAAA) to the cadre of volunteers at the National Council on Alcoholism (NCA), including many who are recovering alcoholics, this segment forms the major anti-alcohol juggernaut.

They excel in the mass media. They play endlessly on the emotional issues of drunk driving and drug corruption of youth. Alcohol is the *bete noir*, the causal agent which is responsible for abusive drinking in adults and the corruption of the young. Public and private agencies push the same agenda.

One of the latest issues of *Prevention Pipeline,* provides a glaring example of how the federal bureaucracy works with the private bureaucrats at the NCA. This publication is produced by the action arm of the Alcohol, Drug and Mental Health Administration (ADAMHA) called the Office for Substance Abuse Prevention, (OSAP). The publication is a splendid source of abstracts of research in the alcohol research field. Haase, the bulletin editor, protests in the January–February issue that OSAP is not for prohibition. Yet this issue carries a two page, anti-alcohol party line set by NCA board member, Jean Kilbourne. Included are such lines as:

> Say "alcohol and other drugs" not "alcohol and drugs"
> Avoid the phrase "responsible drinking"
> Say "drinking and driving"...not "drunk driving"

In the introduction to her penetrating book *The Politics of Alcoholism*, Carolyn Wiener uses the sociological term "actors on the arena" to describe this collaborative, anti-alcohol drama:

The social worlds that interveners represent are themselves constantly in a state of flux, constantly splitting off and reshaping. This is reflected in the continual transformation occurring within the arena...Christie and Bruun, in their paper on the conceptual framework of alcohol problems, talk about the function of vagueness, and how apparent agreements can be reached, for instance, on the disease concept of alcoholism, while the parties who reach that apparent agreement really have very different notions of what is going on. Coalitions are impermanent, and there is a great deal of sliding that goes on between various interests...All the worlds represented by these actors are attentive to their own public relations, and all have stakes — not just economic, but ideological. All of the actors are exchanging time, advice, information, and have concerns for their individual self-respect and status.

NCA originally was not anti-alcohol.

The largest and most articulate of the private agencies is the National Council on Alcoholism. Originally devoted to treatment of the alcoholic, the NCA is now a major political force. Cahalan in *Understanding America's Drinking Problem* recounts this transmogrification from caregiving to political activism:

In the past, the NCA traditionally concentrated exclusively on getting the alcoholic more effective treatment and tried to dissociate itself from movements that might be labeled neoprohibitionist. However, Noble's 1982 leadership in getting the alcohol industry's representatives off the NCA's National Board, and in the issuing of the 1982 manifesto calling attention to the dangers inherent in heavy alcohol advertising budgets and relaxation on controls of availability of alcohol, has been followed up by a strong emphasis on primary prevention on the part of the NCA's national directors. The NCA has now established an active office in Washington, D.C., which devotes much of its attention to lobbying before congressional committees and with individual legislators for increased control over alcohol advertising, for putting health warning labels on containers, and for increasing taxes on alcohol. The NCA has also played a central role in lobbying successfully to induce states to raise the drinking age to twenty-one.

The founders of the NCA had quite different objectives in mind—treatment and care of alcoholics, the establishment of the disease concept, and reducing the terrible moral image of alcoholism. John MacIver was one of the early board members of NCA. In an interview reported in *Moderate Drinking Journal,* he decried this new politicizing of NCA and he recounted the dynamics of National Council on Alcoholism founder Marty Mann:

> Marty Mann believed in fighting the disease not the substance. Marty told me stories of having alcoholism meetings at the bar of the 21 Club in New York City. She was no enemy of alcohol. She believed in and worked within the framework of research, treatment and general education. To the extent that we deliver ourselves and the movement to political solutions, we set up a false sense of security. The real solutions are in prevention and education.

The *University of California Wellness Letter* of March 1986 provides another example of how the public health bureaucracy pushes the concepts of new temperance. The entire agenda of control of availability appears in their March 1986 issue. Here are excerpts:

> 1. Put warning labels on alcoholic beverages...
> 2. Public opinion (a force the media are quick to respond to) can be brought to bear on the communications and entertainment industries...
> 3. Current laws and regulatory authority can be used to motivate the alcoholic-beverage industry to eliminate advertising associating alcohol with driving, sexuality, or celebrity role models...
> 4. Networks, cable companies, and print media that carry alcohol advertising should be persuaded to donate equal time or space for public health messages...
> 5. Increase federal and state excise taxes on alcohol and index them to inflation.
> 6. Revise tax laws to disallow alcohol as a deductible business expense.

New temperance doesn't need a propaganda machine with such a network of media fellow-travellers. There are hundreds of newsletters and bulletins selling the political agenda of new temperance. They have to have an impact on public opinion.

Research Finding 9.2

Conservative religions form
the second temperance group.

> *Any such set of beliefs that are religiously adhered*
> *to but not scientifically proven (be it macrobiotics,*
> *fundamental Christianity, or insistence on daily*
> *jogging) tends to irritate the scientific community.*
> **George E. Vaillant**
> *The Natural History of Alcoholism*

The second faction in the current temperance coalition is
composed of the traditional conservative religious organizations. The
conservative churches are still quite important politically, particularly
in the Deep South, but they no longer can pledge or deliver the
millions of votes that buttressed prohibition forces at the turn of the
century.

Politicians are well aware of the support or opposition to social
issues originating from the fundamentalist churches. While still
important, the influence of conservative religion is ebbing as a major
factor in the alcohol control area. In *Drinking In America*, Lender and
Martin cite the changing statistics on church involvement:

> On the other hand, this same survey reported that areas
> with high concentrations of native-born Americans,
> fundamentalist Protestants, or Mormons had lower
> than average consumption levels. Cahalan, Cisin and
> Crossley ranked only 18 percent of native Americans
> (defined as those with fathers born in the United
> States) who drank as heavy drinkers: 38 percent were
> likely to be abstainers. Among conservative Protestants
> (Methodists and similar denominations, Baptists, or
> other theologically conservative Protestant groups), 48
> percent were abstainers, as opposed to some 20
> percent among liberal Protestants (Lutheran,
> Presbyterians, and Episcopalians), 17 percent among
> American Catholics and 8 percent among Jews.

This is not to downplay the political influence of this huge group
of Americans who have been, at the very minimum, uncomfortable
with alcohol. But, it is to say that there is no Wayne Wheeler of the
prohibition era Anti Saloon league that could deliver millions of
ballots when it counted. Recall that Gallup reported in 1988 the
lowest number of respondents ever, 17 percent, desired a return to

prohibition. The religionists have mellowed somewhat on alcohol. While not discounting the strength and pervasiveness of this grouping for a moment, it can be said that its opposition is secondary to the professional care deliverers.

Research Finding 9.3

Moral entrepreneurs are
the third prohibition group.

> *Operating out of a borrowed office with a handful of volunteers, CSPI was founded in 1971 on a shoestring budget. To Jacobson and his co-founders...CSPI would ideally "serve as a model for scientists on how to get involved in social problems."*
> **Richard M. Hoppe**
> *The Wine Spectator*

In a Hoppe article in the *Wine Spectator*, Dr. Elizabeth Whelan of the American Council on Science and Health is quoted, "Jacobson goes around squashing ants while the elephants run wild."

Ant crusher Michael Jacobson of the Center for Science in the Public Interest (CSPI) is very effective at what he does. Representing the smallest contingent in the new temperance triumvirate, the social entrepreneurs are professional advocates. They are a relatively new phenomena on the political scene. Professional advocates know how the media impacts the political process. They adroitly employ all facets of the public and private media to press their many causes. When Jacobson sets about forming an ad hoc coalition for those specific legislative goals, the world can observe an extraordinarily adept public organizer.

The CSPI National Alcohol Tax Coalition is a classical example. The roster has impressive, high profile organizational names representing a wide spectrum of potential voters:

> **Religion** (Adventist Health Network), the **aging** (American Association of Retired Persons), **youth** (The Children's Foundation, American Youth Work Center, American Medical Students Association), **health** (Doctors Ought To Care, American Licensed Nurses Association, National Association for Public Health Policy), **safety** (National Center for Drunk Driv-

ing Control, National Drivers Association for the
Prevention of Traffic Accidents, Rid Intoxicated
Drivers), **education** (Association of Schools of Public
Health), etc.

The printed materials given legislators and the media by CSPI
are masterfully prepared, full of hyperbole and contorted opinion, but
always fact-filled and science oriented. They overpower by profusion.
"Beer and wine taxes are less than one-fourth of what they were at
repeal...Due to inflation since 1951, the real dollar of value to tax
revenues on alcoholic beverages declined by 75%...Government
reports estimate the annual toll from alcohol abuse at between
100,000 and 200,000 deaths and $120 billion in economic
damage...Doubling liquor taxes and then equalizing the rate of tax on
alcohol in liquor, beer, and wine as proposed by the National Alcohol
Tax Coalition would...etc."

Professor David Pittman coined the term New Moral
Entrepreneurs for this group. I like it because it fits so appropriately
these "actors on the arena" of national alcohol policy. The
professional advocates are not recovering alcoholics (as some are in
the NCA) or tenured civil servants with a personal cause (as some
are at NIAAA). These are opportunistic, issue-oriented, highly
educated entrepreneurs, in the true sense of that word. They are
hustling bucks and attention for their public causes. Often, they seem
more committed to the art of advocacy (and generally against
big-business) than do true partisans in the wet-dry debate.

An example of their selective science is found in the May 1988
issue of CSPI's newsletter *Nutrition Action*. In a generally excellent
article on the good and bad forms of cholesterol, there is no mention
of the positive impact of moderate drinking as outlined in chapter 2.
Even though the American Heart Association recognizes the values
of alcohol to the heart, these "scientists" at the Center for Science In
the Public Interest never say anything positive about alcohol. One
begins to wonder about that kind of objectivity.

Founded in 1971 by alumni of the Ralph Nader organization,
CSPI has grown into a formidable agency. It has a staff of nearly
twenty, a budget in excess of a million-and-a-half to fight what it
deems to be toxins like alcohol, the support of heavyweights such as
the Henry J. Kaiser, the Babcock, the Needmor and the Rockefeller
funds. The subscriber mailing list is said to exceed 80,000 while their
pamphlets, books and news releases reach millions of readers.

CSPI alcohol publications are diatribes. An example is *The Booze Merchants The Inebriating Of America* authored by staffers, Jacobson, Robert Atkins and George Hacker. Everyone who grows, manufactures, distributes and retails alcoholic beverages (no distinctions as to type or size) are *booze merchants*. One presumes, by inference, that those of us who consume are *boozers*. Paul Murphy comments on this tendency to blame the substance (alcohol or drugs) instead of the offender who misuses the substance. In a thoughtful essay titled "Societal Morality and Individual Freedom" in *Law, Alcohol and Order*, Murphy writes:

> One cannot resist speculating on whether it could happen again (Prohibition). One's instinctive reaction is that this is highly unlikely. But the use of the law for allegedly moral ends has had its supporters from that time to the present day. The "Moral Majority" is not all that reluctant to use the same kind of arguments regarding federal imposition of proper standards which the early prohibitionists used — that massive federal authority is necessary to intervene in people's moral behavior, both for their own good and to shame them from themselves; and that, there being no such thing as a victimless crime, individual sin hurts the community and produces disruption and immorality.

Summary of Chapter 9

This tripartite prohibition coalition is definitely winning the current propaganda battle. It's winning, partly because we are in another introspective and self-critical time as a people. Aaron and Musto in "Temperance and Prohibition in America" remind us that the last prohibition came at a time of great concern for ecology and the fragility of the human species:

> Anti-alcohol organizing reached its pinnacle of influence during historical periods in which agitation against the plundering of the social and physical landscape was most intense. Efforts to curb drinking emerged from broad reformist sentiment. The relative obscurity today of any alcohol control movement may be deceptive.

There is nothing obscure about the federal role in developing the alcohol control movement. Wiener in *The Politics of Alcoholism* tells how the NIAAA officials, while preparing the *Third Special Report to Congress on Alcohol and Health*, established these claims as being caused by alcohol abuse without substantive, objective data.

> ...not the least of which was to maintain an "alcohol-
> specific institute" as the rationale for establishing the
> now proto-factual 10 million American problem
> drinkers, the risk of death from disease, accident or
> violence, the involvement of alcohol in one-third of
> suicides, half of murders, half of traffic deaths, and as a
> major factor in child abuse and crimes such as rape...
> Thus do research figures become "public facts."

In the introduction to Harold Fallding's *Drinking, Community and Civilization* written in July, 1974, Charles R. Snyder provided a reach of vision so needed today:

> Having glimpsed, through the study of traditional
> Jewish drinking patterns, something of the power of
> community to give civilized meaning to drinking...To
> those who value pluralism, as I do, perhaps the
> profoundest long-run question raised by Professor
> Fallding's study is how, in America, we can reconcile
> the apparent contradiction between the social reality
> and values of cultural pluralism, on the one hand, and
> the need, on the other hand, for a more embracing com-
> munity to foster civilized meanings of drinking and con-
> strain the pathologies of alcohol.

Fallding's vision of the "civilized meanings" of drinking must help to form our objectives in fighting new temperance. The only antidote to new temperance is a positive, encompassing and compassionate policy on drinking. That's the challenge of consensus.

Part 3

ENGAGING THE PUBLIC MIND

Where Do We Go From Here?

10

The Critical Arena for Debate

> _We must publicly challenge the many oft-repeated half truths and untruths these groups use to increase the dramatic impact of their message. For example, the statement that alcohol is the most abused drug, picked up by the media and given currency by various secondary sources, is a lie based upon the strongly held prejudice of the New Drys that any use whatever of any alcoholic beverage constitutes abuse._
> **David N. Whitten, M.D.**
> _Wines & Vines_

> _The most serious challenge to public health advocates is to recognize that this enormous, vastly sophisticated marketing strategy is still only a part of a larger and continuous effort to "normalize" a highly abnormal commodity—a psychoactive drug with potent addictive properties, one which has for long periods of Western history been marked as dangerous or even sinful._
> **Robert McBride**
> "Industry Structure, Marketing and Public Health"

The editorial and entertainment content in the popular media, seldom portrays alcohol as the "good creature of God" as perceived by Increase Mather. Alcohol is nearly always depicted as a "highly abnormal commodity, a psychoactive drug with potent addictive properties" as suggested above by Robert McBride. Little wonder that American drinkers are schizoid about alcohol. They don't know what to believe. Drinkers carry a heavy burden of guilt and misgivings.

New temperance advocates say that advertising is creating an alluring image for alcoholism. I say that alcoholic beverages and drinking in general are losing the battle of the media by a wide margin. Alcohol advertising will never catch up to the preponderance of negative messages on the editorial side.

The proof of this impact is found in the ambivalence of most drinkers toward alcohol. Nearly all 130 million Americans drink and probably 129 million feel some sense of guilt or uncertainty about the practice. This is not true in France, Italy or Germany where alcohol has a defined and meritorious role in the society. Many objective readers will have difficulty with the message of this chapter. Many will conclude it with lingering doubts about the power of advertising to move the public. Advertising primarily acts as a *follower* rather than a motivator. The essential function of advertising is to aggrandize market shares. Religions motivate people. Advertising sells things to people who already want them.

Research Finding 10.1

The temperance battleground is the popular media.

> *They made a tactical mistake in the White House Conference...they pre-empted the voice and claim to speak for many others where there is much more division and much more distinction.*
> **Interview with John De Luca**
> The Wine Institute

We don't believe everything we read in the papers. We are, nonetheless, influenced every day by what we see and read.

Temperance advocates are exceedingly tenacious when it comes to influencing what people read, see and hear about drinking. They flood the media with newsletters. They are highly visible in the letters-to-editors' columns and they fill many guest spots in print and electronic media. More power to them. They have something to say. They realize they no longer have a Wayne Wheeler with millions of votes organized county-by-county around the country.

New temperance workers know that an aura of public excitement and pressure is essential. They need it to get legislators to enact such sweeping bills as that which forced states to raise the drinking age to twenty-one. News clippings and appearances on the major talks shows can affect the political system by creating a sense of public urgency.

Sinclair in *Era of Excess* says, "For more than forty years before the passage of the Eighteenth Amendment, the press of the United States was flooded with articles and editorials alleging that alcohol was the chief cause of poverty, crime, disease, and insanity." Sound familiar? Glance through any ten popular magazines today, the national newspapers like _USA Today_ or the many health oriented newsletters. This simple exercise will convince you of the universal message that "alcohol and drugs" are the root causes of the evil in our society. Seldom is the criminality of the illegal user mentioned. The agent "alcohol" is the cause rather than the instrument.

Sinclair reports that after the fact — by 1920 — the popular press had largely flip-flopped from dry to wet. People came to their senses as they watched Al Capone become a mover and shaker in their lives. Unfortunately, those recantations came too late.

If the drys are winning the battle of the news releases, it's because they are sending out more and probably better news releases and providing more and probably better informed spokespeople for the talk shows. Until the wets decide to get into the fray, the drys will have the day.

Research Finding 10.2

The media drinking image is mostly negative.

> _So the whole social climate, the media climate, the focus on drugs and drunk driving has created a bad atmosphere. The skillful bureaucrats have been able to exploit the tense climate._
> **Interview with John De Luca**
> The Wine Institute

The negative cast for alcohol should not be very surprising to anyone who reads or listens to the media's general news stories.

There are no alcohol editors (nor should there be) aside from the large contingent of food and wine writers, and they seldom get editorial page space. Many of these food specialists also are negative about some aspects of drinking. They share the general ambivalence of the population.

Little wonder that the media and the public are confused about alcohol. They hear the incessant rat-a-tat-tat of bad news from the major government agencies like National Institute on Alcohol Abuse and Alcoholism (NIAAA), and from the private propagandists like the National Council on Alcoholism (NCA) and the hyper-media-active Center for Science in the Public Interest (CSPI). These attacks have their cumulative effect along with the nearly universal negative tone of media reports on alcohol and drinking.

Pollster's finding reflects America's confusion about alcohol.

In one of the anomalies of our times, most people drink but apparently consider the practice to be bad for them. George Gallup writes in "Majorities for Three Congressional Proposals," "The American people overwhelmingly favor each of three proposals which its sponsors believe would reduce alcoholism and other alcohol-related problems in the nation."

> Eight in 10 (79%) would like to see a federal law that would require health and safety warning labels on alcoholic beverage containers...Three in four (75%) favor a federal law that would require TV and radio stations carrying beer and wine commercials to provide equal time for health and safety warning messages about drinking...Two in three (66%) favor a proposal to double the federal excise taxes on alcoholic beverages to raise revenues to fight drug and alcohol abuse.

The new temperance campaign largely succeeds in the media by default. Such few articles or speakers that appear to favor drinking are said to be flacks for the producers. The nearly universal anti-alcohol bias largely offsets the positive impact sought and paid for through advertising.

As an alcohol journalist, I am sensitive to this prevailing attitude. Here are a few recent examples from my media files:

> *The St. Louis Post Dispatch* on November 14, 1985 gave the alcohol policies director of the Center for Science in the Public Interest fifteen inches of column space to argue that alcohol taxes should be dramatically increased.

> A recent headline in the *Christian Science Monitor* asked, "Is alcohol abuse being ignored in antidrug fervor?" You would expect conservatism here.

> The February 15, 1988 issue of *Time* carried a "Just Say No" story with the typical nearsighted attitude. "Why can't we keep our children from drinking? Many are beginning to conclude that the greatest obstacles are not the kids but the permissive attitudes of all too many other parents." No mention of George Vaillant's

findings that societies that teach their young to drink
have far less abuse by young and old.

The September 13, 1986 column by Ann Landers
repeated a Students against Drunk Driving catalogue of
alcohol "involvement" blamed for 66 percent of fatal
accidents, 60 percent of child abuse, 37 percent of
suicides, and so on. Naturally enough, the sources
quoted for the figures are the Department of Health
and Human Services and the 1982 FBI files. We have
seen that there is no proof of causality in these statistics
but they are spread as fact daily in thousands of media
outlets.

The September 24, 1986 issue of the _New York Times_
carried a letter from the executive director of the
National Council on Alcoholism, asserting, "Alcohol is
by far the most abused illegal drug among young
people. In 1985, an estimated 4.6 million young people
experienced negative consequences of alcohol use."

The Harvard School of Public Health recently
announced a nationwide program designed to insert
anti-alcohol messages into movie scripts, to enlist
actors as spokesmen for temperance and to oversee
production of television commercials.

Prevention magazine's cover in February 1988 promises
"New Ways To Help Your Heart" but the opening
article adds the caveat "There are a lot of ill effects
from drinking even among nonalcoholics."

Bonnie Liebmann, another Center for Science in the
Public Interest associate, asks in _Medical Self-Care_, "Is
a Little Alcohol Good for You?" and concludes,
"Despite the current headlines, the social costs of
promoting moderate drinking far outweigh any possible
public health benefits."

In the _Seattle Post Intelligencer_ in January 1984, a headline, attributed to a report from a national meeting of
pathologists, read "...9 in 10 road deaths may be
alcohol-linked". A Minnesota medical examiner was
quoted in the report as saying, "Of 31 traffic fatalities,

> only three resulted from what he calls 'real accidents' —
> cases where no driver has been drinking."

The overwhelming tenor of these guest articles and news stories is negative. Heath's "A Dither about Drinking" in the *Wall Street Journal* raises the right issue. "Let us be wary that increasing appeals for the control of alcohol do not mask a drive toward more pervasive controls. Why, at this moment in history, is there suddenly such a flurry of opposition to drunk drinking? Could it be, among other things, a newly acceptable way of shaking one's fist and invoking law and order?"

While one expects such treatment in general speech, a pinnacle of sorts was achieved in a governmental publication in 1987 by the Standing Committee on National Health and Welfare of the Canadian House of Commons. The document is titled *Booze, Pills and Dope*. While such solecisms often have their humorous side, they also serve to reinforce deeply felt prejudices.

The electronic media also demeans alcohol inadvertently.

Seattle's TV medical expert, Dr. Bill Crounse conducted a Health Check on KOMO in November 1988 during which viewers answers were rated by numbers. As example, a person smoking ten or more cigarettes loses ten points. Here is the alcohol segment:

> What about alcohol? If you don't drink, or have less
> than 1 drink a day, give yourself 4 points. If you have 8
> to 15 alcoholic drinks in an average week, you get 3
> points. More than 16 (drinks) you score 1 point.

Nothing subtle here. If you drink less you score more points and are more healthy. Forget all the alcohol and health research and go with your friendly TV doctor.

Even National Public Radio, the prototypical liberal outlet, demonstrated this pervasive tendency to disparage alcohol by selecting a negative headline to a generally positive story. All day it billboarded an interview with a doctor by warning that heavy drinking is associated with increased risk of stroke. Quite true, except that the abstract of the medical story, "Stroke and Alcohol Consumption", opened with the much more positive story that light alcohol drinkers experienced less stroke incidences. The reporter could hardly have missed the first line of the study. That should have been the news. "Among men, the relative risk of stroke (adjusted for hypertension, cigarette smoking, and medication) was lower in light drinkers (those consuming 10 to 90 g of alcohol weekly) than in nondrinkers, but was four times as heavy in drinkers (consuming over 300 g weekly) than in nondrinkers."

I could fill the remainder of this book with similar selections. Yes, there are positive contributions to the debate in the press, but they are few and infrequent. An example is "The Third Wave of Prohibition is Upon us" written by Morris Chafetz in the July 21, 1987 *Wall Street Journal* . In it, Chafetz briefly details the history of temperance:

> The first wave of Prohibition began in 1820, when the nation sought virtue in health, and ended in 1861 with the beginning of the Civil War. The second wave, which made Prohibition a household word, started in 1860 and ended with the 18th Amendment's repeal in 1933...The third wave's grass roots groups such as Mothers Against Drunk Driving focused on the innocent victims of drunken driving. The Fetal Alcohol Syndrome adherents lobbied for warning labels. And concerns about alcohol and drug abuse among young people caused a hue and cry to ban all alcohol advertising. The flood gates were opened.

Research Finding 10.3

The media associates alcohol with street drugs.

The media constantly links alcoholic beverages with street drugs and commission of crimes. In any competition with the bad effects of other drugs, alcohol is the heavy favorite to be the champion. The repeated and eloquent comparisons of the damage done by alcohol and marijuana by the pro-pot advocates have again raised the consciousness of the public regarding alcohol.
David F. Musto, M.D.
The Wall Street Journal

There is a simple solution to the problem of alcohol abuse on college campuses. Ban alcohol on college campuses.
Candy Lightner
The Los Angeles Times

Here is an example of how an Associated Press writer set in motion an avalanche of misleading and defamatory headlines in the nation's print media. The *Department of Justice Bulletin* publishes studies of our jails and their inhabitants. "Prisoners and Alcohol" in early 1985 made some telling points on abusive drinking patterns among our criminal element:

> The fact that one inmate out of every four drank very heavily on a daily or near daily basis in the year before incarceration indicates an alcohol problem of staggering size....The relationship between alcohol consumption just prior to the crime and the crime itself has not been sufficiently explored in these data. It is tempting to point to very heavy drinking (again, the equivalent of at least 8 cans of beer, 6 glasses of wine, or nearly 9 ounces of 80 proof liquor) as the proximate causes of many crimes since 30% of the offenders admitted to such large consumptions just prior to their offense. *The survey strongly suggests, however, that for many offenders these are typical daily drinking levels.*
> [Emphasis added.]

The Associated Press news release on November 3, 1985 did print the above disclaimer that drinking was not the cause of crime but a daily practice of most criminals. However, the Associated Press reporter added one small biased phrase, "...the government said Sunday in a grim study of alcohol's role in fueling crimes of passion." There was nothing linking alcohol to crimes of passion in the Justice department bulletin. In fact, the bulletin stressed the opposite conclusion. Here are examples of how this reporter's bias produced shocking headlines.

> "Government study cites alcohol's role in violent crime" was the headline in the *Springfield State Journal Register.* "Report links alcohol to crimes of passion" appeared in the *Fargo Forum.* "Justice report indicates link between alcohol, violent crime" said the *Raleigh News & Observer.* "Alcohol plays part in violent crime" trumpeted the *Mobile Register.* In Pontiac, Michigan, the *Oakland Press* put it this way, "Alcohol plays role in more than 50% of violent crimes". The *Phoenix Times Democrat* in Muskogee was a bit more sedate with, "Study: Alcohol has a big impact on crime."

Alcohol is commonly grouped with tobacco and hard drugs.

Another aspect of the negative media coverage is the linkage of alcoholic beverages with tobacco and the street drugs. This is a primary tactic of the Department of Health and Human Services (DHHS), NIAAA and CSPI. And it works. The September 16, 1987 issue of _USA Today_ demonstrates. In a full page layout under a "Health and Behavior" banner, _USA Today_ told its readers, "Here's a roundup of what is known or suspected about the effects of some of the most common street drugs." There sits alcohol cheek-and-jowl with cocaine and PCP. There is no distinction between alcohol as a daily food and beverage and these terrible street drugs.

News reporting on teenage-drinking is another area of confusion. Never is any distinction made between illegal drinking by youth and that which takes place under parental supervision in the home. This contributes to a subtle reinforcement of the myth that all drinking by youth is bad. _Monday Morning Report_ on January 25, 1988 repeats this inconsistency. "Alcohol is a legal drug, but not for those under 21, yet the ISR [Institute for Social Research] annual survey of youth drinking and drugging conducted for NIAAA] showed that two-thirds of the high school seniors drank in the month preceding the survey."

How many of those teenagers drank in a controlled situation, perhaps with their parents at the supper table. This distinction is of no apparent interest to NIAAA or the media,. Many of these young people are partaking of legal and culturally desirable learning experiences.

No recognition is made of moderate drinking education.

An October news release from Field Publications reported a survey of "more than 500,000 school children showed that 26 percent of children as young as fourth graders believe that their peers are drinking wine coolers, 34 percent feel peer pressure to do so and 50 percent of fourth graders do not think of alcohol as a drug." This message was carried in many of the nation's papers along with commentary by Secretary Bowen of DHHS that, "These statistics...are indeed alarming, but the consequences are even more devastating...Use of alcohol and other drugs by youth is clearly linked to juvenile delinquency, truancy, unwanted pregnancies, poor academic performance, traffic-related fatalities, homicides, suicides and other problems." There was no mention that the "survey" was not conducted under secret ballot as is appropriate, but consisted of raised hands in classrooms where peer pressures could influence kids to claim that they drink. The vote was taken in conjunction with the distribution of the anti-alcohol *Weekly Reader*.

As a journalist, I think the answer to these media problems is better communication by the drinking side. We have a free, open and generally responsive press. In our society, advocates and opponents must contend for that precious space in the journalistic sun. Those who don't contend, don't get. Most of those who grow, make and sell alcoholic beverages just sit back and take their licks.

Research Finding 10.4

The influence of alcohol advertising is overestimated.

> There is virtually no evidence that advertising
> starts anyone drinking. Rather, peer and parental
> influences are the most important
> factors for explaining why teenagers drink.
> **H. Blane and L. Hewett**
> *Alcohol and Youth*
> No scientific evidence exists that beverage alcohol
> advertising has any significant impact on the rate
> of alcohol abuse and alcoholism in American Society.
> **David J. Pittman, Ph.D. and M. Dow Lambert, Ph.D.**
> *Alcohol, Alcoholism and Advertising*

In *The Booze Merchants*, Michael Jacobson of CSPI argues against alcohol advertising. Seemingly, no advertising standard will satisfy him because he doesn't like any alcoholic beverage ads. Producing companies, wholesalers and retailers, nonetheless, have a right to use the prevailing media to sell their goods.

There are two reasons why Anheuser-Busch brewery and E. & J. Gallo winery sell respectively more beer and wine than any other firms in the world. The first is that they make good products. The second is that they are adroit advertisers in this quintessential advertising age.

Public health spokespeople refuse to accept the premise that beer advertising does not create beer drinkers. In fact, many readers may find that statement difficult to accept. In spite of copious research data establishing this fact, alcohol advertising is the favorite target of new temperance. Mosher and Wallack, in "Government Regulation of Alcohol Advertising: Protecting Industry Profits versus Promoting the Public Health," claim the following:

> The usual focus of prevention programs since repeal
> has been the individual drinker, with no attention being
> paid to the producers, marketers, or distributors of
> alcoholic beverages. This has resulted in a narrow
> range of prevention strategies.... programs, no matter
> how well planned and implemented, are unlikely to suc-
> ceed because they exist in an environment that is rich
> with messages that support and encourage the use and
> misuse of alcohol. The major contributor to this anti-
> education environment is clearly alcoholic beverage
> advertising.

The mythical power of advertising is thoroughly entrenched in our popular beliefs. Many may believe that Anheuser-Busch's lovable dog, Spuds MacKenzie, and Miller's huge, huggable ex-football coach, Dan Madden, really do entice youth to drink illegally and adults to drink copiously. But their real _raison d'etre_ is to convince Budweiser drinkers to drink Miller beer, and vice versa.

Advertising cast in bad light by CSPI.

The anti-business bias of moral entrepreneurism is abundantly evident in CSPI publications. They want us to believe that alcoholic beverage advertising is the proximate cause of abuse, by both young and old drinkers. In a tract worthy of the 1920s titled _The Booze Merchants: The Inebriating Of America,_ Jacobson, Atkins, and Hacker tell us:

> Advertising, in general, has a greater effect on young
> people...The great volume of alcohol ads in the media
> can have a gradual, but important, effect on young
> attitudes. Alcohol is presented as the social norm, as
> adult-like, sophisticated, and as a sign of success.
> Before even reaching the drinking age, young people
> are primed for a drinking lifestyle...

But alcohol _is_ a social norm for most of us. It _is_ sophisticated and adult for most of us. Why can't alcohol opponents realize that the majority of consumers want and, in a general sense, pay for the alcohol advertising by their purchases at retail. The campaign called SMART (Stop Marketing Alcohol on Radio and TV) seeks to eliminate all advertising. _The Booze Merchants_ also contends:

> Rather than appealing narrowly to the personality of
> the heavy drinker, some ads aim to increase consump-
> tion all around. These ads suggest to drinkers that
> many nontraditional occasions are appropriate for

drinking. Alcoholic beverages should not be confined
to dinner time, cocktail hour, or weekends, but can be
consumed every day, after work, in the afternoon, or
while working. Such ads clearly encourage daily drinking as a means of increasing consumption. The NIAAA
considers daily drinkers to be problem drinkers and
less than 10 percent of the adult population fits into this
category.

I think this is a fair presentation of the temperance point of view.
It holds that alcohol advertising causes or influences a number of
decisions that would not be made otherwise. The fact that advertising
bans in Canada did not change anything, does not influence those
scientists at CSPI. The fact that there is no advertising in Finland and
Russia, each with major abuse problems, does not influence those
scientists at CSPI. CSPI scientists are just against alcohol advertising.

As a practical matter, advertising is the least important
component in the etiology of alcohol abuse. Consider your own
response to general advertising. Each of us ignores hundreds of ad
exposures daily, thousands annually. We respond on a very selective
basis and generally only to those ads which portray something we
already are disposed to want or need. Nondrinkers ignore Chivas
Regal ads. Teenagers aspiring to achieve macho manhood may well
respond affirmatively to a California Cooler ad, but the disposition to
drink was there before the media exposure. It would be fulfilled in the
absence of the ad.

Advertising has little to do with the decision to drink.

While recognizing the need to maintain high social standards in
alcohol advertisements, Grant and Gwinner in *Alcoholism in
Perspective* state that advertising has little to do with the amount or
degree of problem drinking:

It is proper that the public, and especially vulnerable
sections of the public such as young people, should be
protected from misleading advertising. At the same
time, it should be noted that in those countries where alcohol advertising has been banned, no appreciable difference in rates of alcohol problems has been detected.

An antipathy to alcohol advertising, however, is common and
understandable among recovering alcoholics. A large portion of the
anti-advertising contingent are recovering alcoholics. For them,
advertising may well be a factor in the pathology of their former
addiction. The advertisements may, in this sense, be triggers used by

heavy drinkers to justify their drinking. But we don't run our world solely for a minority. We don't stop candy or ice cream ads because some people are diabetic.

Blane and Hewett in _Alcohol and Youth_ determine, "There is virtually no evidence that advertising starts anyone drinking. Rather, peer, and parental influences are the most important factors for explaining why teenagers drink." Pittman and Lambert in _Alcohol, Alcoholism and Advertising_ find, "No scientific evidence exists that beverage alcohol advertising has any significant impact on the rate of alcohol abuse and alcoholism in the American society."

This is the real world of the media. To put it mildly, drinking suffers a very bad public image. This constant browbeating fosters continuing negative images in the American mind. Media industry· trade agencies should do some real soul searching about their handling of a product that means so much to so many of their readers, listeners and viewers. And to their advertising revenues.

Research Finding 10.5

Alcohol is the most controlled product available.

> _Although we should not lose sight of the need to regulate advertising, nor should we expect that, by doing so, we will have much impact on the extent and severity of alcohol problems..._
> **O. Jeanneret**
> _Alcohol and Youth_

Well planned alcohol advertising offsets the massive editorial negativism to some degree, but it is hardly the dominant force suggested by Mosher and Wallack. The authors conclude their study, not surprisingly, by recommending more advertising constraints:

> The policy question we address is distinct from these issues and quite specific: what is ATF's [Bureau of Alcohol, Tobacco and Firearms] legal mandate and how is it related to the public's need for accurate and informative alcohol advertising as a part of a government policy to reduce alcohol-related problems.

The Bureau of Alcohol, Tobacco and Firearms already does severely restrict the industry. It does this overtly, in terms of what can go on a label or in an ad, and by intimidation in maintaining that the industry cannot say anything whatsoever about a therapeutic aspect of their products. Advertisers are enjoined by BATF rule-making from implying curative, therapeutic, caloric or nutritional values—though those features may be found in profusion.

Here is an example of a line that was denied in an advertisement. "Relax with a _brand or product name_" was held by BATF, "to be curative or therapeutic because the act of relaxing would have resulted from consuming the alcoholic beverage." Physiologically, alcohol is a depressive. Therefore it relaxes. That's science, but it is not permitted in the world of advertising.

It may have many shortcomings and it may lack propriety or good taste at times, but alcoholic beverage advertising does not suffer from lack of control. Wet T-shirt promotions and rock star look-alikes notwithstanding, nothing in our free-market society is more tightly monitored.

Apart from emotional arguments, what is the real impact of advertising. Sobel studied reactions of college students in "Effects of Television Programming and Advertising on Alcohol Consumption on Normal Drinkers" and concluded, "The results provided no support for the widely held assumption that drinking scenes in television programs or televised advertisements for alcoholic beverages precipitate increased drinking by viewers." When is the last time you heard such talk from NIAAA, DHHS or CSPI?

The most compelling evidence that advertising does not affect the amount of drinking exists just north of the border in Manitoba and British Columbia. DHHS, NIAAA or CSPI never mention the Canadian experience when they call for new advertising restrictions. In these Canadian provinces, very much akin in lifestyle to many states, total elimination of alcohol advertising failed to achieve improvements in alcohol-related problems or even rates of drinking. In "Will Restrictions on Alcohol Advertising Reduce Alcohol Consumption?" Ogborne and Smart summarize what happened:

> The effects of restrictions of alcohol advertising in Manitoba, Canada and in the United States are examined using statistical data on alcohol consumption. The relationships between consumption and alcoholism rates for the U.S. and advertising regulations were very weak and not statistically significant. Subsequent to a restriction on beer advertising in Manitoba, beer consumption in that province rose at a similar rate as in a control province of Alberta [where advertising was

allowed]. It is considered unlikely that restrictions will reduce consumption.

Similarly, Kohn and Smart find in "The Impact of Television Advertising on Alcohol Consumption:"

> The results of the present study were interpreted as not supporting strong concern about television advertising's impact on immediate consumption of available alcohol....Over the entire experiment, advertising had no significant effect on total beer consumption.

Strickland, Finn and Lambert in "A Content Analysis of Beverage Alcohol Advertising" conclude:

> The results of the thematic and human-models analyses and the analysis of advertising by type of magazine, in general, provide little support for the claims that supposedly vulnerable groups (blacks, women, youth) are being disproportionately targeted in massive magazine advertising programs, at least through the portrayal of relevant models and the concentration of advertising in certain magazines.

Wine coolers prove the point that advertising follows sales.

The impact of alcohol advertising is not a closed issue. This book does not argue the case that advertising lacks impact. Lacking impact, there would be no ads. In long-term comparisons between ads and consumption, Franke and Wilcox, in "Alcoholic Beverage Advertising and Consumption in the United States, 1964-1984," present the little understood function of advertising as a _following_ rather than a _leading_ medium:

> In relating advertising expenditures to consumption levels, it is difficult to show that advertising "causes" consumption. It is often the case that consumption "causes" advertising, in that many leading consumer advertisers use a percent of past sales or anticipated sales in setting advertising...Nonetheless, these findings increase the plausibility of the argument that reductions in wine and distilled spirits advertising would bring about reductions in consumption, while suggesting that reductions in total beer advertising would have little effect on beer consumption.

Coolers are a good example of how commercial advertising _follows_ rather than leads the consumer. There was a meteoric rise of the wine cooler sales without a dollar's worth of advertising. Millions

of case sales developed in the first year of distribution. Large
producers saw the opportunity and poured millions into the creation
of new cooler brand names. In the space of two years, the major
companies with big advertising budgets like Seagram and Gallo took
over dominating shares of the market. Bourgeois and Barnes frame
the argument more concisely in "Does Advertising Increase Alcohol
Consumption?" with a subtitle, "In Beer, Yes; in Liquor, No." But for
both it was of little influence. " The authors reviewed the literature and
evaluated nearly every influence of alcohol advertising and
concluded:

> The critics of beverage alcohol advertising are of the
> opinion that the volume and content of advertising for
> beer, wine and spirits leads to increased demand...The
> major conclusion is that many factors influence alcohol
> consumption levels. This study produced little evidence
> to support the claim that the level of per capita
> consumption of alcoholic beverage in Canada is in-
> fluenced by the volume of advertising for those
> products.

In the real world, advertising marries a brand name to a human
desire. In the real world, human beings have aspirations and
appetites, some good and some excessive, and advertisers vie to fill
the vacuum. Chafetz reminds us, "The simple fact remains that many
cultures were misusing alcohol, and experiencing severe problems
as a result, centuries before advertising existed."

Research Finding 10.6

Warning labels would be anti-alcohol propaganda.

> *What you have is a small group of people*
> *at the policy level who have a platform*
> *from which to speak. They shrewdly use*
> *press releases...but they haven't got a lot of backing.*
> **Interview with Karst J. Besteman**
> Alcohol and Drug Problems Association

Warning labels and warning posters for alcohol are media
instruments. That's why Strom Thurmond routinely introduces into
the national Congress legislation which would require health
warnings. New temperance has this legislation as its highest priority.
State legislatures like California, Wisconsin and Massachusetts also
have warning label legislation. The pressure is building for a

compromise in Congress. For the record, here is the judgment of the marketing professionals from the *Proceedings of the Human Factors Society* in 1984:

> In spite of the widespread use of warning labels, searches for scientific evidence have yielded virtually no reason to anticipate that warning labels on consumer products serve as effective mechanisms to increase safety. We have yet to identify a product that, when evaluated in an unbiased manner, clearly demonstrates the utility of any warning label which was placed on the product.

That should be sufficient to dissuade legislators. The little messages don't work. Failure Analysis Associates conducted another study called "Product Information Presentation, User Behavior and Safety" which found:

> Findings are examined for implications in the design and use of on-product warning labels for improved product safety through modification of user behavior. No scientific evidence was found to support the contention that on-product warning labels measurably increase the safety of any product.

These authors cited definite reports on the lack of impact of similar warnings on cigarettes, diet soft drinks, hammers, road signs, lawn mowers, poison containers, adhesives, industrial materials and seat belts. What is known now is that commonly used items cannot effectively convey health warnings.

The April issue of *Beer Perspectives* reports that the label issue is hot in Congress. "More than a dozen co-sponsors have been lined up to date, and over 50 national, regional and state organizations have been enlisted by NCA and CSPI as allies in the drive." In addition to declaring my opposition to Congress on labels, I wrote the major spirit, beer and wine producers in 1986 suggesting that they could easily obtain thirty or forty million petition signers in the bars and liquor stores of America who would object to such wording on their favorite selections. I haven't heard from the producers either.

Research Finding 10.7

Alcohol advertising could
be a moderating influence.

*They say society is pushing this drug on them
and they are powerless to resist. I don't buy
that kind of line. A person is exposed to
100,000 beer commercials in his or her lifetime.
But we are exposed to hundreds of thousands of
other commercials and we surely do not become
everything we are exposed to by the mass media.*
Interview with David J. Pittman, Ph.D.
Washington University

Richman and Warren in "Alcohol Consumption and Morbidity in
t

he Canada Health Survey" opened an interesting door for future
research:

> Other aspects of beer drinking lifestyles may enhance
> the health of beer drinkers indirectly, through their
> effect on more distal variables. Within that context, the
> current trends towards "lifestyle-oriented" beer adver-
> tising might well merit special consideration. Healthy
> lifestyles, in particular, fitness and friends are increas-
> ingly present in television portrayal of beer-drinking
> lifestyles. Rarely do these commercials associate nega-
> tive lifestyle habits, e.g. smoking, drug use, stress,
> obesity with the consumption of beer. Additionally,
> there is evidence that the general population is both
> aware of and sensitized to, the pronounced lifestyle
> focus of beer advertising. Thus the positive health levels
> of beer drinkers observed in this study may be simply
> mute testament to the success of mass advertising —
> with healthier individuals increasingly indicating beer
> as their beverage of choice.
>
> Alternatively, beer advertising may even contribute to
> the adoption and maintenance of positive lifestyle
> behaviors, by encouraging individuals who consider
> themselves beer drinkers to emulate the healthy life-
> styles shown in the advertisement.

This is not a beer commercial. These are scientists who found
that beer drinkers had "significantly lower rates of morbidity than
expected." In other words, beer drinkers in Canada are healthier than
others who do not drink. If we are truly interested in better health, we
ought to find out why.

Summary of Chapter 10

The media's trouble with alcohol lies in the public perception of the role of alcohol in society. If alcoholic beverages are dastardly addictive drugs, no advertising should be permitted—the position of CSPI. If alcohol is a pleasant and harmonious component of an adult lifestyle which benefits society, producers should be permitted to sing out the merits of their products in a competitive forum.

In 1974, Fallding wondered in *Drinking, Community and Civilization* whether our people were once again ready for such a consensus such as they enjoyed before temperance:

> It is a crucial problem of this study to ask what sense of meaningfulness in drinking has been recovered by modern Americans in view of this history. It seems not impossible, if the compounded distortions I allude to did occur, that meaningfulness in drinking would only be recovered after a time of searching.

If we moderates cannot convince the media to cover our side of the drinking story, the prohibitionists will have their way once again.

11

New Perspectives on
Drinking and Driving

*Drunk driving is not the activity of a small
deviant minority. Vast numbers of the public
engage in it: a recent Gallup Poll
commissioned by the Wall Street Journal
found that 80 percent of American
business executives admit to the offense.*
H. Laurence Ross, Ph.D.
Deterring The Drinking Driver

*The exaggerations of the alcohol aspect also reduce
the credibility and, consequently, the supportability
of programs to control the alcohol-involved crashes.*
Richard Zylman
"OVERemphasis on Alcohol May Be Costing Lives"

*One or more drugs were detected in 81 percent of
the 440 male drivers, aged 15–34, killed in
motor vehicle crashes in California; two or
more drugs were detected in 43 percent.*
Allan Williams
Drugs In Fatally Injured Young Male Drivers

Nearly everyone who drinks in America drives. That's how they get home from the party or restaurant.

Drunk driving and underaged drinking and driving unfurl the red flag of emotion. This short chapter cannot do justice to these complicated and controversial subjects. But it can jar your own reasoning by bringing out some facts and statistics often lost in the welter of emotion.

The recent tragedy of over twenty Kentucky youngsters burning to death in a school bus emphasizes the stark reality of the problem. The driver of the pickup, going the wrong way, had a Blood Alcohol Content (BAC) of 0.10.

Research Finding 11.1

Temperance plays on the fear of drunk driving.

The problem is the transportation system
The possibilities for ameliorating the problems of
drinking and driving become clearer if the nature
of the problem to be addressed is redefined. I suggest
two definitions that can lead to promising options for
policy: one sees the drinking-and-driving problem as
part of the general problem of controlling alcohol use,
and the other sees the problems as a part of the
general problem of controlling the consequences
of traffic crashes.
H. Laurence Ross, Ph.D.
Deterring the Drinking Driver

Mankind when tipsy has always faced the risk of injury or death on uncertain and precipitous pathways. When employed as the common transport, the horse introduced stability on the roadway but a new peril of falling from an animal's back at full speed, drunk or sober. However, an intoxicated rider seldom injured or killed others. The horse was sober and in command of his or her faculties. Motorized vehicles introduced a new world of mayhem, one which we have yet to adjust to.

Injuries and fatalities under the influence of alcohol, or any other drug, are part of a larger problem involving the way we move ourselves about in a highly mechanized, industrialized society. James Bush in a letter to the editors of the *New York Times* raises critical issues about this brave new automobile world:

> In suburban communities, at least 40 percent of police work is directly related to automobiles, as is one-sixth of fire department runs...drain construction is usually about 40 percent of road building...some suburban communities devote as much as 4,000 square feet of paved road and parking surface for each automobile...[Other issues include] premature obsolescence of the streetcar era...worldwide stagflation caused in part by a fourfold increase in U.S. of imports in the nine years after domestic oil extraction peaked in 1970.

Drunk-driving fatalities and injuries are part of a much broader problem. Vehicles today dominate society when it should be the other way round. Driving While Intoxicated (DWI) fatalities won't be solved by ritualistic vendettas against alcohol, or any other drug. Fatality and injury statistics involving stone–cold sober drivers are seldom mentioned in the anti-alcohol literature. Victims of sober driver accidents are just as dead and those maimed in sober driver accidents hurt as much. Mothers Against Drunk Driving (MADD) represent only half a loaf.

I grew up in that heady time when Henry Ford decreed that the automobile should be available to the common man. My first car was purchased (in my mother's name) at age sixteen, and I had bought and sold probably twenty cars by the age of twenty-one. Those Model A Fords and four cylinder Plymouths dominated my teen years, providing me access to an enticing adult world of power and mobility. I still am in awe of the power, grace, elegance and, yes, of the sexual aura, of a classic automobile.

Michael Marsden in his column "Headlights" in *Motor Trend* provides a modern perspective, the visceral McLuhanesque reality that the accelerator is in reality an extension of the foot itself:

> Our automobile is our passport to the imagined frontier. The driver's seat is no mere transportation bench — it is a fantasy couch on which we live out our dreams of true freedom and mobility — to be free to go where we want, when we want, and in the style we want. What more could you ask from a machine that has become our friend?

Research Finding 11.2

Our highways are the safest in the world.

A recent announcement by the U.S. Department of Transportation showed that in 1985 the traffic fatality rate on U.S. highways declined to the lowest level in history.
U .S. Department of Transportation

Fact 1. Americans are the safest drivers in the world.

Few people seem to know that. When placed in the perspective of two deaths for one hundred million miles traveled, the trade-off in accidents and fatalities seems more tolerable. Nigeria has 33 deaths, Belgium has 6, Chile 17, Portugal 11, Finland 3 and Great Britain 2.3

deaths per hundred million miles traveled. The progress accomplished over the past three decades has been remarkable. It has used what is called a "systems approach," one that involves all segments of the community. Highway deaths have dropped fifty percent since 1966.

Fact 2. Drunk driving deaths are declining.

As bad as they are, both the incidence and the rates of drunk driving are going down. The Insurance Institute for Highway Safety (IIHS) newsletter *Status Report* for January 24, 1987 reports:

> The number of motorists who drive on weekend nights after drinking substantial amounts of alcohol has decreased sharply in the United States, according to the first national roadside survey of this issue since 1973.
>
> Thirty-seven percent fewer drivers in 1986, compared with 1973, had blood alcohol concentrations (BACs) of 0.10 percent or greater — high enough for driving to be defined as a criminal offense in ll states. Thirty-nine percent fewer drivers had BACs of 0.05 to 0.10 percent, which is enough to impair driving and lead to arrest in many states.

This same agency conducted recently a random sampling of 317 on-duty truck drivers and found only two drivers, less than 1 percent, were confirmed as having low levels of blood alcohol. Twenty-nine percent had used marijuana, cocaine or prescription and nonprescription drugs. The report comments:

> Alcohol, the drug whose effects are best known, was found in less than 1 percent of the drivers and in every case the concentration was well below presumptive limits and even below the old 0.04 percent limit for commercial vehicle drivers currently under consideration by the National Academy of Sciences.

Yet another study with IIHS personnel involved an analysis of drugs in the corpses of men aged 15 to 34 in four counties — Los Angeles, Orange, Sacramento and San Diego. The study states, "The major role of alcohol (ethanol) in motor vehicle crashes is well established...The role of drugs other than alcohol — whether prescription drugs, over-the-counter drugs, or illicit drugs — is not established." Their findings raise serious questions about the direction of future traffic safety programs in a polydrug culture. The results were:

> One or more drugs were detected in 81 percent of 440 male drivers aged 15–34 killed in motor vehicle crashes in California; two or more drugs were detected in 43 percent. Alcohol, the most frequently found drug, was detected in 70 percent of the drivers; marijuana was found in 37 percent, and cocaine in 11 percent...Except for alcohol, drugs were infrequently found alone; typically, they were found in combination with high blood alcohol concentrations.

There are many drivers on the road who are affected by too much alcohol, too much fatigue, and too many other legal and illegal psychoactive substances which impair the ability to brake and avoid collisions. A survey in 1986 performed at the University of Michigan found that one-third of Michigan men aged 18 to 24 admitted to, at times, driving after having too much to drink. Based on a sample of 500,000 people, the Michigan study estimated a total of one million drunk-driving episodes in a month. According to these figures, 6,250 full-time police officers would be required to police Michigan streets if a campaign were attempted to eliminate all drunken drivers.

Given the fact that we are dealing with millions of drivers who ingest many legal and illegal mind-altering substances, we are progressing substantially in making our highways safe for travel. The problem is the vehicle and its unencumbered use by all of us at any time of day in any sort of condition. The problem is motorized transportation, not simply alcohol.

Fact 3.   The states with the lowest per capita of alcohol consumption have some of the worst fatality records.

Earlier alcohol-use data linked restrictive alcohol control laws to higher rates of alcohol-related disturbances. The same relation is borne out when per capita consumption is compared to fatalities per 10,000 registered drivers. The February 1987 issue of the _Responsible Hospitality Institute Bulletin_ **reports:**

> ...the states with the lowest fatal crash rate also had a higher per capita consumption, even higher than the total average of 2.617 [per capita alcohol intake.]

The four states with least fatalities — New Jersey, Massachusetts, Connecticut and New York — had one quarter of the rate of fatalities with uniformly higher drinking rates than the four worst states in the comparison—Tennessee, Alabama, Arizona and South Carolina. As the author says, the report is not definitive but it suggests again the shallowness of the control of availability objective simply to lower drinking per capita.

Fact 4.   A high percentage of drunk drivers are repeat offenders.

Any one of us can become intoxicated and endanger society by operating a motor vehicle. But, as with alcoholism and alcohol abuse, most DWIs are people already in trouble from alcoholism, stress, anti-social dispositions or other personal problems. A trade group titled Beverage Retailers Against Driving Drunk (BRADD) commissioned two studies. The second, titled "DWI—Are We Off Track?" contains these statistics:

> Research (both government and independent studies) over the past 20 years shows that 70 to 75 percent of those convicted of driving while drunk have blood alcohol concentrates of at least 0.15 percent and many have levels of 0.20 percent or higher...Half the fatally injured drivers who are legally drunk have blood alcohol contents at or above 0.20 percent...Studies have shown that problem-drinking drivers have other iden-tifiable problems: a record of one or more alcohol related arrests; previous contacts with police or social agencies; reports of marital, employment or social problems.

These repeat offenders are an identifiable sub-culture in our society. A BAC of 0.15 percent requires *10 drinks by a 150 pound person*. The average drinker does not ingest 10 drinks at a sitting. Scoles et al. in "Personality Characteristics and Drinking Patterns of High-Risk Drivers Never Apprehended for Driving While Intoxicated" report:

> There is a surprising consistency with which alcoholism, drug dependency, personality disorders, neuroses and, occasionally, psychotic illnesses are found in those persons apprehended for violation of the vehicle code...In conclusion, the high-risk driver is likely to be married, under 40 years of age, educated, employed in a job earning over $19,000 per year and to have a problem with alcohol, as opposed to other con-trolled substances. In addition, the high-risk driver

appears shrewd, warmhearted, assertive and resource-
ful.

The National Commission Against Drunk Driving "Progress Report" in December 1986 identified the frightening size of this sub-culture which places the entire population at danger:

> Drivers with alcohol problems, very often repeat
> offenders, are responsible for the majority of the
> alcohol-related crashes. The heavy, problem drinker
> fits the description for almost 20 million of some 150
> million licenses drivers.

Fact 5. The NIAAA's claim that half of all traffic fatalities involve intoxicated drivers is a falsehood.

As long ago as 1974, Zylman in "A Critical Evaluation of the Literature on Alcohol Involvement In Highway Deaths" placed the lie to that claim, but the National Institute on Alcohol Abuse and Alcoholism (NIAAA) persists in asserting it to this day:

> The number of traffic deaths "caused by", "related to",
> or "involving" alcohol has been adopted as the key-
> stone to the alcohol counter-measure action and infor-
> mation programs. The statement "half of all traffic
> deaths involve alcohol" appears in one form or another
> in almost every article, radio or TV commercial, or
> public information leaflet on the subject, and figures
> like 27,000, 30,000 or 35,000 are used indiscriminantly
> to dramatize the urgency of the problem...Without
> credibility it is not only ineffective, it is also likely to
> elicit active rejection...*The actual number of alcohol re-
> lated traffic deaths is not known and even the best ap-
> proximations are subject to question*. [Emphasis added].

Table 3 from the National Commission report shown below was taken from thirty-seven "good reporting states" and is therefore as accurate as any data available. Note that the percentage of intoxicated drivers dropped from 30 percent in 1982 to 25 percent in 1985.

Also note that the largest percentage of deaths occur in the 21 to 24 age span attesting to the fact that Congress should have raised the drinking age to 25 if it seriously believed raising the age would solve the problem.

In the IIHS newsletter, Brian O'Neill, president of the Insurance Institute for Highway Safety, estimates that in 1984 not 25,000 as reported by NIAAA but, "...about 12,000 to 13,000 deaths could be attributed to drivers with BACs of 0.10 or higher." Ross and Hughes in "Drunk Driving—What Not To Do" writing in 1986 found:

TABLE 3
Intoxicated Drivers Involved in Fatal Crashes By Age Group

Year	All Ages[1] #	15–17 #	18–20 #	21–24 #	25–34 #	35+ #
1982	16,790	570	2,530	3,600	5,190	4,460
1983	15,830	510	2,280	3,290	5,030	4,290
1984	15,730	470	2,170	3,340	5,030	4,220
1985	14,650	410	1,760	3,180	4,920	4,000

Year	All Ages[2] %	15–17 %	18–20 %	21–24 %	25–34 %	35+ %
1982	30	20	35	40	35	21
1983	29	18	34	39	35	21
1984	27	16	31	37	33	19
1985	25	13	27	35	32	19
Percent Change 1982–1985*	-17	-32	-24	-13	-8	-10

Although drunk driving poses risks to the driver and others, the popular impression of the number of traffic deaths it causes is exaggerated. It is frequently stated that alcohol is responsible for 50 percent of U.S. traffic fatalities, but that statistic has no solid foundation. The figure includes all traffic deaths in which anyone directly involved has consumed any alcohol. That means cases of drunken pedestrians who are killed by sober drivers, or accidents involving a drunk driver properly stopped for a red light and hit by a reckless but sober motorist...Perhaps the most accurate estimate, from the National Academy of Sciences, attributes roughly 25 percent of fatal accidents to intoxication.

Fact 6. Drunk drivers primarily kill themselves and their friends.

Data developed from the U.S. Department of Transportation and reported in the BRADD publication *Straight Talk About the Drunk Driving Problem* by C. F. Livingston, demonstrates the following percentages of individuals involved in alcohol-related traffic fatalities in 1985:

Drunk drivers	52 %
Passengers of drunk drivers	20 %
Drunk pedestrians	11 %
Innocent victims	17%

Every death or injury, drunk or sober, is a lamentable statistic. Livingston's data gathered from six areas of the country is instructive in illustrating that this large sub-culture of drivers endangers first themselves, then their friends and family, and finally society as a whole. They are a segment that specifically and deliberately overdrinks:

> DWI drivers who are arrested consume far more than the social drinking norm. Eleven or more drinks on one occasion would have to be consumed to reach the average BAC of those arrested for DWI (applicable on basis of the fact that most DWIs are men — about 90 percent — body weights of 160 pounds or more being normal). BACs of .18 to .20 are <u>average</u> for this group of offenders; it must be realized that even BAC legal <u>minimums</u> of .10 require <u>abnormal consumption of alcohol</u>.

Much of what we know about our driving problems is ignored in terms of legislation and public policy. A special report in the *Seattle Times* gave the following statistics which might be typical in any other state:

> Men are twice as likely to be killed in accidents as women. The danger age group is 20 to 34. More people are killed in July. Alcohol is involved in one-third (not 50 percent) of these fatalities. Most deaths occur between 11 p.m. and midnight. More die on weekends. Motorcyclists die at ten times the rate of auto drivers.

We know a great deal about the populations that cause the most problems but we are loathe to restrict them. We must find new strategies which focus on the offender, not on the beverage.

Research Finding 11.3

DWI offenders are a small drinking population.

> *...Alcohol/drug-related accidents are highly*
> *concentrated in a small segment (about 20 percent)*
> *of the young adult population which is involved*
> *in multiple illicit drug use and criminal behavior.*
> **1983 National Youth Survey**

As with adults, drunk-driving teenagers are a subculture in the entire population. Should everyone have the privilege of driving? At any hours? Under all circumstances? Without any specific education on drinking aside from "Just Say No?" Pertinent questions.

A decade ago, in a thoughtful article on temperance and the disease concept of alcoholism titled "The Discovery of Addiction", H. Levine posed a vital question that still remains unanswered in 1988:

> The different conditions facing people in the 20th century, in particular the obviousness of giant organizations and of the degree of human interdependence, begin to make it possible to see the "social" nature of what had formerly been viewed as "individual" problems...Take, for example, the issue of drunken drivers. An individualist perspective looks at those who have lost their ability to "manage" in the world because of drink; an alternative view focuses, instead, on the interaction between social life and transportation. If drinking is "normal" activity, then perhaps the phenomenon of drunken drivers is not a drinking problem but a transportation problem. Indeed, if one thinks about it, we live with a bizarre system of transportation: In order to get from one place to another, people are required, at all hours of the day and night, to execute high-speed maneuvers, through a maze of obstacles, with a ton of machinery.

Consider the primary focus of automobile advertising. Promised speed with promised control. Do we really need to achieve the speeds currently in vogue to maintain transportation efficiency in the industrial and commercial age?

Penalties alone haven't solved the driving problems anywhere. Ross in *Deterring the Drinking Driver* reports:

In 1985, a review of the available studies published in the *Journal of Studies on Alcohol* indicated that increasing the penalties for drunk driving was almost totally ineffective...Publicity campaigns and stepped up police activity, combined with harsher punishment, may reduce the amount of drunk driving for a short time. In the long run, however, certainty of punishment is the only true deterrent, and the actual chances of being caught while driving drunk are on the order of one in a thousand such trips.

Ross conjectures that many other techniques could be helpful, such as better training of servers and bartenders, expanded public service broadcast campaigns, and assuring certainty of punishment. But each of these represent band-aids on a festering sore — that of mandated speed and safety provisions for all vehicles.

Seat belts reduce deaths dramatically, but they are only indifferently enforced in this nation. Speed kills with unerring precision, yet our political structure opts for raising speed limits. O'Neill of the IIHS reports flatly, "The facts are compelling. Fifty-five is one of the most effective death and injury preventing programs ever implemented...Fifty-five was responsible for saving 2,000 to 4,000 lives in 1983; it also saved 2,500 to 4,500 serious, severe, and critical injuries." Yet, Congress passes increased speed rules which are already showing a dramatic increase in highway deaths.

The National Commission Against Drunk Driving held a recidivism conference in September of 1986. Ross is quoted in the summary of proceedings. "Passage of legislation requiring air bags would save more lives than all the drunk-driving laws in existence."

Zylman in "OVERemphasis on Alcohol May Be Costing Lives" asks whether the concentration on alcohol-caused and alcohol-related vehicle crashes is not diverting us from attacking the larger transportation issues:

This still represents many unnecessary and tragic deaths. It is important to recognize, however, that if the figure is closer to 30 percent, as my review indicates, than to 50 percent or more as is popularly believed, there must be other major causes for traffic deaths. If we continue the obsession with alcohol as the major cause of crashes, trying to attribute ever increasing numbers of traffic deaths to alcohol when the actual figure is around 30 percent, we may be blinding our-

selves to the possibility that there are other major
causes of traffic crashes responsible for the other 70
percent of all traffic deaths, some of which may even be
more important than alcohol.

Research Finding 11.4

Teenage drunk driving is a unique problem.

> *In 1985,there were 7,462 deaths associated with
> young drinking drivers. This total is down 8 percent
> from the 1984 total of 8,132 and 11 percent from the
> 1977 total of 8,402 deaths. However, it is a 25
> percent decrease from the nine-year high of
> 9,918 deaths in 1980.*
> **Trends in Alcohol-Related Fatal
> Traffic Accidents, DHHS, 1987**

Teenage drunk driving should be treated apart from intoxicated
driving in the general population. Teen drinking is more of an
expression of rebellion and confusion than that of the confirmed,
habituated drinker. Teenage drinking and driving both are erratic,
episodic and highly emotional occurrences.

Nothing in the alcohol spectrum is more loaded with emotion
than teenage drunk-driving. The statistics are shocking and
ubiquitous. *Teenage Drinkers* published by the Insurance Institute for
Highway Safety recites the familiar data, "About half of all deaths of
16–19 year olds from all causes involve motor vehicles...The
nighttime fatal crash rate per mile for 16-year-old boys is four times
their day rate and many times the day rate for girls...The economic
costs also are staggering. About a billion is spent annually to treat
and rehabilitate healthy young people who have been injured in
crashes."

Of course, one seldom considers that 16–19 year olds don't die
much for conventional disease reasons. Logic would have accidents
assuming the largest causal share. But logic does not vitiate the
terrible waste of young people.

Waller in "Spitting In The Ocean" from *DWI Reeducation and
Rehabilitation Programs* flatly debunks the efficacy of alcohol
education as assigned through DWI laws. He seconds Straus'
opinions that society has conditioned the young, particularly the
young male, to drink illicitly:

Realistically, what we spend on educating the public
about the hazards of drinking and driving is minuscule
compared to the dollars committed to communicating
contradictory messages. The young male is caught in
the middle of this hypocrisy, and we are failing
especially to provide adequate guidelines for this most
vulnerable group...The fact remains that driving after
drinking is still widely accepted in the American
society...Or, we might add, as a young male who would
not be living up to the expectations our society has been
communicating to him through his lifetime.

Wagenaar in _Alcohol, Young Drivers and Traffic Accidents_
argues for a more enlightened scenario that would inculcate alcohol
into the social life of young people on a more gradual basis allowing
for a transition from abstinence to total liberty:

Perhaps a differentiated drinking-age policy should be
implemented, gradually allowing youth more freedom
in their use of alcohol as they approach the age of
twenty-one. For example, youth might be allowed to
consume alcohol in their own homes under parental
supervision at any age; consumption in a restaurant
under parental supervision might be allowed for those
over the age of sixteen; drinking under adult (not
limited to parental) supervision might be allowed at age
eighteen.

It is not simply beating a dead horse to once again raise these
issues now that the Congress has bludgeoned the states into a
common twenty-one age. Very soon the consequences of that
ill-considered, but cardinal objective of control of availability, will bear
its fruits of more death and destruction. Wagenaar concludes that
despite the "...potential positive functions of alcohol...It is also clear
that the benefits of alcohol use among youth are diffuse and difficult
to quantify, whereas the tally of deaths, injuries, property damage,
and social disruption that result from drinking continues to
accumulate."

Some states, Wisconsin as example, are reconsidering the
wisdom of raising the drinking age to twenty-one. Even though they
would face loss of highway funds, there is evidence of increasing
misuse of alcohol by the 19 to 21 age group. Roberts et. al. in "An
Evaluation of the Impact of RAising the Minimum Drinking Age from
19 to 21 in Wisconsin" finds:

The annual incidence of liquor law violations among the 18 to 20 age group more than doubled between 1984 and 1986, indicating that the age group which was the target of the drinking law change still continues to use alcohol and/or to provide it to other minors.

A spokesman for the Wisconsin Tavern Association is quoted in *The Milwaukee Journal* as commenting, "People are finally beginning to realize that it was wrong to take young drinkers out of supervised settings." While the report shows a drop in fatalities in that age group, there are drops also in the surrounding age groups indicating the national downward trend is more than a consequence of the new law.

To assume that young adults are incapable of self-discipline in alcohol consumption is to disparage our entire educational system. Instead of "Just Say No," perhaps at long last we should take more seriously the responsibility of teaching *responsible drinking.*

Research Finding 11.5

Raising the minimum purchase age was a mistake.

> *So, what we have is a federal government of limited powers but proving that the limited powers themselves are so great that there is more power than limits.*
> **Mark Meierhenry**
> Attorney General, South Dakota

NIAAA statistics verify that one third of adolescents aged 16 to 18 drink regularly. Few if any of these youngsters will give up drinking when they turn 19 simply because the practice is now officially illegal. This is a social fact that no amount of wishful thinking can alter. Even those who pushed intellectually, emotionally and legislatively for the raising do not hold forth such hopes.

Williams in "Raising the Legal Purchase Age in the United States" acknowledges the legislation's shortcomings. "Raising the alcohol purchase age is one important way to reduce the problem of alcohol-related motor vehicle crashes, but it must be viewed in perspective. It reduces the problem somewhat within one high-risk, but small, segment of the population, but by no means eliminates the problem in this group."

Teenagers drink mostly in their own homes.

Beck and Simmons in "The Social Context of Drinking among High School Drinking Drivers" recall the fact that, "Evidence presented in NIAAA's *Fourth Special Report to Congress on Alcohol and Health* shows that adolescent drinkers list their own homes as the place where they most frequently drink, usually with friends or peers and followed by parents and relatives." The authors continue:

> Finally, the notion of responsible drinking seems to be called for where students, peer leaders, teachers and parents are educated to the fact that a great percentage of high school students drink, drink to excess upon occasion and drink and drive...Peer-based efforts to instill a sense of moderation or responsibility in alcohol consumption seem more likely to succeed...Indeed our earlier finding with high school students was that alcohol abusers tended to utilize their friends as well as their own experience as credible information sources about alcohol and other drugs, as opposed to their teachers.

Then there is the evidence that raising the age will prove futile, as it has in earlier experiments. Males in "The Minimum Purchase Age For Alcohol and Young-Driver Fatal Crashes — A Long-Term View" reports:

> This study suggests that changes in state MLPAs (Minimum Legal Purchase Age) or in a particular MLPA level have no discernable impact on the larger issue of adolescent drinking — a conclusion based not only on the traffic accident data presented earlier but also on national surveys which show that more than 85% of all teenagers drink, and around 20% admit to drinking in vehicles, in states with MLPAs of 21...While the "not one drop before age 21" argument may have appeal, there is no statistical evidence whatsoever that it produces either responsible attitudes or practices by young people with respect to alcohol.

Studies such as "Raising The Alcohol Purchase Age" by Mouchel, Williams and Zador, have shown that lowering the purchase age, "...increased fatal crash involvement among drivers under the age of twenty-one." Others such as Smith et al. in "Legislation Raising the Legal Drinking Age in Massachusetts from 18 to 20" have found to the contrary. These authors claim, "Our analysis did not reveal a significant difference in single-vehicle nighttime fatal accidents among 16–17 yr olds in Massachusetts and New York after enactment of the law." They found that teenaged drinking-and-driving remained serious problems. And the post-high school age group would have to continue drinking in cars or parks since the control and discipline of legal establishments would remain beyond their legal reach.

We are apparently simply shifting deaths to older age groups.

Perhaps the most compelling research to date was published in November of 1986 through a grant funded by NIAAA. Asch and Levy in "The Minimum Legal Drinking Age and Traffic Fatalities" take to task the whole fabric of the current program being sponsored by the alcohol conservatives and public safety officials. The authors contend:

> Our findings with respect to the MLDA [minimum legal drinking age] and drinking experience are not happy ones for public safety officials. It does not appear that the high fatality risk presented by new drinkers can be ameliorated by raising the legal drinking age. Indeed, it is not clear that increasing the MLDA even from 18 to 21 can be expected to have a consistent effect on overall fatality rates.

The authors note that the new drinking age might alter somewhat the positioning of some fatalities. However, their copious evidence suggests it will merely delay most of the same deaths to older ages since it takes a couple of years of drinking before the drinking and driving is manageable..

> Our observations above indicate that the drinking experience effect erodes quickly; it diminishes sharply in the second year of drinking, and by the third year, no positive effect on fatality rates is discernible...The problem arises not because we permit people to drink when they are "too young"; but rather because we permit them to experience the novelty of "new drinking" at a time when they are legally able to drive. If drinking experience preceded legal driving, a potentially important lifesaving gain might follow. The suggestion that people be permitted to drink before they are permitted to drive, is very likely impractical in social and political terms. But if saving lives is the objective, the data indicate that this type of policy change deserves thought.

Research Finding 11.6

Legal deterrence is the short-range solution.

> *Today there are programs that posit that significant numbers of DWIs are sick individuals who need treatment for alcoholism. Many however are irresponsible people who need to learn to be responsible.*
> **Interview with David J. Pittman, Ph. D.**
> Washington University

Drinking and driving is not uniquely American. It is uniquely associated with motorized societies. Drinking is endemic and, therefore, driving while intoxicated is endemic.

Klein reports In "DWI — Are We Off Track?"on the success of such programs as the Stop–DWI program in New York which successfully focuses on the problem drinker. Mandatory fines are returned to the county in which offenses occur and the bulk of deterrence budgets are allocated to enforcement. Nothing works perfectly, but in New York all persons with at least one prior conviction must be screened.

A survey of over 300 convicted drunk drivers in 1985 revealed over 70 percent were considered problem drinkers. This is an identifiable population and it should be the primary focus of prevention.

City Attorney Ira Reiner in Los Angeles commented in 1984 on the punishment of a California man to his eighth term for drunk driving. The man had been sentenced to ten years, the longest sentence then known. "Nothing works. The only think you can do now is worry more about the public and warehouse him...It's clear he has driven thousands of times under the influence of alcohol to have been caught and convicted on 27 separate occasions. It's astonishing that he hasn't killed someone, but he's just a homicide waiting to happen." The story in the September 29th issue of the *Daily News/Idahoan* goes on to report the offender lost fingers years ago curtailing a career as a pro bowler but raises the proper question, "Lots of people have industrial accidents where they lose a finger or two. That does not excuse a lifetime of endangering other people's lives."

We need to rethink driving privileges from a safety viewpoint.

Professor Ross's global solution to rates of damage would be to broaden the issue by surrounding the driver with a safer vehicle and a safer roadway, thereby reducing the damage.

> This is a very broad goal, and it has the advantage over dealing with more narrowly-defined problems in being relevant to crashes with any number of causes. A vehicle and highway that are safe for a drunk driver are also safe for the driver who has a heart attack, one who dozes off, one who drops his lighted cigarette into his lap, one who fails to see a stop sign or a vehicle approaching from an unexpected angle, etc. This perspective has marked the efforts of the National Highway Traffic Safety Administration since its founding and has led to such innovations as seat belts, air bags, removal or modification of fixed hazards on highways, and other programs with clearly cost-effective results.

This is the real legislative challenge.

Summary of Chapter 11

Evidence shows that the vast majority of people are willing to accept some risks to keep their automobiles. Most use public transportation reluctantly. Despite this, we are gaining on the problems. The systems approach to safety is paying dividends, including a lessening of alcohol-related fatalities.

In *Deterring Drinking Drivers*, Ross argues that deterrence methods today are working and they are getting better. Marshall in "Alcohol and Highway Traffic Safety Efforts in the United States" finds a vastly improving atmosphere under the systems approach:

> Since 1923 when motor vehicle accident statistics were first recorded by the National Safety Council, there has been a steady reduction in the motor vehicle death rate...Members of the Alliance for Traffic Safety believe that this increased reduction in motor vehicle death rate since 1966 was due, at least in substantial part, to the development of a comprehensive, balanced highway traffic safety program or a systems approach.

If we provide no other method for the excessive drinkers or druggers to get from point A to point B, they will continue to endanger us all. If we are serious about curtailing drunk driving, we should abandon the goal of lowering per capita alcohol consumption and begin to attack the real problem of how to move people who are stoned or drunk.

Gusfield, Rasmussen and Kotarba in *The Social Control of Drinking-Driving* concludes that we are not really serious about the issue:

> As one example, take the frequent admonition: "If you drink, don't drive," an admonition that takes no account or leads to any provision of specific alternatives to driving. In studies of drinking-driving and in speaking with officials about the phenomenon we have been struck by the lack of policy, research or even exhortations concerning alternative transportation...The general sense of those we observed that drunk driving is just one of the risks attendant to drinking in Southern California appears as quite rational in the face of the practical alternatives available.

As a seminar leader, I have the responsibility of training bar servers on the use of alternative transportation methods to get intoxicated patrons to their homes, I can report authoritatively that these alternatives are now working effectively in many bars. Taxi pools and free rides are commonly offered by alert managers for tipsy customers. Unfortunately, most drunks turn free rides down. They don't fear getting caught since they know the odds are very low—some estimate as many as one in 2,000 at night. The alternative transportation system is not solution we need.

Punishment Befitting the Crime

There is no deterrent devised yet for the crime of drunk driving. t is obvious that heavy-drinking offenders will continue to drive as long as there are no serious consequences. Let me close with my facetious but half-serious suggestions that I make in my seminars to "solve" the riddle of drinking-driving deterrence.

Solution 1. Confiscate all vehicles in DWI arrests and sell them with the proceeds going to victim families. The first few BMWs, Porsches, and business vans confiscated would alert the audience. Federal authorities confiscate real property in drug busts. Why shouldn't the states follow suit for drunk-driving offenses?

Solution 2. Raise the driving age to 25 or severely restrict driving privileges. By that time, all but the confirmed heavy-drinking crowd have settled down. This would not be a popular move among the younger set, but a variation might be the loss of driving privileges for a year for each under-25 offense.

Solution 3. Provide free public transportation anywhere in major urban areas to anyone who calls in drunk or drugged. The costs for this service would be minuscule compared to the costs of accidents and DWIs.

Solution 4. Stop coddling youth or elders who drive drunk or drugged. Treat them as criminal offenders, as repugnant as child molesters. They are breaking laws and endangering us all. Alcohol and drugs are not the cause. These criminals are.

The likelihood of passage of such novel reprisals in legislative assemblies is not likely, but they would certainly send the message home that society is damn sick and tired of the moral indifference of the drunk driver. As it is, drunk drivers don't think they will be caught. And statistically they won't.

I hope these observations on drinking-and-driving have taken you to another level of consideration of an chronic transportation-related problem. Just as we have an endemic problem of drunks, we have an endemic problem of drunks driving. The percentage of alcohol-related crashes is almost identical to what it was in the 1920s. Since the percentages of abusive drinkers haven't changed very much, the alcohol-related crashes have remained fairly constant.

We haven't invented new solutions, only speedier vehicles.

12

Responsible Selling and
New Opportunities for the Industry

I hear many cry, "Would there were no wine!"
O Folly! O Madness! Is it the wine that
causes this abuse? No. For if you say, "Would
there not wine!" because of drunkards, then you
must go on by degrees, "Would there no night!"
because of thieves, "Would there no light!"
because of informers, and "Would there no
women!" because of adultery.
St. John Chrysostom

What I think their book offers us is the
documentation of our common sense: the only
solution is a total, legally enforced ban on the
advertising or promotion of alcoholic products of any
kind to any group of customers at any time.
Nicholas Johnson
The Booze Merchants

The promotion of alcoholic beverages inevitably involves some social risks. But, overall, the alcoholic beverage industry can be commended for its efforts at responsible selling and abuse prevention.

Alcohol should not be sold as if it was an automobile or breakfast cereal. And, it isn't sold that way. There are many merchandising checks and balances in place at the federal, state and, often, municipal levels. No other commercial product is so excessively governed and taxed as alcoholic beverages.

Government officials closely monitor the advertising, marketing and promotion of wines, beers and spirits. Approval must be sought for everything from the size of the lettering on bottle labels to any special inducements offered by point-of-sale cards. The industry has demonstrated extraordinary citizenship in its concern for the alcoholic and the abuser. The public is largely unaware of the scope and variety of industry sponsored programs supporting responsible drinking. Probably no other industry works so hard, spends so much and gets so little credit for its efforts to prevent abuse.

Since the early 1940s, individual companies and their trade associations have sponsored responsible drinking campaigns. In recent decades, distributors and retailers have expanded on this supplier-based leadership with their own aggressive local prevention programs against drunk-driving and alcohol abuse.

Despite this record of public service, the average worker in the beverage industry is poorly equipped to understand or respond to the alcohol hostility that has developed since the mid-1980s. During a two-decade career as a wine and liquor salesman, I was never given any instruction on alcoholism and new temperance. It's virtually a non-subject in marketing, distributing and retail training. Yet, it would be difficult to assemble a more articulate, outgoing and gregarious group than the men and women of the beverage trade. Once instructed and enthused, this army of informed spokespeople could reach out to the millions of contacts they make each week with the good word about moderate drinking.

This chapter is meant to stimulate industry leaders to consider more cooperative information programs. What is needed today is confrontation and argumentation. What is needed is a strong commitment to survival. The good news is that industry today possesses masterful public information and advertising skills. The question is whether those leaders are willing to exercise the skills and employ the army to that worthy end.

Research Finding 12.1

The alcohol industry is controlled by fifty firms.

> *Alcoholic beverage marketing is a complicated and difficult-to-study subject. The marketing of alcoholic beverages does not take place in a simple system, but instead occurs in a complex environment involving a huge assortment of interacting forces and elements.*
> **Marketing Practices**
> Alcoholic Beverage Industry

The fight against new temperance must be waged by the alcoholic beverage industry. In our free society, it can and should protect its own interests. The response to temperance over the past century has been largely reactive and defensive. It is true that wine, beer and spirit interests have worked with government and private prevention agencies for years in meeting the challenges of alcoholism, drunk driving, fetal alcohol syndrome and the problems of underaged drinking. Without fanfare or credit, major firms have cooperatively funded original research, hundreds of thousands of informative brochures, public service advertisements, billboards, posters and participated in hundreds of study programs. Individually, nearly every large firm has its own staff of prevention experts who are involved in hundreds of prevention and care projects.

Some of these efforts are outlined below. I am aware of no other industry in the world that has contributed so generously and worked so vigorously to allay the damage caused by abusers of its products. Lest this sound like an advertisement itself, I am equally critical of the industry's failure to confront the confounding and continuing problems of temperance. However, there are hopeful signs.

Kennedy in the *Alcoholic Beverage Newsletter* quotes Richard Grindal, adviser to the Scotch Whisky Association in a May 1988 speech, that the present international temperance movement is far more menacing than any in the past:

> It seems that backing for prohibition propaganda is being given secretly through charitable foundations...The foundations give money to alcohol misuse agencies and to selected anti-alcohol individual researchers and through them the propaganda is fed into similar organizations around the world...to the World Health Organization and through the WHO to apparently scientific bodies such as the International Association for Research into Cancer [IARC].

Grindal recounted the coalition of British abuse agencies which had signed a consensus which would exact increased excise taxes, continue restricted hours of service in Britain and impose restrictions on advertising. Correspondence to the *Moderate Drinking Journal* confirms similar movements in Canada, West Germany, Italy, South Africa, New Zealand and Australia.

Less than fifty companies control over ninety percent of your favorite wines, beers and spirits. Decision-making about public information and promotion sits on those few desks.

Consolidation and bigness dominate in business affairs today. For the past fifty years, especially since the advent of television and other mass marketing media, the trend in alcoholic beverages has been toward consolidation. Fewer major firms have gained larger shares of the expanding alcoholic beverage market.

There are some interesting exceptions. Beneath the umbrella of consolidation among old-line breweries (the 2,000 brewing firms of the last century have folded into a dozen or so today), a category of tiny microbrewers has emerged. They serve regional markets with European-style, more heavily flavored beers. Small investor wineries continue to pop up each year in such unlikely places as Scranton, Pennsylvania and Lubbock, Texas. But the big news is big business.

Multi-national, multi-line companies control the business.

Patricia Kennedy reviewed some of these recent amalgamations in *Alcoholic Beverage Newsletter:*

> Heublein bought Almaden; Grand Met bought Heublein. Heublein bought McGuinness of Canada and then sold it. Grand Met bought a piece of Martell. Seagram bought a bigger piece. Allied-Lyons bought all the remaining shares of Hiram Walker. Bacardi Corp. and Bacardi Imports bought all their shares back from Hiram Walker. Heileman Brewery bought Schmidt. Bond bought Heileman. Bond bought a stake in Allied-Lyons. Schenley bought Renfield. Guinness bought Schenley. In fact, Guinness bought and sold all over the world. It has been a year when it really has been difficult to tell the players without a scorecard.

Another Kennedy article cites the world's ten largest purveyors of spirits as Grand Metropolitan's International Distillers & Vintners, Joseph E. Seagram & Sons, Pernod Ricard, Allied-Lyons, United Distillers Group, Martini & Rossi, Brown-Forman, Suntory, Bacardi and James Beam. These large firms represent most of the world's most famous name brands. They also represent all kinds of beverages.

Four of the five big brewers are domestic companies.

The Australian Bond corporation recently purchased the fourth largest American brewery, G. Heileman. The remaining members of the big five brewers are domestically based. Anheuser-Busch, Miller Brewing, Stroh Brewing, the Adolph Coors Company and Heileman Brewing produce over ninety percent of America's beer. The beer market is steady to slightly up in recent years with imports showing double-digit annual growth on a five percent market base. Long time import leader Heineken has given ground in recent years to Corona from Mexico. These two brands account for forty-three percent of all beer imports. The sixty tiny microbrews are a side-show with less than one percent of total consumption.

Two dozen wine firms dominate the trade.

The U.S. domestic wine market fluctuates with the strength of the American dollar. Eighty percent or more of the domestic market is shared by a half dozen producers of jug wines. E. & J. Gallo (including Carlo Rossi), Almaden, Inglenook, Paul Masson and Taylor California labels dominate in the California white wine jugs. This category reached its zenith in 1985 and has been gently sliding since as consumers are upgrading to more expensive varietal wine selections. America's giant wine suppliers are E. & J. Gallo, Brown-Forman, Canandaigua, Heublein, Villa Banfi, and Allied Grape Growers.

Immediately below this high volume level come the familiar premium labels such as Robert Mondavi, Beringer, Christian Brothers, Sebastiani, Korbel, Domaine Chandon, Wente Bros., Charles Krug, Chateau Ste. Michelle, Sutter Home, Meier's Wine Cellars, Sonoma Vineyards, Warner, Weibel, Mirassou and Parducci. Several hundred smaller nationally distributed brands round out the over one thousand commercial wineries around the nation today. As with the spirit and beer firms, only a handful of the major firms can afford the type of national advertising that invokes the wrath of the new temperance movement. While there are over two thousand licensed alcohol producers in the United States, the fifty some companies above supply all but a fraction of the goods.

In recent decades, besides the major market shares taken by French and Italian wine imports, there has been a substantial invasion of foreign capital in American wineries. In recent purchases, Grand Metropolitan-IDV has taken market shares with the purchase of the Almaden, Inglenook and Beaulieu Vineyard brands. Moet-Hennessey pioneered the invasion in 1973 with the establishment of Domaine Chandon in Yountville in the Napa Valley. Piper-Heidsieck purchased Sonoma Vineyards in 1979. Today, Freixenet Spanish champagne maker owns Gloria Ferrer, Suntory owns Chateau St. Jean, and Peter Eckes of West Germany owns Franciscan Vineyards.

Beer is the favorite alcohol worldwide.

As pointed out in chapter 4, drinking patterns vary around the world, but beer is the hands-down favorite alcoholic beverage. *Kennedy Newsletter* reports European consumption at 42 billion liters annually with 60 percent beer, 15 percent wine and 2 percent spirits. A recent *Wines & Vines* summary reported U.S. consumption in 1988 at 2.43 gallons of wine per person, 1.74 gallons of spirituous liquors and 23.7 gallons of beer (85 percent of the total). Over the decade, spirits dropped 11 percent, wine soared 47 per cent and beer increased 13 percent.

Europeans drink considerably more per capita than U.S. imbibers. West Germany quaffs 40 gallons of beer per capita alone, nearly double our 23 gallons. Germany has no marked alcohol abuse problems. In Germany, as in Italy and Spain, alcohol is a food as well as a beverage. Per capita consumption, as usual, is the poorest measurement of real abuse. It's not what people drink, but how they drink that matters.

The point in these references is that several dozen firms control the industry just as a dozen firms control the automobile and videocassette fields.

Research Finding 12.2

Alcoholic beverage producers are under siege.

> *On December 21, the U.S. Court of Appeals for the Third Circuit reversed an earlier decision handed down by the U.S. District Court in February 1987 which had dismissed a suite ruling that a brewery has no obligation to warn customers about possible dangers of alcohol.*
> **Market Watch**

> *The moment you go into courts. The moment there's a prospect of product liability, you have a different modem. You're method of operation has to change.*
> **Interview with John De Luca**
> The Wine Institute

If you conclude, as I have, that alcoholic beverages give more than they take from the society, then you must be concerned for the relative health of that industry. In today's frenetic alcohol-baiting atmosphere, it's producers are rarely viewed as truly concerned citizens. New temperance advocacy has placed the alcoholic beverage industry under virtual siege today. Room in "Public Health and the Organization of Alcohol Production" tells how public health research increasingly places alcohol on a par with illicit drugs:

Viewed in the context of studies of other drugs, perhaps the only surprise concerning the new trend in alcohol studies is how long delayed it has been. Studies of the organization of production and distribution and government controls already form an accepted part of the public health-oriented literatures on tobacco, pharmaceuticals, and illicit drugs.

I suggest that the industry defend itself from that imminent threat by joining the research game. The January issue of *Alcohol Health & Research World* features the role of genetics in alcoholism. In "The Genetic Paradigm" National Institute on Alcohol Abuse and Alcoholism (NIAAA) director Enoch Gordis notes:

The practical issues and the ethics of counseling individuals who may have a genetic predisposition toward alcoholism certainly will be topics for debate. A key research issue for the future will be how successful intervention will be with high-risk youth.

Pursch writes in "Genetics and Environment Play a Part in Alcoholism but Result is the Same:"

The present state of knowledge about alcoholism suggests that alcoholism results from a combination of genetic, familial, cultural and psychological factors.

Those are the information issues that the industry should invest heavily in. If genetics and environment are the primary causes of alcoholism and abuse, the focus for prevention ought to be on the family history of heavy drinkers and environmental factors. What use are warning labels, higher excise taxes, lessened retail availability, if we are dealing with an inherited trait and the response to unsavory environments.

The industry should invest millions of dollars in legitimate, full scale, epidemiological and biomedical projects to prove Gordis and Pursch are right. And that new temperance with its repressive governmental restrictions is wrong. Remember that major foundations and conservative forces are investing millions of dollars in the National Council of Alcoholism and the Center for Science in the Public Interest and other agencies in the pursuit of control of availability. This is a war for the minds of the people, and research projects are the major offensive weapons.

The threat of lawsuits has paralyzed the industry.

The industry itself should encourage the research of the positive aspects of drinking because the hatchets of temperance are out for their collective scalp. In Seattle, two sets of parents have filed suits against seven liquor companies including James Beam, Anheuser-Busch and California Cooler (Brown-Forman) claiming that the consumption of various of their products during pregnancies has resulted in fetal birth defects. The plaintiffs assert that product warning labels should have communicated the dangers of excessive drinking to the two pregnant mothers. A Wilkes Barre, Pennsylvania widow has another suit in process against the Stroh Brewing Company claiming that her husband's death resulted from drinking Old Milwaukee beer which also carried no warnings of its potential hazards.

The widespread coverage of these legal actions tends to reinforce an oppressive image for the producers and one of virtuous innocence for the abusers. Is there no personal fault or responsibility anymore? The producing industries have sent out to physicians, through the Licensed Beverage Informational Council, hundreds of thousands of information brochures about fetal alcohol syndrome and alcoholism. But the producers continue to be the bad guys. The good guys, presumably, are the individuals who, of their own free will, ingest excessive amounts of alcohol.

The threat of lawsuits are particularly bothersome to the larger firms because of what plaintiff lawyers call "deep pockets." The incessant campaign of vilification by major agencies such as NIAAA, the Center for Science in the Public Interest (CSPI), the National Council on Alcoholism (NCA) and others have created a crisis atmosphere among producers, and with good reason. Sympathetic juries have made outrageously large awards in recent years in all sorts of liability cases. The larger the company, the more marked the potential for exorbitant awards. This looming crisis was described in a *Barron's* editorial by Robert Bleiberg as early as September, 1984:

> By some standards, indeed, neoprohibition has even uglier implications. In the light of history, of course, both the word and threat tend to be shunned. Nonetheless, as a quick survey of what's going on reveals, the latter-day Carry Nations are making successful assaults throughout the U.S. on the liquor trade...One member of the National Transportation Safety Board recently discarded all pretense. Americans under 21 years of age "will soon be living

under Prohibition." Why not go all the way, he added, (speaking for himself and not the Board), and put the nation's distillers out of business?

BATF rulings constrict industry's ability to respond.

In the *Moderate Drinking Journal,* I have called for a review of the Bureau of Alcohol, Tobacco and Firearm (BATF) ruling on labeling and advertising. It is called "Labeling and Advertising Regulations under the Federal Alcohol Administration Act." I see nothing punitive in the position of the BATF in this matter, only that these regulations, which were last revised in 1984, no longer serve the public. The public is not getting an accurate appraisal of the values and benefits of moderate drinking. The regulations prohibit direct label or media advertising of health and drinking and they should be upheld. They have been extended, however, so that any public airing of valid research data by the industry is also forbidden. I suggest the ruling be changed to permit producers the privilege (the right?) to print and disseminate valid research data found in the professional literature. The industry should be free to engage in the new temperance debate.

As reported in chapter 10, the public hears mostly the bad news. There is little positive reinforcement for the moderate drinkers to offset this blizzard of adverse publicity. Often the charges are salacious and mean-spirited. As example, in his foreword to *The Booze Merchants,* former Federal Communications Commissioner Nicholas Johnson echoes a common theme that beverage producers are deliberate corruptors of public morals:

> Although marketing executives profess the contrary, only they will be shocked by the rather obvious finding that the industry is—in the same way and for the same reasons as the heroin dealer—pushing drugs to addicts....Of course alcoholics are not the only targeted audience....Yes, the industry is trying to increase sales in every possible market—heavy drinkers, light drinkers, young people, women. And it is succeeding. Advertising pays. Sales are up. Its markets are expanding.

Mendelson and Mello in *Alcohol Use and Abuse in America* suggest that prohibition forces today, as in the early years of this century, are constituted of groups of like-minded populists in many nations. They see in government control the enforcement of moral imperatives unachievable in human affairs. Unfortunately, one of the attributes of freedom is the ability to make bad choices. Individuals do choose often to ruin or squander their lives in any number of excesses, overdrinking among them. The authors point to the international sweep of this movement which seeks to stifle alcohol merchandising throughout the world:

> Undoubtedly, many Protestant evangelicals used prohibition as a means to spread salvation, but it seems that the majority of Prohibition supporters were searching for an alternative to the Church's waning moral authority. If the Church could not exert sufficient authority, the alternative was to demand that state governments assume the role of moral steward....
> During the first quarter of the twentieth century, almost every European nation joined North America in viewing alcohol control as an issue of urgent social concern.

If new temperance succeeds in destroying beer, wine and spirit businesses through the virtual elimination of all advertising, our lives and well-being as consumers will be proportionately diminished.

In 1987, the legislatures of fourteen states considered twenty-one bills that would have severely impacted the ability of the supplier to reach the consumer. For example, a Massachusetts bill would have prohibited media advertising altogether. One in North Dakota asked the national Congress to restrict advertising. An Ontario, Canada commission recommended health warnings, or what is called counter-advertising in this country. Counter-advertising would require something akin to "Drink my beer but it could be bad for you."

Gavaghan in "Social Aspects of the Alcoholic Beverage Trade" distinguishes between the affirmative use and the chronic problems in drinking:

> We must keep in sight one vitally important fact: there is a durable persistence in social norms and drinking practices, as verified by wide-ranging social research studies. This is generally affirmative and positive. All too many tend to be diverted from this by control of alcohol availability advocacy and the tendency to confuse alcohol abuse with the responsible use of beer, wine and spirits. The responsible behavior of the vast majority of drinkers is all too often overlooked...

There is a concerted, international effort to demean alcohol and its producers. That industry must mount a concerted, international effort to protect the integrity of their products and the viability of those products in the markets of the world.

Research Finding 12.3

Producers have many alcoholism programs.

Over the years since the Prohibition movement began to take hold, the drys have succeeded in forcing these industries into a constantly defensive position.
Interview with Louis Gomberg
Wine Industry Consultant

If you study the record of the industry since repeal, it has been one defensive move after another. This is not surprising since the temperance movement did not dissipate with repeal. One of the better moves of the industry has been an alliance of their trade agencies to address the challenges of alcoholism, fetal alcohol syndrome, drunk driving and consumption by the underaged. This cooperative agency is called the Licensed Beverage Information Council. Its publications and campaigns have been models of cooperative accomplishment between government and business. They have merited praise by government and private alcoholism leaders alike. Intra-industry efforts to abate alcoholism and abuse are many and diverse. I was not surprised recently to discover that the Wisconsin beer wholesalers conducted their first "Know Your Limits" campaign in 1945.

The wine, beer and spirit segments maintain separate codes of good practice encompassing advertising, merchandising and promotions. Naturally enough, they are voluntary codes but there are review boards to evaluate complaints and to bring industry pressures against offenders. Critics of alcohol advertising will never be satisfied, because the product is inevitably shown in pleasant, life enhancing circumstances. If it wasn't, who would buy it?

Trade agencies for each industry produce materials which encourage moderation and responsibility for both retailers and consumers. The Beer Institute is a good example. It has published many pamphlets describing moderation techniques such as "Cheers: Six Keys to Operating Responsible Pubs," and "Think Twice...about Drinking." The institute also promotes an Alcohol Awareness Program in cooperation with the National Beer Wholesalers

Hanging out shouldn't give you a hangover.

Don't drink too much of a good thing.
The Distilled Spirits Council of the United States.

Wet your whistle but don't drown it.

Don't drink too much of a good thing.
The Distilled Spirits Council of the United States.

A word for the wise: "enough."

Don't drink too much of a good thing.
The Distilled Spirits Council of the United States.

A license to drive doesn't mean a license to drink.

Don't drink too much of a good thing.
The
Distilled Spirits Council of the United States.

Association of America, and it has supported many public service announcements, such as the Kristy McNichol radio ads.

Individual brewery activities in the prevention and alcohol abuse fields are numerous. Stroh Brewing Company has provided start-up financial aid to a number of local prevention programs such as BABES, designed to spur alcohol drug education in grade schools. It also supports existing agencies such as the North Conway Institute, a national program for training bar personnel to recognize and curtail overdrinking called Techniques of Alcohol Management (TAM). Other agencies it supports includes Students Against Driving Drunk and the National Commission Against Drunk Driving.

The Adolph Coors Company formed an aggressive Alcohol Abuse and Misuse Task Force to promote programs both within the company and for the general public. William Coors has chaired this signal program. The group maintains many action programs ranging from a Prevention Center in Boulder, Colorado designed to educate high school youth on the dangers of drunk-driving, to an elaborate Wellness Center for Coors employees and their families in Golden on plant property.

Miller Brewing Company has been active on a number of alcohol education fronts under a program called AIM (Alcohol Information from Miller). These include the production of a film called "The Right Move", which is shown at distributor and civic meetings, and the promotion of the Training for Intervention Procedures by Servers (TIPS) seminars throughout their distributor network. Over 8,000 servers have been given this valuable course on how to avoid service to intoxicated customers. The firm has supported public service announcements in cooperation with the National Sheriff's Association and the American Council on Alcoholism. An informative series of pamphlets and a brochure "Somebody Do Something" are also available from Miller Beer.

Anheuser-Busch also promotes the valuable TIPS training program through its distributors and operates a varied program under an Operation Alert banner. It includes both industry and consumer training programs.

The National Beer Wholesalers Association inaugurated a program in 1982 called Preventing Alcohol Abuse (PAA) which functions through its state wholesaler members. The curriculum has separate teaching units from the second through the eleventh grades These were devised by a professional educational consulting firm. Components include how drinking affects the body, how abusing alcohol can impact the organs, how to handle peer pressures to drink while underaged, and a unit designed to get kids and parents involved in problem solving.

The Canadian and U.S. brewing industries have funded the Alcoholic Beverage Medical Research Foundation since 1982. The foundation operates entirely independent of industry. Individual brewers have invested over $10 million for biomedical, social and behavioral research projects. The Canadian brewers have inaugurated a Responsible User Program with a budget in excess of $6 million. The program elements include research, television advertising and local promotions.

The Wine Institute has also been active in alcoholism and social action programs since the end of prohibition. Its advertising code was adopted first in 1978 and has been strengthened periodically. Recently it expanded the code to include wine cooler advertising standards. The Institute co-sponsored two national conferences on drunk driving with the U.S. Department of Transportation and it has played a major role in the expansion of Students Against Driving Drunk (SADD). The Institute supported the move to a standard age of 21 for drinking. It has been active in a wide range of California Employee Assistance programs and other alcoholism committees.

The most recent Distilled Spirits Council of the United States (DISCUS) public service advertising campaign depicts drinkers sharing food and cocktails under such headlines as "The Perfect Party Mix: Good Friends, Good Refreshments, Good Judgment." The ad copy reminds drinkers to, "1. Know your limits. 2. Stay within those limits. 3. If you have too much to drink, do not drive."

DISCUS has long provided leadership in civic and governmental programs designed to reduce alcohol abuse and alcoholism. Since 1960, the agency has funded as many as 450 research projects, including 30 on fetal alcohol syndrome alone. Over two dozen projects seek answers to the genetic link to alcoholism. In 1980, in one of the largest grants ever awarded by private industry, Joseph E. Seagram & Sons gave $5.8 million to Harvard for scientific research in alcoholism. Officers of DISCUS have participated in dozens of seminars and symposia and the agency has been effectively involved in education against abuse in the public school system.

This brief recounting demonstrates a major investment of personnel and funds in allaying the problems of alcohol abuse. These are not window dressing but generous efforts by the producers to ward off the dangers and social problems created by people who abuse their alcohol. The public should be made aware of these efforts. Gavaghan in "Alcohol and Health" writes:

> To summarize, the principles of sound education
> include the need for validated facts, awareness of and
> respect for different viewpoints, and a balanced discus-
> sion of the pluses and minuses of drinking behavior.

Research Finding 12.4

Licensed Beverage Information
Council addresses key abuse areas.

> *The guiding theme of our*
> *programs is that the answer*
> *to our problems lies in education.*
> **Interview with John Burcham**
> Licensed Beverage Information Council

The programs described above are sponsored by producing companies or their trade associations. These wholesaler/retailing enterprises follow the "systems approach" found so successful in reducing highway fatalities and accidents. Many segments of the community are coordinated in a single program. These will range from tax supported agencies and educational institutions to private media and commercial operations. No alcohol prevention program in the world has a better grasp of alcohol issues than the Licensed Beverage Information Council (LBIC). It is a combined service by the ten major alcoholic beverage trade associations. The Council includes manufacturing, distribution and retailing of wine, beer and spirits.

LBIC was formed in 1979 to mount a national campaign on drinking and pregnancy. It was the first formal and effective warning voice for the dangers of drinking while pregnant. It is ironic that today the anti-alcohol forces are using the fetal dysfunction hazard to attack the very industry that first sought to widely publicize its dangers. Paul Gavaghan in "Conveying Information on Alcohol Abuse to the American Public" recounts the philosophy that has undergirded LBIC efforts:

> All of our DISCUS and LBIC activities are based on
> the comprehensive, factual and affirmative approach
> whose value has been substantiated by a 1980 study con-
> ducted by Group Attitudes Corporation. Its review of

mass communications research literature (published throughout the past 35 years) showed that the public is more receptive to positive messages than to scare tactics or the fear approach. We are also guided by the philosophy first expressed in 1969 by a coalition of religious leaders who declared, "The essence of responsibility in the use of alcohol is to make certain, in every situation, that it is used only in a manner to enhance human life."

Gavaghan pointed to the LBIC mandate to develop programs that can have national impact working with and through such established organizations as the American Council on Alcoholism, the Alliance for Traffic Safety, the North Conway Institute, the Alcohol and Drug Problems Association, the National Association of Broadcasters, the Outdoor Advertising Association, the U.S. Department of Transportation and the U.S. Treasury Department.

As many as 3,000 LBIC sponsored Friends Don't Let Friends Drive Drunk outdoor ads cover nearly all states warning against drunk driving. Public service spots appear on hundreds of radio and television stations reaching untold millions of people. The first pregnancy and drinking campaign placed information pamphlets into the offices of over 260,000 physicians. The literature was developed by Dr. Jack Mendelson of Harvard Medical School. The March of Dimes carried the same message through its 935 chapters. Media kits were distributed by LBIC and workshops were sponsored for expectant mothers.

A pamphlet on "The Most Frequently Asked Questions about Alcoholism" was developed with the National Council on Alcoholism and another was prepared on women in the workplace in cooperation with the Alcohol and Drug Problems Association of North America. The agency has a long-running television series in cooperation with the National Football League. The "Know Your Limits" campaign has distributed hundreds of thousands of cards and posters educating drinkers on the safe limits of consumption.

The organized systems approach has been effective.

Gavaghan, secretary treasurer of LBIC, concludes his paper on an upbeat note and with strong support of the systems approach to alcohol problems:

We believe there is cause for optimism. The vehicle-mile death rate in America has dropped significantly over the years. We believe that a disproportionate

share of the drinking-driving problem is caused by a
relatively small number of problem drinker-drivers who
repeatedly compound dangerous driving by drinking
excessively (Bacon 1979). The health approach, including diagnosis and treatment, offers real potential
toward reducing this hard core of the problem. We
believe that the systems approach to reduce excessive
drinking and driving will reduce fatalities and casualties
(Marshall 1982).
We believe that a balanced mix of enforcement,
rehabilitation, and education is needed to deal effectively with this problem and that the 3 main groups of
offenders — chronic problem drinkers, occasional overdrinkers and inexperienced drinkers — each need carefully targeted, different approaches.

In 1980, the Treasury Department commended the LBIC and
called for continued and expanded efforts by the industry to combat
abuse of its products. These information programs cannot eliminate
all abuse or bad advertising or distasteful merchandising. But they
speak highly of the moral responsibilities of the alcoholic beverage
industry. The "devil" is hereby accorded his due.

Summary of Chapter 12 and Recommendations to the Industry

*Finally, although a recent report by the National
Academy of Science noted, "that benefit results from
drinking is usually conceded even by those who are most
appalled by the damages," few studies have tried to
document those beneficial consequences and even fewer
have tried to evaluate how different beverage types
contribute to them.*
Alex Richman, M.D. and Reg Warren, M.D.

*Let us resolve to become more aggressive in our struggle
with those who would put us out of business and deny
the American people freedom and convenience in enjoying
our products in moderation.*
Douglas Metz
Wine and Spirit Wholesalers of America

All of us who drink have a responsibility to help achieve a new
drinking consensus. Those who manufacture, wholesale and retail
alcoholic beverages have the greatest moral and economic

responsibilities of all. Unless the producers get very serious about telling the story, it won't get told.

The industry has nothing to be ashamed of regarding abuse and alcoholism prevention efforts. Its programs evidence a strong commitment to responsible selling as well as to the vexing problems of alcoholism and abusive drinking. What the industry lacks, despite its monumental expenditures on product advertising and public relations, is a defined program for communicating the values and benefits of *responsible* drinking. Its consumers are confused and in need of more basic information on the health and human values of their drinking.

Anything that the industry does in this field will be said to be self-serving. Of course, it will be self-serving. There is nothing wrong with constructive self-interest.

In a recent *Alcoholic Beverage Newsletter* commenting on the shifting fortunes of the multi-national liquor firms, Patricia Kennedy remarked how recent consolidations had shifted majority control of the liquor trade to United Kingdom companies—IDV-Heublein, United Distillers Group (Guinness), Schenley, and Allied-Lyons/Hiram Walker. Perhaps in one of those ironies of history, the Brits and the Scots, who bequeathed us many of our hard-drinking habits, must now lead an international response to the challenge of new temperance.

In another new book on temperance titled *On The Demon Drink* British writer Robinson relates how most people in England are more Latin or continental in their views about drinking and its dangers:

> Perhaps the most notable aspect of Great Britain's relationship with drink is how close it is. We share with more Mediterranean cultures such a longstanding familiarity with alcohol that, unlike the Scandanavians and Americans, we rarely analyse or scrutinize it. Like some national monument, its position in our society is so entrenched that we hardly even notice it. This state may not be as healthy as it first appears.

Robinson describes a real consensus in Britain about alcohol. It belongs. It brings problems but it belongs. That's why the British are well-prepared to lead the fight against temperance for all the English-speaking world. They appreciate what they have, and now control.

I am pleased with the response to the *Moderate Drinking Journal* from Canada, South Africa and Australia. Each of these nations is facing vigorous new temperance drives. From materials which they have sent, I find the anti-alcohol charges and proposed remedial legislation to be nearly identical between nations. Reading all these frightening evidences, there is only one sensible conclusion. The time for concerted action by the industry is at hand. Publisher Philip Hiaring in an editorial "Alarm" in *Wines and Vines* writes:

> The drys have their MADDs, their SADDs, their consumer advocates with pseudo-scientific pressures for warning labels, their infliction of the 21-year-old drinking age that beckons teenagers to taste what is forbidden. Ranged against them? Not a united front. Not by a long shot. Whiskey interests quarrel with wine and beer over relative alcohol content. Growers and vintners in the most vinous state of all — California — fall out over research and promotion issues. In the U.S. wine industry itself the need to bring together the combined clout of 42 states into a national force is largely ignored. Am I pushing the panic button? No. I am being realistic.

As long as modern day drinkers remain confused about the values of moderate drinking, there will remain the threat from organized temperance forces. New temperance is well financed and tightly organized around a defined political agenda.

New temperance should be fought on two fronts. The first line of resistance is to take the public pulpit away from the drys. Through two long decades, the drys have sought and achieved control of many of the tax-supported public health agencies, those of the federal government in particular. Political pressure must be exerted in Washington, D.C., in Albany and Sacramento, and wherever public service has acquiesced to the propaganda of new temperance. These agencies shape the public mind by their control of the statistics. They use selective, pejorative research to buttress the need for severe control measures. This is a political problem. What we should ask for and receive is objectivity and representation of the interests of moderate drinkers who are the majority.

The second phase involves changing the mores of drinking. That will take time and patience, but the proclivity is there and so is the research. The recommendations below would turn the beverage producing arena into a debating forum. It would be provisioned with the latest scientific data and rationale for reasonable drinking. It would return a sense of pride and purpose to the nearly three million individuals who earn their livelihoods in the sale of alcoholic beverages. The struggle belongs to the consumers, the industry and its workers. It is their free choices, their health and future, their security and their sense of civic well-being. Arm them with information, and the battle will be waged and won.

There are many opportunities to inform the hundred million moderates on the benefits of their moderation. They want to shed the mantle of ambivalence and doubt. Many consumers have genuine interest in wines, beers and spirits and in the lore, history, and problems of their production and use. They will be an attentive audience. An informed, committed and enthused sales force from Sydney to Hamburg could meet and match the arguments of the drys with an abundance of science and sociology. New research on the values of drinking is developed daily. These data need wide distribution within the industry.

Trade associations in Washington and San Francisco cannot react to invidious local issues as well as local businesses can. That is the second part of my agenda for industry. Get involved in the states in which you operate. Educate your executives to be able to appear at Rotary and Chamber meetings, to do their stints on the local talk shows and to communicate when necessary with legislators and administrators. Lacking that sense of awareness and self-drive, the political system generally lays back on alcohol issues giving the drys a much larger platform than they deserve.

How should all this be done? I recommend that the makers of wines, brews and spirits take some simple survival steps:

1. Producers of alcoholic beverages in the United States should create a public information bureau along the lines of the newly formed Beverage Alcohol International Information Centre (BAIIC). The new agency should have the primary responsibility of gathering and making available to the public research data on all aspects of drinking. It should not be a trade organization with its narrow product interest. It should not have direct lobbying responsibilities, though its professional staff could be called upon to testify and to provide reports and documentation before public bodies. Think of it as a true Center for Alcohol Science in the Public Interest.

The autumn 1986 issue of IDV World has an interview with Sue Wilkie, BAIIC director. Wilkie describes the Centre's objectives:

> It is definitely not intended that the Centre be a propaganda device for the industry. The emphasis is

always on the provision of information relevant to the
industry and the needs of the people...The Centre will
be used by medical professionals, researchers, social
workers, teachers, educational advisors and many
others. It is important to stress that BAIIC will be
impartial at all times.

The nine founding firms of the London centre are Allied-Lyons,
Anheuser-Busch, Grand Metropolitan, Guinness, Heublein, Miller,
Moet-Hennessy, Seagram and Whitbread. Each of these firms has
major investments in the American market.

2. Producers of alcoholic beverages in the United States should
make a public commitment to fight new temperance on the basis of
sound medical and social research data. They can do this through
their trade agencies and by member firms on every level available in
the society. A major part of this commitment must be to educate
everyone employed in their own ranks and those in other associated
businesses on the values of responsible drinking to the society.

3. The industry's new information bureau should be coordinated
through an interchangeable data base and document library with the
BAIIC in London and other such information centers developed
throughout the world.

4. Producers, wholesalers and retailers should redouble their
national and regional efforts involved in the major alcohol abuse
issues and prevention programs. The stellar work of the LBIC should
be vastly expanded to provide a model of cooperation between
industry and government in pressing the systems approach to
solving abuse problems. The full range of issues from education
programs for the young to seasonal safe driving campaigns should
be deliberated, planned and shared with the media.

The beverage alcohol industry can be proud of its prevention
programs and its efforts to educate and warn of the abuse or
potential peril of alcohol. Next, it should muster the same kind of
fervor in order to educate its own workers on the positive value of
moderate drinking. The results might be amazing!

13

Toward a Moderate
Alcohol Consensus

_Prevention of alcohol abuse as a major social
policy priority requires a long-term commitment
not only of funds but of personnel over a
generation or longer before one can expect radical
changes in patterns of alcohol misuse in society._
David J. Pittman, Ph.D.
Primary Prevention Of Alcohol Abuse And Alcoholism

_What is almost never mentioned, much less discussed,
is that the system of control and regulation—alcohol
control it was called—which replaced national Prohibition in
the middle of the 1930s, was a political creation. It was
formed with conscious design and intention to do some particular
things and not others, and to meet only certain needs and interests._
Harry Levine
"The Committee of Fifty and the Origins of Alcohol Control"

_In our opinion, we will see major changes in the
years ahead as our society begins to understand alcohol
use from a social learning perspective. Drinking is a
learned behavior. Biological factors will be included
in the learning account, but they will not
occupy the central role they do currently._
Roger Vogler, Ph.D. and Wayne Bartz, Ph. D.
The Better Way To Drink

A responsible drinking consensus is a national imperative.

The alternative will be to drift into a system of alcohol controls
now advocated by many in public health. They could destroy an
important industry and, quite likely, add to the numbers who suffer
alcohol disruption in their lives.

The proposed agenda of legislation suggested by U.S. control
advocates is radical since it would virtually destroy the free-market

trade in alcoholic beverages authorized in the Twenty-first Amendment. These measures include the elimination of normal business deductions, loss of advertising and merchandising privileges, arbitrary high pricing tied to the cost of living index, pejorative bottle labeling, vastly increased excise taxation, limitations on the number and location of retail outlets, and a general denigration of all drinking through identification of alcohol with tobacco and illegal street drugs.

The measures are radical because of their catastrophic economic impact on private enterprise. Because they ignore the rights of two-thirds of American adults who drink without abusing. Because they ignore the munificent dimension of alcohol consumption. The majority's economic and behavioral rights are to be sublimated to the presumed needs of a minority of less than ten million problem drinkers.

Aside from the social, health and therapeutic aspects of drinking, the economic dimensions of alcohol production and distribution are very real and important to nearly every state in the union. The farming, production, distribution and retailing contribute significant employment and very substantial tax and licensing funds to city, county, state and federal governments. The disease concept of alcoholism now is universally accepted, but the agent alcohol is involved not just in the disease pattern but in hundreds of positive social and economic circumstances.

Drinking is not just another disease.

No other agent involved in a major disease contributes legitimate legal employment and vital commercial activity to the communities which it serves. Cancer gives nothing back to society in terms of taxes and jobs. Heart disease depletes personal savings and health-care insurance reserves. Beyond enriching the coffers of organized crime and the street pusher, drug addiction offers a total deficit. Diabetes gives nothing back. And, indeed, the disease of alcoholism and alcohol abuse give nothing back.

But the alcoholic beverage trade does contribute to society. It constitutes a $114 billion dollar annual commercial enterprise (a figure remarkably close to the National Institute on Alcohol Abuse and Alcoholism (NIAAA) total of $116.8 billion cost of abuse. More than a million Americans find dignified and rewarding career employment in the business of alcohol. The Department of Health and Humans Services (DHHS) often makes a specious comparison of alcoholism with other diseases like heart and cancer. The implication is that , like the other major diseases, alcoholism can be eradicated by suppressing alcohol. No mention is made of alcohol's tangible benefits to society.

Research Finding 13.1

Drinking should be an option in a healthy lifestyle.

> *There is also a sense in which drinks perform the other task of ritual. They make an intelligible, bearable world which is much more how an ideal world should be than the painful chaos threatening all the time.*
> **Mary Douglas**
> *Constructive Drinking*

The question was raised in chapter 2, "Is moderate drinking good for you?"

In 1775, that rhetorical question never would have been asked, so fully integrated in daily affairs was the practice of drinking. A new working consensus on the use of alcohol in this society must again answer that questions in the affirmative. Although many in the society should not be embarrassed to continue their abstinent ways. our government policy must say, "Yes, alcohol can be good for you and, yes, it does no harm in moderation, at least insofar as modern science knows." The difference between *good* and *bad* drinking must be found in the *dosage* as it is with all other legal potables.

My argument in this book is not that people should drink to be healthy, though that may be a happy consequence, but that people who drink should learn to do it in a healthy manner. *That is true moderation.*

One of the exciting conclusions of anthropologist Mac Marshall in the cross-cultural review of drinking around the globe titled *Beliefs, Behaviors & Alcoholic Beverages* was that true integration of alcohol in a society lessens its disruptive effects. Drinking has not been integrated in the American society for the better part of two centuries. Alcohol has been merely tolerated in our public proclamations since the 1830s (excepting the 13 years of prohibition). Gusfield's chapter "Passage to Play" in *Constructive Drinking* describes how alcohol, and even drunkenness, had their specific and accepted roles in those bucolic, pre-temperance times:

Before the 1830s, while drunkenness was observed and
condemned, it had an accepted place in American life
in both work and play. With the emergence of
industrial organization, the separation of work as an
area of sobriety and play as an area of permissible
insobriety became more common. The development of
leisure as a contrast to work did much to reinforce the
disapproval of drinking as daytime activity.

Gusfield is telling us is that alcohol was a comfortable partner in
daily affairs. No one questioned the worth or value of drinking. We
shared common feelings about that function. But prohibition
sentiments eventually relegated drinking to the back room, a kind of
limbo, where it has languished for the better part of two centuries.
Gusfield says that this new attitude toward the use of alcohol
compartmentalized it as an after-work, play-time pleasure rather than
an integral part of living:

In America, the segregation of the use of alcohol to the
period of leisure is largely a product of the nineteenth
century. Colonial America did not generally perceive
alcohol as inherently evil. Its consumption was not
limited to special times and places. (Lender and Martin, 1982). Its impropriety as an adjunct to "serious"
utilitarian pursuits arises with industrial and organizational development. The shift from alcohol as the
"goodly creature of God" to "demon rum" was,
however, not simply a response to economic development. The ambivalent feelings about alcohol owe much
to the work of the American Temperance and Prohibition movements in creating the public awareness of
alcohol as a "dangerous commodity" (Gusfield, 1963;
1984).

Marshall writes in _Beliefs, Behaviors & Alcoholic Beverages_
that many countries consume alcohol for centuries without really
deciding upon a positive consensus. Ireland and most of the North
American Indian tribes exemplify this ingrained ambivalence. Yet
Marshall says:

When members of a society have had sufficient time to
develop a widely shared set of beliefs and values pertaining to drinking and drunkenness, the consequences
of alcohol consumption are not usually disruptive for
most persons in that society. On the other hand, where
beverage alcohol has been introduced within the past

century and such a set of beliefs and values has not
developed, social — and sometimes physiological —
problems with ethanol commonly result.

Alcohol was re-introduced politically (though it never really left
physically) following repeal but it was never fully redeemed. That's
what our task is today. Both the Cooperative Commission on the
Study of Alcoholism in 1961 and the Education Commission of the
States in the 1970s found large areas of agreement among
Americans about drinking. That's the place to start.

Research Finding 13.2

There is grass roots support for consensus.

> The Commission proposes the formulation
> of a national public policy on alcohol and believes
> that such a comprehensive policy can be developed.
> **Alcohol Problems: A Report to the Nation**
> Cooperative Commission on the Study of Alcoholism

Americans are apparently ready to come to some agreement on
alcohol usage. A recent finding by Gallup pollsters indicated that only
17 percent of Americans desire a return to prohibition. This is a rather
remarkable number, the lowest since repeal, when you consider that
fully 34 percent of Americans do not drink. It suggests that only about
half the nondrinkers want to close the bar down. Thus 83 percent of
Americans seem willing to settle for some form of controlled drinking.

Evolving public attitude has accepted alcoholism as a disease
and not a moral turpitude. If the addiction is involuntary, then
alcoholics are akin to other members of the society who suffer from
diseases such as diabetes or hypertension in which certain common
foods must be proscribed.

Despite public acceptance of drinking, a virtual stalemate exists
between the beverage producing industries and the current
leadership at DHHS and NIAAA. What had been promising
cooperation in the war against alcohol abuse through several
post-war decades has descended over the past two decades into
open warfare.

A sound foundation for political consensus exists under these
gathering clouds. During the presidency of Jimmy Carter, a study
was conducted by the Education Commission of the States on the

role of alcohol in the society. This commission's recommendations, utilized the positive aspects of the Committee of Fifty, formed at the turn of the century. It also used the findings of the Cooperative Commission on the Study of Alcoholism, which had also outlined a possible consensus. The Carter administration adopted the comprehensive plan of the Education Commission as national policy. The bedrock of agreement has already been put together by nationally representative bodies.

Mutual respect between government and industry is vital.

After World War II, the beverage producers and the care and treatment industry worked together in seeking solutions for alcohol abuse and alcoholism. In a recent interview, Donald Shea of the Beer Institute recalls the general atmosphere of optimism and agreement on shared objectives:

> When I was first involved with the industry, it was the tail end of the consensus years, from the mid-sixties to the mid-seventies. At the mid-point, the NIAAA was formed. Industry favored the initial approach at NIAAA and it wasn't until around 1977 and 1978 that the focus switched from the problems of drinking to the product itself. Until the NIAAA stated its goal to reduce per capita consumption, the consensus in the field and among brewers, vintners and distillers had been working very well through a coalition for adequate alcoholism programs.

In *The Better Way to Drink*, Vogler and Bartz foresee a gradual transition from the current emphasis in government research funds on the biomedical aspects of abuse to a greater stress on learned behavior techniques. This would mean that both industry and the general educational system would place more resources to the task of teaching people how to acquire good drinking habits. Levine reminds us that alcohol control systems are essentially political instrumentalities. Many controls established at repeal really intend to discourage consumption rather than to moderate intake.

Legislators must drop quick fix legislative answers.

Federal and state legislatures should begin to recognize that the public agrees (or at least the majority does) on far more than it disagrees about drinking. First, everyone agrees that adult alcohol abuse, underaged drinking, and driving while intoxicated are pernicious and costly problems that require even more dedication of federal and state funds and energy.

None of the alcohol behavioral problems would evaporate with label warnings, increased alcohol taxes or the elimination of advertising privileges. These anti-alcohol programs are no solution, and they create more havoc than what they seek to cure.

The politician needs and deserves community backing for this new structuring. Prestigious community leaders came together as the Committee of Fifty at the end of the last century with a drinking consensus plan that was rejected. Thoughtful leadership rose up again to throw off the yoke of prohibition during the late 1920s, and briefly flowered again in the 1960s and 1970s. We desperately need that kind of widespread, highly-placed community leadership again to ward off another quick fix by a determined and articulate cadre of extremists.

Thomas Hill in an essay titled "Ethnohistory and Alcohol Studies" identifies this broader, anthropological approach to alcohol in society:

> In contrast, a third approach, which developed out of the culture and personality tradition, places less stress on disruptive and escapist functions of alcohol consumption and emphasizes the ways in which alcohol use contributes to the maintenance of a sociocultural system. This perspective recognizes that native societies have changed through time, but focuses on the manner in which traditional and foreign elements have been incorporated into new viable patterns. Even though some forms of heavy drinking may be perceived as deviant and disruptive, others are seen as normative and may be interpreted as modified expressions of traditional values and activities.

Alcoholics Anonymous (AA) works well for many people because of its functional simplicity. AA works for those who commit to its disciplines as a path to sobriety. Mark Keller tells of a close friend, an alcoholic, who professes to be an atheist but who finds that the commitment to a Higher Will, a tenet of AA, works even for him as an atheist. What works, works.

To me, the most important of those AA disciplines is the mandate that recovering alcoholics stand confidently before strangers or friends and say with candor, "Hi, I'm Gene and I'm an alcoholic." That's what Elizabeth Taylor, Jason Robards and Betty Ford have been able to do for the society They provide inspiration, support and leadership for many others. That is the approach which I am suggesting for moderate drinkers as well. Those of us who believe in responsible drinking have to come out of our own closets of embarrassment and ambivalence.

Research Finding 13.3

Guidelines for consensus have been established.

> *There have been attempts to begin to lay the tracks*
> *toward a consensus of public policy about alcohol and*
> *alcoholism and, in my view, they have failed. The Plaut*
> *commission still stands as one of the best efforts.*
> **Interview with Michael Q. Ford**
> National Association of Alcohol Treatment Programs

A uniquely American approach to the alcohol issue was formulated by the eastern establishment in the late 19th century with the formation of the Committee of Fifty. Thanks to the foresight and endeavor of this citizen group, the idea of a public consensus took shape. This was the philosophy of the possible, one that recognized the inevitability of drinking as well as the need for controls. This same philosophy emerged again in the 1960s with a more definitive agenda in the Cooperative Commission on the Study of Alcoholism.

Membership on the earlier Committee of Fifty included powerful and prestigious representatives of industry, religion and education. In an incisive report on the committee, Levine in "The Committee of Fifty and the Origins of Alcohol Control" points to their praiseworthy though essentially self-serving objectives. "The Committee of Fifty sought the destruction or at least the tight control of the working class saloon, the development of working class respect for law and police, and the reconstruction of working class life along the model of middle class ideals."

This committee representing education, industry and religion shared the vision of a stable American society in which a healthy and happy workforce was free of oppressive drinking. The major contribution of the Committee of Fifty was that alcohol control laws should rely on the public they served rather than the church or government. When repeal did come, it was built upon another thoughtful collaboration of academe, industry and religion, but it achieved political viability by assuring local rule. In many states, Utah and Mississippi, for examples, repeal constituted a slightly more liberal variation of classical prohibition. New York and Nevada were able to construct much more liberal control structures representative of their populations.

As Levine reports in *The Committee of Fifty*, the broad consensus originally proposed by the group persists as a viable program for today's dilemma. Levine concludes:

> Thus, taken as a whole, the Committee did offer a new and authoritative approach to the handling of the liquor problem. And in the long run most of its general ideas and recommendations have triumphed. Present day alcohol policy does work; law is respected and obeyed, the saloon is not thought of as a corrupt institution, and public order is maintained.

The genius of the state level, what-will-work control ethic was embodied in the language of the Twenty-first Amendment. It has gradually developed public support in many states over the sixty years since repeal.

Much better we dust off the blueprints of the Committee of Fifty and restrict federal agencies to research and treatment, functions which require the massive funding and administration. The Cooperative Commission on the Study of Alcoholism recognized the problems inherent in developing a consensus. "A thorough examination is needed for individual and group behavior...The Commission believes that there is substantial, if not conclusive, evidence that such modifications will reduce the rates of alcoholism and other types of problem drinking."

Research Finding 13.4

An independent commission would articulate consensus.

> *It is essential that a single organization or group take responsibility for the creation and implementation of a national alcohol policy, and since no governmental or voluntary organization presently exists that can take a leadership role...a new organization is proposed.*
> **Alcohol Problems: A Report to the Nation**
> Cooperative Commission on the Study of Alcoholism

The answers to our alcohol dilemma are already on paper. The eighteen members of the Cooperative Commission on the Study Of

Alcoholism included prominent professionals in the alcoholism, drug and prevention fields. Despite this insularity in structure, the group rose above partisanship in its far-reaching recommendations. The committee's profound grasp of the overall problem is mirrored in its "Proposals for a Coordinated Approach to Alcohol Problems" in *Alcohol Problems: A Report To The Nation*. Their vision foresaw all segments of a community involved in working out the appropriate role for alcohol in national life:

> A total change is needed in the climate of opinion regarding alcohol use. A wide variety of methods will therefore be necessary to develop and implement a national policy. The issues involved must be discussed in the press, in magazines, and on radio and television, to arouse interest in bringing about the required changes.

The report suggested that the conflicts between wet and dry forces had been "...so energy-consuming that a detached examination of the American drinking patterns and systems of control and intervention has not been possible." That resistance to evaluation and compromise is as recalcitrant now at DHHS and NIAAA as it was in radical circles twenty years ago.

An independent national committee would pursue consensus.

As conceived by the commission, an independent, national committee would be appointed by the President and would receive annual federal funding to carry out its purposes. The new policy group would move beyond the narrow horizons of research, prevention and treatment to represent the moderate drinking and the nondrinker, as well as the abuser. The commission recognized that only with such complete independence could there be true reform and a new acceptable consensus:

> Also shown is the extent to which alcohol problems and issues penetrate contemporary American life. The diversity of interests and points of view is also abundantly clear, and developing consensus in areas where agreement is possible will not be an easy task or soon achieved...A major shift in social attitudes and policies is required to match the prevalence, the persistency, the complexity, and the interrelatedness of alcohol problems.

Research Finding 13.5

Solutions must originate at the local level.

> *Many of us in the alcohol field know that the enlightened educational and comprehensive multi-systems approach works...The current neo-prohibitionist approach is using sensationalism and alarmism as a vehicle to reduce consumption...and to frighten the American public about any use of alcohol.*
> **Larry Monson**
> National Rural Institute on
> Alcohol & Drug Abuse

Drunk is drunk. But there are differences between drunks (and everyone else, for that matter) in El Paso and Brooklyn. Residents in both cities can read the same magazines, listen to the same national news networks, vote for the same presidential candidates, and still be very different folks. And they are. We are a diversified people.

In a personal interview, Michael Ford, executive director of the National Association of Alcoholism Treatment Programs explained the natural tendency for the politician to reach for global solutions without tackling the root causes of problem drinking or the role of alcohol in society:

> Part of the problem is that there has not been an establishment of a basic public policy on alcohol in this country. As a result, policies are often made or offered on the basis of emotion instead of first, on research, and second, on public opinion. In the absence of those factors, it makes the quick fix very appealing. And, if a moral judgment can be the policy, then that's the quick fix.

Alcohol professionals could gain insights from anthropology.

I am impressed with the findings of contemporary anthropologists and sociologists on drinking, particularly the work of Gusfield, Heath and others in *Constructive Drinking* and Mac Marshall in *Beliefs, Behaviors, & Alcoholic Beverages*. Heath writes:

> Emphasis on "social problems" in terms of promising areas for future research should not obscure the fundamental and most important finding that anthropologists have so far contributed to alcohol studies—the fact that most of the people who drink—

> like most of the individuals in Western society who
> drink — do so without suffering in any discernible way.

Many professionals in the alcohol treatment field believe the true successes in alcohol and drug prevention are generated in the local communities by local professionals. Not at desks or in legislative halls in the state or national capitals. Alcoholics Anonymous works because it directly involves the alcohol with his peers. Members reflect similar cultural patterns, points of view and share the wrenching struggles with addiction. Karst Besteman of the Alcohol and Drug Policies Association puts it this way:

> When the rules were coming down from state levels, or
> the federal level down during prohibition, they didn't
> work. Wallace Mandell's studies indicate to us that as
> long as the rules emanated within the counties and
> closely reflected the life style of the residents, then you
> had fewer problems.

We must return to our pre-Revolutionary War belief that drinking can be a wholesome part of daily life. During the earlier colonial times there was much more heavy drinking than would be tolerable today, but alcohol had an accepted role in the society and everyone knew it. It was accepted and it belonged.

Research Finding 13.6

These seven ideas can help achieve consensus.

> *When members of a society have had*
> *sufficient time to develop a widely shared*
> *set of beliefs and values pertaining to*
> *drinking and drunkenness, the consequences*
> *of alcohol consumption are not usually*
> *disruptive for most persons in that society.*
> **Mac Marshall**
> *Beliefs, Behaviors & Alcoholic Beverages*

Everyone's job is no one's job. But consensus needs everyone. It cannot be obtained by a small committee or by a select few leaders. Consensus means compromise, conciliation, agreement and acceptance. So, I have a job for everyone. Here are my major recommendations for the politicians and thought leaders and the media in which they speak..

RECOMMENDATIONS FOR
A MODERATE CONSENSUS

1. That the President of the United States appoint a new commission titled the Committee for a National Alcohol Policy. Its objective would be to formulate public policy on the role of alcohol in the American society.

2. That the President of the United States direct the secretary of Health and Human Services, the director of the Alcohol, Drug Abuse and Mental Health Administration and the director of the National Institute for Alcohol Abuse and Alcoholism to formulate and carry out new policies that incorporate the concept of responsible or moderate drinking along with the choice of abstinence.

3. That the governors of each state appoint similar committees to evaluate the role of alcohol within their borders and to make such new policies and regulations as are necessary to effect proper control and regulation of responsible drinking within the states.

4. That all segments of the media, but particularly those organs that reach the entire nation, convene similar study groups designed to formulate guidelines for fair and comprehensive coverage of alcohol issues.

5. That the President and the governors mandate new language in public communications and documents that differentiates between moderate and abusive drinking.

6. That the President direct NIAAA to undertake new research of non-abusive drinking. Its purpose would be to discover the reasons why moderates are able to maintain a healthy intake and what, if any, health values obtain from that drinking.

7. That Citizens for Moderate Drinking coalitions be formed in all fifty states of existing organizations, groups and agencies for the promotion of responsible drinking at all levels.

Research Finding 13.7

A local level systems approach holds promise.

*Almost overlooked — especially since 1981 —
has been the success of the total traffic
"systems approach" in the U.S. A.*
Paul Gavaghan
Social and Health Issues

Thoughtful citizens and many alcoholism professionals took to heart the recommendations of the Cooperative Commission on the Study of Alcohol. Much was accomplished during the early 1970s, beginning with the establishment of the NIAAA and the appointment of Dr. Morris Chafetz, a consummate moderate, as its first director. There was at least surface cooperation among many alcohol-interest groups (which have since splintered into opposing camps). The National Council on Alcoholism had not yet purged its ranks of moderates. Many in the public health field recognized moderate, responsible drinking as a component in a healthy life-style.

Of course, public education is the key expression of consensus. Professor William Eck in "Important Issues Affecting Alcohol Education: Yesterday, Today, and Tomorrow" in the 1983 *Forum Report* produced by the National Conference of State Liquor Administrators comments on the classic approaches to alcohol education:

> Historically speaking, alcohol education has followed a definitive pattern. Wyatt (1972) has identified four approaches to alcohol education which he considers to represent the major current positions:
> 1) temperance (abstinence),
> 2) objective facts,
> 3) responsible drinking, and
> 4) value clarification. Many of us who have been in education for a number of years could suggest a fifth approach, expedient exhortation, in which specific effort is made in a single session, usually in large assemblies, to satisfy legislative requirements about alcohol instruction.

Eck carefully traces how new temperance conservatives have gained the public podium and have reverted to the classic temperance answer of abstinence through regulation of the system of alcohol supply, limitations on advertising, product warnings and price fixings.

Eck finds that the 1977 report of the Education Commission of the States Task Force also recommended widespread involvement:

> In its first interim report the task force presented its preliminary findings and outlined its goals. Among those findings was that alcohol abuse and alcoholism have a direct relationship to daily living experiences. The task force further stated that prevention of these problems is the responsibility of the total educational system, including the public and private schools, the family, peer and reference groups, mass media, business and industry, government agencies, religious and volunteer organizations.

A systems approach for alcohol similar to traffic control.

So was born the alcohol control "systems approach," which has yielded such rich rewards in the motor vehicle area. The systems approach is credited with reducing deaths on American highways to the fewest per miles traveled on the face of the earth. Hewlett in "Economic and Demographic Factors Relating to Public Alcohol Policy in the United States" points to the progress that has been achieved using such cooperative techniques:

> 1. The American people have gradually come to accept the illness concept of alcoholism...
> 2. It is no longer considered heroic by a growing number of younger drinkers to overindulge...
> 3. Increasingly, no matter what age group is involved, it is no longer considered unsociable to choose non-alcoholic drinks at social functions...
> 4. Drunkenness is no longer considered humorous by a large and growing number of Americans...
> 5. More American businesses are adding alcoholism as a coverable diagnosis in their group health insurance..
> 6. Chronic public drunkenness is now seen as a symptom of alcoholism rather than as a criminal offense...
> 7. Americans are now beginning to take more responsibility for their own personal health...
> 8. Many of America's large industrial corporations have instituted alcoholism-oriented employee assistance programs.

These and many more subtle changes bear witness to the workability of a consensus around an attack on abuse while maintaining the propriety of moderation. Gavaghan in "Social and Health Issues" tells how the comprehensive systems approach was adopted by the Presidential Commission on Drunk Driving with substantial progress resulting:

> Almost overlooked – especially since 1961 – has been the success of the total traffic "systems approach" in the U.S.A. This approach includes but is not limited to enforcement, adjudication, treatment, education, traffic licensing, and emergency medical care services.

Hewlett sees great promise in the systems approach just as he fears the control of availability propensity to muddle the issues. "This same discrepancy between genuine expert opinion and public attitudes may also be found on several other important issues...The true nature, extent, and complexity of these issues are understood by the experts, but they are not known among the policy makers, the media and the public. We have the control advocates to thank for this divisive knowledge gap."

Research Finding 13.8

Moderate drinking is good for society.

> *Clearly, alcohol can serve many purposes*
> *through its pharmacological and symbolic*
> *characteristics. It gives pleasure, reduces pain,*
> *eliminates fear, raises self-esteem, solves conflicts*
> *and so on. But, basically, the pleasurable experience*
> *from alcohol underlies all alcohol problems,*
> *and perhaps all alcohol use.*
> **R. M. Morse**
> *Fermented Food Beverages in Nutrition*

David Pittman, one of my mentors in this writing and a long-time scholar of temperance movements warns in a recent personal letter to avoid making any health claims for alcohol in this book:

> I, however, would like to caution you again about making any health claims about alcoholic beverages; there have appeared in the last two years two significant critiques (Knupfer in the *British Journal of Addiction* and by Ferrence, Truscott and Whitehead in

the _Journal of Studies on Alcohol_) of the studies which posit a relationship between light drinking and decreased rates of myocardial infarction and consumption of alcoholic beverages.

Caution well advised. The research that I have presented in this book speaks volumes about people who do drink moderately. Their better health may be due, as Knupfer argues, more to their easy-going lifestyles than to their drinking. At the very least, daily alcohol use doesn't seem to put them in harm's way. It's as simple as that. I did not set out to prove that life could be extended by moderate drinking, only that there were tangible benefits to it. If those benefits are limited to social ease, better appetite and wholesome commerce in some of our states, so be it. Those are goods. Those are benefits.

However, it seems to be a well-kept secret in anthropology that alcohol problems are, in the sweep of human history, rarities in terms of the total human experience. Heath in "A Decade of Development in the Anthropological Study of Alcohol Use 1970–1980" from _Constructive Drinking_ argues:

> Without in any way belittling the importance of human suffering that does occasionally stem from toxic or other effects of alcohol, however, it deserves mention that a long-term strength of anthropological studies has been that they have paid attention not only to "alcoholism" but rather to alcohol as an artifact and to the complex of attitudes, values, and actions that are associated with it. A major finding, in cross-cultural perspective, is that alcohol-related problems are really rare, even in many societies where drinking is customary, drunkenness is commonplace.

This positive side is seldom considered. But it's there.

Research Finding 13.9

Achieving consensus will not eliminate health concerns.

> _We have the same problem that Russian has_
> _with drinking. We are not an integrated society._
> **Interview with Karst Besteman**
> Alcohol and Drug Problems Association

A political consensus on drinking will bring no nirvana. We will still have drunks on our highways and tragic indiscretions among intemperate young people. Alcoholism will continue to plague mankind at all social levels. These problems will still cost the nation dearly, though perhaps in a better comparative light than at present when only the costs and not the benefits are presented.

However, the objections to the methodology need follow-up. Ferrence does not deny a positive relationship in some instances but points to the obvious dangers in establishing a public policy which would recommend drinking. The fact is that no one, not even the industry spokespeople, has recommended that everyone drink. Here is a Ferrence warning statement:

> In summary, there is evidence that moderate levels of consumption of alcoholic beverages bestow a protective effect, under some circumstances, when compared with abstinence. Evidence is inconsistent across studies, however, and the mechanism is not yet understood. Given the negative health consequences associated with higher levels of drinking, there is considerable reason to be wary of either altering the scientific or public focus on the damage caused by alcohol or supporting changes in policy that might make drinking more socially acceptable.

This is an important and reasonable medical debate. But my conclusions, following a study of the same material, are vastly different. I think that Americans are sufficiently adult to make personal lifestyle choices given proper data.

Both drinking and abstention are healthy choices.

No one needs to drink. There are many effective regimens and satisfactory diets for the maintenance of healthy hearts, minds and bodies that do not include alcohol. Abstention is not just for sissies, alcoholics or religious fanatics. Abstention is a perfectly logical and appropriate choice for many. There are dozens of reasons not to drink ranging from alcoholism in the family to moral precepts, all of them quite as reasonable as my own choice to drink.

However, Ferrence further states, "As for liberalizing control measures, the weight of evidence indicates that restricting increases in per capita consumption of alcohol will bestow much greater health benefits than will encouraging increases, however small."

To this statement I ask what facts and what evidence? No compelling evidence is offered in her paper. The preponderance of the evidence I have been able to unearth in the professional literature demonstrates little if any effect on heavy drinkers (where the ill effects of drinking occur) from a lowered per capita consumption. Indeed, the major criterion of alcoholism for decades has been the cirrhosis rate. Cirrhotic deaths in the United States dropped a dramatic 34 percent from 1974 through 1985 — from 14.7 per hundred thousand to 9.6 — a period in which total alcohol intake steadily escalated.

Knupfer's "Drinking for Health: the Daily Light Drinker Fiction" expresses concern that positive data on alcohol and heart disease will be used to recommend drinking. Dr. Thomas Turner responds to these criticisms in the Alcoholic Beverage Medical Research Foundation's _Monthly List of Pertinent Abstracts_:

> A third point that seemed to concern Knupfer was "should physicians recommend that abstaining patients take up light drinking." I am not aware that the authors of any of these papers cited made such a suggestion, and indeed a number caution against such action.

The relation of alcohol to health needs more research.

While Knupfer correctly states that the causal relationship between alcohol and health has not been established, Turner cites the review by Moore and Pearson (see chapter 2), which finds sufficient evidence of alcohol and heart health to state, "The consistency, strength and independence of the inverse relationship argues persuasively for a causal association."

To these concerned researchers, I ask how suffering is to be measured? If light or moderate drinkers are influenced to lower their per capita drinking thereby losing whatever present health protection they might be enjoying, could not these lowered per capita drinkers suffer increasing heart attacks, morbidity and mortality from other diseases? There are far more of these moderate drinkers likely to be impacted negatively than there are problem drinkers.

Certainly Americans ought to be entrusted with the knowledge that one to two drinks a day may have a positive relationship to the nation's number one killer, heart disease. Turner questions this unseemly reticence by comparing it to relatively unrestrained support of other unproved regimens for heart health in the medical community:

> It should be noted that the same limitations obtain in evaluating the effect on health of exercise, smoking, fat in the diet, caffeine, late hours, workaholism, etc.

Without making presumptuous and unprovable health claims, I conclude that moderate consumption of alcohol is of value to society and adds to the well-being of its users. At the same time, those who choose to abstain are in no danger from that choice. A healthy consensus on alcohol use would recognize and support both choices without prejudice.

Research Finding 13.10

Name-calling reinforces the bias against alcohol.

> *Health promotion campaigns are typically designed to elicit fear, yet fear is often ineffective in achieving the desired behavior change.*
> **R. F. Soames Job**
> *American Journal of Public Health*

> *Not since the days of prohibition has the federal government been so involved in controlling American life. In the alcoholic beverage industry, there is an urgency to coalesce and to speak with a single voice. Our opposition knows that it is easier to change one federal law than fifty sate laws.*
> **Personal Interview with Ronald Rumbaugh**
> National Beer Wholesalers Association

An important first move toward consensus lies in cleaning up the official language. Calling alcohol a dirty drug, as an example. The "Just Say No" literature and propaganda notwithstanding, alcohol has as much relation to cocaine as an automobile to a torture rack.

Among legal drugs, sugar, coffee, and tranquilizers are more abused than alcohol. Among controlled substances, cigarettes and medicines are abused by more than the estimated ten million alcohol abusers. The abuse of alcohol may be among the most costly of human indiscretions. But the *good* use of alcohol shows another side of the ledger in saved marriages, forgotten quarrels, and jobs more fully accomplished.

I recommend the President and the governors insist that federal and state officials use conventional language when referring to alcoholic beverages. This language should reflect alcohol's comprehensive role in society as a food which supplies nearly ten percent of the energy used by a majority of Americans, as a beneficial social drink, and as an important economic commodity.

This process should begin at DHHS. In November 1987, secretary Bowen at DHHS instituted a policy in which the common term "substance abuse" would be replaced by the longer and more lugubrious term "alcohol and other drug abuse." The Secretary directed all departments to use this pejorative "...unless legislation requires otherwise." I suggest the policy be rescinded or the corrective legislation passed. Using "alcohol" to preface every reference to illegal drugs is absurd. We cannot expect private agencies like the National Council on Alcoholism or the Center for Science in the Public Interest to refrain from hyperbole. That's their ploy, but it is bad public policy for government employees to do so.

We live in a polydrug culture.

We are experiencing more problems with therapeutic drugs than with alcohol. Naturally psychoactive herbal drugs have always been in widespread use, but the last three or four decades have seen an explosion in manufactured drug therapies. This era of chemical solutions is a legacy of Pasteur's work and the development of the science of microbiology. By the time we reach the toddling stage, we know that something can be taken orally for anything that hurts. Name the ill and there are a dozen over-the-counter and two dozen prescription drugs to provide instant assuagement. Kaptchuck and Croucher in _The Healing Arts_ show that drug abusers are not limited to the lost generations on the streets:

> Of the 200 most common drugs used today, only nineteen were developed before 1940. The Second World War provided not only incentives — for discovering quinine substitutes, for example, for the large numbers of troops going into areas in which malaria was still endemic — but also funding for research....Is the drug approach that our society has apparently embraced the ultimate answer or just another crest of the wave?

The drug problems will not disappear with alcohol consensus.

This wholesale surrender to the lure of drugs bears another bitter fruit, loss of personality consequent to surrendering to drugs' good times. Cohen in _The Drug Dilemma_ finds:

> Many of us suffer from a serious disease of affluence: directionless. No longer need large segments of this society focus on the struggle to avoid hunger, thirst, and the extremes of temperature which preoccupied their fathers. Unfortunately, new directions and new goals have not yet been acquired. Meanwhile, for others the

crushing diseases of poverty remain, and these enhance
escape in the form of bedrugged existence. Although
we cannot agree with the means, we can try to understand that attractiveness of oblivion, the distancing
from hurt, of the fabulous fantasies that drugs can bring.

It is my belief that when a person becomes a "head," —
be it "pothead," "hophead," "acidhead," "pillhead," or
"rumhead" — he has relinquished a core aspect of his
existence. He has surrendered his human freedom, his
individuation — the potion has become the master.

Ironically, this loss of individuation may well contribute to abuse
of alcohol among so many for whom hope and future are empty
words. To characterize alcohol as the most abused drug in society is
absurd. Therefore, the problem of public language is a serious one,
not simply a semantic dispute. The official language of public health
should include the values of responsible drinking.

Research Finding 13.11

Consensus must involve everyone.

> *I see us within the next two to four years*
> *forging a new consensus in America about*
> *our products. There will be a confluence of*
> *thinking about alcoholic beverages in America*
> *and this all will come out of a shifting of the*
> *issues such as Proposition 65 and carcinogenicity.*
> **Interview with John De Luca**
> The Wine Institute

Alcohol abuse is everybody's problem.

The *Moderate Drinking Journal* seeks to involve more of those
115 million moderate drinkers in the process of consensus. I remain
convinced that the 65 percent who drink would be more than willing
to support a political consensus on responsible drinking if they could
be convinced of the correctness of their own personal decisions to
drink.

The people who grow, produce and sell beverages have a
unique responsibility. I am urging the people involved in farming,
production, distribution and retailing of these beverages to start

telling their story in public. That's the American way. Statistically, the majority of these suppliers and merchants are also moderate drinkers.

The cities and states in which wines, beers, and spirits are grown and produced will suffer the most by depression of the legitimate, nonabusive alcoholic beverage commerce. These large producing states have a right to protest the generation of new temperance programs by federal agencies which will severely impact their economic well-being.

I say to the farmers who raise the barley, grapes and hops that this is their fight. I reach out to the individuals who sell tractor tires, batteries, forklifts and beer barrels to the breweries, wineries and distilleries. I want to inform the one million salespeople who represent spirit, beer and wine brands in countless stores and bars. Their jobs, products and services are at risk. I speak to the restaurant associations, the chambers of commerce and convention bureaus. They share a legitimate concern for the commerce in beverages that serve the tourist and convention trade. Anti-alcohol forces care little for conventions and trade.

Citizens coalitions are the logical response to temperance.

There is a potential for effective coalitions of Citizens for Moderate Drinking. Or coalitions travelling under any of a dozen names. They could forge a new regional recognition of the positive contributions of alcohol production and trade. In my own state, there are 70 wineries, seven small and two large breweries, over two billions in annual commerce and over thirty thousand jobs at stake. Much larger figures pertain in New York and California. Normally liberal politicians in many of these large states support control measures which, in effect, will kill their golden geese.

The problem is one of focus and communication. Barsby, as reported in the _Kennedy Newsletter_, expressed this problem at a recent convention of the National Licensed Beverage Association (liquor store owners):

> Retail sales of alcoholic beverages are double those of the wholesalers and triple those of the producers and importers...This diversity in size and business focus, and the secondary importance given to alcoholic beverages by many of your fellow retailers, makes it more difficult for you to tell your story...on-premise retailers provide over 999,000 of the 1.2 million jobs throughout the industry...Your $4.1 billion in direct tax

payments to state and local governments expands to over $6 billion by the time the direct income you helped generate is taxed again and again.

A team of Mondavis is needed to reach the drinking public.

The alcohol beverage industry needs more leaders like Robert Mondavi, the Napa Valley vintner. He recently trained his marketing and sales staff to tell the story of responsible drinking, and he plans a series of informational seminars around the nation with prominent health and research panelists to argue the case.

The *Napa Register* quoted Mondavi as saying that the wine industry should have been engaged long ago in research designed to "show the healthful effects of moderate wine consumption." Responding to the recent public coverage about aspirin's impact on the health, Mondavi declared:

> We know historically that wine is better than aspirin for the heart — in moderation of course. But doctors are afraid to expound on it — to say that — because we don't have research to back it up, because of the threat of lawsuits. We're in a vacuum.

Mondavi's leadership should encourage others to speak out. There is no more important health issue in the nation today than alcohol use and abuse. Senator Thurmond and I concur at least on that point. No matter whose figures you use, alcohol abuse costs us dearly. It drains limited human and financial resources and it pits normally cohesive groups into bitter and hostile camps. Moderates need to come out of their closets with the strength and conviction of the recovered public alcoholic.

Summary of Chapter 13

According to tradition, when a Jew takes a drink, which is often in the company of friends and family, a simple prayer is silently offered, "Thank God for the fruit of the vine." We can all learn from this wonderful practice which not only celebrates the gift of wine itself but the great God who provided this good creature for our comfort.

If you have read this far and are convinced that something must be done to temper new temperance, then don't shrug and look over your shoulder. You must help spread the following messages:

> In most societies, drinking is essentially a social act and, as such, it is imbedded in a context of values, attitudes and norms. **Dwight Heath.**

...alcohol is an accompaniment of social solidarity. Precisely because it possesses a meaning of contrast to organized work, it is a dissolver of hierarchy. **Joseph Gusfield.**

When alcoholic beverages are defined culturally as a food and/or a medicine, drunkenness seldom is disruptive or antisocial. **Mac Marshall.**

Getting drunk is what's wrong. That's the thing to teach. You drink to a reasonable limit for any one of a variety of reasons but you don't get drunk. **Mark Keller.**

It makes sense that a small amount of alcohol relieves tension and thereby alleviates whatever destructive impact tension imparts, both physically and psychologically. **Leonard Gross.**

Drug-related laws and policies center too often on the drugs themselves and not often enough on the problems of the people misusing them...Drug policies should instead be primarily focused on people and their problems. **Drug Abuse Council.**

However, people are not generalizations, and hundreds of individual responses pop up to defy the statisticians. In one case, the solace and support an abstainer finds in following his religious or ethical principles are more important to his well-being than a statistical probability that he will live longer if he drinks moderately. **Morris Chafetz.**

For more than 6,000 years, wine has been the companion of man. His affection and concern for it are shown in the written records of all ages, coming from such diverse sources as the utterances of kings and cardinals, the advice of philosophers, and the wishes of journalists. **S. P. Lucia.**

The death of prohibition was not the death of prohibitionism. The body still twitches. **John Kobler.**

It is interesting to speculate on the effects of the complete elimination of alcohol abuse: what would be the

economic cost of the consumption of alternative substances and/or of the anti-social behavior which would
then occur? **Donald Light.**

Anthropologists bring several challenges to the assumptions of other writers on alcohol. They challenge the
common view that some races are, because of their
inheritance, peculiarly vulnerable to ill effects from
alcohol...They find no clear relation between the use of
alcohol and a tendency to aggressive or criminal
behavior. **Mary Douglas.**

By far, the lion's share of attention has been devoted to
alcohol, and the more restrictive the controls have been
and the more people covered by such controls, the
more profound have been their failures. **Augustus
Hewlett.**

Dimas in the _U.S. Journal_ for November 1984 writes that no
national agenda will be complete unless:

(1) There is renewed emphasis on the issue of
alcoholism as a treatable disease;
(2) NIAAA again becomes responsive to its
constituency;
(3) the voluntary alcoholism movement is revitalized;
(4) there is greater application of existing knowledge to
prevention programming;
(5) funding for alcoholism research becomes a serious
priority in the field; and
(6) methods of conflict resolution are again applied on
an effective democratic basis.

This book has presented a review of the prolific, profound,
thought-provoking literature of beverage alcohol—its uses and
abuses. It is largely a literature on the shelves, known only to the
academics. It speaks with a quiet voice, rarely heard in the popular
media. When it does, it is quickly drowned out by the strident wail of
new temperance radicals. I believe it is, nonetheless, the voice of
reason and moderation.

I hope you agree.

To your health. Moderately!

BIBLIOGRAPHY

Aaron P, Musto D, Temperance and Prohibition in America, in Alcohol and Public Policy:Beyond the Shadow of Prohibition, National Academy Press, Washington,D.C., 1981

ADAMHA News, National Conference on Alcohol Abuse and Alcoholism, 1988

ADAMHA News, Statistics on Alcohol Abusers, A National Conference on Alcohol Abuse and Alcoholism, November 1987

Adams J, Drink To Your Health: Alcohol Without Alcoholism, Harper & Row, N.Y., 1976

Alcohol Health & Research World, The Homeless, Spring 1987, Vol. 11, No. 3

Alcohol Health & Research World, RTI Economic Costs of Alcohol Abuse and Alcoholics, Winter, 1984/1985

Alcohol Problems A Report to the Nation, Cooperative Commission on the Study of Alcoholism, Oxford University Press, 1967

Alcohol Research Report, Johns Hopkins Alcohol Research Center, Vol.1, Issue 1, 1985

Alcohol Use in the United States, Statistical Bulletin, Metropolitan Life Insurance Co., N.Y. Jan/March 1987

Alcoholic Beverages Advertising Ban, Washington State Medical Association House of Delegates, Resolution: #23, September, 1984

Allen S, Alcoholics Deserve our Sympathy, not Glamour Treatment, the Seattle Times, May 4, 1988

Amatteti S, Bass R, Inner City Youth: A Challenge for Drug Prevention Efforts, ADAMHA News, Vol. XIV, No. 4, April, 1988

The American Assembly, Public Policy on Alcohol Problems, Columbia University, University of Georgia, April 26-29, 1984

The American Assembly, The Southeastern Regional American Assembly on Public Policies Affecting Alcoholism and Alcohol-Related Problems, April 29, 1984

American Automobile Association, Alcohol, Vision and Driving, 1975

American Automobile Association, One Drink Can Be Too Many, 1975

American Heart Association, Dietary Guidelines for Healthy American Adults, American Heart Association, Undated

American Heart Association, News Release NR88-3647, (Aspirin), Dallas, January 28, 1988

American Heart Association, News Release NR87-3651 (Hennekens/Buring) Dallas, November 19, 1987

American Heart Association, News Release NR88-3672, Dallas, January 17, 1988

American Heart Association, Report of Inter-Society Commission for Heart Disease, Circulation, Volume 70, 1984

American Medical Association, Manual on Alcoholism, 1968

American Public Health Association, Alcohol Tax Policy Tax Reform, January, 1987

Amerine M, Absorption of Ethanol from Alcoholic Beverages, Proceedings, Wine Health and Society, The Wine Institute, November, 1981

Ames B, Cancer Scares Over Trivia, Los Angeles Times, May 15, 1986

Ames B, Dietary Carcinogens and Anticarcinogens, Science, Vol. 221, September 1983

Ames B, Six Common Errors Relating to Environmental Pollution, Regulatory Toxicology and Pharmacology, 7,379-383 (1987)

Ames B, Gold L, Response, Science, December, 1987

Ames B, Gold L, Response, Science, July 17, 1987

Ames B, Magaw R, Gold L, Ranking Possible Carcinogenic Hazards, Science, Vol., 236, April 1987

Ames B, Magaw R, Gold L, Response, Science, September 18, 1987

Amis K, Kingsley Amis On Drink, Harcourt Brace Jovanovich, N.Y., 1970

Andrianopoulos G, Letter to the Editor, New England Journal of Medicine, Vol. 317, No. 2, November, 1987

Annis A, Is Alcoholism Treatment Effective? Science, Vol. 236, April 3, 1987

Antze P, Alcoholics Anonymous, in Constructive Drinking, Cambridge University Press, Cambridge, 1987

Asch T, Levy D, The Minimum Legal Drinking Age and Traffic Fatalities, Rutgers University, NIAAA, 1986

Ashley M, Alcohol Consumption, Ischemic Heart Disease and Cerebrovascular Disease, Journal of Studies on Alcohol, Vol. 45, No. 9, 1982

Ashley M, Alcohol Use During Pregnancy:A Challenge for the '80s, Journal of the Canadian Medical Association, 25, January 1981

Auth J, Warent G, Estimating the Prevalence of Problem Drinking in the General Population, Alcohol Health & Research World, Winter 1982/83

Babor T, Kranzler H, Louerman R, Social Drinking as a Health and Psychosocial Risk Factor Anstie's Limit Revisited, Alcoholism, Marc Galanter,ed Vol.5, Plenum Press, 1987

Bacon S, The Classic Temperance Movement in the U.S.A.:Impact Today On Attitudes, Action and Research, British Journal of Addiction, Vol 62., 1967, pp. 5-18

Bales R, Cultural Difference in Rates of Alcoholism, Quarterly Journal of Studies on Alcohol, Vol. 6, 1946

Barboriak J, Anderson A, Hoffmann R, Alcohol And Coronary Arteries, Clinical And Experimental Research, 3, 1979

Barleycorn M, Moonshiner's Manual, Oliver Press, Willets, California, 1975

Barnes G, Farrel M, Caine A, Parental Socialization Factors, Journal of Marriage and the Family, 48, February 1986

Barsby S, The Economic Contribution of The Beer Industry to the States, The Beer Institute, Washington, D.C., 1984

Barsby S, Alcoholic Beverage Retail Business, As quoted in The Kennedy Newsletter, November 13, 1988

Baus H, How To Wine Your Way To Good Health, Mason & Lipscomb Publishers, New York, 1973

Beck J, A Sensible Ruling on Alcoholism as 'Misconduct', Chicago Tribune, May, 1988

Beck K, Summons T, The Social Context of Drinking Among High School Drinking Drivers, American Journal of Drug and Alcohol Abuse, 13(1&2), pp. 181-198

Beer Perspectives, National Beer Wholesalers Association, Vol.1, No.11, April 27, 1988

Bennett W, This World, March 20, 1988

Bennett W, The Drink-a-Day Lore, the New York Times Magazine Section,(also in Harvard Medical School Health Letter), January 10, 1988

Berridge V, Drinking Sensibly. Defining the Historical Context, British Journal of Addiction, 1988 January;83(1): 36-9

Berry R, Boland J, The Economic Cost of Alcohol Abuse, The Free Press, 1977

Besteman K, Personal Interview, Alcohol and Drug Policies Association

Blane H, Hewitt L, Alcohol and Youth: An Analysis of the Literature, 1960-1975, NIAAA, Springfield, VA, 1977

Bleiberg R, Sober Second Thoughts, Barrons, September 24, 1984

Blose J, Holder H, Liquor-by-the-Drink and Alcohol-Related Traffic Crashes, A National Experiment Using Time Series Analysis, Journal of Studies on Alcohol, Vol.48, No. 1, 1987

Blum R, The Journal of the American Medical Association, as reported in the Seattle Times, Living Fast and Dying Young, August 26, 1987

Blume S, Levy R, Kannel W, Takamine J,, The Risks of Moderate Drinking, Journal of the American Medical Association, Vol. 256, No. 23, December 19, 1986

Bonnet J, The Culinary System in the Encyclopedia, in Food and Drink in History, Johns Hopkins Press, Baltimore, 1979

Mr. Boston Official Bartender's Guide, Warner Books, N.Y., 1984

Booz, Allen Public Administrative Services, The Parameters of Responsible Alcohol Taking, NTIS, 30 July, 1973

Booze, Pills & Dope, House of Commons, Issue No. 28, 1986-87

Bottom Line, Alcohol Use in the United States, 1986

Bottom Line, If All Heavy Drinkers Switched to Two Drinks A Day, Vol. 8, Fall, 1987

Bottom Line, New Developments in the Battle for Stomach Share, Winter 1988

Bourgeois J, Barnes J, Does Advertising Increase Alcohol Consumption?, Journal of Advertising Research, Vol. 19, No. 4, August 1979, pp. 19-29

Bowden S, Brain Impairment in Social Drinkers? No Cause for Concern, Alcoholism: Clinical and Experimental Research, Department of Psychology, University of Melbourne, 15:1985

Bowden S, Cerebral Deficits in Social Drinkers and the Onus of Proof, Australian Drug and Alcohol Review 6,1987

Braunschweig H, Das Buch du Distilleren, 1519

Brent D, Perper J, Allman C, Alcohol Firearms and Suicides Among Youth, Journal of the American Medical Association, June 26, 1987

Brewers Association of Canada, Brewing In Canada, Ronalds- Federated Ltd, Montreal 1965

Brewers Digest, World Beer Production 1982-1986, December, 1987

Brown J, Early American Beverages, Charles E Tuttle Company, Rutland, 1966

Brown P, Skiffington E, Patterns of Marijuana and Alcohol Use Attitudes for Pennsylvania 11th Graders, The International Journal of Addiction, 22(5), 1987

Bruun K, Edwards G, Lumio M, Makela K, Pan L., Popham R, Room R, Schmidt W. Skog O, Sulkunen D. Osterberg E, Alcohol Control Policies In Public Health Perspective, The Finnish Foundation for Alcohol Studies, Vol.25, 1975

Bryant C, Effects of Sale of Liquor by the Drink in the United States, The Society of the Medical Friends of Wine, Vol. 15, 1954

Burcham J, Personal Interview, Licensed Beverage Information Council, March, 1988

Bureau of Justice Bulletin, January, 1983

Business Week, Sobering of America, February 25, 1985

Cadoret R, Troughton E, O'Gorman T, Haywood E,, An Adoption Study of Genetic and Environmental Factors in Drug Abuse, Archives of General Psychiatry, Vol. 43, December, 1986

Caetano R, Drinking Sensibly. The Resistance Also Comes from Within, British Journal of Addiction, 1988 January; 83(1); 39-41

Caetano R, Public Opinions About Alcoholism and Its Treatment, Journal of Studies on Alcohol, Vol., 48, No. 2, 1987

Cahalan D, Cisin I, Crossley H, American Drinking Practices, College and University Press, New Haven, 1967

Cahalan D, Cisin I, Drinking Behavior and Drinking Problems, in the Social Aspects of Alcoholism, Plenum Press, N.Y., 1976

Cahalan D, Understanding America's Drinking Problem, Jossey-Bass Publishers, San Francisco, 1987

Cahalan D, Why Does the Alcoholism Field Act Like a Ship of Fools?, British Journal of Addiction, 74, 1979

Cahalan D, Room R, Problem Drinking Among American Men, College & University Press, New Haven, 1974

Camargo C, Williams P, Vranizan K, Albers J, Wood P, The Effect of Moderate Alcohol Intake on Serum Apolipoproteins A-I and A-II, Journal of the American Medical Association, Vol.253, No.19, 1985

Carson L, Mondavi to Lead Fight Against New Prohibition, the Napa Register, February 23, 1988

Cashman S, Prohibition:The Law of the Land, The Free Press, N.Y., 1981

Center For Disease Control, Morbidity and Mortality Weekly Report, DHHS, Public Health Service, February 1987

Chafetz M, Liquor: The Servant of Man

Chafetz M, Why Drinking Can Be Good For You, Stein and Day New York, 1976

Chafetz M, The Third Wave of Prohibition is Upon Us, The Wall Street Journal, Tuesday, July 21, 1987

Chafetz M, Young People and Alcohol, Youth Alcohol and Social Policy, Plenum Press, N.Y., 1978

Chalke H, Moderate Drinking-Moderate Damage, British Journal on Alcohol and Alcoholism, Vol. 16, No.3, Autumn 1981

Charen H, Surgeon General Invites Smokers to Feel Helpless, the Seattle Times, May 23, 1988

Christian Science Monitor, Is Alcohol Abuse Being Ignored In Antidrug Fervor, September 24, 1986

Chu S, Centers for Disease Control, as reported in University of California Wellness Letter, June, 1988

Cinzano C, in Alcoholic Beverage Executives Newsletter, No. 2503, March 4, 1988

Coate D, Grossman M, Change in Alcoholic Beverage Prices and Legal Drinking Ages, Alcohol Health & Research World, Fall, 1987

Cohen S, The Drug Dilemma, McGraw-Hill Book Company, N.Y. 1969

Cohen S, The Drug Free Act of 1986: Will It Work, Vista Hill Foundation, Vol. XVI, No. 2, February, 1987

Colditz G, Branch L, Lipnick R, Willett W, Rosner B, Posner B, Hennekens C, Moderate Alcohol And Decreased Cardiovascular Mortality In An Elderly Cohort, American Heart Journal 109, 1985

Colquitt M, Fielding P, Cronan J, Drunk Drivers and Medical and Social Injury, The New England Journal of Medicine, Nov., 12, 1987

Connors G., O'Farrell T, Cutter H, Logan D, Dose-Related Effects of Alcohol Among Male Alcoholics, Problem Drinkers and Nonproblem Drinkers, Journal of Studies on Alcohol, Vol. 48, No. 5, 1987, pp. 461-466

Cooperative Commission on the Study of Alcoholism, see Alcohol Problems A Report to the Nation

Cowan R, Mosher J, Public health implications of beverage marketing: alcohol as an ordinary consumer product, Contemporary Drug Problems, Winter 1985, 12(4), pp. 621-657

Crawford A, Attitudes About Alcohol: A General Review, Drug and Alcohol Dependence, 19(1987), pp. 279-311

Dabney J, Mountain Spirits, Copple House Books, Lakeview GA, 1974

Darby , Wine and Medical Wisdom Through The Ages, The Beverage Analyst, May, 1979

De Luca J, Personal Interview, The Wine Institute, March, 1988

DHHS, Second Special Report to the U.S. Congress on Alcohol & Health, June, 1974, Morris E. Chafetz, Chairman Task Force; Third Special Report on Alcohol & Health. Ernest P. Noble, Editor June, 1978: Fourth Special Report on Alcohol & Health, John R, De Luca, Editor, January, 1981; Fifth Special Report on Alcohol & Health, Robert G. Niven, Director, December, 1983; Sixth Special Report on Alcohol & Health, Enoch Gordis, Director, January, 1987

DHHS, Alcohol, Drug Abuse, and Mental Health Administration, Fiscal Year 1989 Budget

Be Smart! Don't Start Just Say No, Publication No. ADM 87-1502, 1987

DHHS, Drug Abuse And Drug Abuse Research, The First Triennial Report to Congress, DHHS, 1984

DHHS, Drug Abuse And Drug Abuse Research, The Second Triennial Report to Congress, DHHS, 1987

DHHS, Health Hazards Associated with Alcohol and Methods to Inform the General Public of these Hazards, 1980

DHHS, My Baby...Strong and Healthy, ADAMHA, NIAAA, U.S. Government Printing Office, Washington, D.C.

DHHS, Report #7, Apparent Per Capita Alcohol Consumption: National, State and Regional Trends, Alcohol Epidemiological Data System, September, 1987

DHHS, Trends in Alcohol-Related Fatal Traffic Accidents, 1987

Department of the Treasury, Labeling and Advertising Regulations under the Federal Alcohol Administration Act, Federal Register, Vol. 49, No. 154, August, 1984

Diehl A, et al., The Relationship of High Density Lipoprotein Subfractions to Alcohol Consumption and Other Lifestyle Factors, and Coronary Heart Disease, Atherosclerosis 69:1988

Dimas G, Rebuilding An American Consensus For Alcoholism, U.S. Journal, November 1984

DISCUS, Know Your Limits, 5th Edition, Washington,D.C. 1986

DISCUS, Moderation is in the Public Interest, Washington, D.C., November 13, 1984

DISCUS, Public Service Advertising, 9th Edition, Washington D.C.

DISCUS, Social and Health Issues, Washington, D.C.

DISCUS, The Annual Statistical Review, 1984/85

Donovan J, Jessor R, Jessor L, Problem Drinking in Adolescence and Young Adulthood, Journal of Studies on Alcohol, Vol. 44, No.1, 1983

Douglas M, Constructive Drinking, Cambridge University Press, 1988

Drug Abuse Council, The Facts About Drug Abuse, The Free Press, New York, 1980

Duffy J, Commentary on the Single Distribution Theory of Alcohol Consumption, Journal of Studies on Alcohol, 39:1648-1650, 1978

Dull R, Giacopassi D, An Assessment of the Effects of Alcohol Ordinances on Selected Behaviors and Conditions, The Journal of Drug Issues, 16(4), 1986, pp. 511-521

Du Mouchel W, Williams A, Zador P, Raising The Alcohol Purchase Age, Journal of Legal Studies, 16(1), 1987, pp. 249-266

DWI Colloquium, AAA Foundation For Traffic Safety, Falls Church, VA, 1983

Dyer A, Stamler J, Berkson P, Lepper M, McKean H, Shekeele R, Lindberg H, Garside D, Alcohol Consumption, Cardiovascular Risk Factors And Mortality In Two Chicago Epidemiological Studies, Circulation 56, 1977

Eck W, Important Issues Affecting Alcohol Education, Forum Report, National Conference of State Liquor Administrators, Mauai, Hawaii, 1983

Eckhardt M, Harford t, Kollber C, Parker E, Rosenthal S, Ryback R, Salmoiragi G, Vandermeer E, Warren K, Health Hazards Associated With Alcohol Consumption, Journal of the American Medical Association, Vol. 246, 1981

Education Commission of the States, Final Report, 1977

Engs R, Fors S, Drug Abuser Hysteria: The Challenge of Keeping Perspective, Journal of School Health, January 1988, Vol 58, No. 1

Erickson K, Wayward Puritans: A Study in the Sociology of Deviance, John Wiley & Son, New York, 1966

Ewing J, Rouse B, Drinking, Nelson-Hall, Chicago, 1978

Failure Analysis Associates, Evaluation of the Effectiveness of On-product Warning Labels, San Francisco, February, 1987

Fallding H, Drinking, Community and Civilization, Rutgers Center of Alcohol Studies, New Brunswick, 1974

Farb P, Armelagos G, Consuming Passions: The Anthropology of Eating, Houghton Mifflin Company, Boston, 1980

Fein, R, Alcohol in America:The Price We Pay, Care Institute, Newport Beach, 1984

Female Trouble, Scientific American, 257:24 July, 1987

Ferrence R, Truscott S, Whitehead P, Drinking and the Prevention of Coronary Heart Disease: Findings, Issues and Public Health Policy, Journal of STudies on Alcohol, Vol. 47, No.5, 1986

Field Publications, New Release, Children Report Less Peer Pressure to Try Marijuana but New Pressure to Try Crack, Wine Coolers, Makovsky & Co, N.Y., April 23, 1987

Fingarette H, Heavy Drinking: The Myth of Alcoholism as a Disease, University of California Press, Berkeley, 1988

Fisher M, Brillat-Savarin's The Physiology of Taste, Harcourt Brace Jovanovich, NY, 1949

Fitzgerald E, Hume D, The Single Chemical Test for Intoxication: A Challenge to Admissibility, Massachusetts Law Review, Vol. 66., No.1., Winter, 1981

Fleming A, Alcohol:The Delightful Poison, Dell Publishing Co., Inc., N.Y., 1975

Forbes R, Short History of the Art of Distillation, Brill, Leiden, Holland, 1948

Ford, G, Moderate Drinking Journal, Vol. 1, Nos. 1-5, 1987

Ford G, Safe Service Of Alcoholic Beverages, Alcohol Awareness Training, Gene Ford Publications, Seattle 1985

Ford G, Ford's Illustrated Guide to Wines, Brews and Spirits, Wm. C. Brown, Dubuque, 1983

Ford M, Personal Interview, National Association of Alcohol Treatment Professionals

Ford M, from Private Sector, as quoted in the Moderate Drinking Journal, March/April, 1987

Franke G, Wilcox G, Alcoholic Beverage Advertising and Consumption in the United States, 1964-1984, Journal of Advertising, Vol. 16, No. 3, 1987, pp. 22-30

French R. The History and Virtues of Cyder, St. Martin's Press, N.Y. 1982

Funk L, Prescott J, Study Shows Wine Aids Patient Attitudes,The Modern Hospital

Galanter M, Recent Developments in Alcoholism, Plenum Press, N.Y., 1984

Gallup G, Majorities For Three Congressional Proposals, Alcoholism And Addiction, January-February, 1987

Gardner G, Kannel W, Drinking Habits and Cardiovascular Disease: The Framingham Study, American Heart Journal, April 1983

Gardner R, Stewart H, Blood Alcohol and Glucose Changes After Ingestion of Ales, Wines and Spirits, Brewers Association of Canada, 468 (B-112)

Gastineau C, Darby W, Turner T, Fermented Beverages in Nutrition, Academic Press, N.Y., 1979

Gavaghan P, A Decade Of Change, North American Congress On Alcohol and Drug Problems, September 10, 1986

Gavaghan P, Change: And a look ahead, Speech to North American Congress on Alcohol and Drug Problems, DISCUS, Washington, D.C.

Gavaghan P, Conveying Information on Alcohol Abuse to the American Public, DISCUS, Washington, D.C.

Gavaghan P, Moderation Is In The Public Interest, White Paper, DISCUS, Washington, D.C., November 13, 1986

Gavaghan P, National Coalition for Jail Reform: Panel on DWI, Arlie House, Virginia, November 12, 1986

Gavaghan P, Personal Interview, DISCUS

Gavaghan P, Social and Health Issues, DISCUS

Gavaghan P, Social Aspects of the Alcohol Beverage Trade, DISCUS, February 18, 1988

Gavaghan P, The Comprehensive Approach To Alcohol Abuse Problems, DISCUS, Washington, D.C., June 5, 1987

Gavaghan P, Threats To Brand Advertising In North America, Dublin, DISCUS, May 25, 1987

Gavaghan P, What Can Local Licensees Do, Nightclub & Bar Expo, Atlanta, April 14, 1987

Gerstein D, Olson S, Preface in Alcohol in America: Taking Action to Prevent Abuse, National Academy Press, Washington, D.C., 1985

Getlin J, Tobacco Firms Accused of Exporting 'Cancer Epidemic', The Seattle Times, May 2, 1988

Getz O, Whiskey, David McKay Company, Inc. N.Y. 1978

Gill J, Zezulka A, Shipley M, Gill S, Beevers D, Stroke and Alcohol Consumption, the New England Journal of Medicine, Vol. 315, No. 17, October, 1986

Gilmore T, Equivocal Spirits: Alcoholism and Drinking in Twentieth Century Literature, University of North Carolina Press, Chapel Hill, 1987

Gilson C, Alcohol and Coronary Heart Disease: An Update, The ACA Journal, Spring, 1988

Glenn J, The Congressional Record, March 14, 1988

Gliksman L, Rush B, Alcohol Availability, Alcohol Consumption and Alcohol-Related Damage, II, The Role of Sociodemographic Factors, Journal of Studies on Alcohol, Vol. 47, No. 1, 1986

Goldstein D, How Ethanol Really Works, Bulletin of the Society of the Medical Friends of Wine, Vol. 26, 1981

Goldstein D, The Pharmacology of Alcohol, Oxford University Press, N.Y., 1983

Gomberg L, Personal Interview, Wine Consultant

Gordis E, Alcoholism and the Medical Cost Crunch, Science 235, March 6, 1987

Gordis E, The Genetic Paradigm, Alcohol Health & Research World, Vol. 12, Nol. 2, Winter, 1987/1988

Gordon A, Alcohol Use in the Perspective of Cultural Ecology, in Recent Developments in Alcoholism, Plenum Press, N.Y., 1984

Gordon T, Doyle J, Drinking and Coronary Heart Disease, The Albany Study, 1985

Gordon T, Doyle J, Drinking and Mortality: The Albany Study, American Journal of Epidemiology, Vol. 125, No.2, 1987

Gordon T, Kannel W, Drinking Habits and Cardiovascular Disease: The Framingham Study, American Heart Journal, April, 1983

Grant M, Gwinner P, Alcoholism In Perspective, Croom Helm, London, 1979

Greeley A, McCready W, Thiesen G, Ethnic Drinking Subcultures, NIAAA, 1976

Gross L, How Much Is Too Much: The Effects of Social Drinking, Random House, New York, 1983

Gusfield J, The Culture of Public Problems, the University of Chicago Press, 1981

Gusfield J, Passage to play, in Constructive Drinking, Cambridge University Press, Cambridge, 1987

Gusfield, J, Rasmussen P, Kotarba J, The Social Control of Drinking-Driving, Law & Policy, Vol. 6, No. 1, January 1984

Gusfield J, Symbolic Crusade:Status Politics and the American Temperance Movement, University of Illinois Press, Urbana, 1983

Grant M, Gwinn P, Alcoholism In Perspective, Croom Helin, London, 1979

Haase T, News from OSAP, Prevention Pipeline, ADAMHA, January/February 1988

Haberman P, Alcohol Use and Alcoholism Among Motor Vehicle Driver Fatalities, The International Journal of Addiction, 22(11), 1987, pp. 1119-1128

Hacker G, Collins R, Jacobson M, Marketing Booze to Blacks, Center for Science in the Public Interest, Washington, D.C., 1987

Happy Hour Therapy, Editorial, Human Behavior, June, 1974

Harburg E, Parent and Offspring Alcohol Use, Journal of Studies on Alcohol, Vol.43, No.5, 1982

Harper R, The Code of Hammurabi, King of Babylon, The University of Chicago Press, 1904

Harris L, Inside America, Vintage Books, N.Y., 1987

Harrison B, Drink and the Victorians, Faber and Faber, Ltd., London, 1971

Heath D, A Critical Review of Ethonographic Studies of Alcohol Use, in Gibbons et.el., Research Advances in Alcohol and Drug Problems, Vol.2, John Wiley & Sons, N.Y., 1975

Heath D, A Decade of Development in the Anthropological Study of Alcohol Use, 1970-1980, in Constructive Drinking, Cambridge University Press, N.Y., 1987

Heath D, In A Dither About Drinking, Wall Street Journal, February 25, 1985

Heath D, Cooper A, Lesson on Drinking: The Italians Can Do It Best, Wall Street Journal (Europe), January 13, 1988

Heien D, Pompelli G, Stress, Ethnic and Distribution Factors in a Dichotomous Response Model of Alcohol Abuse, Journal of Studies on Alcohol, Vol.48, No.5,1987

Hennekens C, Rosner B, Cole D, Daily Alcohol Consumption And Fatal Coronary Heart Disease, American Journal of Epidemiology 107,1978

Hennekens C, Drink A Little And Help Your Heart, American Heart Association, New Release, November 19, 1987

Hennekens C, Physicians' Health Study, American Heart Association, February, 1988

Henriques E, Should Wine Advertising Be Banned, California Wine Press, July, 1987

Hewlett A, Economic and Demographic Factors Relating to Public Alcohol Policy In The United States, Alcohol Policy Council, Waterford, VA, 1985

Hewlett A, Moderate Drinking Journal, Vol.1, No.3, 1987

Hewlett A, Personal Interview, Alcohol Policy Council, August, 1987

Hewlett A, Public Policies For Alcohol-Related Problems, Arden House, N.Y., April, 1984

Hewlett G, Public Policy In The United States, International Council On Alcohol And Addictions, June 1984

Hewlett G, Economic And Demographic Factors Relating To Public Alcohol Policy In The United States, Alcohol Policy Council, Waterford, VA, 1985

Hiaring P, Alarm, Wines & Vines, San Rafael, Vol. 69, No. 4, April 1988

Hill T, in Ethnohistory and Alcohol Studies in Recent Developments in Alcoholism, Plenum Press, N.Y., 1984

Hilton M, Clark W, Changes In American Drinking Patterns And Problems: 1967-1984, Journal of Studies On Alcohol, Vol. 48, No.6, 1987

Hodgson T, Meiners M, Cost-of-Illness Methodology: A Guide to Current Practices and Procedures, Health & Society, Vol.60,No. 3, 1982

Holden C, Alcoholism and the Medical Cost Crunch, Science, Vol. 235, 1987

Hooker R, Food And Drink In America, The Bobbs-Merril Company, Inc., NY, 1981

Hoppe R, Warning: Michael Jacobson Wants To Save You From Wine Drinking, The Wine Spectator, March 15, 1987

Hughes S, Dodder R, Alcohol Consumption Indices: Format Comparisons, Journal of Studies on Alcohol, Vol. 49, No. 1

Human Behavior, Happy Hour Therapy, 3(6), 1974

Human Factors Society, Proceedings, See McCarthy

Hunter B, Fermented Foods and Beverages, Keats Publishing, Inc., New Canaan, 1973

IARC, Monographs Programme on the Evolution of Carcinogenic Risk of Chemicals to Humans, IARC Monographs, Vol. 38, 1987

Insurance Institute for Highway Safety, Facts, 55 Speed Limit, Washington, D.C., February, 1987

Insurance Institute for Highway Safety, Teenage Drivers, Washington, D.C., 1985

Jackson R, Stewart R, Beaglehole R, Scragg R, Alcohol Consumption And Blood Pressure, American Journal of Epidemiology 122, 1985

Jacobson M, Atkins R, Hacker G, The Booze Merchants, Center for Science in the Public Interest, Washington, D.C, 1983

Jeannerete O, Alcohol and Youth, 1983

Jellinek E, The Symbolism of Drinking: a Culture-Historical Approach, Journal of Studies on Alcohol, Vol. 38, 1977, pp. 852-866

Job R, Effective and Ineffective Use of Fear in Health Prevention Campaigns, American Journal of Public Health, Vol. 78, No. 2, February, 1988

Jones S, Jones Complete BarGuide, BarGuide Enterprises, Los Angeles, 1977

Josephson E, An Assessment of Statistics on Alcohol-Related Problems, Trends in Problem Drinking, Columbia University School of Public Health, DISCUS May 5, 1980

Kalant H, Le Blanc A, Wieson A, Homatidis S, Sensorimotor and Psychological Effects of Various Alcoholic Beverages, CMA Journal, April 19, 1975

Kane J, Atherosclerosis, High Density Lipoproteins

Kaplan J, The Hardest Drug Heroin and Public Policy, University of Chicago Press, Chicago, 1983

Kaplan N, Personal Interview, University of Texas Medical School

Kaptchuck T, Croucher M, The Healing Arts, Summit Books, N.Y. 1987

Katz S, Personal Interview, University of Pennsylvania

Katz S, Voight M, Bread and Beer, Expeditions, Vol. 28,, No. 2, 1986

Katz S, The Evolution of Wine and Cuisine, American Wine Society Journal, Winter, 1987, Vol. 19, No. 4

Kaufman E, The Relationship of Alcoholism and Alcohol Abuse in the Abuse of Other Drugs, American Journal of Drug and Alcohol Abuse, 9(1)

Keller M, Alcohol Problems and Policies, in Law, Alcohol and Order, Greenwood Press, Westport, 1985

Keller M, New Inhibitionists Ignore History Lessons, The U.S. Journal of Drug and Alcohol Dependence, January, 1985

Keller M, Personal Interview, Alcohol Historian

Keller M, Problems of Epidemiology in Alcohol Problems, Journal of Studies on Alcohol, Vol. 16, No. 24, 1974

Kellner E, Moonshine, Weathervane Books, N.Y., 1971

Kendell R, Drinking Sensibly, British Journal of Addiction, (1987), 82, pp. 1279-1288

Kennedy P, Alcoholic Beverage Newsletter, Omaha, 1987

Kennedy P, Balance of Power in Industry Shifts to UK Companies, Alcoholic Beverage Newsletter, December 4, 1987

Kerr K, Organized for Prohibition, Yale University Press, New Haven, 1985

King H, Letter to ADAMHA, United States Brewers Association, July 23, 1985

Kissin B, The Disease Concept of Alcoholism, in Alcohol and Drug Problems, Vol. 7, Plenum Press, N.Y., 1983

Kivlahan D, Coppel D, Fromme K, Secondary Prevention of Alcohol-Related Problems in Young Adults at Risk, Original Manuscript

Klatsky A, Alcohol Better Than We Thought, American Health, December, 1986

Klatsky A, A Ten Year Study of Alcoholic Beverage and Cardiovascular Mortality, Proceedings, Wine and Health Symposium, The Wine Institute, San Francisco, November, 1981

Klatsky A, Friedman G, Seiglaub A, Alcohol And Mortality: A Ten-Year Kaiser-Permanente Experience, American Journal of Internal Medicine 95, 1981

Klein T, DWI-Are We Off Track?, Straight Talk About The Drunk Driving Problem, Part 2, Washington, D.C., June, 1986

Knupfer G, Drinking for Health: The Daily Light Drinker Fiction, British Journal of Addiction, 82, 1987

Kobler J, Ardent Spirits, Fawcett Books, Greenwich, CT, 1973

Koch J, Alcohol: Gift of God, Original Manuscript, The Samach Institute, Lakewood, CO, 80226

Kohn P, Smart R, The Impact of Television Advertising on Alcohol Consumption: An Experiment, Journal of Studies on Alcohol, Vol. 45, No. 4, 1984

Kozarevic D, Vojvodie N, Kaelber C, Gordon T, McGee D, Zukel W, Drinking Habits And Death: The Yugoslavian Cardiovascular Disease Study, Internal Journal Of Epidemiology 12, 1983

Kusin B, Begleiter H, Social Aspects Of Alcoholism, Plenum Press, NY, 1976

Kyvig D, Law, Alcohol and Order, Greenwood Press, Westport, 1985

Kyvig D, Repealing National Prohibition, The University of Chicago Press, 1979

Kyvig D, Sober Thoughts: Myths and Realities of National Prohibition After Fifty Years, in Law, Alcohol and Order, Greenwood Press, Westport, 1985

Landers A, Alcohol abuse leads to violence, The Seattle Post Intelligencer, September 13, 1986

Lang A, Alcohol:Teenage Drinking, Chelsea House, 1985

La Porte R, et. al., The Relation of Alcohol to Coronary Heart Disease and Mortality, Journal of Public Health Policy, 1980, 1 (3), pp. 198-233

La Porte R, Cresanta J, Kuller L, The Relationship of Alcohol Consumption to Atherosclerotic Heart Disease, Preventive Medicine, 9, 22-40, 1980

La Porte R, et al., Coronary Heart Disease and Total Mortality, Recent Developments in Alcoholism, 1985, 3

Lauderdale M, An Analysis of the Control Theory of Alcoholism, Denver, Colorado: Education Commission of the States, June, 1977

Ledermann S, Alcool, Alcoolism, Alcoolisation, Donnees Scientifiques de Caractere Physiologique, Economique et Social, Institute Nationale d'Etudies Demographique, Cah. No. 29, Paris Universitaires de France, 1956

LBIC, Alcohol And Health: Education, Warning Labels And Responsibility To The Public, Washington, D.C., June, 1987

Lender M, Martin K, Drinking In America, The Free Press, N.Y., 1982

Levin M, Alcohol Can Be Good For Your Health, Southern Beverage Journal, May, 1982

Levine H, The Committee of Fifty and the Origin of Alcohol Control, Journal of Drug Issues, Winter, 1983

Levine H, The Discovery of Addiction, Journal of Studies on Alcohol, Vol. 19, No. 1, 1978

Levy D, Sheflin N, The Demand for Alcoholic Beverages: An Aggregate Time Series Analysis, Journal of Public Policy & Marketing, 4, 1986. pp. 47-54

Lewis R, Drunk Driving Tests in Fatal Accidents, Crime Control Reports, Washington, D. C., 1986

Lewis J, Washington Report, Journal of Studies on Alcohol, Vol.37, No.9, 1976

Lichine A, Wine and Health, Encyclopedia of Wines and Spirits, Alfred A. Knopf, N.Y., 1969

Liebman B, Is A Little Alcohol Good For You?, Medical Selfcare, Spring 1985

Light D, Costs and Benefits of Alcohol Consumption, Society, September/October, 1975

Lightner, C, Los Angeles Times, May 6, 1984

Lindegard B, Letters to Editor, Alcohol and Breast Cancer, New England Journal of Medicine, Vol. 317, No. 2, November 1987

Linsky A, Colby J, Straus M, Drinking Norms And Alcohol-Related Problems In The United States, Journal of Studies On Alcohol, No.5, 1986

Lister C, The 21st Amendment: Realities and Myths, Beverage Marketing, January, 1987

Livingston C, Straight Talk About The Drunk Driving Problem, BRADD, Washington, D.C., September, 1985

Lolli G, Serianne E, Golder G, Luzzatto-Fegiz P, Alcohol In Italian Culture, Monographs of the Yale Center of Alcohol Studies, The Free Press, Glenco Illinois, 1958

Longmate N, The Waterdrinkers: A History of Temperance, Hamish Hamilton, Ltd., London, 1968

Longnecker M, MacMahon B, Associations between Alcoholic Beverage Consumption and Hospitalization, 1983 National Health Interview Survey, American Journal of Public Health, February 1988, Vol.79, No.2, p.153

Los Angeles Times, Alcohol Cancer Link Eased, May 28, 19898

Lucia S, A History of Wine as Therapy, J. B. Lippincott Co., Philadelphia, 1963

Lucia S, Wine And Your Well Being, Popular Library, N.Y.1971

MacAndrew C, Drunken Comportment, Aldine Publishing Company, N.Y., 1969

Macdonald D, Drugs, Drinking and Adolescents, Year Book Medical Publishers, Chicago, 1984

MacIver, J, It's Time for Congress, the Press and the People to Develop a National Consensus, quoted in the Moderate Drinking Journal, March/April, 1987

Males M, The Minimum Purchase Age for Alcohol and Young Driver Fatal Crashes: A Long-Term View, Livingston, MT, 1984

Mann P, Arrive Alive, Woodmere Press, N.Y., 1983

Market Watch, U.S. District Court to Hear Consumer Suit Against Stroh, April, 1988

Markinovich V, Wine and Allergies Research, The Wine Institute News Release

Marlatt G, Alcohol, the Magic Elixir: Stress, Expectancy, and the Transformation of Emotional States, in Stress and Addiction, Brunner/Mazel, N.Y., 1987

Marlatt G, Gordon J, Relapse Prevention, Guilford Press, Lancet 1, 1981

Marmot M, Shipley M, Rose G, Thomas B, Alcohol and Mortality: A U-Shaped Curve, Lancet, 1:580-83, 1981

Marrison L, Wines and Spirits, Penguin Books, London, 1970

Marsden M, Headlights, Motor Trend, January, 1987

Marshall M, Beliefs, Behaviors & Alcoholic Beverages, The University of Michigan Press, Ann Arbor, 1979

Marshall R, Alcohol and Highway Traffic Safety Effects in the United States, Alcoholism Treatment Quarterly, Vol.3, No. 2, Summer, 1986

Marshall N, Raising Alcohol Purchase Age, Journal of Legal Studies, 16/1, 1987

Marshall R, The Systems Approach to DWI Reduction, Forum Report, National Conference of State Liquor Administrators, Mauai, Hawaii, June, 1983

Marrison L, Wines & Spirits, Penguin Books, N.Y., 1970

Maury E, Wine Is The Best Medicine, Sheed Andrews and McMeel, Kansas City, 1977

Marketing Practices in the Alcoholic Beverages Industry, U.S. Department of Commerce, September, 1981

Maus A, Hopkins R, Weisheit R, Kearney A, The Problems and Prospect for Prevention in the Classroom: Should Alcohol Programs be Expected to Reduce Drinking by Youth?, Journal of Studies on Alcohol, Vol. 49, No. 1. January, 1988

McBride R, Industry structure, marketing and public health: a case study of the U.S. beer industry, Contemporary Drug Problems, Winter 1985, pp. 593-619

McCarthy P, Finnegan J, McCarthy G, Product Information Presentations, User Behaviors and Safety, Proceedings of Human Factors Association, 28th Annual Meeting, 1984

McConnell C, McConnell M, The Mediterranean Diet, W.W. Norton & Company, New York 1987

McDonald J, Wine and Human Nutrition, A Symposium On Wine, Health and Society, Wine And Nutrition, Wine Appreciation Guild, San Francisco,1986

McNulty H, Drinking In Vogue, Vendome Press, NY, 1978

McMichael A, member of International Agency for Research on Cancer, University of Adelaide, as reported in Alcohol Insights, October, 1987

Mead J, Health Warning, WINO Newsletter, Vol. I, No. 5, October, 1987

Meierhenry M, The 21st Amendment: Realities and Myths, Beverage Marketing Management, January, 1987

Meister F, Consumer Attitudes about Beverage Alcohols, Speech, DISCUS, January 20, 1986

Mendelson J, The Future of the Word 'Alcoholism,'. Problem Thinking, British Journal of Addiction, (1988) 82; 1061-1071

Mendelson J, Mello K, The Diagnosis And Treatment Of Alcoholism, McGraw-Hill Book Company, N.Y., 1979

Mendelson J, Mello K, Alcohol Use And Abuse In America, Little Brown and Company, Boston, 1985

Metz D, Alcoholic Beverage Executive's Newsletter, No. 2511, April 29, 1988

Metz D, Personal Interview, Wine and Spirits Wholesalers of America

Michaels M, Stay Healthy With Wine, New American Library, New York, 1981

Mills J, Grauberd B, Is Moderate Drinking During Pregnancy Associated With An Increased Risk For Malformation, Pediatrics 80, 1987

Minnesota Department of Public Health, Review and Cost of Alcohol Abuse in Minnesota, July, 1985

Mishara B, Kastenbaum R, Alcohol and Old Age, Grune & Stratton, New York, 1980

Monday Morning Report, Vol. 12, No. 2, January 25, 1988

Monday Morning Report, Vol. 12, No. 2, January 18, 1988

Monday Morning Report, Vol. 11, No. 24, December 21, 1987

Mondavi R, as quoted in Mondavi to Lead Fight Against New Prohibition, the Napa Register, February 23, 1988

Monson L, The Myths of Control of Availability Theory, Original Manuscript

Moore M, Gerstein D, Alcohol And Public Policy, National Academy Press, Washington, D. C., 1981

Moore R, Research Discloses Alcohol's Possible Protective Effect on Heart, Alcohol Research, Vol.1, Issue 1, Summer, 1985

Moore R, Pearson T, Moderate Alcohol Consumption and Coronary Artery Disease, Medicine, Vol. 65, No. 4, 1986

Morse R, Alcoholism: How Do You Get It? as cited in Fermented Food Beverages in Nutrition, Academic Press, N.Y., 1979

Moser J, Alcohol Policies in National Health and Development Planning, World Health Organization, Geneva, 1985

Mosher J, Wallack L, Government Regulations of Alcohol Advertising Protecting Industry Profits versus Promoting the Public Health, Journal of Public Health Policy, December, 1981

Mothers Against Drunk Driving, Alcohol and Driving, Channing L. Bete Co., Inc. Deerfield, MA, 1985

Murphy P, Societal Morality and Individual Freedom, in Law, Alcohol and Order, Greenwood Press, Westport, 1985

Muscatine D, The Maturing of Wine-Related Culture in the United States, The Society of the Medical Friends of Wine, Vol. 28, February, 1986

Musto D, The American Disease, Oxford University Press, N.Y., 1987

Musto D, New Temperance VS Neo-Prohibition, The Wall Street Journal, June 25, 1984

Musto D, Understanding America's Temperance Movement, Wine East, May/June, 1986

Mydans S, Gorbachev Wants Russia to get Sober and Stay Sober, The Seattle Post-Intelligencer, August 15, 1985, A-11

National Alcohol Tax Coalition, Impact of Alcohol Excise Tax Increases on Federal Revenues, Alcohol Consumption and Alcohol Problems, Washington, D. C., September 18, 1985

National Beer Wholesalers Association, Washington Update, Vol.7, No.7, 1987

National Commission Against Drunk Driving, Zeroing In On Repeat Offenders, Atlanta, September 16, 1986

National Commission Against Drunk Driving, Progress Report, 1986

National Health Policy on Alcohol in Australia, Ministerial Council on Drug Strategy, November 6, 1987

National Highway Traffic Safety Administration, How Much Do You Know About Drinking and Driving?, USDOT, Washington, D. C., 1983

National Institutes for Mental Health, Alcohol and Alcoholism, Washington, D.C.

NCALI, Alcohol and Aids, Alcohol Resources: Update, February, 1987

NIAAA, Alcohol and Alcoholism, Chevy Chase, Pub. No. 1640

NIAAA, Report of the 1986 Ad Hoc Scientific Advisory Board, Bethesda, June, 1986

NIAAA, Research and Research Training Grants, FY 1986 Grants, USDHHS, Rockville, MD

NIAAA, Review of the Research Literature on the Effects of Health Warning Labels, June, 1987

NIMH, Alcohol and Alcoholism, Chevy Chase, Publication No. 1640

Noble E, Prevention By and For All to Make a Safer Future, The Bottom Line, 1986

North R, Orange R, Teenage Drinking, Collier Books, N.Y., 1980

Neuendorf K, Alcohol Advertising And Media Portrayals, The Journal of the Institute for Socioeconomic Policy, Vol. X, No. 2, Summer, 1985

Norton R, Batey R, Dwyer T, MacMahon, S, Alcohol Consumption and the Role of Alcohol-Related Cirrhosis in Women, British Medical Journal, 295:80-82, 1987

Office of Technology Assessment, The Effectiveness and Costs of Alcoholism Treatment, U.S. Congress, March 1983

Ogborne A, Smart R, Will Restrictions on Alcohol Advertising Reduce Alcohol Consumption? British Journal of Addiction, 75(1980), pp. 293-296

Olsen R, Wine and Health, Society of Wine Educators, 1985

Olsen S, Gerstein D, Alcohol in America: Taking Action to Prevent Abuse, National Academy Press, Washington,D.C., 1985

O'Neill B, Williams A, Dubowski K, Variability in Blood Alcohol Concentrations, Journal of Studies on Alcohol, Vol. 44, No.2, 1983

O'Neill B, Myths and Misconceptions About 55 MPH Speed Limits, IIHS Status Report, Vol. 21, No. 5, April 26, 1986

O"Neill B, Separating Fact from Fiction, IIHS Status Report, Vol. 20, No. 14, December 7, 1985

Ornstein S, Control of Alcohol Consumption Through Price Increases, Journal of Studies on Alcohol, Vol, 41, No. 9, 1985, pp. 807-818

Pace N, Cross W, Guidelines To Safe Drinking, McGraw-Hill Book Company, New York, 1984

Parachini A, Surgeon general puts tobacco on par with cocaine, heroin, Seattle Times, May 11, 1988

Parker D, Harman M, The Distribution of Consumption Model of Prevention of Alcohol Problems: A Critical Assessment, Journal of Studies on Alcohol, 39:372-399, 1978

Pearl R, Alcohol and Longevity, Alfred A. Knopf, New York, 1926

Pearson D, Shaw S, Life Extension, Warner Books, New York 1982

Peele S, Harsh Penalties for Drunk Driving May Miss the Target, Los Angeles Times, June 6, 1979

Peele S, Introduction to "Visions of Addiction": The Nature of the Beast, Journal of Drug Issues, Winter, 1987

Peele S, The Limitations Of Control-Of-Supply Models For Explaining And Preventing Alcoholism And Drug Addiction, Journal Of Studies On Alcohol, Vol. 48, No. 1, 1987

Peele S, The Meaning of Addiction, Lexington Books, Lexington, MA, 1985

Peele S, The Limitations of Control-of-Supply Models for Explaining and Preventing Alcoholism and Drug Addiction, Journal of Studies on Alcohol, Vol. 48, No.I, 1987

Peele S, The Pleasure Principle in Addiction, Journal of Drug Issues, Spring, 1985

Peele S, What Does Addiction Have to do with Level of Consumption: A Response to R. Room, Journal of Studies on Alcohol,Vol. 48, No1. 1, 1987

Pelletier K, Wine & Health, A Symposium on Wine and Health, the Wine Institute, February 24, 1986

Peters J, Higher Per Capita--Lower Fatality Rate, Responsible Hospitality Institute Bulletin, February, 1987

Peters J, The New School of Politics, Restaurant Business Magazine, February, 1988

Pickering J, The Multiple Risk Factors Intervention Trial, Quoted in Southern Beverage Journal, May, 1982

Pidgeon W, Many Nonprofits Still Depend On Others, The ACA Journal, Spring, 1988

Pikaar N, Wecel M, van der Beek E, van Dokkum W, Kempen H, Klift C, Ockhuizen T, Jermus R, Effects of Moderate Alcohol Consumption on Platelet Aggregation, Fibrinolysis and Blood Lipids, Metabolism, 36(6) 1987

Pittman D, Lambert D, Alcohol, Alcoholism and Advertising, Social Science Institute, St. Louis, 1978

Pittman D, Drinking Sensibly, British Journal of Addiction, (1987), 82, pp. 12889-1300

Pittman D, Personal Interview, February, 1988

Pittman D, Primary Prevention Of Alcohol Abuse And Alcoholism, Social Science Institute, Washington University, St. Louis, 1980

Pittman D, Snyder C, Society, Culture and Drinking Patterns, John Wiley & Sons, Inc., N.Y., 1962

Plaut T, Alcohol Problems: A Report To The Nation, Oxford University Press, 1967

Polkis A, Maginn D, Barr J, Drug Findings In 'Driving Under The Influence of Drugs' Cases, Drug and Alcohol Dependence, 20:, 1987, pp. 57-62

Presbyterian Church (USA) Task Force on Alcohol Policy Recommendations

Proceedings of the Human Factors Society, see McCarthy

Pursch J, Alcohol's Effect on the Brain is Easy to See, Seattle Post Intelligencer, February 3, 1988

Pursch J, Few Doctors Understand Alcoholism, the Seattle Post Intelligencer, September 25, 1984

Pursch J, Genetics and Environment Play apart in Alcoholism but the Result is the Same, Seattle Post Intelligencer, March 24, 1988

Ramsey L, Alcohol and Myocardial Infarction in Hypersensitive Men, American Heart Journal, 1979,

Rawn I, The Control-of-Consumption Approach to Alcohol Abuse Prevention I. A Reconceptualization, and The Control-of- Consumption Approach to Alcohol Abuse, II. A Review of Empirical Studies, The International Journal of the Addictions, 22(9), 1987, pp. 813-823 and 22(10), 1987, pp. 957-979

Reid L, Factors Associated with Drug Use of Fifth Through Eighth Grade Students, Journal of Drug Education, Vol. 17 (2), 1987

Richman A, Research Insights, Information From a Canadian Health Survey, United States Brewers Association, Fall 1984

Richman A, Warren R, Alcohol Consumption and Morbidity in the Canada Health Survey: Inter-Beverage Differences, Drug and Alcohol Dependence, 15, 1985

Ritter H, Link of Alcohol to Breast Cancer Disputed, the Seattle Post Intelligencer, March 21, 1988

Roberts D, et. al., An Evaluation of the Impact of Raising the Minimum Legal Drinking Age From 19 to 21 in Wisconsin, Wisconsin Department of Transportation, January, 1988

Robinson D, Drinking Behavior, in Alcoholism in Perspective, University Park Press, Baltimore, 1979

Robinson D, Factors Influencing Alcohol Consumption, in Alcoholism New Knowledge and New Responses, Croom Helm, London, 1977

Robinson J, Evaluation of the Effectiveness of On-Product Warnings, FAilure Analysis Associates, Boston, February, 1987

Robinson J, On the Demon Drink, Mitchel Beazley, London, 1988

Ronan L, Alcohol-Related Health Risks Among Black Americans, Alcohol Health & Research World, Vol. 11, No.2, 1987

Room R, Alcohol Control, Addiction and Process of Change: Comment on "Limitations for Explaining and Preventing Alcoholism and Drug Addiction, Journal of Studies on Alcohol, Vol. 48, No.i, 1987

The Future of the World Alcoholism. Bring Back Inebriety?, British Journal of Addiction, (1987) 82; 1061-1071

Room R, Public health and the organization of alcohol production, Contemporary Drug Problems, Vol. 12, No. 4, Winter, 1985

Room R, The Supply Side of Drinking: Alcohol Production and Consumption in the United States before Prohibition, Contemporary DRug Problems, Winter, 1985

Rooney J, Schwartz S, The Effect Of Minimum Age Drinking Laws Upon Adolescent Alcohol Use And Problems, Vol. 6, 1977

Rorabaugh W, The Alcoholic Republic, Oxford University Press, 1979

Rosett H, Patterns of Alcohol Consumption and Fetal Development, Journal of the American College of Obstetricians and Gynecologists, Vol. 61, May 1983

Rosett H, Weiner L, Alcohol and the Fetus: A Clinical Perspective, Oxford University Press, New York, 1984

Ross L, Deterring the Drinking Driver, Lexington Books, Lexington, 1982

Ross L, Hughes G, Drunk Driving--What Not To Do, The Nation, December 13, 1986

Roueche' B, Alcohol:The Neutral Spirit, Grove Press, Inc. New York, 1960

Royce J, Alcohol Problems and Alcoholism, The Free Press, N.Y., 1981

Rubin E, An Overview of the Evidence Concerning the Hypothesis that Alcohol Causes Cancer, The Wine Institute, Delivered to the California Hearing on Proposition 65, 1988

Rumbaugh R, Personal Interview, National Beer Wholesalers Association

Saltz R, The Role of Bars and Restaurants in Preventing Alcohol-Impaired Driving, Evaluation and Health Professions, Vol. 10, No1. 1, March, 1987

Sarley V, Stepto R, Wine Is Fine for Patient's Morale and Helps Stimulate Their Appetites, Modern Nursing Home, January/February 1969

Schatzkin A,Jones Y, Hoover R, Taylor P, Brinton L, Ziegler R, Harvey E, Carter C, Licitra L, Dufour M, Larson

D, Alcohol Consumption and Breast Cancer in the Epidemiologic Follow-up Study of the First National Health and Nutrition Examination Survey, New England Journal of Medicine, Vol. 316, No. 19, May, 1987

Schnellinger L, A grim report on state's emotionally disturbed students, Seattle Post Intelligencer, May 4, 1988

Scientific American, Medicine, 257: July, 1987

Scoles P, Fine E, Steer R, Personality Characteristics and Drinking Patterns of High-Risk Drivers Never Apprehended for Driving While Intoxicated, Journal of Studies on Alcohol, Vol. 45, No1. 5, 1984

Seattle Post Intelligencer, War On Drugs A Loser Say Mayors, Oct 29, 1987

Segal B, Russian Drinking, Rutgers Center of Alcohol

Selzer R, Mortal Lessons: Notes on the Art of Surgery, Simon & Schuster, New York, 1976

Seward D, Monks and Wine, Crown Publishers, Inc., N.Y., 1979

Shaefer J, Drunkenness and Culture Stress: A Holocultural Test, in Cross Cultural Approaches to the Study of Alcohol, Mouton Publishers, The Hague, 1976

Shea D, Personal Interview, The Beer Institute, March, 1988

Sherman L, Drunk Driving Tests In Fatal Accidents, Crime Control Reports, Washington, D.C., December, 1986

Sherman S, America's New Abstinence, Fortune, March 8, 1985

Siegel R, Changing Patterns of Cocaine Use: Longitudinal Observations,, Consequences and Treatment: In Brabowski J, Cocaine: Pharmacology, Effects and Treatment of Abuse, NIDA Monograph, No. 50, 1984

Sinclair A, Era of Excess: A Social History of the Prohibition Movement, Harper & Row Publishers, N.Y., 1964

Skegg D, Alcohol, coffee, fat and breast cancer, British Medical Journal, London, October 24, 1987

Smart R, The Alcohol Advertising Ban in British Columbia, Problems and Effects on Beverage Consumption, British Journal on Addiction, Vol., 71, 1976

Smith J, Up Your Spirits, Atheneum/SMI, New York, 1978

Smith C, The Wrath of Grapes: The Health Related Implications of Changing American Drinking Practices, AREA, March 2, 1985

Smith C, Harham R, Alcohol Abuse: Geographical Perspectives, Resource Publications in Geography, 1982

Smith R, Hingson R, Morelock S, Heeren T, Mucatel M, Mangione T, Scotch N, Legislation Raising the Legal Drinking Age in Massachusetts from 18-20, Journal of Studies on Alcohol, Vol. 45, No.6, 1984

Snyder C, Alcohol and the Jews, The Free Press, Glencoe, Il, 1958

Sobel L, Effects of Television Programming and Advertising on Alcohol Consumption on Normal Drinkers, Journal of Studies on Alcohol, Vol. 47, 1986

Sokol R, from the Journal of the American Medical Association as quoted in BRADD Bulletin, July 20, 1987

Stall R, Research Issues Concerning Alcohol Consumption Among Aging Populations, Drug and Alcohol Dependence, 19(1987) 195-213

Stamler J, Coronary Heart Disease: Doing the "Right Thing," New England Journal of Medicine, Vol. 312, No. 16

Status Report, Motor Vehicle Crashes Cost Nation $74.2 Billion in 1986, Insurance Institute for Highway Safety, January 30, 1988

Status Report, Congress Appropriates $92.8 million for NHTSA Operations and Research, Insurance Institute for Highway Safety, January 30, 1988

Staudenmeier W, Context and Variation In Employer Policies on Alcohol, The Journal of Drug Issues, 17(3), 1987

Steinman B, Alcohol Issues Insights, Vol.4,1987

Stepto R, Clinical Uses of Wine, New Physician, January, 1965

Straus , An Historical Perspective on the Clinical Uses of Wine, Vintage, August, 1979

Strickland D, Finn T, Lambert M, A Content Analysis of Beverage Alcohol Advertising, Journal of Studies on Alcohol, Vol. 43, No. 7, 1984

Stroh P, Speech to National Conference, National Beer Wholesalers of America, 1987

Temple M, Trends in Collegiate Drinking in California, 1979-1984, Alcohol Research Group, Berkeley, 1985

Thomas D, Breast Cancer Studies, Moderate Drinking Journal, Vol. 1, No. 3, May/June, 1987

Tierney J, Not to Worry, Hippocrates, January/February, 1988

Time Magazine, November 30, 1987, February 1, 1988

Time Magazine, When Parents Just Say No, February 15, 1988

Throwback A, The Great Dry War, MacMillan Publishing Co., N.Y., 1987

Trebach A, The Great Drug War, MacMillan Publishing Company, London, 1987

Turner T, Bennet V, Hernandez H, The Beneficial Side of Moderate Use, Johns Hopkins Medical Journal, 148, 1981

Turner T, Editorial Comment, Monthly List of Pertinent Abstracts, Alcoholic Beverage Medical Research Foundation, Vol. 18, No. 189, September 15, 1987

Turner T, Personal Interview, Alcoholic Beverage, Medical Research Foundation, October, 1987

Turpin E, Governors Commission on Children, Washington State, Post Intelligence, May 4, 1988

Tuyns A, Drinking Sensibly. The Search for a 'Limit,' British Journal of Addiction, 1988 Jan:83(1): 35-36

Ummel D, as quoted in Teen Pregnancy Facing the Challenge, Human Life News, Vol. 17, No. 1, January, 1987

University of California Wellness Letter, Low Risk, High Risk, Vol. 4, Issue 9, June, 1988

University of California Wellness Letter, Wellness Prospects, Alcohol Policies, March, 1986

USA Today, Health and Behavior, September 16, 1986

USDOT, You Alcohol And Driving, Washington, D.C.

U.S. Supreme Court, South Dakota VS Dole, No. 86-260, 1987

Vaillant G, The Natural History of Alcoholism, Harvard University Press, Cambridge, 1983

Vatz R, Weinberg R, Disease Idea is an Obstacle, Special to The Lost Angeles Times, 1984

Vogler R, Bartz W, The Better Way To Drink, New Harbinger Publications, Oakland, 1982

Wagenaar A, Alcohol, Young Drivers and Traffic Accidents, Lexington Books, Lexington, 1983

Walker L, Is Wine A Toxin or Tonic?, The Wine Trader, Vol.1, No. 1, February 1988, p.6

Wallack L, Do Mass Media Report Alcohol Problems, OSAP Meeting, ADAMHA News

Wallack L, Drinking and Driving: Understanding the Role of the Mass Media, Journal of Public Health Policy, December, 1984

Waller P, Spitting in the Ocean, in DWI Reeducation and Rehabilitation, AAA, August, 1983

Warburton C, The Economic Results of Prohibition, Columbia University Press, N.Y., 1932

Washburne C, Primitive Drinking, College & University Press, N.Y. 1961

Wasson R, Ruck C, Hofmann A, The Road To Eleusis, Harcourt Brace Jovanovich, NY, 1978

Webster L, Alcohol Consumption and the Risk of Breast Cancer, Lancet, Vol.2, 1983

Weil A, Rosen W, Chocolate to Morphine, Houghton Mifflin Company, Boston, 1983

Weinberg R, Personal Interview, Washington University

Whelan E, Personal Interview, American Council on Science and Health

Whelan E, To Your Health, Across The Board, The Conference Board, January, 1988, p.49

Whelan E, Consumerism and the Misdirected War Against Alcohol Advertising, Speech, Boca Raton, DISCUS, 1984

Whipple A, The Big Squeeze, California Farmer, February 10, 1988

Why the Draft National Health Policy On Alcohol, Wine & Brandy Co-operative Producers Association of Australia, January 11, 1988

Whitten D, Wine and Health: a physician's view, Wines & Vines, April, 1988

Whitten D, Proceedings, Wine, Culture, and Healthy Lifestyles, The Wine Institute, May, 1987

Wiener C, The Politics of Alcoholism, Transaction Books, New Brunswick, 1981

Wiley J, Camacho T, Life-Style and Future Health: Evidence from the Alameda County Study, Preventive Medicine 9,1980

Williams A, Peat M, Crouch D, Wells J, Finkle B, Drugs in Fatally Injured Young Male Drivers, Public Health Reports, October, 1984

Williams A, Raising the Legal Purchase Age in the United States, Alcohol Drugs and Driving, Vol.2, No.2, 1986

Williams G, Stinson F, Parker D, Harford T, Noble J, Demographic Trends, Alcohol Abuse and Alcoholism, Epidemiological Bulletin No. 15, Alcohol Health & Research World, Spring, 1987

Williamson D, Forman M, Binkin N, Gentry E, Remington P, Trowbridge F,, Alcohol and Body Weight in the United States, American Journal of Public Health, Vol. 77, No. 10, 1987

Willett W, Stampfer M, Colditz G, Rosner B, Hennekens C, Speizer F, Moderate Alcohol Consumption and the Risk of Breast Cancer, New England Journal of Medicine, Vol. 316, No. 19, May, 1987

Williams G,, The Greening of the Northwest, Pacific Northwest, April, 1988

The Wine Institute, A Symposium on Wine, Health and Society, San Francisco, 1986

The Wine Institute, Wine and America, San Francisco, 1986

The Wine Institute, Wine and Medical Practice, San Francisco, 1979

The Wine Institute, Wine, Health and Society, San Francisco, 1981

Wine Spectator, 1986 Consumption by Household, Nov 15, 1987

World Health Organization, Problems Related To Alcohol Consumption, WHO, Geneva, 1980

Yankelovich, Skelly and White, Inc., Family Health in and Era of Stress, 1979

Yankelovich, Skelly and White, Time Poll, May, 1985

Yano K, Reed M, McGee D, Ten-Year Incidence Of Coronary Heart Disease In The Honolulu Heart Program, American Journal of Epidemiology 119, 1984

Young G, The Diet-Cancer Link Takes Hold Across America, Seattle Post Intelligencer, February 21, 1987

Zinberg N, Drug, Set and Setting, Yale University Press, New Haven, 1984

Zinberg N, Heroin Use in Vietnam and the United States, Archives of General Psychiatry, 20:486-488, 1972

Zinberg N, Social Sanctions and Rituals as a Basis for Drug Abuse Prevention, American Journal on Drug and Alcohol Abuse, 2(2) 1975

Zucker R, Developmental Aspects of Drinking Through the Young Adult Years, High School Practices and Problems, Psychiatric Opinion, 16 (n.3), 1975

Zylman R, A Critical Evaluation of the Literature on Alcohol Involvement in Highway Deaths, Accident Analysis & Prevention, Pergomen Books, Great Britain, 1974

Zylman R, OVERemphasis on Alcohol May be Costing Lives, Police Chief, 41(1), January, 1974

Zuker R, Noll, R, Precursors and Developmental Influences in Drinking and Alcoholism, USDHHS, Alcohol & Health, Monograph No.I, 1982

Index